TRADE, POLITICS, AND REVOLUTION

The Carolina Lowcountry and the Atlantic World
Sponsored by the Program in the Carolina Lowcountry
and the Atlantic World of the College of Charleston

TRADE, POLITICS, AND REVOLUTION

SOUTH CAROLINA AND BRITAIN'S ATLANTIC COMMERCE, 1730–1790

HUW DAVID

THE UNIVERSITY OF SOUTH CAROLINA PRESS

© 2018 University of South Carolina

Published by the University of South Carolina Press
Columbia, South Carolina 29208

www.sc.edu/uscpress

Manufactured in the United States of America

27 26 25 24 23 22 21 20 19 18
10 9 8 7 6 5 4 3 2 1

Library of Congress Cataloging-in-Publication Data
can be found at http://catalog.loc.gov/.

ISBN 978-1-61117-894-4 (cloth)
ISBN 978-1-61117-895-1 (ebook)

This book was printed on recycled paper with
30 percent postconsumer waste content.

For my parents,
Rhys and Susan David

CONTENTS

CHAPTER FIVE

THE VOYAGE OF THE *LORD NORTH*

American Independence, Anglo-Carolinian
Trade, and Unfinished Business

131

CONCLUSION

"Let me have done with American lands"

176

LIST OF ILLUSTRATIONS

ACKNOWLEDGMENTS

Like the business of the eighteenth-century merchants who populate this book, writing it has been a hugely rewarding enterprise. And, to push the analogy a little further, in the process I've run up many outstanding debts to colleagues and friends who have made the book possible.

Special thanks must go to Perry Gauci for his tireless enthusiasm, insight, and generosity. He really is a "conscientious, vigilant and accessible man of action," as he has defined the archetypal eighteenth-century merchant. At Oxford University the Rothermere American Institute is an exceptional place to study America and its relations with the world, and it has been a wonderful academic home. I am very grateful to colleagues at the RAI for their advice and encouragement, in particular its outstanding directors Nigel Bowles and Jay Sexton, and Gareth Davies, Pekka Hämäläinen, and Stephen Tuck. Each year one of America's great historians visits as Harmsworth Professor, and I am grateful to all of them who have shared ideas and recommendations, in particular Peter Onuf and Philip Morgan. Peter Thompson and Betty Wood also gave invaluable feedback on my thesis. Experts in British history have helped fill many gaps in my knowledge of the "mother country" and opened up new lines of enquiry, and I am especially grateful to Bob Harris, Joanna Innes, Erica Charters, Stephen Hague, and Benjamin Heller for their advice and recommendations. The camaraderie of RAI's graduate community, especially Ken Owen, Will Pettigrew, David Sim, Joe Merton, Ursula Hackett, Tom Packer, Sebastian Page, and Steve Tuffnell, too helped make this a thoroughly enjoyable project.

I benefited from the friendliness, helpfulness, and expertise of staff in all the libraries where I spent time doing research for this project. Top of the list must be Jane Rawson and her colleagues—Judy Warden, Martin Sutcliffe, Johanna O'Connor, and Richard Purkiss—at the Vere Harmsworth Library in Oxford for tracking down books and innumerable visits to the stacks on my behalf. This book would also not have been possible without the assistance of librarians at the South Caroliniana Library in Columbia, the South Carolina Historical Society in Charleston, the South Carolina Department of Archives and History, the National Archives in London, and the Huntington Library in San Marino, California. Graham Duncan and Brian Cuthrell at the South Caroliniana, Mary Jo Fairchild at the S.C. Historical Society, and Juan Gomez at the Huntington merit special mention for making their institutions such welcoming places.

Research led me to many new and fascinating places. I've been blessed with great hospitality on my travels. First and foremost, Vennie Deas-Moore and

Keith Moore have been wonderful hosts, making Columbia, S.C., a home away from home; thanks too to Joe Renouard in Charleston, and to Louise McLaren and Phil Killingley, and Gavin Pape for accommodation and good company on visits to the National Archives in southwest London.

Financially, grants from the Arts and Humanities Research Council made my research possible, supplemented by an invaluable writing-up scholarship from the Rothermere American Institute. I am grateful to both institutions for their assistance, and at the RAI for the support and encouragement of Vyvyan and Alexandra Harmsworth, David and Maria Willetts, Nicolas Ollivant, and the anonymous donor who funded my writing-up grant. Travel awards from Lincoln College, Oxford; the College of Charleston; and the Huntington Library have been vital in supporting visits to far-flung archives.

I was honored to receive the Hines Prize for the manuscript of this book in 2015. I am very grateful to Carolina Lowcountry and the Atlantic World Program at the College of Charleston and the prize committee for reading my work and awarding me the prize, and in particular to Samuel Hines for so generously creating the prize. Thanks go also to Bill Adams, Linda Fogle and their colleagues at the University of South Carolina Press and especially the two anonymous readers whose insightful comments on the manuscript have much improved it.

Friends have listened patiently and with apparent interest to my stories of historical detective work. A special mention here to Seth and Kate Sinclair, Robert and Laura Burley, and David and Carin Peller-Semmens. Louisa Hotson injected love, laughter, and irrepressible enthusiasm into the final push. Finally, and above all, the love and support of my parents, Rhys and Susan David, have been instrumental. Early trips to castles, churches, and museums laid the foundations for a fascination with history and proved to be time very well spent. For that, and for so much else, I will always be grateful.

NOTES ON THE TEXT

During the eighteenth century the words "Carolina" and "South Carolina" were used synonymously, particularly in Britain. North and South Carolina were formally made separate colonies in 1712; before and after the separation, "Carolina" generally referred in Britain to South Carolina, the wealthier of the two and, in its interaction with the British state, the more prominent. The term "Carolina traders," for example, was used to denote merchants trading specifically to South Carolina.

After the Revolutionary War, Charles Town became Charleston. For authenticity, I have followed this change and use Charles Town when referring to the town before the Revolutionary War and use Charleston afterward.

Prices are given in pounds sterling unless otherwise stated. Throughout the period between about 1730 and the end of British control, one pound sterling was equivalent to about seven pounds in South Carolina currency (see John J. McCusker, *Money and Exchange in Europe and America, 1600–1775: A Handbook*).

To retain authenticity, spellings in quotations from primary sources have not been corrected unless essential to convey meaning. Italicization and underlining are from the original texts. Any words added to quotations appear in brackets.

CHRONOLOGY

1660	First Navigation Act is passed, governing the terms of trade within the British Empire. Further acts in 1663, 1673, and 1696 codify and reinforce the strictures.
1670	Foundation of North and South Carolina follows the granting of land between Virginia and Spanish Florida by King Charles II to eight English aristocrats, the Lords Proprietors, and the arrival of the first English settlers.
1680	Charles Town, named in honor of the king, is relocated from its original site at Albemarle Point on the Ashley River to its current site on a peninsula between the Ashley and Cooper Rivers.
1690s	The first successful experiments in cultivating rice in the colony are made through a combination of European and African knowledge and techniques and the labor of slaves brought to South Carolina from Africa and the West Indies.
1704	Rice is added to the Navigation Acts' list of "enumerated commodities."
1710	South Carolina's enslaved black residents first outnumber the colony's white settlers at this approximate date.
1712	South Carolina's first official agent in London, Abel Kettleby, is appointed with instructions to secure the continuation of a bounty on naval stores and to gain South Carolina the right to export rice to foreign markets.
1714–27	George I reigns.
1715	The Yamassee War breaks out. During 1715 and 1716 as many as four hundred traders and settlers living south of Charles Town are killed in an uprising of the region's Yamassee Indians, in alliance with Creeks, Choctaws, and Cherokees.
1727–60	George II reigns.

1727–31 Samuel Wragg serves as South Carolina's agent in London.

1729 South Carolina becomes a Crown colony after the colonists rejected proprietorial government a decade earlier and the Lords Proprietors formally surrendered ownership of the Carolinas to the British government.

1730 Rice Act permits direct rice exports from South Carolina to European ports south of Cape Finisterre (that is, Spain and Portugal).

1732 Georgia is founded on South Carolina's southern frontier.

1733–49 Peregrine Fury serves as South Carolina's agent in London.

1735 Rice Act is amended to allow direct rice exports to Spain and Portugal from Georgia.

September 1739 Stono Rebellion, South Carolina's largest slave insurrection, occurs. As many as one hundred slaves seek to escape to Spanish Florida and kill about forty white settlers living south of Charles Town before the revolt is suppressed.

1739–48 War of Jenkins' Ear and the War of the Austrian Succession: Britain is at war with Spain (1739–48) and France (1744–48) in continental Europe, the Mediterranean, North America, and the Caribbean.

late 1740s Large-scale cultivation of indigo begins in South Carolina.

1748 London's Carolina lobby, led by James Crokatt, secures a bounty of sixpence per pound on imports of indigo from South Carolina.

1749–55 James Crokatt serves as South Carolina's agent in London.

1750 Growth of Raw Silk Act removes the duties on silk imported from the American colonies.

1751 Pot Ash and Pearl Ashes Act removes the duties on potash and pearl ashes, used in glass and soap making and in the textile industry, which are imported from America.

1753 James Crokatt attempts to resign metropolitan agency but is retained in the post for a further two years.

1756–63	Seven Years' War: Britain is at war with France and Spain in continental Europe, North America, the Caribbean, and India.
1757–60	James Wright serves as South Carolina's agent in London.
1760–1820	George III reigns.
1762–75	Charles Garth serves as South Carolina's agent in London.
1764	Rice Act permits rice to be exported directly from South Carolina and Georgia to foreign colonies in the West Indies and South America.
1764	Hemp Act places bounties on imports of hemp and flax, essential to rope making, from the American colonies of eight pounds per ton.
1765–66	Charles Garth and London's Carolina merchants lobby against the Stamp Act, which requires that printed material in the colonies should bear official stamps produced in Britain; and the Mutiny Act, which contains provisions relating to the quartering of troops in America.
1767	Parliament passes the Townshend Duties (Revenue Act), which impose new duties on colonial imports of tea, glass, lead, paints, and paper.
1770–82	Lord North is prime minister.
1774	Parliament passes the Coercive (or Intolerable) Acts, four punitive acts made in response to the Boston Tea Party.
1775–82	American Revolutionary War takes place.
January 1775	South Carolina's Provincial Congress meets for the first time, succeeding the colonial assembly.
September 1775	British control in Charles Town ends with the departure of Governor Lord William Campbell.
December 1775	Parliament passes the Prohibitory Act, which outlaws British trade with the thirteen colonies in rebellion and permits the Royal Navy and British privateers to seize American produce as prizes of war.
March 1776	General Assembly of South Carolina succeeds the Provincial Congress.
May 1780	British forces under Sir Henry Clinton recapture Charles Town from Patriot control.

February 1782	South Carolina's General Assembly, meeting in Jacksonborough, passes legislation penalizing Loyalists and owners of Carolinian land living in Britain, including confiscations.
March–June 1782	Marquess of Rockingham is prime minister.
June 1782–February 1783	Lord Shelburne is prime minister.
December 1782	British forces evacuate Charles Town, leaving it to Continental troops under General Nathanael Greene and the establishment of civil government led by Governor John Mathews.
1783	Charles Town is formally incorporated as a city and becomes Charleston.
April–December 1783	Fox-North coalition forms British government.
July 1783	An Order-in-Council limits trade between the United States and the British West Indies to vessels built and owned in Britain or its colonies.
September 1783	Treaty of Paris is signed, formally ending the war between Great Britain and the United States.
December 1783–1801	William Pitt the Younger is prime minister.
1791	British merchants present their claims for prewar debts in the United States to the British government.
1794	Jay Treaty between Great Britain and the United States attempts to resolve the two countries' ongoing territorial, commercial, and financial disputes but arouses hostility in Charleston and elsewhere in the United States.

JOHN BESWICKE (?–1764) Merchant of Charles Town and London. Beswicke was in business from 1735 in South Carolina, where he was considered by one contemporary as a man "who bears a Good Character . . . & is Considerably Concern'd in Trade." He relocated in 1740 to London, where he became one of the capital's leading Carolina traders and maintained successive partnerships with merchants in Charles Town. Beswicke owned several oceangoing ships and invested his mercantile profits in a country house outside London called Little London. After withdrawing from trade in 1763, he died the following year, leaving his nephews, William Greenwood and William Higginson, to continue his trading house.

JAMES BOURDIEU (1715–1804) Major London merchant, principally in the French and Caribbean trades before the Revolutionary War; active in trade to South Carolina after 1783. Bourdieu was in trade in London from 1753 and in partnership with Samuel Chollet in the firm of Bourdieu & Chollet by 1763. He was noted for his sympathy for the American cause during the war and regularly visited his friend and business associate Henry Laurens during Laurens's imprisonment in London in 1780–81. Bourdieu attempted to intercede in the Anglo-American peace talks in Paris in 1782–83 and was a strong advocate for free trade with the United States.

SAMUEL BRAILSFORD (1728–1800) Charles Town and Bristol merchant. Brailsford was born in South Carolina and followed his father into commerce. In three partnerships, he was among Charles Town's largest importers of slaves during the 1750s and owned several oceangoing vessels. He also invested in plantation land in the colony. Brailsford moved in the late 1760s to Bristol, where he continued in transatlantic trade to South Carolina and appears to have been politically supportive of the American colonies in the early 1770s. However, his partnership from 1771 with two Loyalist Charles Town merchants, Robert Powell and John Hopton, stymied his attempts to reclaim the firm's prewar debts.

EDWARD BRIDGEN (?–1787) London merchant in the firm of Bridgen & [James] Waller, which was in trade by 1763. The firm specialized in textile exports and had particularly strong connections to North Carolina, though also sent goods to Charles Town. Bridgen was noted for his strong pro-American sympathies before and during the war. He cultivated friendships with John Adams and Benjamin

Franklin and associated with prominent British radicals. His politics gained him trade to America after the war, and helped him recover lands in North Carolina that had been confiscated from him.

JAMES CROKATT (1701–77) London's leading Carolina trader in the 1740s and 1750s. Born in Scotland, he went in the late 1720s to Charles Town, where he prospered in trade, bought extensive properties, married into an important planting family, and was appointed to the Royal Council. He relocated to London in 1739. Besides his trade to South Carolina, he promoted agricultural diversification in the colony, notably with a campaign for a bounty on Carolinian indigo, and was the colony's London agent from 1749 to 1755. A young Henry Laurens was one of his apprentices. Crokatt withdrew from trade in the early 1760s, leaving much of his business to his son, Charles, and his son-in-law, John Nutt, but continued to take an interest in South Carolina and in agricultural improvement from his country estate in Essex.

CHARLES CROKATT (1730–69) The son of James Crokatt, he followed his father into London's Carolina trade. He entered partnership with his father in 1755 and began trading in his own right from 1760, using the title James & Charles Crokatt to lend the firm his father's prestige. Despite extensive trade to South Carolina, he lacked his father's commercial nous and ran into financial difficulties. These were compounded by an expensive and unsuccessful attempt to run for Parliament in 1761. His creditors included firms in Charles Town and his own father, and his losses forced him to stop trading in 1766. He was declared bankrupt and committed suicide in 1769.

CHARLES GARTH (1734–84) South Carolina's official agent in London between 1762 and 1775. Garth was appointed because of his family connections to the colony, particularly the fact that his cousin Thomas Boone was governor. Arguably the most assiduous of all the North American colonial agents during the 1760s, he represented South Carolina's interests on a range of commercial matters and was at the forefront of lobbying against the Stamp Act. Garth was also an MP from 1764, replacing his father for the West Country seat of Devizes, and served briefly as agent for Maryland and Georgia.

WILLIAM GREENWOOD (c. 1733–86) London Carolina merchant. Greenwood was trained in the capital by his uncle, John Beswicke, and with his cousin, William Higginson, inherited Beswicke's firm in 1764, thereafter trading as Greenwood & Higginson. The partners were London's largest Carolina traders in the decade before the American Revolution, operating from a grand countinghouse and owning several ships; Greenwood also inherited Beswicke's Little London estate in Middlesex. He was widely seen as hostile to the American cause before and during the American Revolution and had great difficulties in recovering his firm's large debts in South Carolina, efforts that Higginson continued after Greenwood's death in 1786.

RALPH IZARD (1742–1804) Scion of a major South Carolina planting family with extensive landholdings in the lowcountry. Izard was educated in England before returning to South Carolina in 1764. Back in England with his wife from 1771, Izard remained in London for several years. During this time he observed and reported on political developments in Great Britain, including the politics of the capital's Carolina merchants. After the outbreak of war, the Izards moved to Paris, where they remained until peace was restored. After returning to South Carolina, Izard became the new state's first U.S. senator.

ISAAC KING (?–1797) London Carolina trader from the mid-1750s, in partnership with Sarah Nickleson. Besides his trade to the colony, King visited South Carolina several times during the 1760s and 1770s as he sought to recover debts owed to the firm, and he went to Charles Town while it was under British control in 1780. He also acquired land in the colony, which he struggled fruitlessly to recover after American independence. King's losses compelled him to move from London to Bristol in 1783 in search of a fresh start in more modest accommodations.

HENRY LAURENS (1724–92) South Carolinian merchant, planter, statesman, and diplomat. Born in Charles Town, Laurens spent time in London in the 1740s as an apprentice to James Crokatt. He returned in 1747 to Charles Town, where he became one of the port's leading merchants, especially in the slave trade. His correspondance is a leading source on South Carolina's commerce and politics during the colonial era and the American Revolution. After cutting back on trade in the early 1760s, Laurens spent time in Europe supervising his sons' education and witnessed British political debate as the American crisis mounted. At the forefront of South Carolinian politics in the 1760s and 1770s, he was a delegate to and president of the Continental Congress, spent fifteen months imprisoned in the Tower of London, and was a delegate at the Paris peace talks.

WILLIAM MANNING (?–1791) One of London's leading merchants during the 1770s and 1780s. He had earlier spent time as a merchant on St. Kitts, where he had acquired plantations and traded to South Carolina. In London he was heavily involved in the West Indies trade and continued to trade to South Carolina. His daughter Martha married Henry Laurens's son John in 1776. Manning was regarded as pro-American, and he regularly visited Laurens in the Tower of London and held money on his account in London. Two of his sons-in-law, Benjamin Vaughan (with whom he became partner) and Henry Merrtens Bird, benefited from his reputation and connections in South Carolina and became leading British traders to the state in the 1790s.

WILLIAM MIDDLETON (1710–85) Major landowner in South Carolina and England. Middleton was born into one of South Carolina's leading planter families and owned some fifteen thousand acres in the colony. On inheriting large landholdings near London and in Suffolk, England, he left the colony in 1754 and lived in England for the rest of his life. He retained close interests in South Carolina, however, extending his landholdings with the aid of his brother, Henry. He also gave evidence to Parliament on the colony's behalf and joined an appeal as one of "several Natives of America" against the so-called Intolerable Acts in 1774.

EDWARD NEUFVILLE (fl. 1740s–87) Merchant of Charles Town and Bristol. Neufville was in trade in Charles Town during the 1740s and 1750s, principally in partnership with his brother John. He relocated to Bristol in 1764, apparently maintaining a transatlantic connection with his brother. He also went into partnership with the London merchant Christopher Rolleston, trading to South Carolina. Neufville returned to South Carolina in the 1780s to try to recover prewar debts.

JOSEPH NICHOLSON (?–1783) Merchant originally from Yorkshire in northern England. During the 1750s and early 1760s, Nicholson was in partnership in the Charles Town firm of Downes & Nicholson and with William Bampfield. In 1764 he relocated to Britain, where he remained in the Carolina trade in premises in the City of London and owned a house in Hackney, just north of London. He signed a petition to the king in 1775 urging conciliation with the American colonies. He died in 1783, leaving his family to pursue significant debts owed to him in South Carolina.

JOHN NICKLESON (?–1754) Charles Town and London merchant originally from Poole in the southwest of England. After captaining transatlantic ships, Nickleson began in trade in Charles Town in 1739 in partnership with his brother-in-law Richard Shubrick. Nickleson, Shubrick & Co. was a prominent trading house and secured valuable contracts to supply the colony's government and the Royal Navy. Nickleson relocated in 1743 with his wife and children to London, where he continued to trade with South Carolina. On his death in 1754 he left an estate valued at over twenty thousand pounds; his business was continued by his widow, Sarah (née Shubrick).

JOHN NUTT (?–c. 1814) Originally from Yorkshire, England, Nutt captained transatlantic ships before becoming one of London's leading Carolina traders during the 1760s and 1770s. He was James Crokatt's son-in-law through marriage to Crokatt's daughter Mary and took on much of Crokatt's trade after his father-in-law's retirement in the early 1760s. Nutt was particularly known for handling Carolinian indigo and for exporting British and European goods on credit to the colony, through which he amassed great wealth. He gained a reputation for hostility toward America during the 1770s and because of this struggled in vain during and after the war to recoup his extensive losses in South Carolina.

CHARLES OGILVIE (c. 1731–88) Charles Town and London merchant. Born in Scotland, Ogilvie followed his elder brother James to South Carolina in 1751 in search of commercial fortune. He traded in two partnerships in Charles Town during the 1750s and married the daughter of the colony's chief justice, a major heiress. In 1761 Ogilvie relocated to London, where he continued in the Carolina trade. He had acquired substantial plantations in South Carolina through his wife and continued to add to his landholdings there while living in Britain. He served briefly as an MP in 1774–75. He periodically visited his widely spread estates in South Carolina and employed a nephew, George Ogilvie, as a resident manager. His lands were confiscated during the American Revolution.

JAMES POYAS (?–1799) Charles Town and London merchant. The son of a silk spinner from the Italian Piedmont, Poyas was raised in South Carolina and traded in Charles Town before relocating to London in 1767. He traded to South Carolina in the decade before the Revolutionary War and was owed sizable debts in the colony, which he continued to claim in the 1790s. Despite his losses in South Carolina, Poyas continued in trade in London, though he was shunned by prewar connections in the colony on account of his purported hostility to the American cause.

ROBERT PRINGLE (1702–76) Charles Town merchant. Born in Scotland, Pringle served an apprenticeship in a West Indian merchant firm in London before going to South Carolina in 1725. He became one of the colony's most prosperous merchants, operating mostly as a sole trader after being involved in some partnerships in the 1740s. Much of his transatlantic trade was with his brother Andrew, a ship's captain turned merchant in London. He exported rice and deerskins and imported British and continental European goods for sale from his store on Tradd Street. He served in South Carolina's Assembly in the 1750s.

ROBERT PRINGLE JR. (1755–1811) Son of Robert Pringle Sr., the leading Charles Town merchant. Pringle Jr. trained as a doctor in Britain before entering trade in Charles Town in 1783. He went into partnership with William Freeman, who was married to his younger sister. Under their arrangement, Freeman represented the firm in Bristol, where his uncle, also called William Freeman, had been a prominent merchant during the 1760s and 1770s.

ROBERT RAPER (1709–79) Charles Town lawyer, naval officer, and agent for several absentee owners of land and property in South Carolina who lived in Britain, including James Crokatt, John Beswicke, and the Colleton family. Raper also pursued and collected debts on behalf of his clients in Britain and advised them of commercial and political affairs in South Carolina. Raper's letterbook, covering 1759–70, is an invaluable source on transatlantic commerce and land management in South Carolina.

CHRISTOPHER ROLLESTON (1739–1807) London merchant. Born in Derbyshire, about 150 miles north of London, Rolleston came from an important local family and was active in trade by the early 1760s. He entered partnership with Edward Neufville in 1772, principally in the Carolina trade, and apparently managed the firm's commerce in London while Neufville operated in Bristol. Rolleston was identified by American radicals in London as being particularly opposed to their cause. He and Neufville later pursued substantial prewar debts owed to them in South Carolina. His partnership with Neufville seems to have ended in 1785, though he continued in trade in London before retiring to Nottinghamshire, near his birthplace.

RICHARD SHUBRICK II (1707–65) Born in London, Shubrick followed his father (also Richard) into the Carolina trade, first captaining an oceangoing ship. From 1739 he traded in Charles Town with John Nickleson, who was married to his sister Sarah; later Shubrick's younger brother, Thomas, joined the partnership, having also served a spell as a ship's captain. Shubrick married a wealthy widow and heiress, Elizabeth Vicaridge (née Ball), and through her and by other investments amassed sizable landholdings in the colony. After her death, Shubrick returned to London in 1747, where he became one of the capital's leading Carolina merchants and had prominent charitable and company directorships. His substantial wealth allowed him to buy houses outside London at Mile End and in Greenwich.

RICHARD SHUBRICK III (1741–97) Son of Richard Shubrick II. He was born in South Carolina but moved to London as a child. He followed his father into London's Carolina trade and served on the board of the London Assurance Company. By the American Revolution he was owed substantial debts in South Carolina but, despite his difficulties in recovering these after the war, remained prosperous with a large fortune and a sizable estate in Enfield, north of London.

THOMAS SHUBRICK (1710–79) Ship's captain and younger brother of Richard Shubrick II. He plied a route between London and Charles Town before joining his brother and brother-in-law, John Nickleson, in partnership in Charles Town in 1742. Though both Richard Shubrick and Nickleson returned to Britain in the

1740s, Thomas Shubrick remained in Charles Town, handling the South Carolina end of the business. He helped manage his brother's landholdings in the colony and became a major landowner in his own right. By his death he was one of the colony's largest slaveholders, owning 333 slaves. He also held numerous civic positions and served in the South Carolina Assembly.

JOHN WATKINSON (?–1742) Mariner and merchant in the Carolina trade. Watkinson operated during the 1720s as a merchant in Charles Town, where he acquired several properties. He retained these after returning late in the decade to London, where he continued to trade to South Carolina and lobby on the colony's behalf.

SAMUEL WRAGG (?–1750) London's foremost Carolina trader during the 1720s and 1730s. Wragg went from Britain to join his brother Joseph in Charles Town around 1710. During the next ten years their partnership, Joseph Wragg & Co., was probably the town's biggest trading house, particularly in the slave trade. Samuel Wragg also became a member of South Carolina's Assembly before relocating to trade in London from the early 1720s. Besides being one of the largest exporter of slaves to South Carolina in the next two decades, Wragg served as South Carolina's official agent in London between 1727 and 1731 and regularly appeared before the Board of Trade during the 1720s and 1730s. Wragg also became one of South Carolina's largest landowners.

TRADE, POLITICS, AND REVOLUTION

INTRODUCTION

"A large territory on the Atlantic Ocean, in a temperate latitude"—South Carolina and Great Britain

"Patience is a necessary ingredient to pass thro' life with tolerable quiet, but very few [are] embued with a sufficiency of it to combat Carolina disappointments," reflected Isaac King in 1790, looking back on a thirty-year career as one of London's foremost merchants in the "Carolina trade."[1] King had been one of a group of merchants in the British capital who specialized in handling South Carolina's staple exports of rice, indigo, deerskins, and naval stores, and who arranged the shipment of the merchandise, equipment, and slaves on which South Carolina and its economy depended. Like their counterparts in Charles Town, the merchants had grown rich on the back of their trade—in the words of one observer in South Carolina, "in general & almost to a Man by means of their Commissions & profits arising from such Trade, risen from humble & moderate Fortunes to great affluence, from walking upon foot to the command of Conveniences which render their legs and feet almost useless."[2] From King's vantage point in 1790, such wealth seemed a longtime past. The Revolutionary War and American independence had severed his links with South Carolina. Fruitless efforts to reclaim debts and land in the state that had been confiscated after the war had exhausted his patience and consumed him with "Carolina disappointments." King was not alone. In the previous ten years the relationship between Britain and South Carolina had been marked first by the colony's dramatic rejection of imperial authority, then by a war of often bitter savagery, and then by a resumption of trade at the war's end that was as quick—and in many ways quicker—as had been the breakdown of trade at the start of the war and as hard for many in the state to comprehend. This book tells the story of how commerce and politics combined to bring the relationship between Britain and South Carolina to this point.

Why South Carolina's merchant-planter elite class—one of the British Empire's wealthiest groups and ostensibly among the chief beneficiaries of the imperial system—came to reject British authority has long been debated by historians. Interpretations stressing the importance of ideological convictions have proposed how political objections overrode material economic arguments for maintaining the status quo.[3] Conversely, materialist interpretations of why Anglo-American relations broke down in the 1760s and 1770s attribute a powerfully provocative role to trade, and some in particular to the symbolic "meanings" that goods carried.[4] According to one consumerist interpretation, "British merchants bore as much responsibility as did members of Parliament for the growing unhappiness of American consumers from the 1760s."[5] In exploring how the commercial activities of London's "Carolina merchants" intersected with their political lobbying on South Carolina's behalf and how this dual role was understood by their correspondents in the colony, this book shows how economic and political forces were interrelated in the growing disenchantment of South Carolinians with their metropolitan trading partners and the system they represented.[6]

Sixty years before Isaac King's lament, London's Carolina merchants had proved their value to the colony in the first of many political interventions on South Carolina's behalf. They had successfully lobbied the British Parliament in 1730 to achieve a long-cherished ambition for the colony: the liberalization of rice exports. As bureaucratic as it sounds, this was a major achievement. Rice was South Carolina's principal export crop, in the words of one of its earliest historians, "the staple commodity of Carolina . . . the chief support of the colony, and its great source of opulence."[7] It was also the cornerstone of South Carolina's slave economy, with its cultivation reliant on the labor of enslaved Africans to plant and harvest the grain, and the source of good profits for planters, merchants, and—through duties—the British government. The 1730 Rice Act allowed South Carolina's planters and merchants and their British correspondents to ship the grain directly to Spain and Portugal for the first time, opening a significant new market for the crop and marking an important exemption within the strict Navigation Laws that governed trade in the British Empire.[8] For their lobbying, London's Carolina traders duly received the thanks of their counterparts in the colony. The passage of the legislation appeared to vindicate a system in which colonial interests could be effectively represented at the empire's heart by lobbyists and interest groups who themselves stood to benefit from a colony's greater well-being and development—a variant of the "virtual representation" by which British politicians would in the years before 1776 justify the colonies' lack of electoral representation in Parliament. Such a system depended on colonial and metropolitan interests being aligned and, as importantly, the perception that these interests were aligned.

The 1730 Rice Act heralded a series of successful political interventions by the "Carolina lobby" in Britain on the colony's behalf over the next thirty years. London's Carolina traders were to the fore. Financial stimuli were secured for the cultivation of silk, naval stores—the hemp, pitch, tar, turpentine, and certain types of lumber used to build and equip shipping—and indigo—the blue dye extracted from the indigo plant, which was from the 1750s second only to rice among South Carolina's exports. Military resources were sought to protect the colony and its trade. The merchants often found a receptive audience in Britain's political circles. From British policy makers' point of view, South

Carolina mattered commercially and strategically. Founded in 1670, it was throughout most of its colonial period Britain's southernmost colony of real size in North America. In comparison, Georgia, established in 1732, had a population of less than one-tenth of South Carolina's until as late as 1760. South Carolina was a vital link in the chain of imperial defense, a bulwark against threats from the rival French and Spanish Empires and from the Indian tribes on the southern frontier of British North America. It needed a robust economy and a population that could not only defend the colony but also provide a ready market for British goods and services and supply Britain with much-needed commodities. The fact that throughout the period from 1730 to 1783 more than half of South Carolina's residents were enslaved did not trouble British policy makers. In line with the precepts of mercantilism that governed British economic policy—that the nation's economic interests could best be strengthened by government intervention, through protection of domestic industries by tariffs, monopolies, and a favorable balance of overseas trade, and that colonies should support, benefit, and strengthen the "mother country"—these considerations underlay South Carolina's value to Great Britain.

Rice had taken its place as South Carolina's staple cash crop in the 1720s. Exports of the crop trebled during that decade, and with further steady growth throughout the colonial era, by the 1770s rice was behind only tobacco and the grain of the northern colonies as the third most valuable commodity export from British North America.[9] Rice's rise to preeminence followed the settlers' earlier ventures in trading with the region's Native Americans—Creeks, Cherokees, Choctaws, and Chickasaws—for deerskins to export, a trade that remained important to South Carolina for much of the eighteenth century and linked the colony's transatlantic trade to Indian trading networks stretching far into the North American continent. Other enterprises in supplying beef and pork, wood, and enslaved Indians to Britain's Caribbean colonies connected South Carolina to markets and communities across the Atlantic Ocean and around its shores from its earliest British settlement.[10] Connections to the West Indies were especially formative—many of South Carolina's first white settlers had come from Barbados—and would continue to be vital throughout the colonial period and beyond.[11]

Visitors to South Carolina were struck by its similarities with the West Indies in its climate, the characteristics of its elite white society, and above all by its demography. Enslaved black people were a majority of South Carolina's population from about 1710. In the words of one visitor from England, "with a few Exceptions, [they] do all the Labour or hard Work in the Country, and are a considerable Part of the Riches of the Province."[12] Such characteristics meant that the colony more closely resembled the plantation societies of Barbados and Jamaica than it did Britain's other mainland slave colonies, such as Virginia and Maryland. Back in London even officials responsible for overseeing Britain's colonies had difficulty distinguishing between South Carolina and the Caribbean islands.[13] Before the American Revolution marked the political separation of thirteen colonies from Great Britain, South Carolina was one of more than two dozen British colonies in the Western Hemisphere. Its connections for much of the eighteenth century with Jamaica and Barbados were at least as strong as those with Massachusetts, New York, or Virginia—a fact that histories of the American Revolution have often failed to emphasize.[14]

Not only were South Carolina's connections with the West Indies economically essential to the colony, with slaves on the islands' sugar plantations being major consumers of its rice, but they also reinforced the colony's strategic significance within the British Empire. South Carolina was both a leading source of provisions for the West Indies—in British policy makers' eyes, the jewel of the empire—and important to their defense. Charles Town was the largest town and the most important harbor in the southern half of British North America. Its population by 1730 numbered about four thousand residents, split almost equally between free whites and enslaved blacks. Within a decade this grew to six thousand, placing Charles Town behind only Boston, New York, and Philadelphia among the most populous towns in British North America. As well as being a major port, it was an important station for the Royal Navy in its defense of Britain's possessions in the Americas. In the warfare between Britain, France, and Spain that punctuated the eighteenth century, the port's value was magnified. The navy could use Charles Town as a base for patrols against the enemy privateers that preyed on British shipping and could itself disrupt rival nations' Atlantic commerce. Further enhancing its value to Great Britain, South Carolina's semitropical climate, abundant cultivable land, and slave labor force could provide Britain with much-desired commodities such as naval stores and, later, indigo that the country could not produce itself and which therefore did not compete with domestic industries. The significance of this point was not lost on South Carolina's governor James Glen when he characterized the colony in a report to his superiors in London in 1751. It was, he told them, "a large territory on the Atlantic Ocean, in a temperate latitude, the soil of which is found by experience capable of producing many commodities no way interfering with the product of the mother country, whose ports are good, and whose rivers are many of them navigable."[15]

The merchants who handled the fruits of South Carolina's land and labor, the produce shipped downstream on the colony's rivers from plantations to Charles Town, are this book's central characters. For a group of such importance in South Carolina's development, the colony's merchants and their counterparts across the Atlantic have been surprisingly neglected by history. "The role of merchants is often derided or devalued, when not dismissed altogether or assumed away . . . the area's precocious and prepossessing economic experience was due in large part to markets, merchants, and merchant capital," the historian Peter

Coclanis has observed; and for another, R. C. Nash, "our knowledge of the role of British merchants and capital in the South Carolina trade is very limited."[16] In the titles of two articles considering Anglo-American relations and the nature of Atlantic trade in the eighteenth century, the historian Jacob Price posed two questions: "What did Merchants do?" and "Who Cared about the Colonies?"[17] The answers to both these questions are interrelated.

The merchants at the forefront of London's Carolina trade—men such as Isaac King—cared about South Carolina for reasons that were commercial, economic, and social. The way they managed and manifested these concerns had profound implications for the stability of the imperial-colonial relationship between Britain and South Carolina, for that relationship's eventual collapse, and for the reconstitution of the relationship in a new form after American independence. In London, Carolina merchants had an important role as political as well as commercial connections in the fabric of the British Empire. They were South Carolina's leading lobbyists, operating alongside official agents employed by the colony to represent its interests. Not only was the British capital the country's most important port and the center for Britain's trade to South Carolina, but in addition the London Carolina merchants' location placed them close to the imperial corridors of power, facilitating their access to the political decision makers they sought to influence. Their lobbying was part and parcel of their regular business activities. As did merchants in other branches of Britain's colonial trade—but more actively and with greater success than most—the Carolina traders organized and signed petitions to the key institutions of imperial government: Parliament, the Treasury, and the Board of Trade, a committee of Great Britain's Privy Council that formally reported to the monarch and was charged with overseeing all matters relating to Britain's trade and colonies. They gave evidence to parliamentary committees investigating South Carolina's trade and defense and provided statistics to inform government policy. They reported all this back to their correspondents in Charles Town.

London's leading role in South Carolina's commerce was well known to contemporaries. "There are between Two and Three Hundred sail of shipping yearly Loaded from this port," the Charles Town merchant Robert Pringle told a prospective British entrant into the Carolina trade in 1738, "& the Chief part are Large ships for London & to London especially."[18] The capital's preeminence in South Carolina's transatlantic trade and the consequent influence of its merchants continued up to and beyond the American Revolution.[19] London was the most important destination for South Carolina's exports throughout the eighteenth century: it received the lion's share of the colony's indigo exports, the majority of its deerskins, and a large proportion of its rice. In terms of exporting goods to South Carolina, London's preeminence was still more pronounced, and it increased during the colonial period to account for between 85 and 90 percent of British merchandise exports to the colony between 1760 and 1774. In addition, while London's position in the Atlantic slave trade is often overlooked, with the roles of Bristol and Liverpool better known, the capital's merchants and shipping played a pivotal organizational and financial role in supplying the labor upon which South Carolina's economy and wealth were founded. London was the most important British port in the slave trade to South Carolina during the 1720s and 1730s, a dominance that declined only gradually in the second half of the eighteenth century. Throughout the period slave importers in Charles Town relied heavily on credit advanced by London merchants.[20]

The composition and structure of London's Carolina trade made the merchants within it especially active in their engagement with government. The trade was concentrated in relatively few hands. Most of the merchants at the forefront of the trade until the 1760s had lived and worked in Charles Town; many had bought houses and lots in the town and plantations across South Carolina's lowcountry and continued to hold on to these after leaving the colony. In contributing to the merchants' particular political activism on South Carolina's behalf, these compositional features would be a force for stability for much of the colonial period. As Anglo-American relations deteriorated from the 1760s, however, they took on very different implications. The merchants' activism with the government on commercial issues contrasted with inaction on more explicitly political matters. Concentration of trade became synonymous with domination of trade. Ownership of property and land in South Carolina became less a symbol of a benevolent stake in the colony than a facet of remote control. As British officialdom increasingly encroached into the lives of South Carolina's leading merchants and planters, they found that the system of lobbying and representation that had long proved effective could no longer provide relief. Their interests were no longer aligned with the men with whom they traded. Disputes between British merchants and their correspondents in South Carolina reflected in microcosm the geopolitical shifts of the time and show at an individual level how disenchantment with and then resistance to imperial authority developed.

Between the 1730s and the 1760s the lobbying, petitioning, and legislative initiatives mounted by London's Carolina merchants to gain favorable treatment for South Carolina and its goods sent important signals to their counterparts in Charles Town. These initiatives were seen to manifest the traders' commitment to the colony from which their wealth derived; even if unsuccessful, the intent behind the lobbying was itself significant.

Exploring the commercial trajectories of London's leading mid-century Carolina merchants is also vital to understanding the lobby's development. It was in South Carolina's own "metropolis," Charles Town, that these traders began their careers before relocating to London in search of still greater profits. In the capital they dominated Britain's trade with South Carolina and became the colony's principal advocates. Their routes into trade, such as through commercial apprenticeships and by captaining transatlantic shipping, and the influence of their early careers in Charles Town had lasting consequences. Experiences in South Carolina helped them build the capital and connections needed to prosper in transatlantic business and propelled them to the forefront of London's Carolina trade.

The lobby reached its zenith during the middle decades of the eighteenth century. Charles Town's merchants looked to their "Friends at Home"—a doubly revealing epithet—to represent mutual interests in imperial political forums. The structural features of London's Carolina trade strengthened its political impact. Chief among these features were its concentration in a relatively small number of hands, the personal experience that most of the merchants had of living and working in Charles Town, and the emergence of dynamic leadership within the trade. These distinguished the capital's Carolina lobby from other North American interest groups and contributed to its effectiveness. Merchants settled into business in London and came to dominate Britain's trade with South Carolina. The commercial activities of individual merchants were closely linked with their collective lobbying. James Crokatt's rise as London's leading Carolina merchant and the colony's foremost advocate in the capital revealed how shrewd traders could combine economic patriotism with commercial gain. The lobby's successes in securing a bounty—a supplementary sum paid by the government to incentivize production—on South Carolinian indigo and stimuli for the colony's silk, potash, and hemp came as it tapped into a favorable ideological environment in British politics.

The spells that London's leading Carolina traders—up to the 1760s at least— had spent in the colony distinguished them from many of their counterparts in other sectors of North American trade in Britain. This followed a practice more common in London's West Indies trade, in which many of the capital's merchants had honed their commercial expertise in the Caribbean. Absenteeism was typically associated in eighteenth-century Britain with ownership of lands in the West Indies or Ireland, and with harmful consequences. For the London Carolina merchants, ownership of property and plantations reinforced their commercial interests in the colony and contributed to their particular assiduity in promoting the colony's interests in Britain: absenteeism helped to amplify South Carolina's voice in the imperial corridors of power. Initially treated with ambivalence in the colony, by the eve of the American Revolution, however, this absenteeism had come to assume more negative political connotations.

The composition and structure of the transatlantic Carolina trade broadly served as a force for stability in relations between Great Britain and South Carolina. However, there was a multidimensional breakdown of trust within the trade during the 1760s and 1770s. Viewed retrospectively, the lobbying achievements of London's Carolina merchants over the previous thirty years took on a new dimension as the merchants' previous activism contrasted with their apparent inactivity and reluctance to intervene in the political disputes that exercised South Carolinians from the 1760s onward. Commercially, the concentration of London's Carolina trade in relatively few hands—once a factor in the efficiency of its lobbying—came to be seen as domination. While historians have assessed the economic implications of how specific trades became concentrated in fewer hands during the eighteenth century, this work assesses the political ramifications of this process. London merchants were held to be increasingly unsympathetic or even hostile to South Carolina's interests. As tensions between Britain and its American colonies mounted, the perceived commercial and political dependence on these uncertain London "friends" seemed no longer either effective or wise to many Carolinians. Their complaints were not expressed as explicit challenges to the mercantilist precepts that governed the British Empire's trade. However, critiques of supposed commercial malpractice were a tacit or at least incipient rejection of the systemic constraints that the empire imposed on the colony, constraints that had—many believed—led to the malign concentration of trade in London, furnished the capital's traders with great and excessive wealth, and allowed these traders to manipulate business in their own favor.

Events during the decade following American independence cast fresh light on the discord leading up to 1776. The postwar resumption of Anglo-Carolinian trade was marked both by commercial upheavals and by continuities. This book explores how trading links between South Carolina and Great Britain in the 1780s were strongly influenced by prewar politics. Britain remained the new state's largest overseas market, but this structural continuity—much bemoaned by many observers in Charleston—masked pronounced discontinuities within Britain's postwar Carolina trade. London's leading prewar Carolina merchants, nearly all of whom had come to be considered by Patriot observers as hostile to South Carolina's interests by the eve of the war, were spurned in postwar commerce because of their supposed prewar politics. Conversely, London merchants who had sympathized with or actively supported the American cause were favored. Exercising commercial choices in this way, South Carolinians confounded contemporary jeremiads that decried ongoing subservience to monolithic British business interests. Investigating how London's Carolina merchants continued to press and lobby the British government during and after the Revolutionary War also demonstrates the centrality of commercial matters in British policy making toward the United States during the 1780s and, accordingly, to Anglo-American relations in this critical decade of uneasy and hesitant rapprochement.

Like Isaac King, having conducted "a considerable Trade as a Merchant to the then Province of South Carolina" before the war, Joseph Nicholson was another merchant reduced by debts "from a Situation of comparative Elevation in which he and his Family enjoyed every comfort that affluence could afford to one of embarrassment and distress."[21] His family submitted a claim to the British government after the war for compensation for his losses. His and King's experiences typified the trajectories of the merchants whose commercial and political roles were crucial in South Carolina's development between 1730 and 1790. This development was achieved on the backs of displaced Native Americans and enslaved Africans, through agricultural innovation, economic stimulation, and political encouragement. At every stage of the process, merchants on either side of the Atlantic were central. Their trade and their lobbying had once brought South Carolina and Great Britain together. These activities also sowed the seeds for an irrevocable falling-out. The merchants' stories of political activity and inactivity, profits and losses, and reputation and notoriety are at the heart of this book.

CHAPTER ONE

"THE METROPOLIS OF SOUTH CAROLINA"

London Lobbying and Charles Town Commerce

In May 1730 the British Parliament passed the Rice Act, "granting Liberty to carry Rice from His Majesty's Province of Carolina, in America, directly to any port in Europe Southward of Cape Finisterre."[1] In an important amendment to the Navigation Acts that governed the empire's trade, the act allowed merchants to export the grain directly from South Carolina to Spain and Portugal and marked the culmination of twenty years of on-off activism by South Carolina's "friends" in London.[2] Renewed efforts had begun in February 1730. A petition from "several Merchants, Factors and Traders to *Carolina*" was presented to the House of Commons, recapitulating arguments made over the previous two decades in favor of direct exports to the Iberian Peninsula. The petition identified the demand for the colony's rice in Iberian markets but complained that the legal requirement that South Carolinian rice be landed in British ports before being reexported to Spain and Portugal made the trade uncompetitive: reexportation added to shipping costs and delayed the rice's arrival in Iberian ports until after the annual Lent peak in demand. As a consequence, the Iberian rice trade was "in the Hands of Foreigners, to the detriment of the *English* Merchants, and Planters." The London merchants who traded to South Carolina and comprised the "Carolina lobby" adopted a shrewd strategy. They strengthened their case by co-opting other commercial interests: petitions in support followed from merchants in the capital trading to Spain and Portugal and from Bristol merchants, manifesting a grouping that was both cross-sectoral and combined metropolitan and regional trading interests. Broadening the appellant base followed long-established precedents for petitioning Parliament in the eighteenth century and signified the Carolina lobby's tactical astuteness. The choice of two MPs to introduce the Rice Bill to Parliament demonstrated this again: Peter Burrell, MP for Haslemere in Surrey, was a leading London merchant in the trade to Portugal and a director of the South Sea Company; and Abraham Elton was MP for Bristol and regularly presented petitions from the city's merchants.[3]

Over the previous two decades, the Carolina lobby's regular petitions to Parliament had raised British political awareness of South Carolina. The lobbying coincided with rapid population and economic growth in the colony, which, coupled with profound political changes, had powerful implications for South

Carolina's transatlantic trade and its relationship with the British state. In the twenty years before 1730, South Carolina's population of free white and enslaved black residents had almost trebled, from 10,300 in 1710, roughly when the number of black slaves first exceeded that of free whites, to 30,000 in 1730 (table 1). Black slaves formed the clear majority of the population in 1730, numbering approximately 20,000 people. More than 9,000 enslaved black people had been brought into South Carolina over the previous ten years.[4] Rice underlay the dramatic demographic growth. Planted, harvested, and processed by slaves in the irrigated fields and swamps of South Carolina's lowcountry, the colony's rice exports had increased threefold during the 1720s. Most went via Britain to Holland, Germany, and Portugal and to the West Indies. At the same time, South Carolina's exports of deerskins had doubled, the volume of shipping clearing Charles Town harbor had grown by more than 100 percent, and per capita exports to Britain had risen by 37 percent.[5] Politically, in 1729 the British Crown had taken formal control of South Carolina as the authority of the colony's proprietors—the descendants and inheritors of the original eight Lords Proprietors who had founded the colony in 1670—was revoked after ten years of impasse.[6] South Carolina was more closely integrated into Britain's political and trading empire than ever before. As a colony that lacked the public and political profile of its northern neighbors, however, not to mention the West Indies sugar islands, its advocates in London needed to maneuver carefully to make their voices heard.

Petitioning between 1715 and 1730 that culminated in the Rice Act helped to put South Carolina on the political map in Britain. It also shaped the assumptions and expectations that would hold sway in South Carolina for the next half century about the responsibilities to the colony of London's "Carolina merchants." These were the capital's traders in South Carolina's exports of rice, naval stores, deerskins, and later indigo; they arranged the shipment of manufactured goods, textiles, foodstuffs, and other commodities to the colony and in some cases also supplied the slaves whose labor formed the basis of South Carolina's economy. Aside from their commerce, these were the men who would be the colony's leading interlocutors and lobbyists on matters of trade, regulation, and government in the empire's corridors of power. Understanding the commercial trajectories of London's leading Carolina merchants is essential in making sense of how this lobbying developed. It was in Charles Town—the "Metropolis of South Carolina"— that London's leading Carolina merchants cut their commercial teeth before relocating to the capital.[7] Their routes into trade were various. Some served apprenticeships with established merchants in Charles Town; others arrived on British North America's southern frontier as captains of oceangoing ships and opted to stay. For all, the time spent in Charles Town in their early careers was formative, garnering them the capital and connections that would enable them to prosper in Atlantic trade and would propel them to the forefront of the Carolina trade in London.

Table 1. Population of South Carolina, 1680–1790

	Total population	Black population	White population	Black population as % of total population
1680	1,200	200	1,000	16.7
1690	3,900	1,500	2,400	38.5
1700	6,260	3,000	3,260	47.9
1710	10,300	5,700	4,600	55.3
1720	18,328	11,828	6,500	64.5
1730	30,000	20,000	10,000	66.7
1740	54,200	39,200	15,000	72.3
1750	74,000	49,000	25,000	66.2
1760	94,074	57,334	36,740	60.9
1770	124,244	75,178	49,066	60.5
1780	180,000	97,000	83,000	53.9
1790	249,073	108,895	140,178	43.7

Source: Susan B. Carter et al., eds., *Historical Statistics of the United States: Millennial Edition* (New York: Cambridge University Press, 2006), I, 337; V, 651–55.

Mercantilism and "Interest"

South Carolina's value to Britain, like that of the other American colonies, was for most of the eighteenth century understood and articulated in terms of mercantilist orthodoxy. Since the sum of the world's wealth was finite, trade was seen as what modern theorists would call a "zero-sum game": the advantages Britain drew from economic growth would necessarily be to the disadvantage of rival nations. In practical terms, since a favorable balance of trade would augment Britain's wealth, the government's economic role was conceived as being to promote the nation's exports and restrict its imports in order to achieve this. For the first three-quarters of the eighteenth century, advocates of the free-trade liberalism advanced by Adam Smith in 1776 were in a distinct if occasionally vocal minority.[8] Articulations of South Carolina's value within Britain's Atlantic empire were accordingly mainstream. Extolling the colony's economic contribution to Britain to the Board of Trade in 1751, South Carolina's governor James Glen noted how "twenty five thousand [South Carolina's estimated white population] are wholly subsisted and supplyed by the produce of the land, without manufactures of any kind . . . a circumstance that makes us perhaps more valuable to our mother country than any other province on the continent."[9]

Glen echoed earlier assessments. Francis Yonge's 1722 *View of the Trade of South Carolina* suggested boosting the colony's trade in ways that reflected the prevailing political-economic climate. Directed at the Board of Trade, the tract appealed for permission for the colony to export rice directly to foreign markets, making its case in a series of conventionally mercantilist claims. Higher rice exports would redound directly to the benefit of the mother country: rice did not compete with any of Britain's crops, and therefore "every Hundred Weight sold to a Foreign market, is as much Money . . . added to the riches of Great Britain." A surge in risiculture would bring greater prosperity to South Carolina and thereby nourish greater demand for British manufactured goods. Yonge suggested that the government might reasonably require all ships in the rice trade to be wholly owned in Britain, stimulating British shipbuilding and elevating demand for colonial timber—a prime example of the presumed mutuality of domestic and colonial economic interest that his audience wanted to hear.[10]

South Carolina's productive potential was not lost on the more widely read economists of the day. Joshua Gee ruminated on the matter in his influential 1729 treatise, *The Trade and Navigation of Great Britain Considered.* Stressing the value of Britain's colonies through their production of staple crops for which Britain otherwise had to rely on foreign rivals, as well as the colonies' consumption of British manufactured goods, Gee highlighted the potential of the Carolinas and Virginia, "the most desirable of any in America for Latitude, Air, Soil, and navigable Rivers, and [which] lye so commodiously for corresponding with Europe." Naval stores, potash, and indigo were commodities ripe for cultivation in South Carolina and vital to Britain. Growing these in the colony would reduce Britain's dependence on foreign sources, improving the country's balance of trade with rival European powers and stimulating domestic manufacturing through height- -ened colonial demand.[11] Gee's was perhaps the best-known elaboration of a mercantilist refrain that was enshrined in law. Broadcast in published tracts and pervading the rhetoric of ministers and officials of state, his arguments were a staple of eighteenth-century political-economic discourse. It was no coincidence that they would also suffuse the appeals made with increasing frequency by South Carolina's commercial advocates in London.

For London's leading merchants, informing and influencing the state on commercial matters was part and parcel of their business. Merchants in the different branches of trade to the American colonies, whether the "New England trade," "Virginia trade," or "Carolina trade," were no exception.[12] One element of merchants' interactions with the state was giving evidence to inquiries by the Board of Trade or to parliamentary committees on issues about which they had knowledge or expertise. To shape or propose legislation relating to their trade, merchants turned to petitioning. Since the restoration of the monarchy in 1660, petitioning had been the main way for interest groups to make requests and express grievances to Parliament. Petitions were means of either introducing legislation or challenging existing laws. Circulated among and signed by interested parties, petitions were presented to Parliament by sympathetic MPs and then received readings. They were then either discussed in committee and ultimately informed new or amended laws or, in the face of opposition or lack of parliamentary time, were lost into the oblivion of unpassed legislation.[13]

The two decades before 1730 were formative years for Britain's nascent Carolina trade. In these years trade to South Carolina developed as a distinct specialism alongside longer-established branches of American trade—to New England, Virginia, or the West Indies. "Carolina merchants," as they came to be known, emerged as an identifiable group within the capital's panoply of traders. Their interactions with the British state were galvanized by South Carolina's appointment of its first formal representative in London, Abel Kettleby, in 1712. The appointment of a colonial agent followed precedent. Longer-established American colonies such as Virginia, Rhode Island, and Connecticut had long employed agents on a temporary and, from the 1680s, a permanent basis to represent their interests in the imperial metropolis—for example, lobbying the government on laws affecting the colonies, on trade regulations, and to encourage new settlement in America.[14] Kettleby's main task as South Carolina's agent was to ensure that Britain maintained a bounty on naval stores such as pitch, tar, and turpentine exported to Britain. A further objective was to gain South Carolina the freedom to export naval stores and rice to all foreign markets.[15] The position of a permanent colonial agent provided a figure around whom merchants could coalesce, and this Carolina lobby in London—mirroring the colony's rapid economic and demographic growth—became more and more active. The issues raised by the lobby reflected the exigencies of a young colony on the vulnerable southern frontier of British North America. Defending South Carolina from Indian and rival imperial threats and establishing a viable export-based economy were the two most pressing, and mutually reinforcing, priorities.

Who were the merchants who composed London's Carolina lobby? Capturing the membership of any branch of trade in eighteenth-century London is an inexact science; even defining the parameters of any given trade poses difficulties. No statistical records exist to reveal which merchants handled what goods, in what quantities, and at what frequency, and a lack of surviving commercial letters and accounts from either side of the Atlantic further complicates the study of the transatlantic Carolina trade before the 1730s. In light of these limitations, the petitioning activity of London's merchants offers the best guide to the size, composition, and organization of London's early Carolina trade. Thirteen surviving petitions signed between 1715 and 1730 by London merchants trading to South Carolina and two official lists of merchants identified as being involved in the trade reveal how a discernible Carolina lobby began to develop in London during the 1710s and 1720s. Although an imprecise guide to commercial activity, the frequency with which merchants signed the petitions implies the scale of their involvement in the trade. In total, some 113 different names appear on the handwritten petitions and lists.[16] This would seem to point to widespread involvement in London's Carolina trade, making it structurally analogous to the capital's Chesapeake trade—the only branch of London's American trades for which statistics on merchant participation have been assembled.[17] Closer analysis of the petitions suggests, however, that London's Carolina trade may have been concentrated in many fewer hands than the Chesapeake trade was. Among the 113 merchant signatories, some 69 appear on only one petition or list, 15 on two, 11 on three, and 8 on four petitions. Just 10 appear five or more times. Among the 10 most recurrent signatories, David and Stephen Godin were cousins, and William and Samuel Wragg were uncle and nephew, strongly suggesting that they were in trade together.[18]

The pattern of petitioning suggests that London's Carolina trade was relatively open to new entrants during the early eighteenth century, but that a much smaller number of merchants were involved over the long term and on a large scale. Other evidence corroborates this. The papers of Charles Town merchant Robert Pringle, the earliest major set of correspondence on Anglo-Carolinian trade, show his extensive dealings with specialist London retailers such as wig makers, gunsmiths, pewterers, and hatters. Specialist textile wholesalers—generically termed "warehousemen"—too supplied Charles Town trading houses throughout the colonial era, while hopeful exporters in London sent out unsolicited cargoes to Charles Town merchants in their eagerness to claim a share of South Carolina's growing market. "I have good friends enough in London that would send me more Dry goods than I could possibly Vend here, if was so Inclin'd without being so particularly Tied down in the Terms you propose," Pringle rebuked one hopeful London warehouseman.[19] Regular and large-scale London import-export merchants in the Carolina trade were scarcer. Although many in London had the capacity to send out cargoes of goods to be sold on commission in Charles Town—and were often accused in return of dumping outmoded, unseasonal, or unusable merchandise on the local market—fewer had the inclination or skill to receive and market remittances in the colony's principal exports of rice, deerskins, and naval stores.[20]

One of those who did, and who rose to preeminence in London's Carolina trade, was Samuel Wragg. Writing to the Board of Trade in 1724 to protest against a petition from London merchants that had complained about the colony's issuance of paper currency, South Carolina's governor Francis Nicolson testified to Wragg's status. "Mr. Samuel Wragg mercht. in London is more concerned in trade to this H.M. Province than all the petitioners and that his brother [Joseph Wragg] here with Messrs. Gibbon and Allen are by farr the greatest traders here [in Charles Town]," he reported.[21] Wragg's route to becoming London's leading Carolina merchant was a path that successors in the trade would follow. He was born in England and emigrated with his brother, Joseph, to South

Carolina in the first years of the eighteenth century. The pair soon emerged as two of Charles Town's leading traders. Samuel Wragg invested heavily in land and slaves, and he was elected to South Carolina's Commons House of Assembly, the lower house of the colony's legislature. In 1718, however, he returned to Britain, transferring his business to London. His connections in Charles Town and in particular his transatlantic trade with his brother, who remained in South Carolina, seem to have underpinned his commercial success in the capital.

In London, Wragg was the city's most prominent exporter of goods to South Carolina and recipient of the colony's produce, with some twenty different vessels that he owned or part-owned landing in Charles Town between 1717 and 1739.[22] He was also the largest single supplier of slaves to South Carolina during the 1720s and 1730s, with his ships bringing more than thirteen hundred enslaved Africans to the colony between 1725 and 1739. Wragg was the sole owner of several of these ships, a notable characteristic in a trade in which capital requirements made joint ownership of vessels the norm, pointing to the resources at his disposal.[23] His brother's presence in Charles Town facilitated his slaving ventures. Just as Samuel Wragg was the leading supplier of slaves to South Carolina, Joseph Wragg was the leading importer, handling twenty-two of the sixty-seven cargoes of slaves advertised in the *South Carolina Gazette* between 1733 and 1740, far more than any other trading house. Joseph Wragg paid £39,995 in duties on the slaves he brought into Charles Town between 1735 and 1739.[24] With an average duty of £10 currency on each adult slave brought directly into South Carolina from Africa, his firm may have been responsible for the importation of up to four thousand enslaved Africans in these years. Samuel Wragg's strong involvement in the slave trade distinguished him, however, from the next generation of London's leading Carolina traders, who nearly all concentrated on the commodity import and export trades and left human trafficking to specialist slave traders in London, Bristol, and Liverpool.

The regularity of the petitioning by London's Carolina merchants between 1715 and 1730 contrasted starkly with the inactivity of their counterparts in London's trade to Virginia, once the most energetic North American lobby. Having petitioned Parliament fourteen times in the quarter century before 1716, Virginia merchants did so just twice between 1716 and 1732 and not at all between 1733 and 1754. This reflected contrasting structural conditions in the two trades. Regional ports, particularly Glasgow, gradually supplanted London as the centers for Britain's tobacco business, while the capital's Virginia merchants lacked the effective leadership that had shaped the group's earlier lobbying. The diminishing political engagement of London's Virginia merchants has been attributed to the consolidation of the trade in fewer hands; in contrast, the concentration of London's Carolina trade among a small number of merchants appears to have had the reverse effect, fueling their lobbying activity.[25] The period between the 1710s and the 1730s was a time when strong leaders emerged in London's

Carolina trade. London controlled the largest share of Britain's imports of rice, deerskins, and naval stores from South Carolina and of the country's exports of manufactured goods to the colony; London also played a pivotal organizational role in the slave trade to South Carolina, as it did to Britain's other slave colonies. During this period there was a rise in the number of issues that called for effective advocacy in the imperial capital.

Defense, Rice, and the Emergence of a Carolina Lobby in London

The substance of the early petitioning in London on Carolinian matters reflected the colony's relative youth. Petitions were concerned in particular with trade and defense. Of the thirteen petitions between 1715 and 1730, five concerned British financial support for specific export produce as South Carolina searched for a staple cash crop on which to base an export-driven economy: three of these petitions were about naval stores, and one each about rice and potash. Four petitions concerned the issuance of paper currency in South Carolina, intermittently a source of friction between planters and merchants within the colony and between merchants in South Carolina—usually debtors who benefited from inflationary currency printing—and London's Carolina merchants—usually creditors hurt by inflation. Two were on colonial defense, one concerned judicial process in pursuing debts in the colony, and one sought generally to "retrieve the desolation of Carolina, to strengthen that frontier of our colonies on the continent & to encrease its Inhabitants & Trade."[26] In their subjects, their style, and for the most part their tactics, they foreshadowed the petitioning by the Carolina lobby in London until the Revolutionary War.

The grave threat to South Carolina during the Yamassee War in 1715–16 gave rise to London's Carolina merchants' first display of their ability to effectively conduct information about the colony to the Board of Trade and to petition on South Carolina's behalf. After years of growing indebtedness to white traders and of progressive encroachments on their lands, the Yamassee Indians, who lived along the Savannah River on South Carolina's southern frontier, attacked the white settlements in the south of the colony in April 1715. Over the following months as many as four hundred settlers and Indian traders were killed and the survivors driven from lands to the south of Charles Town. They withdrew to Charles Town, where a defensive perimeter was established, and all white men and hundreds of enslaved black men were mobilized. With the Yamassees in alliance with the region's Creeks, Choctaws, and Cherokees, the entire colony appeared in imminent danger of being overrun. "At no other time in colonial America," one historian has written, "did a colony face the danger that South Carolina did."[27]

In urgent response to the crisis, the colony's London agent Abel Kettleby organized some twenty-one "Planters and merchants trading to Carolina" in an appeal to the Board of Trade in July 1715 for immediate military aid for the colony: "Unless it is speedily relieved it must inevitably perish & all his Majesty's

Subjects there fall a prey to their barbarous Enemies," the petition warned. This appeal is a significant document in South Carolina's history that deserves to be better known. It powerfully asserts the inadequacy of South Carolina's proprietorial government; it is an early exposition of South Carolina's economic and strategic rationale; and it is the first coherent expression of British commercial advocacy on the colony's behalf. In stating the nature of their interests in South Carolina, the merchant signatories prefigured the financial and territorial commitments that future London Carolina traders would have in the colony, as they reported that "Most of us have great Debts and Effects there, some of us large Plantations; & the Loss of these would be Considerable." Beyond their own investments in South Carolina, the merchants were at pains to elide personal and British national interest, following mercantilist orthodoxy in pointing out the colony's commercial and fiscal contributions to Great Britain. South Carolina, they asserted, had "for many years taken off so much of our English manufactures, & brought such a large Revenue to the Crown, by the Duties upon Rice, Skins, Pitch, Tarr, & other Naval Stores & Commodities imported from thence, & yet from the first Settlement of it has not put the Crown to one Penny Expence." Besides its economic significance to Great Britain, South Carolina occupied a crucial strategic location on the frontier of the British Empire and was a vital bulwark in a North American chain of defense. If the colony were to be overrun by Indians, behind whose revolt the guiding hand of France and Spain was discerned, "all the other Colonies would soon be involved in the same Ruine & the whole English Empire, Religion & Name be extirpated in America." The petition was also an early acknowledgment of South Carolina's worrying racial imbalance, with black slaves already outnumbering white settlers. The petitioners counted some two thousand white men in the colony able to bear arms, plus about sixteen thousand blacks, "some of which might be armed in our Defence if we had any Arms to supply them withal; But in that too there must be great Caution, least our Slaves when armed might make themselves Masters."[28]

The lobbyists persuaded Parliament to promise aid, although in military terms it was the raising of the local militia, the arrival of men and arms from New England and Virginia, and a diplomatic alliance with the Cherokees that were the critical factors in suppressing the Yamassee revolt.[29] Two petitions to the British government in July and September 1715 against Virginia's trade in guns and ammunition to Indians were significant too in planting South Carolina in Britain's political consciousness.[30] As the House of Commons committee that heard the July petition reported, South Carolina's ruin would be "to the great Prejudice of his Majesty's Subjects, and the Trade of this Kingdom." The consideration of the petition by the Commons demonstrated the efficacy of the Carolina lobby's political advocacy, leading to the first recorded discussion in Britain of the inadequacy of South Carolina's proprietorial government in the face of Indian and concerted French and Spanish threats. In the Commons on 10

August 1715, the revocation of the proprietors' charter was subtly mooted: "That the Proprietors not being able, at their own Charges, either to send the necessary Succours for the present Relief of the said Province, or to support it under the like for the future, your Committee submit, in what manner it may be most proper to preserve and maintain this so valuable a Province, which is a Frontier of the British *Plantations* on the Continent."[31]

The duties on colonial naval stores, South Carolina's issuance of paper currency, and—in particular—the liberalization of rice exports further stimulated the development of London's Carolina lobby. Rice would be, as one of South Carolina's first historians, David Ramsay, later put it, "the chief support of the colony . . . of more value than mines of silver and gold."[32] More than any other commodity, rice furnished South Carolina with export earnings and—for its white elites—wealth; embedded slavery at the colony's economic, demographic, and social heart through the reliance on slave labor for cultivating the crop; and connected the colony with markets around the Atlantic. The first successful experiments in risiculture during the 1690s had shown South Carolina's early white settlers the grain's economic potential, and from the early eighteenth century they had sought favorable legislative and fiscal treatment for it. Merchants in London, who stood to benefit from enlarged rice exports and the consequent increase in demand in South Carolina for imported goods, were willing catalysts. The eventual passage of the Rice Act in 1730 represented the culmination of twenty years' campaigning by South Carolina's official agents and London's Carolina merchants.[33]

As rice had not originally been one of the "enumerated commodities"—colonial produce such as sugar, coffee, and tobacco that according to the Navigation Acts could be exported only to Britain—Carolinian planters had at first been able to export their crop directly to Portugal and to foreign colonies in the West Indies. In 1704, however, this trade was outlawed. Direct rice exports were, the prohibiting statute observed, "contrary to the true Intent and Meaning" of the Navigation Acts, and rice was added to the list of enumerated commodities.[34] For Joshua Gee, the ban was due to the machinations of a ship's captain, who "possessed a Member of Parliament . . . with an Opinion that carrying Rice directly to Portugal was a Prejudice to the Trade of *England*, and privately got a clause into an Act to make it an enumerated Commodity." Gee condemned this rigid extension of the law, exposing the fault lines between mercantilist precepts as enshrined in the Navigation Acts and—as he saw it—the true spirit of mercantilism. "This could not have happened," he claimed, "if that Gentleman who brought in that Clause had understood the Nature and Circulation of Trade, he would have then known, that it is much more the Interest of the English Merchant to sell his Rice in Portugal, and have the money remitted thence, than it is to have it brought to England, and afterwards shipp'd to Holland, Hamburgh, or Portugal; for the Difference in the freight and Charges is at least 50 per Cent."[35]

After Abel Kettleby's efforts to have rice removed from the list of enumerated commodities had come to naught, such attempts continued intermittently during the 1710s and 1720s. In March 1715 three British merchants trading in Oporto, Portugal, told the Board of Trade that South Carolina might export some six thousand barrels of rice a year to Portugal if direct exports were allowed. With sound mercantilist logic, they insisted that the direct trade "might be a considerable benefit to Great Britain, and his Majesty no loser in his duties by their being paid in South Carolina."[36] The Portugal traders' evidence hinted at the incipient sophistication of the campaign, both in the arguments they deployed and in co-opting wider trading interests. Over the next decade, members of South Carolina's London lobby would seek and gain the support of their counterparts in the capital's Iberian trade in their efforts against the restrictions. In a striking gesture, South Carolina's Assembly—as the Portugal merchants had hinted—even offered to offset the losses in customs duty that would be caused by rice exports not landing in British ports before reexportation.

In appointing Francis Yonge and John Lloyd as joint agents for South Carolina in 1722, the colony's government made one of the agents' principal duties to "endeavour to get the enumeration of rice taken off." To help achieve this, they were instructed, "You may propose that the same duty may be pay'd upon the exportation of rice from hence for a revenue to the King in this Province, as is now reserved to the Crown after allowing the rebate upon the exportation from South Britain [Britain's south coast reexport ports such as Poole and Cowes]."[37] This would make the liberalization of rice exports revenue-neutral to the British Treasury: a duty would be paid in South Carolina equivalent to that which would have been paid had the rice landed in England. The agents coordinated a petition signed by twenty-seven "merchants & traders to Carolina, Spain & Portugal" urging that rice be taken off the list of enumerated commodities; however, after the petition was introduced to Parliament in November 1722, it failed to progress through committee hearings.[38]

A further attempt in 1725 indicated the Carolina lobby's growing tactical sophistication. While the previous effort had sought permission for direct rice exports to Spain, Portugal, and the West Indies, the renewed attempt had a more limited goal, seeking direct rice exports only to European ports south of Cape Finisterre in Spain. A more powerful coalition of interests was aligned behind the proposal. Samuel Wragg, London's leading Carolina merchant, sought to harness the influence of the South Sea Company, which had a monopoly on the slave trade to Spain's American colonies, to "get off the Enumeration on Rice." He paid some £33 to the company's secretary and a further £150 "to Solicitors, Clerk's Fees and other Servants of both Houses of Parliament."[39] Although the effort was again unsuccessful, the potential efficacy of London lobbying was not lost on South Carolinians. Wragg had been, observed South Carolina's Assembly, "very Serviceable to this Province in endeavouring to get the Enumeration of rice taken off, and the bounty again given on Pitch & Tarr and in several other negotiations tending to the benefit and advantage of this Province."[40] The partial removal of rice from the list of enumerated commodities in 1730, allowing it to be sent directly to Spain and Portugal, would be the ultimate reward for Wragg's efforts.

If achieving the 1730 Rice Act showed London's nascent Carolina lobby the benefits of cooperating with other interest groups that had connections in Parliament, the value of these connections was confirmed five years later. As was common in trade legislation, the permission for direct rice exports to Iberia had been granted for a limited period, so that its effects might be reviewed. It was due to expire in September 1735. In spring 1735 Peregrine Fury, who had been appointed as South Carolina's official agent in London two years earlier, led moves to get Parliament to prolong the act. His efforts were facilitated by the establishment of Georgia on South Carolina's southern flank and by the new colony's prominent supporters in Parliament. Fury attended a meeting of the Georgia Trustees and, in the words of their president, the Earl of Egmont, asked "that we would befriend them in a Bill they are endeavouring to procure. . . . We replied in writing that we should always contribute our endeavours for the advancing the interests of Carolina."[41] With backing from Georgia's supporters in Parliament, an act prolonging direct rice exports from South Carolina to southern Europe and extending this privilege to Georgia was quickly made law.[42]

Growing in volume and, through the London Carolina merchants' interactions with the state, in prominence, the Carolina trade was recognized by the 1730s as a distinct branch of the capital's trade. Contemporaries distinguished it among the various groupings of London merchants. A writer to the *Universal Spectator and Westminster Journal* in 1734 listed the "Meetings of Clubs of Particular Merchants, either fix'd or occasional . . . the Turkey and Italian Merchants, the Spanish, the Portuguese, the French, the Flandergan, the German, the Danish, the Swedish, the Muscovite, the Dutch, the Irish, the West India, the Virginia, the Carolina, New York and New England Merchants."[43] In their composition, tactics, and rhetoric the Carolina merchants' petitioning efforts between the 1710s and 1730s laid the foundations for lobbying in London on Carolinian matters over the next fifty years. These initial efforts also shaped how London's Carolina merchants understood their interactions with the state. Theirs was not a formal political role: with a few exceptions, they did not become MPs, nor did they even seek political positions within the City of London. Instead their efforts were intermittent and issue-driven. South Carolina's lobby in London interacted with the Board of Trade, the British Treasury, and with Parliament as and when necessary on specific issues, providing information, giving expert advice, and asking supportive MPs to propose and guide legislation. It was not unusual in this, but in its energy during the 1720s, the Carolina lobby stood out. As significantly, these early efforts were also important in the way they informed expectations in South Carolina of the attentiveness and efficacy of London's Carolina merchants as the colony's informal representatives in the capital.

From its outset in the first decades of the eighteenth century, London's Carolina trade was concentrated in the hands of a small number of merchants. Its coherence made it a particularly responsive and productive lobby. The trade's domination by a small number of merchants remained a feature after Wragg and the capital's other leading Carolina merchants of the 1720s and 1730s retired or died. Close personal connections with South Carolina from having lived and worked in the colony was a defining feature of the group of merchants who came to the fore of London's Carolina trade during the 1740s and 1750s, as had been the case with Wragg. In this, London's Carolina trade appears to have been exceptional among the different branches of the capital's North American trade in the mid-eighteenth century. It was common for merchants in ports across Britain's Atlantic empire to have spent part of their training or early careers elsewhere. A number of merchants in London's various North American specialisms—the New York, New England, or Virginia trades, for example—had had such experiences.[44] But in that all of London's leading Carolina merchants during the 1740s and 1750s had spent time in Charles Town, and especially in the long duration and nature of their spells working there, they were distinct. This made the capital's Carolina trade closer in composition to its West Indies counterpart than to other branches of trade to mainland North America. Many, perhaps most, of London's West Indies merchants had commercial or planting experience on the Caribbean islands, building capital and connections there before relocating to Britain.[45] Early commercial experiences in Charles Town were similarly formative for the leading merchants in London's Carolina trade in the 1740s and 1750s.

Getting into the Carolina Trade

The career of James Crokatt, who would become London's foremost Carolina merchant and advocate during the middle decades of the eighteenth century, exemplifies how a savvy merchant could prosper in the Carolina trade. Crokatt was born in Edinburgh in July 1701, but his early life is obscure before his arrival in South Carolina sometime before 1728.[46] In Charles Town, Crokatt would have found a rapidly growing Atlantic seaport. Perched on a peninsula between the Ashley and Cooper Rivers, Charles Town in 1730 had a population of around four thousand, split almost equally between free whites and enslaved blacks. With a regimented grid of streets and wharves along "the Bay"—the strip of waterfront facing the Cooper River and the center of Charles Town's commercial life—it was the only town of note in South Carolina and comfortably the largest urban center in the southern colonies. Charles Town's growth was fueled by South Carolina's dramatic economic expansion. Rice exports had trebled in the previous ten years. Thousands more enslaved Africans had been brought to South Carolina during the 1720s to labor in the growing rice plantations, and the colony's combined population of free white people and enslaved black people had grown by three-quarters. It almost doubled again during the 1730s as forced and free immigration continued apace. Charles Town's population grew to over six thousand by the end of the decade, making it the fourth largest settlement in British North America, behind only Boston, Philadelphia, and New York. South Carolina's risicultural boom continued through the 1730s. As exports flourished, imports reached new heights as well: by the end of the 1730s, Charles Town received at least 15 percent of all imports into North America from England measured by value. A growing community of merchants handled the increasing volume of trade: the rice, deerskins, and naval stores that flowed out of the port, and the slaves and goods that arrived at its wharves. Between 1732—when the weekly *South Carolina Gazette* became the colony's first newspaper—and 1737 some 122 different merchants advertised their wares. Prospective merchants and tradesmen arrived from Britain and from other American colonies to claim a share of Charles Town's burgeoning commerce.[47]

An Exact Prospect of Charles Town, the Metropolis of the Province of South Carolina, 1762. Unattributed, engraved for the *London Magazine.* Library of Congress.

Crokatt's was perhaps a family migration. One brother, Daniel, owned land in Jamaica; other siblings, John and Elizabeth, were both in Charles Town by the late 1730s. Like James Crokatt, they were drawn to trade: Elizabeth Crokatt married the merchant William Woodrop, while John Crokatt also traded, though the two brothers were apparently not formally connected in business. Another John Crokatt, possibly a cousin, traded in Charles Town in the 1730s too.[48] By 1731 James Crokatt was operating from a grand countinghouse and store on Broad Street, Charles Town's premier commercial thoroughfare, where he built up one of the town's leading trading houses. John Beswicke was another Charles Town merchant who would later dominate London's Carolina trade. His entry into commerce in Charles Town also shows the importance of family connections. A native of Yorkshire, he went to South Carolina around the turn of the 1730s, where another John Beswicke—his father or uncle perhaps—was already established as clerk of the markets. The younger Beswicke opened a store near Crokatt's on Broad Street, possibly having inherited the premises from his relative, who died in 1735.[49]

Although the exact details of how Crokatt and Beswicke began in trade are obscure, the routes taken by fellow Charles Town traders—several of whom, like them, later relocated to London—are better documented. They illustrate the allure of the Carolina trade, the opportunities it offered, and the means by which time and experience in Charles Town laid the foundations for future commercial fortunes in London. Captaining a ship offered one path into trade in Charles Town. Mariners gained special insights into market conditions through supervising the handling and exchange of goods at either end of a voyage, and the trustworthiness and skill of ships' captains were vital to successful transatlantic commerce. Knowledge of winds and oceanic currents and the art of "seamanship" reduced crossing times and ensured that cargoes arrived safely, making experienced navigators highly valued. "The good of the Voyage depends [on] having a Clever Brisk Commander that is a good Seaman & well Qualified for his Business," observed Charles Town merchant Robert Pringle.[50] Besides making the Atlantic crossing in a safe and timely fashion, a captain in the Carolina trade was required to make technical decisions about the commodities on board. Errors of judgment in loading a ship could damage or even destroy precious cargoes. When his brother's ship *Susannah* arrived poorly stowed in Charles Town, Pringle offered a warning: "It certainly requires a great deal of Judgment & Experience in the Stowing of a Ship with dry Goods which is a Main Matter in Regard to the Voyage. The *Susannah* will get a bad name here by haveing Goods Damaged every Voyage & people wont care to Ship on her."[51]

Able captains gleaned valuable insights into the business of Atlantic trade through being exposed to the factors influencing supply and demand, the profitability of different commodities, the appropriate storage and packing of goods, and the seasonality of voyages. Their role also offered them a foothold in trade itself, even if they did not have the capital to invest in a large cargo or the connections to supply with goods. With some personal space on board ship, a captain could stow goods that he could sell on his own account at the ship's destination. With judgment and good timing, he could accumulate sufficient capital over time to set up as an independent trader or become an agent in the port for an overseas trading house. John Watkinson typified the latter path. A mariner in the Carolina trade, he settled in the 1720s in Charles Town, where he acted as a factor for the Rotterdam firm of Hope & Hope, importing and selling the firm's goods on commission and brokering cargoes for export to Europe. He invested his profits in several properties in the town. He had returned to London by 1730 and became one of the capital's leading Carolina traders in the 1730s.[52]

A decade after Watkinson, brothers-in-law Richard Shubrick and John Nickleson followed a similar route: from captaining Atlantic shipping, to commerce in Charles Town, to prominence in London's Carolina trade. Both Shubrick and Nickleson began their trading careers as ship captains. Originally from Stepney, just east of London and home to many of the city's mariners and their families, Richard Shubrick took over command of the *Loyal Jane* from his father. During the 1730s he plied a regular trade between London, Charles Town, and the West Indies. Besides supplying goods to Charles Town's merchants, Shubrick also sold merchandise during his spells in Charles Town between voyages and bought land in the colony.[53] At the same time John Nickleson made regular transatlantic crossings in charge of the 100-ton *Pelham* and its eleven crew members and then the 160-ton *Minerva*. From London the ships most often brought textiles and clothing for Charles Town's stores, though sometimes they carried more exotic goods too, such as umbrellas, "Squire's elixir, spirit of lavender, anchovies, olives, walnuts and capers." Nickleson and Shubrick went into partnership together in Charles Town in 1739. The firm became one of the town's leading retailers, selling a familiar mix of textiles, plantation tools, and consumables, while Shubrick's younger brother Thomas took over the command of the *Minerva*.[54] After several years in Charles Town, Nickleson and Shubrick relocated to London in 1743 and 1747 respectively, and there they became two of the capital's leading Carolina merchants.

If captaining an oceangoing vessel was one common route into trade in Charles Town, an even more prevalent path was by serving a commercial apprenticeship, as was true in London and in British regional ports. A clerkship was a sound footing through which to learn a trade, establish a network of contacts, and build a reputation. Writing later in the century, the merchant, planter, and statesman Henry Laurens set out the advantages of learning at an established merchant's elbow. "I would advise a Young Gentleman rather to serve as a Clerk than to dabble as a petty Merchant," he explained to a correspondent in Savannah; "in the former case he is always loose & open to good offers & very often rises with great experience into considerable trade. In the Latter I have often observed worthy young Men by precipitate engagements in Trade confine themselves within a narrow compass & remain in a state little better than stagnant, for many Years."[55] Laurens's advice was grounded in personal experience. Born in South Carolina in 1724 and raised in the colony, he had spent time in London in the 1740s as a clerk to James Crokatt, by then established as the capital's leading Carolina merchant. Although Laurens's connection with Crokatt ended in disappointment, as his attempts to become a partner in Crokatt's firm were denied, he nonetheless valued his commercial training highly.[56] Having returned to Charles Town and established himself in trade, Laurens took on a number of young apprentices himself. Working alongside an established trader, an apprentice learned the negotiations and bargain-striking of daily routine, calculations of price and risk, weights and measures, and strategic decisions on the freighting and destinations of vessels. Practical responsibilities supplemented his observational gleanings. Besides making invoices, copying letters, and manning retail stores, young clerks were also tasked with marking rice barrels or transporting goods to and from the town's wharves.

Apprenticeships, at least with Charles Town's more conscientious merchants, also incorporated training in the theory of commerce. Alongside learning on the job, an apprentice was expected to spend a portion of his leisure time studying manuals on aspects of trade such as accounting and commercial regulation. Didactic literature such as Malachy Postlethwaite's *Universal Directory of Trade and Commerce* or Henry Saxby's *The British Customs* found a place on Charles Town's countinghouse shelves just as they did in contemporary London. During his commercial training, a young clerk could also expect to make himself known to potential future trading partners. Introductions to fellow Charles Town traders were one part of this; still more beneficial was the chance to join his master on trips to other ports, even across the Atlantic, where he might meet important correspondents. In contrast, setting up independently as a small trader—though superficially more alluring—carried greater risks with fewer opportunities to make connections. As Laurens counseled, following this avenue would "seldom intitle you to an acquaintance with Men of consequence & at the same time are generally attended with most trouble."[57]

To grasp fully the complexities of transatlantic commerce, it was thought particularly advantageous for merchants-in-training to spend part of their early careers on the other side of the Atlantic. Those seeking to trade from Britain to South Carolina would benefit from a grounding in Charles Town's commercial scene, and vice versa. After he had relocated from Charles Town to London in 1747, John Beswicke secured a four-year apprenticeship for a nephew at a prominent Charles Town trading house.[58] Another young man, Peter Taylor, spent several years as an apprentice at his uncle's Charles Town countinghouse and lowcountry estates. Though admonished by his uncle for his hedonistic lifestyle and "rough, forward and noisy carriage," he became a substantial merchant on his return to his native Whitehaven, a port in northern England.[59] Even South Carolina's minor ports could furnish a good commercial education for trainees coming to the colony from Britain. One young Londoner went into partnership in a small trading house in Georgetown, some eighty miles north of Charles Town, where it was noted that he "will not spend his time unprofitably by a few Years residence in this part of the World where he will probably gain more knowledge of Men & business than he could have done in twice the time in London."[60]

In the late 1730s Robert Pringle had looked across the Atlantic for a bookkeeper. Like many of his fellow traders in the town, Pringle had been born in Scotland, and he had served an apprenticeship with a West Indies merchant in London before traveling to South Carolina in his early twenties. His particular requirements in any new clerk, sobriety and honesty, were perhaps qualities he identified in his younger self. He set out the terms for the bookeeper's engagement to a London correspondent, asking that "if you should happen to hear of a good Sober Young Man that writes a good hand & is a good Accomptant & can be well recommended & inclinable to come over here for his Encouragement, [I] shall be willing to give him at the rate of Forty Pounds Sterling (as the Exchange goes) Sallary per annum & Lodging & board & if he behaves to my liking will encrease his salary & keep him for a term of years." As he was a shrewd trader, Robert Pringle's generosity toward his new charge had limits, however: the clerk would have to be willing "to come over on the terms above mention'd & pays his own Passage & c."[61] The last stipulation was perhaps a deterrent to would-be apprentices: when two young clerks, James Ogilvie and George Inglis, arrived with Pringle three years later, their £21 passage had been paid for them on Pringle's behalf by his London-based brother, Andrew.[62]

Ogilvie and Inglis would have starkly contrasting experiences of apprenticeship with Pringle. Ogilvie's apprenticeship began inauspiciously and went downhill. Having been captured by a Spanish privateer en route to Charles Town, delaying his arrival and adding greatly to the cost of his crossing, he was unprepared for the cut and thrust of trade in the port. He found his master hard to please and ruthless in his pursuit of profit. "It was not long that he [Pringle] treated me with common Civility," Ogilvie complained to his brother in Scotland; "I soon began to experience the Effects of his Temper. It is impossible to do anything to please him, and he is continually finding fault with the smallest Trifles . . . Mr. Pringle himself has a most villainous temper, and is a Man I have not the least reason to expect anything from, for his own Interest, and a Desire of Scraping up Riches at any Rate is his only aim." Overwhelmed by loneliness, he advised his brothers that any of them wishing to enter commerce should seek training nearer to home. Nonetheless he persevered in trade in Charles Town and went into partnership with Pringle's former business partner in a store "on the bay."[63] By contrast, Inglis adapted more easily to his commercial training with Pringle. In 1745, two years after Inglis's arrival, Pringle reported his "Good Behaviour Since he has Liv'd with me, so much to my Satisfaction & of the Great Regaurd & Esteem I have for him." That same year Inglis began investing his own capital in joint cargoes with Pringle, and in 1749 the pair entered formal partnership.[64] Both Ogilvie and Inglis chose to remain in Charles Town to make their fortunes with established merchants. Illustrating the breadth of commercial opportunity around the Atlantic littoral, other apprentices in the town sought to further their commercial education elsewhere. After beginning as a clerk to a merchant in Charles Town, one trainee, John Brown, received a better offer and decamped to join a firm of traders in New Providence, Bahamas.[65]

For many young men entering trade in Charles Town, partnerships were both logical and financially essential. Partnerships reduced the start-up capital required of an individual; allowed the pooling of knowledge, experience, and contacts; and spread the financial risks of trade. However, capital and some experience were needed to entice a potential partner into a formal connection. These requirements led some would-be merchants to pursue a different strategy: the alluring if risky approach of going it alone, which offered greater flexibility, autonomy, and the whole share of future profits. To do this required carefully accumulating one's own capital to invest in a cargo of imported goods. Another young Scottish apprentice in Charles Town, Alexander Cumine, vacillated between going into partnership and going it alone. Having served two years in his mentor's trading house and living with his employer at his premises—as was customary—he weighed his options. He first considered investing his spare cash in a cargo of imported textiles. However, "if you get a substantial partner you will do very well," he mused, before striking upon a strategy that would provide him with the means to achieve this. Buying some two hundred or three hundred pounds in goods on credit from his connections in London would, he believed, "enable me to enter into partnership with some Merchant here. I might make a perhaps pretty good Fortune for myself in a short time; and this is the way all the Merchants here have begun viz. by Credit & if one be diligent & industrious & make proper Remittances the Merchants at home [Britain] will trust him more; and so enable him to extend his trade further. There is plenty of money to be got here if one was once in the way of making it."[66]

As Cumine appreciated, access to credit was vital in entering trade. Some young merchants were able to call on family wealth. After completing a five-year apprenticeship in Charles Town, one aspirant trader was promised a "very pretty foundation" of two thousand pounds by his father to set himself up; this money would allow him "to live genteely in the Character of a Young Merchant."[67] In preparation for setting up in business in Charles Town, he made visits to Jamaica "to make an acquaintance with Gentlemen in Trade at Kingston" and to Europe "to form some Connections with Men in Trade in Portugal, Spain, Great Britain, and Holland." Illustrating the range of markets for Carolinian produce and the breadth of connections required by an ambitious Charles Town merchant, his various ports of call included London, Bristol, and Liverpool; Amsterdam, Rotterdam, and Hamburg; and Oporto, Lisbon, and Cadiz. James Habersham, one of the leading merchants in Savannah, Georgia, set aside five thousand pounds in start-up capital for his sons' new partnership; he believed this amount to be "a sufficient Fund to carry on Business in a respectable Manner."[68] Another new partnership aimed to muster a starting capital stock of five thousand pounds. "'Tis enough," reckoned Henry Laurens, advising its young partners, that "you shall not want, nor make a mean Entrance."[69]

For many would-be Charles Town traders, however, raising the money needed to enter trade was no easy feat. After James Ogilvie had eventually established himself in trade in Charles Town, his twenty-year-old brother Charles decided to follow from Scotland to seek his own fortune in the town. Perhaps mindful of his brother's initial problems, Charles Ogilvie opted not to take an apprenticeship but to raise capital in London before going to South Carolina. He was unsuccessful. He first approached George Udney, both a fellow Scot and a London merchant in the capital's Carolina trade, "believing he would have something for me . . . but I happened to be mistaken, for he absolutely refused me Credit."[70] Undeterred, Charles Ogilvie traveled to Charles Town anyway. As he lacked an established partner or any capital of note, his first ventures in trade came to nothing. He complained to his brother of "the difficulty of getting a tolerable maintenance in this country . . . I endeavoured to push a little in Trade myself & sent two or three small Adventures to the West Indies, but without success."[71]

House of Robert Pringle, 1774. Tradd Street, Charleston. Photograph by author.

No branch of Atlantic trade offered greater dividends than the slave trade, and with an entrepreneurial mind-set and an eye for a profit, Ogilvie was drawn toward it. He was offered a job as a supercargo—a shipboard agent charged with managing deals on a merchant's behalf—on a vessel that was bound from Charles Town for Guinea on the coast of West Africa to collect a cargo of ninety slaves. The position offered the possibility of one hundred pounds in commission for Ogilvie and for the ship's captain. For Ogilvie, the notorious morbidity of West Africa and the horrors of the Atlantic Middle Passage aboard a slave ship—the mortality rate among slave ships' crews approached that of the ships' enslaved occupants—were worth the risk since the proceeds he would make from the voyage would give him the chance to establish himself in Charles Town.[72] He noted glibly that "all that go upon the Coast of Guinea run a great risk. But I believe 'tis not so bad as 'tis represented, & likewise I believe Dread & Debauchery kill as many as the Climate." He asked his brother, "Who in my situation would not run a risk, for the Prospect of getting into Business, which if we meet with Success, in all probability would make our Fortunes in a few years."[73]

When the partnership backing the venture pulled out, Ogilvie and the captain took matters into their own hands. They agreed to fit out a small, sixty-ton vessel at their own cost, estimated at three hundred pounds, and to go to the Guinea Coast anyway. There they hoped—wildly unrealistically—to buy and bring back to South Carolina a cargo of six hundred slaves.[74] Although the outcome of Ogilvie's first slaving venture is unknown, he eventually succeeded in becoming a leading merchant in Charles Town. The three different partnerships he was a member of imported slaves from Africa and merchandise from the West Indies and from Britain's other North American colonies. Through marrying the daughter of South Carolina's chief justice, he became a large landowner in South Carolina. Maintaining the entrepreneurialism that propelled his rise in Charles Town's commerce, he transferred his business to London in 1761 in search of the even greater profits offered by trade in the capital. His early commercial rise is one of the best documented and most eventful among all South Carolina's Atlantic traders. In its motivations and trajectory, from relative obscurity in Britain to prominence in Charles Town and on to commercial zenith back in London, it was entirely typical.

Trading in Charles Town

Having established themselves in business in Charles Town, Crokatt, Beswicke, Nickleson, and Shubrick conducted their trade in ways typical of the town's commercial scene in the 1730s. Evidence suggests that they were all independent merchants in the goods import trade, among the growing number of Charles Town merchants who by the 1730s were importing manufactured goods and consumables on their own account and risk. In the rice export trade, they acted either as correspondents for British merchants, assembling cargoes of the grain from local planters and their agents in Charles Town and shipping them on commission to British, continental European, and West Indian destinations, or purchased and shipped rice on their own accounts. Most rice was exported between November and May.[75] Trading independently carried greater financial risks but offered higher returns, which would later finance these merchants' relocation to London and their trade in the capital. Beswicke, Shubrick, and particularly Crokatt all acquired extensive land and property holdings in South Carolina that further point to a level of profits generated by independent trading. Such was the scale of Crokatt's trade that he acquired a wharf in Charles Town harbor that came to bear his name. Occupying a prime location on the Cooper River, Crokatt's Bridge was the northernmost of only eight such "bridges," as the wharves were known locally.[76]

Merchants sold an array of imported goods on credit, which was typically extended for a year, to South Carolina's planters and tradesmen from their

stores in the town. In return they either took rice directly from planters in payment or, as was increasingly common, received remittances in cash or notes,
which they used to buy rice sold by planters on the open market. However they
acquired the rice, the merchants then exported it to their connections in Britain
and continental Europe or the British West Indies, where rice was a staple food
for slaves on the islands' sugar plantations. Merchants also bought deerskins
from specialist traders who often operated up to hundreds of miles inland and
who received the skins from the region's Native American tribes in exchange
for goods such as guns, garments, and alcohol. Although trade in deerskins was
less important to South Carolina's economy during the 1730s and 1740 than it
had been two decades earlier, deerskins remained a significant export and were
shipped by nearly all Charles Town's export merchants. To attract customers
in Charles Town's crowded retail market, merchants sought competitive advantage by two principal means. The length of credit a trader could offer his
customers was one important differentiator. Running one of Charles Town's
leading trading houses from large premises on Broad Street, James Crokatt had
enough capital reserves to allow him to offer particularly generous terms to
buyers. He extended up to two years' credit and accepted produce in receipt of
goods sold.[77] His customers were spread across the South Carolina lowcountry
in at least five different parishes, from St. Bartholomew's in the south to Prince
Frederick's in the north, reflecting the scale of his trade.[78]

Besides their terms of sale and credit, retailers also distinguished themselves
from their competitors through the range and quality of their goods. The diver-
sity of wares advertised for sale at John Beswicke's store was typical. In addition
to foodstuffs such as "Herefordshire Cyder," wine, and coffee and "a choice Parcel
of Fans, China Ware, super fine Green Tea, Mens silk Stockings, Shoes and other
sundry goods," he sold a range of plantation hardware: one notice publicized his
"good assortment of very best hard metal pewter, oznabrigs [coarse cloth] and
other thread, British made sail canvas, 4, 6, 8 and 20 penny nails, hinges and
locks of most sorts and variety of ironmongery ware."[79] Customers at Crokatt's
store on Broad Street or at Nickleson & Shubrick's store "on the Bay" would
encounter similar assortments, with different stock for different seasons: "gawse
for Pavilions [mosquito screens], and almost every other kind of Goods proper
for Summer" on sale in Crokatt's store in May and June, and "most kinds of
Woolen and other Goods proper for the Winter season" in September.[80] These
were general stores catering in full to the needs of country visitors and town
dwellers alike. Legal suits filed against recalcitrant debtors reveal customers'
buying habits: one planter had acquired goods including fabric, buttons, knives
and forks, and a broom; another small debtor had been able to purchase fabrics,
rum, wine, sugar, gunpowder, bullets, and tea.[81]

Supplying the Indian trade and South Carolina's government provided profitable sidelines to consumer retail. James Crokatt was particularly active in the

deerskins trade, shipping more cargoes of skins from Charles Town between 1735 and 1739 than any other exporter. In exchange for the skins, he offered suppliers a conventional range of goods that they could exchange with their Native American connections—"guns, hatchets, caddis, beads & most other kind Indian trading goods"—and he provided the colonial government with goods to trade with Creeks and Chickasaws. [82] Beswicke too was regularly contracted by the colonial government to supply goods "for the Use of the Indians" as Britain's wars with France and Spain between 1739 and 1748 and the threats these posed to South Carolina heightened the importance of securing Native American alliances. [83] Nickleson, Shubrick & Co. in particular benefited from the expansion of government spending during the war, becoming one of the colonial government's leading contractors. In 1743, for example, the firm received £1,851.10s. currency, "being for Sundries supplied for the Use of the Indians and for victualling the Spanish Prisoners"; this was more than three times the amount received by the next largest supplier and nearly four percent of the colonial government's total expenditure in 1742–43. The following year the firm supplied the government with a smaller but still substantial £557.3s.7d. of "sundry Goods for the Use of the Public."[84] Even more lucratively, the firm was made the official naval victualler in Charles Town, through which it supplied Royal Navy vessels in the port with provisions and equipment.[85]

In contrast with their extensive ventures in handling rice, deerskins, military supplies, and consumer goods, the leading Charles Town merchants who later relocated to Britain—Crokatt, Beswicke, Shubrick, and Nickleson—had little direct involvement in the slave trade during their time in South Carolina. Imports of enslaved Africans into Charles Town reached record levels during the 1730s as planters sought more and more slaves to work in the colony's growing rice plantations: more than twenty thousand slaves were brought into South Carolina between 1730 and 1739. Slave trading was the basis of some of the greatest fortunes made in Charles Town. Merchants such as Joseph Wragg, Benjamin Godin, and Benjamin Savage were "slave factors," receiving cargoes of African slaves whose trafficking had been arranged by the merchants' correspondents in Britain and on the coast of West Africa. In Wragg's and Godin's cases, their relations Samuel Wragg and David Godin in London played a vital role.[86]

In total, more than ninety-two thousand slaves were brought into South Carolina in the seventy years before the American Revolution—a higher number than in any other British colony on the North American mainland (table 2). Most slaves were imported directly from Africa; the vast majority came in ships owned by merchants living in Britain.[87] The greatest number of slaves arrived in the colony between May and November, timing that was influenced by climate, seasonal demand for labor on plantations, and relative demand for slave imports in the West Indies.[88] Charles Town merchants sold the slaves at auction, keeping a commission. It was more likely for commercial than for moral reasons that

Crokatt, Beswicke, Shubrick, and Nickleson largely avoided the slave trade. The greater risks involved in importing slaves from Africa compared to goods from Britain and Europe, although offset by the potential for very high profits, were the most probable deterrent. The chief risk was inherent in the high monetary value attached to the slave ships' human cargoes. If a ship was lost at sea or if the mortality rate among the slaves on board was exceptionally high, even by the standards of a trade in which the deaths of one in seven slaves during an Atlantic crossing was normal, losses incurred by a merchant and his connections in Britain would far exceed those resulting from lost or damaged goods.[89]

Table 2: Slave Trade to South Carolina, 1706–76

Years	Total number of slaves imported	Slaves imported on British vessels	Total number of slave voyages by British ships
1706–19	3,034	1,064	13
1720–29	9,029	3,860	20
1730–39	20,647	18,656	82
1740–49	1,980	1,775	12
1750–59	15,775	12,694	72
1760–69	21,360	16,744	89
1770–76	20,967	14,972	83
Total 1706–76	92,792	69,765	371

Source: David Richardson, "The British Slave Trade to Colonial
South Carolina," *Slavery and Abolition* 12.3 (1991): 170–72.

All Charles Town's merchants were, however, by the nature of their business inextricably entwined in the wider slave economy. Crops cultivated by slaves provided the bulk of their export trade and much of their wealth. The merchants' stores supplied the equipment that slaves used in the rice and indigo fields, the textiles that clothed them, and the devices used to control them. Slaves were also a feature of the merchants' domestic and commercial lives. They formed the labor force at the merchants' plantations in South Carolina's lowcountry, and Crokatt owned at least two domestic slaves who were "used to wash and dress Linnens."[90] In addition slaves were a mainstay of the workforce on Charles Town's wharves and in stores. Crokatt's reliance on slave laborers at his warehouse was documented in a June 1735 story in the *South Carolina Gazette*. Telling readers of a large theft he had suffered, the newspaper reported that "a discovery was made of a Theft committed by some Negroes belonging to *Mr. James Crokatt,* a *Charlestown* Merchant; they had stolen out of their Master's

Store a considerable Quantity of Goods to the Value of above 2000 Pounds, hid and buried several of them under Ground in his own Yard, carried others to such Houses and Persons as they knew would receive and conceal the same, and gave some to other Negroes of their Acquaintance. It is supposed a great many Negroes are concern'd in this robbery, and no doubt but some white Persons that are concealers of such Goods, will be detected at the Trial of these Negroes."[91]

May the 10th, 1736.

This Day is imported in the *Mary*, from *London*, and to be sold by *James Crokatt* a large variety of all kinds useful Summer goods with a very great assortment of the newest fashion china ware, shoes, gauze and thread Pavillions, Painters colours.

I am unwilling to put any Person to needless Expences, I chuse again to give notice to those who are owing me for what was due last *January*, that if the same is not payed or otherwise satisfied in 5 Weeks from this date they will be directly sued I have neither time nor opportunity to give any other than this publick notice, therefore such as are put to any trouble or expence must blame themselves for their negligence in not at least settling their Accounts with
James Crokatt.

Whereas Mr. *Richard Hill* Merch: who is lately gone off the Province, has appointed us, *Benjamin Whitaker* Esq; and *John Guerard* his Attorneys to transact his Affairs in his absence, we therefore hereby give Notice pursuant to his direction to the several persons whose Debts are now due to his former partnership of *Richard Hill* and Company, as well as to him in particular, that if they do not forthwith comply with payment of their respective Debts, they will be prosecuted by
Benj. Whitaker.

IMported in Capt. *Surry* and Capt. *Raggles* from *London*, by John Beswicke, a good Assortment of Loaf Sugar, Almonds, Bohea Tea, Vermilion, white Lead, ditto ground in Oyl, Allspices, Raspins Dry &c. Sugaries, Barragons, ready made Bed-Ticks, Pavilion &c. torto bello Perty cating, Buttons and Trimmings, white Crppel and other Needles Haberdashery Womans and Girls silk cambrick muco, worsted, damask and laced Shoes, Shammoonees &c. of lard Ware, Mens, Womens, Boys and Girls thread Stockings &c. and Womens silk ditto, Bibles, Common Prayers, Testaments, &c. 3, 4th, 7 8th and yard wide cotton and linen Checks &c. Dimities and other Fustians, Turky Esmil &c. Tape, Nonso pretties Oznabrigs, Crocus, Buckrams &c. Liners, couch and Irish Linnens, Sheeting, Russia Di per, Diaper 3 4th, 7 8th and yard wide Garlix, Platillas brown Hol and &c. Bag and other Hollands, clouting Diapers Cambricks Kentings, Muslins, white Callimancoes, silk Handkerchief Callicoes, Chints, Corderoys, Seersuckers, Pennisfees, Taffeties, Grograms, flower'd Damasks, &c.

PUblick Notice is hereby given, That if any Persons who have made any Silk-Worms this Year, will send them to John Lewis Poyas, at Madam Trott's Point, in Charles-Town, they shall have Four Pounds a Bushel, provided they have been baked in an Oven, and not in the Sun; and that in eight Days after they have done working.

Advertisement by James Crokatt, *South Carolina Gazette*, May 1736

Advertisement by John Beswicke, *South Carolina Gazette*, April 1741

Rarely were the merchants' regular appearances in the *Gazette* so dramatic. Most notices concerned the arrival of new goods in their stores or appealed for recalcitrant debtors to come forward. Newspaper articles also recorded the merchants' social fortunes in South Carolina, charting how they joined clubs and societies, assumed civic duties, and married into the colony's landowning elite class. All of these stories served both to reflect and to reinforce their commercial standing. Most young traders were unmarried when they arrived in South Carolina from Britain. With their growing capital and good prospects, they were able to marry into more established families in the colony, marriages which in turn could facilitate commercial progress by supplying the merchants with extra capital and influential family connections. James Crokatt's marriage to Esther Gaillard, from a notable Huguenot family, linked him to some of South Carolina's most important planters with extensive landholdings in St. James Santee Parish. Her stepfather, James Kinloch, was an active merchant, politician, and major planter.[92] Richard Shubrick married into the wealthy Ball family in 1740, in the process acquiring a large rice plantation, Quenby, about twenty miles upstream from Charles Town on the Cooper River.[93] In 1742 John Beswicke married Mary Hill, the daughter of a wealthy merchant and planter and, in the *Gazette*'s estimation, "an agreeable young Lady, of great merit and a large Fortune."[94]

WHEREAS many Planters have as yet
neglected paying their Debts due to me, and as an
Excuse says they can't fell their Rice, &c in order
to remove this Impediment, I give Notice, That
*I am willing to take their Rice if good, in
Payment at Forty Shillings per Cent. from
this Date to the Tenth Day of June next,*
at which time I propose to go from this Province, and all
such Notes, Bonds or other Debts as are not then paid or
settled to my Content, will be left in the Hands of the
Gentlemen of the Law by
JAMES CROKATT.
Charles Town, April 16, 1739.
N.B. I have two Slaves used to wash and dress Linnens,
and several kinds of Houshold Furniture, also a Chaise and
Horse to be sold

Notice by James Crokatt,
South Carolina Gazette, April 1739

With successful commerce and marriages came civic duties. Crokatt's status in the town was reflected by his officeholdings and social responsibilities. In 1738 his commercial and social standing was translated into political status with appointment to the Royal Council, the twelve-man upper house of the colonial legislature, which advised the governor and acted as a court of appeals.[95] Crokatt was also prominent within Charles Town's community of Scottish merchants—part of an association with Scottish causes that lasted throughout his life—as treasurer of the St. Andrew's Society, a social and charitable club.[96] Further enmeshing his social and commercial connections, and reflecting his status, Crokatt also became the master of the town's Masonic lodge. Besides these charitable commitments, civic and parochial duties offered a public way of cementing status. In 1735 Crokatt helped establish the Friendly Society, the first fire insurance company in North America, and was one of its five directors.[97] As churchwarden of St. Philip's, Charles Town's parish church, he turned his organizational skills to the task of refashioning the system of poor relief for the town's most impoverished white residents. He oversaw a switch from "outdoors" relief, with the poor provided for in their own homes, to "indoors" provision, hiring a house and "proper Attendance" for "all such as are real Objects of Charity."[98] Putting it more bluntly, the parish vestry minutes noted that "all the Poor that are to be present on the Parish, be remov'd from their Several Lodgings to the Work House immediately."[99] John Beswicke, for his part, was appointed one of three tax inquirers for St. Philip's Parish; and Richard Shubrick served as one of five commissioners of Charles Town's market.[100] Yet for Crokatt, Beswicke, and Shubrick, and for many other Charles Town merchants, wealth and respectability in South Carolina paled in comparison with the attractiveness and profitability of commerce in the empire's capital.

Relocating to Britain

After having arrived in Charles Town from Britain and risen to the forefront of commerce in the town, how and why did these men—who were well established, wealthy, and socially and politically connected in South Carolina—choose to up-root their businesses and families and go back to Britain? Writing about the careers of Charles Town merchants, the historian R. C. Nash described how most followed one of two paths on ceasing trade in the town. The most common route, particularly among merchants born in South Carolina, was to invest trading profits in plantation land and slaves and to seek greater fortunes from cultivating rice and indigo. Another group withdrew from trade altogether to retire to country estates in England.[101] There was also a third path, which was profoundly important for South Carolina's commercial and political connections with Britain, and which was pursued by mid-career merchants who had been born in Britain and drawn to Carolina between the 1720s and the 1740s. This group returned to Britain with their trading profits and reentered the Carolina trade in London. Among this group were most of the men at the forefront of London's Carolina trade between the 1740s and the early 1760s, notably James Crokatt, John Beswicke, the brothers-in-law John Nickleson and Richard Shubrick, and Charles Ogilvie.

Merchants relocated from Charles Town to London throughout the colonial era. They had various motivations: some sought to restore their health in Britain's more temperate climes; others left for family reasons. John Burn, a merchant whose assets in South Carolina included some 2,750 acres of land and at least seven properties in Charles Town, left the colony to improve his ailing health and for his son's education.[102] Richard Shubrick's decision to return to London in 1747 was probably influenced by his wife's death the previous year. Inheriting land in Britain led to other departures. William Middleton was one of South Carolina's leading landowners, with some 15,314 acres in the colony, and a member of the colony's Royal Council.[103] In 1754 he was bequeathed an estate in Suffolk and properties in Chelsea and Mortlake, just west of London, which together produced an annual income of twelve hundred pounds. Informing him of his inheritance, a correspondent in London fully expected him to quit South Carolina for landed life in England, writing that "on the receipt of this I presume you will come to England with Mrs. Middleton & your family."[104] Middleton duly did, the allure of a country seat and London houses outweighing considerations of social and political prestige in South Carolina, though with the help of a brother who stayed in South Carolina, he would retain and expand his landholdings in the colony and in Georgia.

For most merchants who relocated to Britain, however, their decision was driven by commercial rationale. They left in search of the greater profits to be made in London from exporting goods on credit to South Carolina. In exchange they received rice, deerskins, naval stores, and from the late 1740s indigo. Trade between merchants across the Atlantic from each other was largely financed in so-called bills of exchange, a legal instrument that allowed for the payment of goods without hard currency changing hands. Merchants could transfer and discount bills, enabling them to offset their own financial liabilities in London against the outstanding debts of traders in Charles Town, and vice versa. Assets that would otherwise be temporarily frozen in a merchant's accounts or as unsold goods could thereby be liquidated. Other remittances were made in promissory notes, written promises to pay sums of money in specified periods for value received; more rarely paper money and specie—coin—changed hands.[105]

The rationale for relocating to London was best articulated by Charles Ogilvie. After his early ventures in the slave trade, Ogilvie established a partnership in Charles Town, exporting rice and deerskins to Europe and selling merchandise from premises "on the Bay." In 1760 he decided to leave South Carolina for Britain. As he explained to his brother, his plan was to "establish matters here [Charles Town] & at home on such a footing as will enable me to live in London & transact the Business there while my partner remains here." He reckoned that he could avoid paying 500 guineas (£525) a year in commission to London merchants if he settled in the capital and sent goods personally to his partner in Charles Town.[106] Ogilvie's calculation was echoed by a fellow Charles Town trader, Samuel Carne, who thought that by moving to London he could "supply Carne & Wilson's shop [in Charles Town], I believe, on better terms than hitherto it has been done."[107] This is what modern economists would term "reverse integration" or "backward integration." Ogilvie and Carne hoped to extend their control up the supply chain to achieve cost-efficiencies in the supply of goods, cutting out the middleman. Their logic echoed the reasoning that underlay the comparable move that many of their fellow merchants in Charles Town made up the supply chain into planting. By buying plantations, these merchants took a stake in the means of production, allowing them—they hoped—to reduce their transaction costs and get a more reliable supply of crops for export.[108]

For his part, Ogilvie predicted that, besides the savings he would make, he could increase the quality of his trading goods by personally selecting the products he would export from London to South Carolina. He would take "more pains with [the goods] than can be expected from many of our present Correspondents." The only constraints to his leaving South Carolina were financial. His profits in 1759—some one thousand guineas after taking account of debts—were lower than expected, forcing him to delay his departure while he accumulated more capital. Moreover, he owed a debt of four thousand pounds to John Beswicke, who had relocated to London more than a decade earlier. This was the remainder of a much bigger debt that Ogilvie had accrued through importing goods from Beswicke for sale in Charles Town. Ogilvie therefore sought a loan of five hundred pounds from his brother to supplement his existing funds and to enable him to send his first cargo of goods from London to Charles Town. He explained that his financial shortfall was one of cash flow, not credit. His debtors could not discharge their debts to him immediately, and many "I have no right to ask for perhaps 6, 9 or 12 months."[109] To reassure his brother of his own credit-worthiness, Ogilvie instructed him in how commercial credit worked and how his business was organized: "You may be surprised that men who have so considerable a Capital should want to borrow Money. The Reason of which is the long credit given & the great Value of Goods always on hand to keep up a proper assortment [of goods]. Ogilvie & Ward and Ogilvie & Forbes [his two partnerships in Charles Town] together have been due them by good men upwards of Ten Thousand Guineas and O & F have on hand Merchandise on their own Account at least the amount of £4,000." Whatever the true state of his finances and for all his cash-flow difficulties, Ogilvie moved from Charles Town to London in 1761. Before leaving, he made arrangements with several merchants in the town to be their supplier in London, as well as maintaining a partnership with one particular merchant.[110]

Relocating from South Carolina to Britain was a drawn-out process, complicated by the need to run down inventories and to call in customers' debts. Before leaving Charles Town, merchants sold off their remaining stock and household goods that were no longer required or could not be shipped to Britain. Usually they did so through their stores, but when their departures were imminent, merchants were willing to accept the lower prices received at auction. Shortly before leaving Charles Town in 1747, John Beswicke announced that he would be selling "at Vendue [auction], under the New Market, what Shop-Goods he has on Hand, together with his Household Goods."[111] James Crokatt's sell-off eight years earlier had been far more extensive, illustrating his standing in the town as well as the wealth and grandeur that success in Charles Town commerce could bring. His remaining dry goods were to be sold "at public Vendue" together with his household fittings; these included "A New England Chaise never used, Good Vidonia Wine, A Marble Chimney Piece compleat, An Iron Hearth with Brass Facings, and Brass Shovel and Tongs, also several kinds of Household Furniture, not much the Worse for use." Closer to his departure, Crokatt would sell his family's more indispensable possessions, among them household furniture, horses and a chaise, and two domestic slaves. Later still, Crokatt sold more furniture, books, and "a Negro man."[112]

Off-loading unsold merchandise, personal goods, and even household slaves was simpler than winding up credit lines that stretched far and wide across South Carolina. Merchants planning to leave placed repeated notices in the *South Carolina Gazette* demanding that debtors come forward. None were more frequent, insistent, and ultimately threatening than Crokatt's, typifying a flair for self-promotion that ran throughout his career and in particular the aggressive commercial approach that would propel him to the top of London's Carolina trade. By the time he left South Carolina in June 1739, the *Gazette* had carried notices alerting readers to his departure in every weekly edition for nearly eight months. Not only did they stand out from other advertisements in the same editions, but they were also far more prominent than other departure notices:

Vendue Range, Charles Town, pictured in 1865. Location for auctions in colonial Charles Town. George N. Barnard, 1839–1902. Library of Congress.

located at the tops of pages and spanning two column widths, they were among the most striking advertisements the newspaper had ever carried.[113] Readiness to sue defaulting debtors further marked Crokatt's combative approach. Poor rice harvests limited the ability of many customers to make their remittances to Charles Town merchants and could leave the merchants with extensive debts. While many traders' notices in the *Gazette* noted the loss of crops, Crokatt was unique in alleging that a number of planters were using this as a cunning ploy. One of his adverts claimed that "several have made Excuses for not paying me last year, by losing, or pretending to have lost their crops."[114] After months of reminders, Crokatt's patience wore thin. He announced, "And whereas many who were indebted to me before last January, have not yet paid or settled their Accounts, either by cash, bond or otherways, which it is in every Man's power to do, all such as don't settle their Accounts due to me some time in this Month, may depend they will be sued for the same the 1st week in July, having now had *six months* notice in the most publick manner from James Crokatt."[115] Crokatt's actions matched his rhetoric, and he hired Charles Town's leading attorneys, Charles Pinckney and James Wright, to recover his dues in a series of lawsuits.[116]

Crokatt's care in settling his commercial affairs before leaving South Carolina illustrates the complexity of relocating a business across the Atlantic. Besides employing the attorneys to collect debts, he also took on an agent to manage his property investments in the town.[117] In a shrewd commercial move, Crokatt, like other departing merchants who sought to retain a commercial foothold in Charles Town, entered partnership with two local merchants, Ebenezer Simmons and Benjamin Smith. The partners invested equal capital in the firm and agreed "to be equally concerned in all Profits & loss accruing, growing, happening or arising" over the partnership's duration, set at seven years. Crokatt's choice of partners was astute. Both were native-born South Carolinians; Simmons was already a trader of some status, while Smith, just twenty-one years old, had worked for Crokatt for at least three years. Smith would go on to be one of Charles Town's foremost merchant-bankers and speaker of South Carolina's Assembly. Terms were agreed in February 1737, and the partnership became effective beginning in September 1738. Having partners in Charles Town would give Crokatt a trusted outlet to which to send goods from London and a reliable supplier of exports from South Carolina. Operating from Crokatt's old premises on Broad Street, where the regular range of imported goods was sold and the same terms Crokatt had given as a sole trader were offered—receiving planters' produce in exchange for merchandise and up to two years' credit—the store also offered commercial continuity, helping it to retain Crokatt's existing customers in the colony.

Having made his arrangements, Crokatt left the humid climes and commercial bustle of Charles Town—a booming port on the frontier of Britain's empire—to further his business at the heart of the empire. As was the case for

I GIVE THIS LAST PUBLICK NOTICE TO ALL THOSE WHO HAVE HAD ANY DEALINGS OR NOW HAVE ANY DEMANDS UPON ME in my own Affairs or as Attorney Executor or Adminiftrator for others, THAT I SHALL GO FROM THIS PROVINCE WITH MY FAMILY IN THREE MONTHS FROM THIS DATE. And as to thofe who are indebted to me after fo long Notice, they muft only blame themfelves for what Expence they are now put to in recovering what is due to JAMES CROKATT. *Charleftown, March* 10, 1738.

Notice by James Crokatt,
South Carolina Gazette,
March 1739

other leading merchants in Charles Town who forsook the competing allure of actively managing and buildings plantations in South Carolina in favor of returning to Great Britain, London's Carolina trade offered Crokatt the chance of even greater profits and wealth than could be reaped by remaining in the colony. The elite status that these merchants would enjoy in London would bring with it responsibilities to the colony that had "made" them—responsibilities as conduits of colonial grievances and as political-economic advocates on its behalf. An earlier generation of London's Carolina merchants had between the 1710s and the 1730s understood these responsibilities and offered a model of activism to emulate. Like the merchant lobbies representing London's other branches of American trade, this first generation of Carolina merchants in London had lobbied the government on issues where their commercial interests intersected with matters of concern to the colony, notably on defending South Carolina from Indian and rival imperial threats and on rice exports. Their advocacy influenced how South Carolinians conceived the role of London's Carolina merchants as representing the colony and its interests in Britain. It also conditioned how during the 1740s and 1750s a more prominent group of London's Carolina traders would petition and lobby the British state. James Crokatt, John Beswicke, Richard Shubrick, and John Nickleson would be at the forefront of this group at a time when the North American colonies came to figure larger in the British political imagination and when Britain's politicians paid closer attention to the colonies' productive potential.

CHAPTER TWO

"FRIENDS TO ASSIST AT HOME"

London's Carolina Trade in the 1740s and 1750s

In 1744 South Carolina's Assembly revived a law that placed extra duties on imports of Madeira wine, rum, molasses, flour, and sugar. Charles Town's merchants tried to persuade the colony's governor James Glen to strike it down. When their attempts were rebuffed, they turned instead to the Board of Trade in London, which could advise the Crown to veto laws made by colonial assemblies. To do so, the merchants needed the aid of their counterparts in London. The capital's Carolina traders were asked to petition for the law to be disallowed on the grounds that it was not just harmful to business in Charles Town but "only a Prelude or Introduction for Our Assembly to Tax and Cramp the Trading Interest for the future more & more." Many of Charles Town's traders would write to their "Friends at Home" to ask them to press their case.[1]

The merchants' campaign and the assumptions that underlay it expose the political economy of South Carolina's transatlantic trade. Residents of the colonies and merchants in London alike understood political lobbying to be an integral activity of a London merchant who traded to one of Britain's colonies. Representing the colony and its trade in political circles was a corollary of a merchant's regular commercial activities. It was also his responsibility to his colonial correspondents. Since merchants in South Carolina lacked direct representation in or access to Britain's political forums, they relied on their British counterparts alongside the activism of the colony's official agent. London's Carolina traders were expected to lobby the relevant political institutions—the Board of Trade, the British Treasury, and Parliament—for commercial preferment for the colony, for legislative action, and for military protection. To achieve these goals, they might orchestrate petitioning and, where possible, galvanize cross-sectoral pressure. Two fundamental conceptions underpinned this: that imperial authorities had the ultimate control over the terms of South Carolina's trade; and that the interests of London's Carolina merchants correlated with those of the colony. During the next thirty years both conceptions would be tested, challenged, and eventually overturned. In the 1740s and 1750s, a period of relative political harmony between Britain and South Carolina, Charles Town's merchants looked to their "Friends at Home"—a doubly revealing epithet—to represent mutual interests in the imperial corridors of power.[2]

Just as during the formative years of Carolina lobbying, there were compelling reasons for Carolinians to look principally to London merchants as their advocates. One was the capital's dominant share of the colony's overseas trade, giving its Carolina merchants particular authority in presenting concerns or conveying information to the British state. Being in London, close to the institutions of government, enhanced the merchants' access to political decision makers. Structural and compositional features within London's Carolina trade in the 1740s and 1750s augmented its political-economic significance. Chief among these were the concentration of the trade in a small number of hands, the personal experience that most of its leading figures had of living and trading in Charles Town, and the emergence of dynamic leadership within the group. Distinguishing the Carolina lobby from other North American interest groups, these features contributed to its particular effectiveness between the late 1740s and the early 1760s. Capitalizing on prevailing political and economic theory, its accomplishments included securing a bounty on colonial indigo in 1748 as well as stimuli for the production of silk and potash in South Carolina. Later, from the mid-1760s, the same features would have important consequences in a less harmonious political environment.

"Carolina merchants":
The Composition and Organization of London's Carolina Trade

London's Carolina trade had, since its origins in the first decades of the eighteenth century, been concentrated in relatively few hands. Petitions, letters, and tax assessments reveal how this concentration remained one of the trade's chief features throughout the middle decades of the century. Its structure paralleled or even prefigured that of other branches of London's overseas commerce, where the sugar, tobacco, and slave trades were all becoming dominated by fewer and larger trading houses.[3] Visiting London in 1749, Henry Laurens identified three trading houses in the capital as being preeminent in the Carolina trade: James Crokatt & Co., John Nickleson, and Richard Shubrick.[4] Together with John Beswicke, these three firms dominated exports to the colony during the 1740s and 1750s. Through the commercial foundations they laid for their successors, their influence would persist after their retirements or deaths. Other London partnerships specializing in the Carolina trade mostly either sprang from these firms or were closely connected to them. Evidence from merchants' petitioning and from the registers of ships docking in Charles Town supports a picture of a concentrated trade.[5]

Fourteen years after Laurens's observations, the concentration of London's Carolina trade was again made clear in 1763 in *Mortimer's Directory,* the first London trade directory to classify merchants by their sectoral or geographic focus. Of the forty-six merchants listed by *Mortimer's* as being in North American trade in the capital, just six firms were categorized as "Carolina merchants." Listings were probably made on the basis of self-identification, with each firm classifying itself by its primary trading concerns, making *Mortimer's* a fairly reliable guide to specialization in each branch of trade.[6] In contrast to the six Carolina traders listed, the directory classified forty-nine firms as West India merchants, nineteen as Virginia merchants, and nine as New England merchants. The connections between the capital's different Carolina trading houses further emphasize the group's stability and unified character. Three of the six firms listed in *Mortimer's* were James & Charles Crokatt, John Beswicke, and Richard Shubrick. The other three were John Nutt, Crokatt's son-in law; Grubb & Watson, formerly junior partners in Crokatt's trading house; and Sarah Nickleson, the sister of Richard Shubrick and widow of John Nickleson.[7] John Nickleson had died in 1754 of an "Apoplectic Fit" caused, according to one friend, by "the Disobedience of his Children, which he took too much to Heart."[8] After his death, Sarah Nickleson took control of the firm, making her one of just a handful of female merchants in an overwhelmingly male business. The other leading Carolina merchants in London during the 1760s and 1770s, William Greenwood and William Higginson, were nephews of John Beswicke who inherited their uncle's business on his death in 1764.

As in previous decades, London's trade with South Carolina was not entirely limited to these firms, as warehousemen and other specialist retailers too sent their wares to correspondents in Charles Town on credit.[9] Other merchants who relocated from Charles Town to London between the 1750s and early 1770s, such as Charles Ogilvie, Samuel Carne, James Poyas, Benjamin Stead, and William Stone, continued trading with the colony; in addition elite London merchants whose trading portfolios stretched across the colonies did business with counterparts in Charles Town.[10] However, the clear majority of London's Carolina trade by volume and, as importantly, the principal voice of the South Carolina "interest" in the empire's capital was concentrated among a select group of specialist Carolina merchants.

The choice by merchants such as James Crokatt, John Beswicke, Richard Shubrick, and John Nickleson to establish themselves in London after leaving Charles Town was driven by the capital's commercial supremacy. London's sheer size set it apart from all other cities in the British Empire. Its population in 1750 was about 675,000, making it the largest city in western Europe and more than ten times more populous than Britain's next biggest city, Bristol, with its roughly 50,000 inhabitants. It had around one hundred times more residents than Charles Town.[11] In terms of trade, in all of Britain's overseas commerce in the first three-quarters of the eighteenth century, London never had less than double the combined share of all the country's regional "outports" such as Bristol, Liverpool, and Lancaster put together. The dominance was mirrored in trade with Britain's colonies. London's share of Britain's imports from its colonies was more than 64 percent of the total and its exports to the colonies above 70 percent of the total throughout the period.[12] The same was true in trade with South Carolina.

In the rice trade, London was the largest single destination for South Carolina's exports of the crop between the 1730s and the 1750s, receiving significantly more than either Bristol or Cowes, the two next biggest British rice ports. Most rice was carried on the account and risk of London "principals," who employed agents in Charles Town and sometimes South Carolina's minor ports, Beaufort and Georgetown, to buy the grain from local planters or intermediary "country factors" and to arrange its shipment across the Atlantic. After being landed and taxed in Britain, most rice was reexported to Holland and Germany, where it was eaten by people and livestock, especially in winter and particularly when poor European harvests led to shortages of cereal products.[13] Smaller amounts were retained in Britain for sale to wholesale grocers. London merchants also controlled much of the rice that was shipped on to continental Europe through England's channel ports such as Cowes and Poole.[14] The capital was also the main recipient of South Carolina's exported deerskins and naval stores, and it was the destination for an overwhelming share of its indigo after the dye became the colony's second largest export from the late 1740s.[15]

In the indigo trade, the commission system was more common. Through this, Carolinian planters or Charles Town merchants acting for several small producers shipped indigo to merchants—overwhelmingly in London—on their own account and risk, matching the system by which Chesapeake tobacco and West Indies sugar were marketed in the capital. The British merchants sold the dye to specialist dealers or to grocers on their correspondents' behalf and remitted the proceeds in bills of exchange, promissory notes, or goods. London also dominated Britain's export trade to South Carolina, principally owing to the more generous credit offered by the capital's merchants and their better access than merchants in Britain's regional ports had to the European and Asian goods, especially fabrics, that colonial consumers sought. Most cargoes were sent on credit—by the 1740s typically at 5 percent interest from six months after date of invoice—to Charles Town merchants who either traded independently or were involved in transatlantic partnerships.[16] Evidence from other branches of Anglo-American trade suggests that exporting goods was a particularly profitable line of business, with goods selling for several times their cost price and giving London merchants profit margins of up to 10 percent on export cargoes. However, against these potential rewards the colonial export trade also involved substantial risks, particularly of recipients defaulting on payments and the loss or damage of goods in transit.[17]

Following their commercial practice when they had lived and worked in Charles Town, where they had concentrated on exporting produce and importing British and European goods, London's major Carolina traders mostly avoided direct involvement in the slave trade. This was not for lack of resources or opportunity. London and Bristol together dominated Britain's slave trade to South Carolina in the first half of the eighteenth century, with ships beginning their journeys in the two ports supplying nearly 25,000 enslaved Africans to South Carolina between 1710 and 1749. Although Bristol and Liverpool would take an increasingly large share of Britain's Atlantic slave trade as the century progressed, London's ships and merchants remained major suppliers of enslaved Africans to Britain's plantation colonies, including South Carolina.[18] Given the merchants' complicity in South Carolina's slave system through their willingness

The Thames and the Tower of London Supposedly on the King's Birthday, 1771. Samuel Scott, 1701/2–72. Yale Center for British Art, Paul Mellon Collection.

St Paul's and Blackfriars Bridge, between 1770 and 1772. William Marlow, 1740–1813. Yale Center for British Art, Paul Mellon Collection.

to export goods used to clothe, equip, and restrain slaves in the colony and to import slave-made produce such as rice and indigo, their general avoidance of the slave trade was surely due to commercial rather than moral reasoning—perhaps an aversion to the greater risks involved in the traffic in human cargoes. Timing may also have been a factor. The commercial ascent in London of Crokatt, Beswicke, Shubrick, and Nickleson during the 1740s coincided with a decade-long hiatus in the Atlantic slave trade to South Carolina. After the Stono Rebellion in September 1739, in which as many as one hundred slaves seeking to escape to Spanish Florida had killed about forty white settlers living south of Charles Town, South Carolina's Assembly introduced prohibitively high duties on slaves brought into the colony in an attempt to curb the growth of its black population. Between 1740 and 1748 just eight slave ships, of which only two were registered in London, arrived in Charles Town, landing 1,550 slaves from Africa. In the previous ten years, 1730–39, eighty-two slave ships had, by contrast, arrived in South Carolina, landing more than 20,000 slaves. Of these voyages, thirty-four were made by ships registered in London.[19]

The Atlantic slave trade to South Carolina began to reach its previous heights from 1748. A reduction of the high import duties four years earlier and surging European demand for rice and a takeoff in indigo cultivation led planters to demand more slaves. By this point London's leading Carolina traders were well established in profitably importing South Carolinian produce and exporting goods from Britain, continental Europe, and beyond to the colony. They were not inclined to diversify into the slave trade, a riskier though very profitable field. James Crokatt responded to a proposal from Henry Laurens for a joint venture "in a Guinea Vessel with Slaves to Carolina" by explaining that he was "fully employ'd with Business on Commission & chuses to be confin'd in that way." Signifying his lack of moral qualms about the trade, however, Crokatt willingly gave Laurens letters of introduction to slave traders in Bristol and Liverpool.[20] After Crokatt, Beswicke, Shubrick, and Nickleson retired or died, their commercial successors for the most part followed the same trading model, concentrating on exporting goods and importing commodities, and left the traffic in human cargo to specialist slave traders. This aversion to the slave trade among London's Carolina traders from the 1740s contrasted with the earlier generation of the capital's Carolina traders. The likes of Stephen and David Godin and Samuel Wragg had combined commodity and slave trading. By comparison, of the six Carolina specialists listed in Mortimer's in 1763, only Richard Shubrick and John Nutt were recorded to have had stakes in slaving voyages to South Carolina. Shubricks & Co., the Charles Town trading house in which Richard Shubrick was in partnership with his brother Thomas, intermittently imported slaves into Charles Town, including 220 slaves brought from Gambia and the Windward Coast in 1755. Nutt was part of an eight-man consortium that owned the slave ship Cape Coast in 1758.[21]

Just as London's Carolina traders mostly eschewed diversifying into the slave trade, they seem to have largely avoided other geographic branches of trade and focused predominantly on South Carolina. This was probably a function of the difficulty all merchants in long-distance overseas trades encountered in maintaining trust, reputation, and accurate market intelligence, considerations that were easier to control by trading predominantly to a single location or region.[22] Diversifications into different branches of trade appear to have been supplementary or speculative ventures. James Crokatt conducted some trade with the West Indies and joined other London merchants, including fellow Carolina traders Andrew Pringle and Charles Ogilvie, in beginning a trade with Guadeloupe and Martinique, the Caribbean islands captured from France during the Seven Years' War. The three signed a petition to the government in 1762 against restoring the islands to France on the grounds that they would be unable to recover debts owed to them by planters on the islands.[23] The import-export trade with South Carolina was, however, the merchants' principal concern; it generated large enough profits to discourage them from diversifying much into other sectors.

These profits translated into status and wealth. London's Carolina merchants often owned the ships that plied the Atlantic, crossing from west to east with rice, indigo, naval stores, and deerskins or in the other direction with textiles, ironwork, furniture, and other goods to be sold in Charles Town. Owning these ships generated extra profits for the merchants from hiring out space on the vessels to smaller traders for their goods and by avoiding the costs of chartering vessels themselves. Buying an oceangoing ship required substantial capital, further pointing to the Carolina merchants' wealth, especially when—as was often the case—one merchant was a ship's sole owner.[24] Directorships of London institutions, especially the capital's limited liability insurance companies, also reflected the wealth and status that London's Carolina merchants enjoyed. John Nickleson, for example, was a director of Royal Exchange Assurance; his brother-in-law, Richard Shubrick, was for fifteen years a director of the London Assurance Corporation and on account of his maritime expertise was an "elder brother" of Trinity House, the body responsible for the upkeep of Britain's lighthouses.[25]

Philanthropic service and donations further signaled the wealth and status of London's Carolina merchants. Sitting on charitable boards, they moved among the capital's commercial elites. As with commercial lobbying, their philanthropic activities indicated how they understood the overlapping roles of commerce, private initiative, and government. Through membership on charity boards, London's Carolina merchants epitomized the well-established belief that private initiative could directly stimulate Britain's "national interest." Several of them directed their philanthropy—a by-product of their commercial profits—toward nautical causes, reflecting the maritime character of their business and the contemporary preoccupation with Britain's naval prowess. A number subscribed to the Marine Society, which funded poor boys to join the Royal Navy. Sailors' welfare organizations such as the "Hospital for decay'd Seamen in the Merchants' Service" and the "Corporation for the Relief and Support of Sick, Maimed and Disabled Seamen, and of the Widows and Children of such as shall be Killed, Slain, or Drowned in the Merchants' Service" were other favored causes.[26] Most explicitly yoking social concern with patriotic ends—and in this case in the expectation of financial dividends for himself—James Crokatt invested one thousand pounds in the Free British Fishery Society, an organization formed in 1749 to promote herring fishing in the hope of boosting Britain's shipping fleet, training sailors, and alleviating poverty.[27] Charity in the "national interest" also complemented the Carolina traders' political lobbying. Both reflected the idea that it was the role and responsibility of the concerned individual to promote economic and social well-being. Moreover, the desired outcomes would lead to national advantages—whether a better manned and more active Royal Navy or more productive colonies—which would in turn benefit the individual donor or lobbyist. For London's Carolina merchants, this benefit might be an Atlantic Ocean made safer by an empowered navy or, thanks to their lobbying for favorable treatment of South Carolina's produce, more rice or indigo to trade. Philanthropy, advocacy, and self-interest went hand in hand.

"Transactions with a few well chosen Friends": The Concentration of London's Carolina Trade

The way businesses were organized in the transatlantic Carolina trade reinforced the concentration of trade in relatively few hands. One aspect of this was the manner in which partnerships were formed. Making transatlantic partnerships with traders in Charles Town offered London's Carolina merchants assured outlets for their goods and reliable suppliers of rice, indigo, naval stores, and deerskins for British and continental European markets. It also gave London traders reliable "market intelligence" on local conditions in South Carolina: which imported goods were in demand—increasing their price—and which were oversupplied and therefore to avoid sending; spot prices for the colony's agricultural exports; details of shipping movements in Charles Town; and the threats of privateers along the Carolina coast during wartime. Partnerships also reduced a trading house's exposure to the age-old problems of principal-agency: the liability of agents on the ground to mismanage the firm's affairs, to trade on their own account, or at worst to actively defraud the firm. Retaining a family member as a business partner in Charles Town, as Richard Shubrick arranged with his brother Thomas, was, at least in theory, the most effective form of mitigating these problems and, more generally, of assuring trust—a commodity critical to success in a long-distance and precarious business environment.

Fraternal partnerships spanning the Atlantic, whether legally binding or more informal, were a feature of British trade with South Carolina and Georgia throughout the eighteenth century. Besides Richard and Thomas Shubrick, this was also the case in the connections between Samuel Wragg in London and his brother Joseph in Charles Town during the 1720s and 1730s, between Robert Pringle in Charles Town and his brother Andrew in London in the 1730s and 1740s, and within Graham, Clark & Co., leading merchants in Georgia's Atlantic trade during the 1760s and early 1770s, in which John Graham represented the firm in Savannah and his brother James controlled business in London.[28] For traders unwilling or unable to rely on a brother on the other side of the Atlantic, long-standing and trusted friends could fill the breach. Having entered transatlantic partnership with Ebenezer Simmons and Benjamin Smith, James Crokatt confined his export trade to the port almost exclusively to his partners.[29] From London, John Beswicke entered into a series of partnerships with Charles Town traders, again showing the value attached to trusted and reliable correspondents "on the spot."[30]

Against the security offered by formal transatlantic partnerships, conducting trade with a number of different correspondents in South Carolina offered competing advantages, not least of which were the greater volumes and higher profits that might be achieved as a consequence. James Crokatt's partnership with Simmons & Smith in Charles Town ended as planned in 1745, when its seven-year term expired, and the firm's assets were liquidated and divided among the three men, each receiving just under seven thousand pounds. The end of the partnership prompted a shift in Crokatt's trading strategy.[31] From 1745 he shipped goods on credit—ranging from textiles to building materials—directly to a multitude of independent traders and storekeepers in Charles Town, receiving remittances in cash, bills of exchange, or rice in a fleet of vessels either co-owned with Charles Town merchants or owned solely by him.[32] Reaching consumers in the interior of South Carolina and Georgia, Crokatt also sent merchandise directly to lowcountry planters for their use.[33] Having gained expertise and reputations, London's principal Carolina merchants found that new firms in Charles Town clamored hard to get business from them, thereby reinforcing their grip on the capital's Carolina trade. The traders in one start-up business asked Robert Raper, the long-serving agent in the port for John Beswicke and James Crokatt, to tell Charles Crokatt, who inherited his father's business, that they were setting up in trade and "want much to deal with him." Raper assured Crokatt that the traders were "honest industrious young men" who would, moreover, "not live extravagantly as too many of our Merchants here." He provided a similar service to William Greenwood and William Higginson after they took over Beswicke's firm, telling them of a new partnership in Charles Town whose members were keen to do business with them. The partnership would "apply to you for Goods & desired I would recommend them," Raper related. Furthermore, they were creditworthy, solvent, and had a reputation for being in good "Circumstances," essential attributes for would-be Atlantic traders touting for connections in London.[34]

For aspiring merchants in Charles Town, choosing the right trading correspondents in Britain required careful deliberation. Confidence and trust were hard-won commodities based on reputation and recommendation; having forged a link with a particular London trading house, a Charles Town merchant often directed the bulk of his trade to it. Moreover, there were economies of scale in shipping rice, indigo, or deerskins in a single consignment to one trading house rather than in several consignments to many. Doing so reduced transaction costs in shipping charges and insurance and simplified making remittances. Reflecting in 1755 to a London correspondent on the successful campaign for a bounty on Carolinian indigo that James Crokatt had led seven years earlier, Henry Laurens described his Charles Town counterparts' partiality to particular trading houses. Some might have expected that Crokatt's endeavors would have persuaded all the town's traders to switch their commercial allegiances to him. Because of the traders' established connections, however, they had not. "You may Possible think the Mercantile Men ought to consign all their Indigo to him [Crokatt]," he explained, "but as every one has his Perticular Freind that sends out all his goods it cant be expected that they would send part of their Remittance to a different hand."[35] Long-term and relatively exclusive trading relationships between Charles Town and London reflected the belief that the greatest stability and surest profits came from confining one's trade to a small circle of correspondents. This persisted throughout the colonial era, again helping to perpetuate the concentration of London's Carolina trade. As Laurens counseled a young trader, he should not be "anxious to obtain a numerous Correspondence, it will plague you in the Carolina Trade, sometimes perplex you to discharge all the business consign'd to you, and what is worse than all, it will sometimes draw Censure upon you for Partiality or Neglect, when in fact you have acted with the strictest Candour and the greatest Diligence. And finally the Profits arising from it, will not be so clear as those which result from transactions with a few well chosen Friends."[36]

The process of forming partnerships within London's Carolina trading houses also helped to maintain the trade's concentration in a small and self-perpetuating circle. Just as commercial logic encouraged the formation of partnerships in Charles Town and between merchants on either side of the Atlantic, there were sound business reasons for merchants to go into partnership in London. For established traders, it reduced workload by spreading tasks and lessened their personal financial exposure; for aspiring merchants, it reduced the capital barriers to entering trade and, by offering the prospect of gaining a financial stake in the firm, incentivized clerks and apprentices. James Crokatt employed at least four apprentices as clerks and bookkeepers in his Cloak Lane countinghouse in the late 1740s. In 1749, being "desirous of easing himself of some part of the Fatigue of so great a concern," he brought two of his apprentices, Richard Grubb and Alexander Watson, into a seven-year partnership. Crokatt invested sixteen thousand pounds, four-fifths of the firm's total stock of twenty thousand pounds, with his junior copartners each putting in two thousand pounds for one-tenth stakes. The partners drew on the firm's joint stock for their subsistence, with these deductions reckoned in the annual accounts. As the partnership was based at Crokatt's house, its terms allowed him to deduct ten pounds a year from the firm for coal and fifty pounds "for the entertainment of strangers"—an early corporate hospitality account. With an eye to the future, the terms of partnership also included a provision for Crokatt's son Charles to take a share in the firm when ready. He duly did, becoming copartner in 1755 and taking over the firm in his own right in 1760.[37] Other Carolina traders as well perpetuated their businesses by bringing sons or other young relatives into their firms. Richard Shubrick's son, also Richard, inherited his father's firm, while John Beswicke trained his nephews William Greenwood and William Higginson. Beneath this veneer of stability, however, were profound contrasts in the merchants' experience, with important consequences for the character of London's Carolina trade. Unlike their predecessors, who had each personally lived and traded for several years in Charles Town, this new generation of London's Carolina merchants had spent their formative years in trade in the capital itself.

The Carolina merchants' geographic concentration within London meant that the trade was doubly concentrated in a small number of hands and, with just a few exceptions, in a small area within the historic City of London. Their close proximity reflected a common pattern within the different sectors of London's overseas commerce. Traders in longer-established branches of American trade had long congregated in particular city wards: Virginia traders, for example, mostly operated in Tower and Aldgate Wards.[38] Propinquity was valued for several commercial reasons. It enabled traders to relay information easily about ships' sailings, to exchange intelligence on matters such as anticipated crop yields and prices and the creditworthiness of transatlantic correspondents, and to arrange shared cargoes. Such clustering took place from the 1740s among London's Carolina merchants, reflecting both the increasing volume of trade between London and South Carolina and the trade's growing prominence as a sector of London business.

When James Crokatt transferred from Charles Town to London, he established himself in premises on Coleman Street, north of St. Paul's Cathedral. He probably chose this location because it was near the trading house of his longtime associate Samuel Wragg. As he supplanted the elderly Wragg as the capital's leading Carolina trader, Crokatt triggered a congregation of Carolina merchants. After Crokatt moved in 1747 to premises on Cloak Lane, closer to the River Thames, nearby streets straddling Dowgate, Vintry, and Walbrook Wards became the nexus for London's Carolina traders. The area gave easy access to Thames-side wharves and warehouses immediately to the south. A short walk north led to the Royal Exchange, the hub of London's trading and a vital stop on a merchant's daily rounds, where cargoes could be brokered, insurance agreed, and commodity trades arranged. By 1760 the Carolina trade occupied a special "walk" in the Royal Exchange alongside dedicated sections for Virginia, New England, and West Indies traders; for specialist commodities; and for other branches of trade such as to Turkey, Portugal, and Italy.[39]

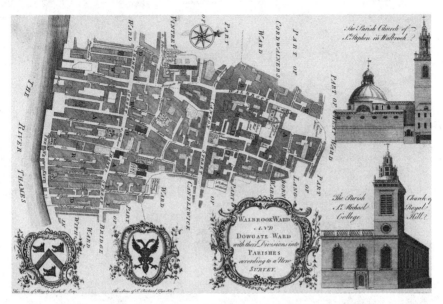

Walbrook Ward and Dowgate Ward, 1756. Cloak Lane, site of James Crokatt's countinghouse, is south of Cannon Street. Benjamin Cole, 1697–1783, after an unknown artist. Yale Center for British Art, Paul Mellon Collection.

Like other fields of commerce, the Carolina trade had its own special coffeehouse. Besides providing coffee, it was a venue for merchants to meet, receive correspondence, read newly arrived copies of colonial newspapers, and do business. A Carolina Coffee House had existed in London since before 1749, when it could be found on Birchin Lane, at the heart of the area where the Carolina merchants had their premises. Together, the Royal Exchange, Carolina Coffee House, and the proximity of trading houses facilitated another of the Carolina traders' activities: petitioning. A petition could be quickly circulated among traders living and working near one another and meeting one another daily at the coffeehouse, at the Exchange's Carolina "walk," and at riverside wharves. Signatures could be rapidly collected and the group mobilized.[40] While this was true in other branches of trade, the concentration of the Carolina trade in a relatively small number of hands along with the traders' geographic congregation seem to have expedited these processes and made London's Carolina lobby particularly responsive. Britain's wars with Spain and France between 1739 and 1748 and the political-economic climate in their wake would test the ability of London's Carolina merchants to capitalize on the group's internal coherence and respond to the political opportunities that arose.

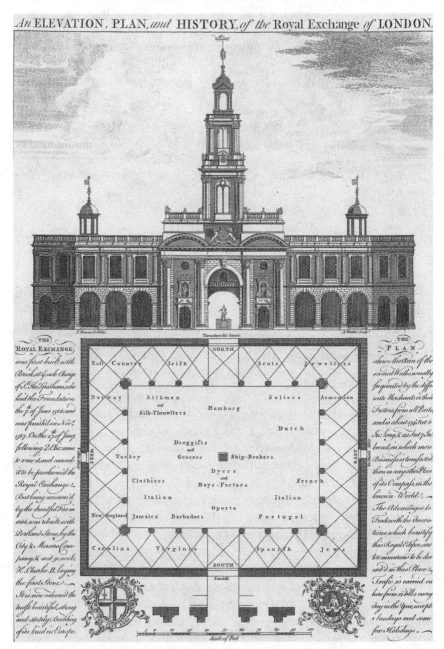

An Elevation, Plan, and History of the Royal Exchange of London, c. 1760. The Carolina "walk" is bottom left. Anthony Walker, 1726–65, after John Donowell, active 1753–86. Yale Center for British Art, Paul Mellon Collection.

A View of the Royal Exchange, London, 1754. After Thomas Bowles, ca. 1712–53.
Yale Center for British Art, Paul Mellon Collection.

"For which this Province is Greatly Oblig'd":
London Lobbying in the Early 1740s

In 1715 the Yamassee War had led to the first organized lobbying by merchants in London on South Carolina's behalf. Given the colony's exposed position on the southern frontier of British North America, Spanish, French, and Indian threats continued to loom large in the minds of its residents and its supporters in Britain. These threats were made all the more serious after the outbreak of war with Spain in 1739 and France in 1744. As they had thirty years earlier, Carolinians seized upon colonial defense as an issue on which London's Carolina traders could particularly influence British government policy. Wartime increased the traders' usefulness to the British government as a source of information on South Carolina, as the government sought news of military dispositions and the colony's defensive readiness. This gave the traders particular access to government, enabling them to lobby for extra protection for the colony. Charles Town's merchants could exert leverage on the government, Robert Pringle suggested, by galvanizing their connections in London. As he wrote to his brother Andrew in the capital in 1743, "the Merchants & trading people [of Charles Town] ought to be Inform'd of & their Opinion ask't & advis'd with in all affairs of that nature, & that they may advise their Friends to assist at Home." London merchants had formed a committee the previous year to lobby for three army companies to defend South Carolina against any Spanish attack.[41] Andrew Pringle, a former ship's captain turned Carolina trader in London, was one of the "Friends at Home" who successfully pressed for greater military and naval protection for the colony. His brother thanked him in March 1744 for his "Good Offices to have the Companies and Gallies Granted to us, for which this Province is Greatly Oblig'd to you." While the irascible Robert Pringle regretted that not all the capital's Carolina merchants were as diligent in serving the colony, his complaint that "if all the Gentlemen in this Trade has as just Concern for it as you, things would goe better here than they doe" nonetheless emphasized the common belief in how effective London lobbying could be.[42]

The Inside View of the Royal Exchange at London, 18th century. Unknown artist. Yale Center for British Art, Paul Mellon Collection.

The forcible impressment of merchant seamen in Charles Town into the Royal Navy particularly vexed the port's traders. As with military protection for the colony, it was a matter where they felt their London counterparts could profitably intercede with government. Whether naval officers could legally force merchant seamen in the American colonies to join the navy was a moot point of law during the 1730s and 1740s. The 1708 "Act for the Encouragement of Trade to America" had prohibited any impressment in America except for naval deserters, but it was subject to differing legal interpretations in Britain. Some jurists believed that the law gave colonial governors residual powers to impress in emergencies and as such banned only impressment by naval officers; others believed that the statute had expired at the conclusion of the War of the Spanish Succession in 1713.[43] Whatever its precise legal status, impressment was taking place in Charles Town even before war broke out with Spain in 1739. Traders in the port felt its impact strongly. "The Merchant Shipping here sufferr very much by the King's Ships that are from time to time Stationed here, who Instead of Encouraging & being a Help & protection to our Navigation are a Nusance & very much Distress same in a great many Respects," Robert Pringle told a London correspondent in 1737; "Captain Collcott, notwithstanding he is all Clear & Ready to sail & waits only for a Wind to carry him over the Bar, has this Day had three of his best Sailors Impress'd on board his Majesties Ship the *Rose*, Capt. Charles Windham, Commander when there is no manner of Occasion for Same neither any law or Authority for so Doeing." Such a complaint might have come from any number of ports in Britain that suffered the incursions of the press-gang. But without parliamentary representatives to present Charles Town's grievances or direct access themselves to the government in London, Charles Town's merchants looked to their counterparts in the capital to make special solicitations. Demonstrating the imperfections of the system in practice, however, little assistance had come from that quarter: "it is a great pity the Merchants of London, who are the most proper persons to Represent [the] same, Did not make immediate Application to Parliament, in order to have so great a Hindrance & grievance to Trade Effectually Remedied," Pringle complained.[44]

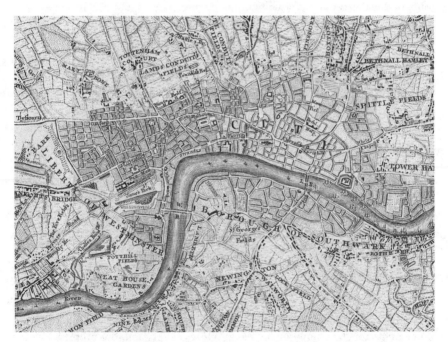

A Map of London and the Adjacent Country 10 Miles Round, (detail) 1748, showing the City of London. Richard Parr (fl. 1723–51) after John Rocque (d. 1762). Yale Center for British Art, Paul Mellon Collection.

If naval impressment was an annoyance to Charles Town's merchant shipping in peacetime, it became a far greater problem in wartime. Having loaded a ship with rice for London in May 1740, Pringle was alarmed to discover that the day before its scheduled departure, all its sailors had been impressed onto the HMS *Tartar,* stationed in the port. Fortunately for Pringle—and no doubt for the sailors too—he managed to secure their release the following day.[45] Impressment disrupted trade by depriving ships of manpower in an intermittent and unpredictable way. In terms of its cost, its impact was more sustained as labor shortages put merchant sailors at a premium. They were able to command higher wages, thereby raising freight costs. With naval demands increasing as the war continued, trading vessels were forced to leave Charles Town shorthanded or were unable to sail at all during the winter of 1742–43. Pringle reported how one ship in January 1743 had been "Detain'd sometime since he has been Loaded & Clear'd at all the Offices purely for want of Sailors, having had Two impress'd on board one of the Kings Ships with whom we have had a pretty Deal of Trouble & Charge before had them [the seamen] Return'd, having oblig'd them to Return them, 'tho one happen'd to be Drown'd in Endeavouring to make his escape by Swimming a Shoar." Pringle had apparently secured the surviving seaman's return by threatening to sue under the 1708 law, which levied a twenty-pound fine on any Royal Navy captain who impressed merchant sailors, and he believed he was the first person in the port to do so.

Perhaps because of the uncertainty surrounding the act, redress from Parliament was once again sought through the lobbying and solicitations of Carolina merchants in Britain. Sending copies of the *South Carolina Gazette,* which carried reports of the Royal Navy's impressments in Charles Town, to his brother in London, Pringle hoped that they would "be taken Due Notice of by all our Merchants & Trading People at Home, & by which they may judge of how Little Service & how Little the Trading Interest is Regarded or Taken Notice of by the Commanders of the Kings Ships sent on this Station." Once again, however, merchants in Britain failed to meet the standards of advocacy that Pringle, at least, expected. He observed that "Merchant Ships are Greatly Oppress'd here by the King's Ships Impressing their Hands, which makes Sailors Wages Run very high" but regretted that "It is pity that it is not taken Notice of by the Gentlemen in Trade at Home in order to have it Remidied."[46]

The success of earlier lobbying had perhaps heightened expectations of the Carolina lobby's efficacy and influence, and indeed of the willingness of the British government to meet its demands. Pringle's comments are revealing: London's Carolina traders simply had to ask for redress, whether for military reinforcements for the colony or for naval impressments, and the problems would be "Remidied."[47] The same applied to commercial privileges. Permission to export rice directly to Madeira might have been "Obtain'd by proper Application," he complained to correspondents on the island in 1742.[48] In reality, South Carolina's advocates in Britain operated in a more complex environment. Carolinian demands for commercial privileges would need changes to the Navigation Acts, while policy makers had to balance the demands against the claims of other colonial lobbies. The permission to export rice directly to Spain and Portugal, for example, granted to South Carolina in 1730 and extended to Georgia in 1735, had set a precedent for other colonial lobbies to exploit. In March 1739 West Indies merchants and planters petitioned Parliament for freedom to send sugar, coffee, indigo, cocoa, and ginger directly to continental Europe. They cited the fact that South Carolina had "received a Liberty of the same Nature, with regard to Rice" and hoped that this precedent would "be a farther Inducement to this House, to grant this Liberty to our Sugar Islands."[49]

Compared to securing the amendment to the Navigation Acts that allowed direct rice exports to southern Europe in 1730, the ambitions of London's Carolina merchants and the colony's official agent in London, Peregrine Fury, during the 1740s were more modest. Fury was a professional bureaucrat with strong military ties, and unlike South Carolina's other agents before and after him, he appears not to have had personal links with the colony. His spell as agent typified the potential for the conflicts of interest that were inherent in the system of colonial agency. He combined his service to South Carolina with being agent for several army regiments, which sometimes conflicted with his duties for the colony and explains the South Carolina Assembly's eagerness to replace him on more than one occasion—the role was offered to James Crokatt in 1746 and to another London resident, John Sharpe, the following year. Most notably, in 1742–43 the assembly believed that Fury had suppressed the colonial government's critical report of the military expedition which James Oglethorpe had led in 1740 against St. Augustine in Spanish Florida, a document which his employers in South Carolina had explicitly instructed him to publish in London. Fury was accused of acting "too much like a courtier" and was charged by the assembly with being "more a Friend to Generall Oglethorpe than to this Province."[50]

Despite Fury's inauspicious leadership, London's Carolina lobby enjoyed some success in the 1740s. In 1740 the British government sought to put an embargo on exports of British and colonial foodstuffs to foreign markets, in the hope of both weakening Spain and France and preventing scarcity in Britain. In collaboration with their colleagues in Bristol, the capital's Carolina merchants successfully lobbied for rice to be excluded from the list of embargoed produce.[51] Their petitions emphasized the benefits that South Carolina's planters and Britain's shipping alike had derived from direct rice exports to Spain and Portugal. They also stressed the colony's strategic significance and precariousness. Fears of Spanish attack and slave insurrection, heightened by the Stono Rebellion—widely attributed to Spanish incitement—the previous year were uppermost. Such was the climate of fear and economic depression in South Carolina that, the traders reported, "the Number of their Inhabitants is so greatly decreased, that the Planters have been scarce able to keep in Subjection their own Slaves, who have been encouraged, and are much too disposed to rebel." An embargo on rice exports would "occasion a total Stagnation of their Trade and Commerce," with dire consequences for the colony. The rhetoric was persuasive, and the act eventually passed by Parliament banned exports of corn, grain, malt, flour, bread, and biscuits, along with other foodstuffs, but specifically excepted rice. The preferential treatment of rice was made all the more impressive by the failure of the agents of Britain's more northerly American colonies to get corn exports similarly exempted.[52]

When the House of Commons debated renewing the embargoes in 1742, South Carolina's lobby in London again secured the continued exemption of rice. Particularly vociferous in Parliament in support of the colony were Sir John Barnard, MP for the City of London and a staunch advocate of merchant interests, and William Bowles, a merchant as well as an MP. Arguments about the harm that an embargo on rice exports would cause to British shipping and manufacturing and about South Carolina's strategic and economic peril were again to the fore. The *Gentleman's Magazine* recorded the debate, substituting names of places and individuals with barely disguised alternations to circumvent official restrictions on parliamentary reporting. The account offers a rare insight into Commons debates. According to the magazine, Barnard warned that "by prohibiting the Exportation of Rice, we shall . . . in one Year, reduce the Colony of *S. Carolana* [sic] below the Possibility of subsisting; the chief Product of that Country, the Product which induced us originally to plant it, and with which all its Trade is carried on, is Rice. With Rice the Inhabitants of that Province purchase all the other Necessaries of Life, and among them the Manufactures of our own Country. This Rice is carried by our Merchants to other Parts of *Degulia* [Europe], and sold again for large Profit." Bowles was still more direct: "The Province of *Carolana* [sic] . . . has already suffered the Inconveniences of this War beyond any other Part of his Majesty's Dominions, as it is situate upon the Borders of the *Iberian* Dominions, and as it is weak by the Paucity of the Inhabitants in Proportion to its Extent; Let us therefore pay a particular Regard to this Petition, lest we aggravate the Terror which the Neighbourhood of a powerful Enemy naturally produces, by the severer Miseries of Poverty and Famine."[53] Having again secured the exemption of rice from the export embargo, London's Carolina lobby achieved further legislative success in 1742 when permission to export rice directly to Spain and Portugal was extended.[54]

Trade and the "National Interest"

Changes in Britain's political environment during the late 1740s would fuel a surge in the Carolina lobby's activity. The Treaty of Aix-la-Chapelle in 1748 brought nine years of war with Spain and four years of war with France to an inconclusive end. Peace allowed British policy makers to scrutinize the country's American colonies and their trade with new purpose. British naval dominance in the war had kept French victories on land in check, preserving a rough balance of power. Throughout the first half of the eighteenth century, however, Britain's politicians had watched the development of French naval power and overseas trade with growing alarm. In the immediate postwar years Britain was gripped by a conviction that France would heed the lesson of its wartime naval defeats and build up its marine forces to challenge Britain's naval hegemony, threaten the country's overseas empire and trade, and undermine the domestic prosperity that was believed to stem from these. Stimulating Britain's overseas trade would catalyze a national revival to combat France's naval and commercial menace. Seizing the initiative, Parliament passed a flurry of legislation between 1748 and 1751 to promote specific trades and manufacturing, ranging from banning the importation and sale of French textiles to bounties to promote whale and herring fishing.[55]

Promoting trade between Britain and its American colonies was a particular priority. First, an increase in the volume of colonial trade would enlarge Britain's merchant fleet, training more sailors whose labor could be diverted to the Royal Navy in wartime. Second, greater colonial output would lead to higher demand in the colonies for British-made goods, stimulating the domestic economy. Third, colonial economic expansion would encourage new settlement and population growth. This would increase the colonies' ability to defend themselves and reduce both their susceptibility to foreign attack and the onus on British regular armed forces to come to their aid—at high cost to the British state. Greater Atlantic trade would also satisfy fiscal ends. Fighting the war had raised Britain's national debt to an unprecedented £68 million. The cost of servicing it was widely seen as a millstone around the neck of the national economy by perpetuating high taxes, by disrupting credit markets since the profitability and security of lending to government deterred lending to private enterprise, and by discouraging holders of government debt from engaging in more productive economic activity.[56] Higher volumes of trade would yield greater customs revenues from the taxes paid on imports and reexports. Customs duties amounted to about 20 percent of government revenue in 1747, when the general rate of customs duty on imported goods and produce was raised from 15 percent to 20 percent of an import's official value. Such a rise, together with increases in extra duties on specific imports, was politically preferable to raising the land tax or introducing an income tax as a means of filling the national coffers.[57]

At the end of war in 1748, government policy sought to make the American colonies pay a greater indirect fiscal contribution to the costs of empire. They would do so through yielding more taxable output. The approach contrasted with the policies that would be adopted after 1763, following the Seven Years' War. An even more costly conflict for the Exchequer, the Seven Years' War would lead the British government to turn—with profound repercussions—to its American colonies for a direct fiscal contribution for the debts incurred in their defense and the anticipated future costs of their protection. The two approaches were different means to the same end—the principle that the colonies should pay their way—and the strategy of indirectly augmenting revenues taken immediately after 1748 was an important precursor to the more direct and controversial approach taken a decade and a half later. Leaving aside its long-term portents, however, the strategy of stimulating colonial production was in the short term one on which South Carolina and its advocates in London were well placed to capitalize.

Despite the end of hostilities in 1748 and the gradual growth of Georgia on its southern frontier, which provided a buffer of sorts against external threats, South Carolina remained perilously exposed to the intrigues of rival imperial powers. The colony was a vital link in the chain of colonial defense. It was also a major producer of staple commodities that yielded much-needed customs duties; a market for British manufactured goods, supporting domestic industry and employment; and crucially, a vital source of the shipping and marine training that were seen as essential to British naval supremacy in future wars. The prevailing spirit of national revivalism—and the inseparable imperial-maritime-commercial rationale that underlay it—gave South Carolina and its advocates in London a particular opening. The political climate coincided with more vigorous leadership within London's Carolina lobby and then roused the lobby to new levels of activity, further enhancing its ability to take advantage of these opportunities. Since relocating to London in 1739, James Crokatt had acted as the capital's de facto expert witness on Britain's most southerly North American colonies, and he invariably was called to give evidence when Parliament investigated their condition or trade. His status reflected his personal experience in South Carolina, particularly the distinction conferred by being a member of the Royal Council, and the extent of his trade with the region.[58] Through his commercial and political standing, Crokatt also assumed effective leadership of London's Carolina traders during the late 1740s, supplanting the colony's official agent, Peregrine Fury, in representing South Carolina and its trade in the capital's political arenas.

At the end of hostilities in 1748, the British government proposed reducing military forces in its southernmost North American colonies, despite the continuing latent threat from Spain. Crokatt took a petition from London's "principal Traders" in the Carolina trade to ministers "Praying that the Forces in Georgia & So. Carolina be kept in Pay & continued"—a protest against the disbanding of a regiment of British regulars in the region. Although the protest was unsuccessful, the lobbying was noted in South Carolina.[59] Crokatt also had a long track record of promoting agricultural innovation and diversification in South Carolina. Dating back to his days in Charles Town, he had urged planters and traders to take advantage of the stimuli on offer from the British government. Back in February 1737 the *South Carolina Gazette* had devoted its front page to a letter from Crokatt reminding readers of the bounty on pitch and tar made in a particular "Swedish" fashion. Two weeks later he had backed up his advice with a personal pledge to buy for at least fifty shillings a barrel any Swedish-style tar.[60] With his customary eye for profit, Crokatt saw both the economic benefits for South Carolina of a revitalized trade in naval stores and a commercial opportunity for himself. From London he continued to promote a more diverse agricultural base in the colony, urging experimentation with cochineal, cotton, hemp, and tar. Cotton, he wrote, is "known to grow well in Carolina and is now worth double the Price it was six Years ago. . . . Hemp, I am told, grows well there, and we know Tar is no where cheaper; it is a simple Manufacture, few Tools required, and easily taught even to Negroes."[61] In 1747 he sent to South Carolina a model of a mill for extracting sesame oil, and the next year he sent a model of an all-purpose plough for cultivating grain or indigo. Both were displayed at the public treasurer's office in Charles Town.[62]

"Indefatigable in the service of this Province": The 1748 Indigo Bounty

"Rice and Indigo are the two pillars on which our future prosperity must be built. In Rice we are unrivalled, let us try to excel in Indigo as well," Governor Glen declared to a joint session of the South Carolina Assembly and Royal Council in March 1749.[63] His call to arms followed Parliament's decision the previous year to grant a sixpence-per-pound bounty on imports of indigo from South Carolina into Britain. Indigo was poised to become South Carolina's second most important crop, behind rice, heightening the colony's importance to Britain as a supplier of key commodities, bringing further wealth to the colony's merchant and planter elites, and deepening the colony's reliance on slavery (table 3). Indigo was much in demand in Britain as a dye, but the country relied on imports from French and Spanish colonies. South Carolina had long been identified as an ideal source to meet Britain's needs: "The Indigo Plant grows exceeding well [in South Carolina]; and 'tis thought, if rightly improv'd, we might be supplied . . . not only to answer our Home-Consumption, but with large Quantities for Re-exportation," the mercantilist theorist Joshua Gee had proposed in a popular treatise in 1729.[64] Besides having the right climate for growing indigo, the colony's lowcountry topography was suitable, as the dye-producing plants thrived in the sandy, higher-lying soil where rice could not be grown. Planters also found that the annual cycle of slave labor for planting and harvesting the crop, in April and May, and then beating and draining the plant's leaves and stems in vats to extract the dye, between July and September, coincided with seasonal lulls in rice cultivation. This allowed them to work their slaves year-round: for these reasons, South Carolina's Assembly declared in May 1749 that "Indico proves an excellent colleague with Rice."[65]

Spearheaded by James Crokatt, the campaign for the indigo bounty was his greatest achievement as South Carolina's leading advocate in London. Historians have debated the bounty's long-term economic significance for South Carolina; politically it had important symbolism as the most significant of several parliamentary interventions on South Carolina and its trade during the late 1740s and early 1750s, and in the way it reasserted the efficacy of the Carolina lobby in London.[66] Crokatt took a two-pronged approach to promoting the cultivation of indigo, seeking both to improve its production quality and to incentivize its growth to meet robust existing demand in Britain. In 1746 and 1747 he published two pamphlets on growing, processing, and marketing the crop under the pseudonym "a Friend to Carolina." He sent them to South Carolina in the hope that they would be "useful in assisting the Planters in Carolina, to excel all others, as much in the Indigo, as they have done in Rice."[67] The second element of his approach was to capitalize on the British government's receptivity to measures that promoted colonial economic development.

Crokatt set about lobbying Parliament for a bounty on imports of South Carolinian indigo by writing a pamphlet, *Reasons for laying a Duty on French and Spanish Indigo, and granting a Bounty on what is made in the British Plantations.* He sent it to the Board of Trade and, unusually, went to the lengths of having it printed, a rarity among petitions to the board and indicative of his sophisticated lobbying tactics. The petition articulated a familiar rhetoric of economic patriotism, carefully attuned to prevailing political-economic discourse. An indigo bounty, it claimed, would boost Britain's textile industry by delivering the vital dye more cheaply and reliably, would alleviate South Carolina's economic depression and promote population growth in the colony, and would increase British shipping and consequently naval power. Bounties were a tested economic stimulus for fledgling industries: colonial naval stores had long been incentivized in this way. Indigo making was similarly deserving, the petition argued, requiring the helping hand of state before it could flourish independently. As Crokatt's pamphlet observed, "All new Manufactures should like weak Children be carefully nursed at first, tho they afterwards increase without assistance."[68]

In galvanizing the lobby, Crokatt assembled a broad array of interest groups behind the application. The approach recognized the value of consolidated, cross-sectional advocacy in petitioning Parliament even if, in the political-economic climate that followed the peace in 1748, the proposals were effectively pushing at an open door. The ad hoc lobby encompassed sectors involved in every stage of indigo's journey from its raw state to usable dyestuff: the planters growing the crop; Atlantic merchants shipping it; commodity dealers; and dyers and clothiers from Devon in the southwest of England to Yorkshire in the north. In all, Parliament heard more than twenty separate petitions in support of an indigo bounty. Their content fused claims for the supply requirements of British industry, benevolent concern for South Carolina's welfare, and arguments for competitive advantage over France. Particularly compelling were statistics revealing Britain's heavy dependence on the French West Indies for its indigo. This, it was said, augmented French marine power while reportedly siphoning some £150,000 from British to French coffers.[69] The range of witnesses who gave evidence to the parliamentary committee considering the matter further showed the comprehensiveness of Crokatt's campaign. Indigo brokers; captains of transatlantic shipping; three Carolinian planters, including Robert Pringle, on a short visit to Britain; and representatives of both the linen and woolen industries—two sectors whose interests were more often opposed than united, but which each relied on regular supplies of good indigo—all testified. "All the

Table 3: Exports of Indigo from South Carolina and Georgia (lbs.), 1747–67

	South Carolina	Georgia	Total
1747	138,300	0	138,300
1748	62,200	0	62,200
1749	138,300	0	138,300
1750	63,100	0	63,100
1751	19,900	0	19,900
Average 1747–51	**84,360**	**-**	**84,360**
1752	3,800	0	3,800
1753	28,500	0	28,500
1754	129,600	0	129,600
1755	303,500	4,500	308,000
Average 1752–55	**116,350**	**1,125**	**117,475**
1756	222,800	9,300	232,100
1757	876,400	18,200	894,600
1758	563,000	9,600	572,600
1759	695,700	600	696,300
Average 1756–59	**589,475**	**9,425**	**598,900**
1760	507,600	11,700	519,300
1761	384,100	1,600	385,700
1762	255,300	9,100	264,400
1763	438,900	8,700	447,600
Average 1760–63	**396,475**	**7,775**	**404,250**
1764	529,100	14,200	543,300
1765	335,800	16,000	351,800
1766	491,800	14,400	506,200
1767	570,600	12,900	583,500
Average 1764–67	**481,825**	**14,375**	**496,200**

Source: Carter et al., *Historical Statistics,* V, 749–50; Robert C. Nash, "South Carolina Indigo, European Textiles and the British Atlantic Economy in the Eighteenth Century," *Economic History Review* 63.2 (2010): 317, table 3.

Note: Terminal dates for the years are 1747–52, March to March; 1752–53, March to January; 1753–67, January to January.

Witnesses agreed," concluded the official report of proceedings, "that there is an absolute Necessity for the Use of Indico in the Dyeing Trade; and that no good Blue can be dyed without it."[70] Faced by such a sectionally and geographically broad coalition and given the prevailing appetite for patriotic commercial measures, Parliament quickly approved the proposals. In May 1748 it legislated for a bounty of sixpence per pound on imports of indigo from South Carolina, to run for seven years.[71]

The introduction of the bounty vindicated Crokatt's labors. It also gave South Carolina's residents renewed and compelling evidence of the practical benefits of commercial advocacy. Securing the bounty signaled that the British government was alert to South Carolina's interests and that a lobby in London could effectively represent the colony's claims. Reaction in South Carolina to the bounty was celebratory. The assembly and council jointly drew up an address of "humble and hearty Thanks" to George III in March 1749; having received from Crokatt an account of the lobbying and copies of the petitions presented to Parliament, the assembly expressed its thanks to him and voted unanimously to reimburse him the £215 he had spent from his own pocket on orchestrating the campaign.[72] "He [Crokatt] is indefatigable in the service of this Province & I think every Inhabitant indebted to him," reflected his onetime apprentice Henry Laurens.[73] Even Governor Glen, who was no friend of Crokatt, told the assembly that he was "no stranger to the Character and Abilities of Mr. Crokatt," adding, "He well deserves the Reputation he is known to have."[74] Alongside his commercial experience and longtime spokesmanship in London for South Carolina's interests, Crokatt's management of the indigo campaign in 1748 was instrumental in his selection by the assembly the following year to replace Peregrine Fury as the colony's agent in London.

Success in securing the indigo bounty was followed by further lobbying campaigns attuned to the mood of patriotic commercialism in Britain. In 1750 Crokatt and his fellow Carolina traders were to the fore in a campaign seeking financial encouragement for colonial silk cultivation—one of several attempts throughout the colonial period to promote sericulture in South Carolina and Georgia.[75] Their lobbying strikingly echoed the indigo bounty campaign two years earlier. Parliament was petitioned by weavers, dyers, and merchants and heard evidence from expert witnesses including Crokatt and John Nickleson. The political-economic rhetoric they used mirrored the indigo campaign too. It lamented Britain's reliance on foreign silk, in this case purportedly leading to an outflow of four hundred thousand pounds annually; trumpeted the greater population and security that silk would bring Britain's southern colonies; and suggested the virtuous economic feedback that Britain's manufacturers and exporters would enjoy through extra colonial demand for their goods. Recognizing that "to encourage the Growth and Culture of Silk in his Majesty's Dominions in America . . . will greatly tend to the Increase and Improvement of the Silk

Manufactures of this Kingdom," a line of reasoning that highlights where Britain's main priorities lay, Parliament agreed to remove duties on all silk imported from the American colonies.[76]

Crokatt again took the lead in a campaign the next year to promote colonial potash manufacturing. Potash could be made from the ashes of trees that were cleared to make land for growing crops in North America and offered a useful supplementary income for Carolinian planters. It was vital in Britain for making glass and soap and as a bleaching agent in the textile industry. A petition to Parliament in May 1751 reflected these mutual interests on either side of the Atlantic. Like the indigo and silk petitions before, it presented an alliance of cross-sectoral and both domestic and colonial interests. The petition was signed jointly by agents for several of Britain's North American colonies, "Merchants trading thither, Soapmakers, Dry Salters [dealers in chemicals], Whitsters [bleachers], and others," and sought incentives for colonial ash making.[77] Their arguments reiterated a familiar blend of commercial patriotism and colonial promotion: Britain's reliance on Scandinavian supplies of ash harmed the nation's balance of trade—a favorite political preoccupation; while Britain's heavily forested North American colonies were a source of abundant ashes that could both supply domestic demands and promote colonial development. Only expertise and parliamentary encouragement were needed to create a flourishing industry. The plans were described in the House of Commons as "Mr. Crokatt's proposals," indicating his authorship and his guidance of the petitioning and lobbying campaign. Together with Robert Dinwiddie, recently appointed lieutenant governor of Virginia, and James Abercromby, who was North Carolina's official agent and a former resident of South Carolina, Crokatt assured Parliament of the southern colonies' productive capacity. The campaign succeeded in getting colonial produce exempted from Britain's 6s.2d. duty on ash imports.[78] Further emphasising to his colonial employers his commitment to South Carolina's agricultural diversification and economic development, Crokatt wrote to the Committee of Correspondence, the subcommittee of South Carolina's Assembly charged with communicating with the colony's London agent, to urge the colony to take advantage of the act. He enclosed a pamphlet explaining how to make ashes and expressed hope that "some Planters . . . would soon turn their Thoughts and Hands that Way."[79]

Not all of the Carolina lobby's efforts in the late 1740s and early 1750s guided by Crokatt proved as successful. They nonetheless were further signals of metropolitan commitment to the colony's economic development. The British state might not always be amenable, but the London merchants' efforts to alter imperial laws and regulations suggested an alignment of commercial interests between the capital's Carolina traders and their transatlantic counterparts. Crokatt's first instructions as agent in 1749 had been to secure direct rice exports to additional foreign markets besides Spain and Portugal, but he was no more successful than Fury had been in this: South Carolina would have to wait until

1764 for further relaxations in the law. He was also asked, as Fury had been, to press for South Carolina to be given the right—as Newfoundland, the New England colonies, New York, and Pennsylvania enjoyed—to import salt directly from Portugal.[80] In petitioning the Board of Trade, Crokatt carefully fused South Carolina's interests with broader imperial priorities: "The Sea Coast and all the Rivers in the Province of South Carolina abounds with great Plenty of Fish, as Bass, Sturgeon, Herrings & c. whereby a very Considerable Fishery might be established to the great Benefit of that Province in particular, and of these Kingdoms in general, but the Difficulty of obtaining Salt proper for Curing Fish has prevented that Branch of Commerce from being extended further than for their own private Consumption." The best salt for curing fish and other provisions came from mainland Europe. As a perishable commodity, however, it did not survive the journey—as required by law—from Europe first to Britain and then on to South Carolina. Direct shipments were needed. Furthermore, since ships often sailed from Britain to Europe laden with corn and then crossed the Atlantic laden only with ballast to South Carolina "in order to return with the Produce of that Province to Great Britain," carrying salt would not only supply the ships with freight income but would also save them the expense of buying ballast.[81]

Crokatt organized petitions from "several merchants in London, trading to his Majesty's Colonies in America" and, alongside London's Carolina traders, from London merchants and shipowners involved in trade to Virginia and to Nova Scotia, two other colonies seeking direct salt imports.[82] Such cross-trade coherence was rare and pointed to the sophistication of the lobbying. Crokatt also testified in support of the petitions in Parliament, where he was joined by fellow Carolina traders Andrew Pringle and Richard Shubrick. Their personal testimony of living and trading in Charles Town was central to their appeal as they set out the alignment of imperial and domestic interests. Crokatt reported that he had lived for more than ten years in South Carolina and spoke of the difficulty of procuring salt there for preserving fish and beef. Shubrick told the Commons that he had "lived for some time in Carolina, and had cured great Quantities of Provisions for the Use of his Majesty's Navy." Referring to Nickleson & Shubrick's service as "agents victuallers" in Charles Town for the Royal Navy, he shrewdly conflated colonial and naval-imperial imperatives.[83] In response to strong opposition from Britain's salt manufacturers, who stood to lose an important market, the proposals were rejected, however. Domestic pressure had trumped colonial interests, a telling exposition of the balance of power in lobbying in Britain when domestic and colonial interests were not aligned or were contradictory.[84] Though the failure of this campaign revealed the limitations of commercial lobbying, through it the capital's Carolina merchants had once again shown their commitment to the colony's development and a willingness to advocate on its behalf. For Crokatt personally, his reputation as an ardent representative of South Carolina's commercial interests was reinforced.

It is through Crokatt that the value that authorities in South Carolina attached to effective commercial-political lobbying in London can be seen most clearly. In particular, the controversy that was sparked when he tried to resign as South Carolina's official agent in London in 1753 reveals perceptions of his personal effectiveness and the influence of the role more generally. In attempting to give up the position, Crokatt complained that "the Service and Duty required is more than is Compatible with my Present Plan of Life." He had never wasted so much time, he told the Committee of Correspondence, as he had in waiting on the Board of Trade.[85] Despite his success as a lobbyist, his relations with authorities in South Carolina had not always been harmonious. Before being appointed as agent, he was accused of prioritizing his own interests above those of the colony when, with eight other London merchants, he had appealed to the Board of Trade against South Carolina's emission of paper currency, which the merchants feared would depreciate the value of debts they were owed in the colony.[86] More controversial still was his support for a rogue Indian trader, Charles McNair, whose claims for financial reimbursement from the Crown were opposed by South Carolina's Assembly and its governor James Glen but which Crokatt—allegedly owed money by McNair's partner—supported.[87]

For the merchant-dominated South Carolina Assembly in Charles Town, these blemishes on his record were outweighed by his achievements in commercial matters. Refusing to accept Crokatt's resignation, the assembly instructed the Committee of Correspondence to ask him to reconsider, and it continued to treat him as South Carolina's official agent. Even though several years had passed since he had secured the indigo bounty, Crokatt's efforts to promote agricultural diversification and innovation and as an advocate in London for South Carolina's trade were central to the high reputation he enjoyed in the colony. He was, Henry Laurens wrote, "not lightly esteem'd by the People." When Crokatt eventually retired from the post in 1755, his former apprentice judged that "a good deal was due from this Province to Mr. Crokatt for his unwearied Endeavours to serve us in Promoting the Culture of Indigo beside other matters . . . but its impossible in such a Country as this to get all the People to be of one mind. He has some very strong Opponents in the Councell who wont allow him that Merit as the Commons House thought his due."[88]

Crokatt's resignation was a pivotal moment in South Carolina's political development. Underlying the dispute was the recognition by each branch of government—the governor, the Royal Council, and the assembly—that it was vital for the colony to be effectively represented at the heart of the empire. Who should be agent and who should appoint him set the assembly at loggerheads with the council and the governor. The constitutional wrangling that followed marked the assembly's growing political ambitions and paralyzed South Carolina's government for nearly three years. Culminating in the assembly's refusal to pass a tax bill until its rights were recognized, the dispute was an early example of the brinksmanship that would be a hallmark of South Carolina's politics for the next hundred years.[89] In the short term, the assembly's determination to keep Crokatt in post between 1753 and 1755 signaled the significance it accorded the London agency, and in particular the benefits that an assiduous and well-connected agent could bring.

A combination of factors gave the Carolina lobby in London particular energy in the late 1740s and early 1750s. The ideological environment ushered in by the end of war with Spain and France made the institutions of state—the Board of Trade, the British Treasury, and Parliament—unusually receptive to the lobbying of colonial interest groups. The government's agreement was not guaranteed: the failure of the salt lobbying in 1750 showed the overriding traction of domestic interests. Insofar as it promoted Britain's own economic, strategic, and military priorities, however, colonial economic development assumed a new degree of importance for British politicians. Initiatives that could help colonies pay a greater share of the cost of their defense were especially welcome. As a producer of staple commodities that could not be supplied domestically and with its orientation toward export markets, South Carolina was well placed to capitalize on the political-economic climate. Proposals such as a bounty for colonial indigo and duty-free status for colonial silk and potash were directed at a sympathetic audience. Strong and effective leadership, which the Carolina lobby found in James Crokatt, gave the proposals direction and authority. Crokatt not only skillfully marshaled the Carolina lobby but was also able to assemble cross-sectoral coalitions, most broadly and effectively in support of the indigo bounty.

Crokatt also exemplified the traits that gave London's Carolina lobby particular energy and influence, setting it apart from the capital's less active Virginia and New England lobbies. Like other leading London Carolina merchants who petitioned and testified in Parliament, he had lived and traded in South Carolina. This gave their evidence added credibility; moreover, the deep personal and social links that London's Carolina traders had with the colony help to explain their assiduity in lobbying. Property holdings in South Carolina further reinforced their ties with the colony, deepening their commercial and economic stake in its development. The consolidation of London's Carolina trade in relatively few hands contributed as well to the lobby's industriousness, by permitting rapid mobilization and imbuing the merchants' claims with authority. The concentration stemmed from structural and compositional features within London's Carolina trade, including the pattern of merchant relocations from Charles Town to London, the formation of transatlantic partnerships, and the networks of credit that extended from Great Britain to South Carolina. The concentration facilitated London's Carolina lobby at a time of relative political harmony between Britain and its American colonies. It would, however, have very different consequences as political-economic attachments were tested and challenged from the 1760s onward. There would be a small step from *concentration* of trade to *domination* of trade.

CHAPTER THREE

"CANKERS TO THE RICHES OF A COUNTRY"?

Transatlantic Absenteeism in Colonial South Carolina

"Cankers to the riches of a country": in this judgment of absentee landowners, made in 1744, the economic theorist Sir Matthew Decker typified contemporary opinion on absenteeism. In his influential *Essay on the Causes of the Decline of the Foreign Trade,* Decker equated absentee landholders with foreign subscribers to Britain's national debt who leeched money away from Britain in interest payments.[1]

But what did he and his contemporaries understand by "absenteeism"? To most, it meant the ownership of Irish lands by nonresidents.[2] Samuel Johnson thus defined an absentee as "He that is absent from his station or employment, or country. A word that is used commonly with regard to Irishmen living out of their country."[3] Half a century earlier, the British economist Josiah Child had observed in his *New Discourse on Trade* the prevalence of absentee landowners in Ireland and how they had hindered Ireland's economic development by repatriating the profits from its land. He similarly attributed the poverty of Cornwall, in the southwest of England, despite its mines and fisheries, to the fact that "a great part of the Stock imployed in the aforesaid great Trade, is taken up at Interest, and consequently owned by Londoners, and other Absentees."[4]

A rare dissenting voice among eighteenth-century economic theorists on the economic consequences of absenteeism was Joshua Gee. In his widely read treatise *The Trade and Navigation of Great-Britain Considered,* he lauded absentee planters in the West Indies for their personal investment in the mother country, besides the broader economic dividends their plantations brought to Britain. But if Gee's positive take on absenteeism was unusual, he nonetheless reflected contemporary opinion in assessing its prevalence. "If there is enough to support the Family," he noted of Caribbean planters, "they come here, and only an Overseer is left upon the Plantation to direct, and the whole Produce is remitted Home; and if enough to purchase an Estate, then it is laid out in *Old England.*" More succinctly, among plantation owners "nothing but the Want of Means to live at Home, keeps them Abroad."[5] Landownership by nonresidents was seen by contemporaries as a defining and, for most, malign feature of the British imperial polity in the West Indies, retarding the islands' social development and, by siphoning money away, hindering their economic progress. The historian Trevor

Burnard has noted the value-laden nature of the term "absenteeism," which, "signifying abstention, neglect of duty, and indifference to one's native country conveys a strong sense of moral culpability."[6]

Less obvious to contemporaries than its Irish or West Indian guises, absentee landownership was a feature too of colonial South Carolina and a powerful force alongside the bonds of ethnicity, kinship, culture, and governance in connecting the colony with Great Britain. British residents owned plantation land and urban property in South Carolina for the financial returns they offered in agricultural output and rental yields. These plantations and properties also demonstrated a symbolic commitment to South Carolina, supplementing their owners' interest in the colony's trade and commerce. Many of Britain's leading Carolina merchants, the colony's most active advocates in Britain, were among these absentees. In practical terms, this property ownership contributed to the particular activism of South Carolina's London lobby during the eighteenth century.[7]

Conceptions of Absenteeism in Colonial South Carolina

Throughout the eighteenth century nonresidents owned tracts of lands in South Carolina. Absenteeism dated to the colony's establishment, when several Barbadian merchants and planters bought lots in Charles Town and left them in the care of resident attorneys, while the family of only one of the original Lords Proprietors, the Colletons, settled permanently in the colony.[8] Petitioning the Board of Trade in 1715 for military aid for the colony, twenty-one "Planters and merchants trading to South Carolina" in London had avowed that "Most of us have great Debts and Effects there, some of us large Plantations."[9] Absenteeism existed, however, in more than one form in eighteenth-century South Carolina, since it had both domestic and overseas guises. Unlike Virginia's tobacco planters, who largely lived full-time on their estates, most of South Carolina's planter elites spent much of the year in Charles Town.[10] A range of factors lay behind their congregation. Charles Town was the colony's commercial and social hub, while the chronically high mortality rates in the rice-growing lowcountry gave a strong epidemiological incentive to seek refuge in the town, particularly as the environmental influences on the spread of diseases were better understood from the mid-eighteenth century.[11] These planters might be defined as domestic or seasonal absentees, living in the colony but often physically remote from their lands and their cultivation of those lands. Many historians have considered the implications of this phenomenon for South Carolina's political, social, and cultural development and how absenteeism affected plantation management.[12]

South Carolina's overseas or transatlantic absentee landowners were owners of agricultural tracts, urban plots, or both who, except perhaps for occasional visits to South Carolina, were permanently absent not just from their lands but from the colony.[13] The group is difficult to quantify and categorize, since it was not until after the American Revolution that any list or record of absentee land

and property owners was made.[14] This is not to say that opinion in South Carolina was wholly ambivalent toward nonresidency. Critiques of the practice were certainly more muted than in the British sugar islands, though fear of the consequences of absenteeism for managing and controlling slaves underlay responses to the phenomenon in both the West Indies and South Carolina. In the Caribbean absenteeism was publicly credited with heightening the risk of slave insurrection. Jamaica and Antigua imposed extra taxes on absentee-owned estates to deter proprietors from leaving the islands, and the Jamaica Assembly petitioned George II against absenteeism in 1749 explicitly on the grounds that slave revolts were more common on absentee-owned estates.[15]

In South Carolina disdain for absenteeism was expressed more tacitly, such as in the slave-patrolling laws passed after the Stono Rebellion in 1739. "All persons, as well women as men, who are . . . owners of settled plantations in any district, ought to contribute to the service and security of that district where their interest lyes," the law stipulated, mandating plantation owners to join regular patrols to apprehend runaway slaves and deter slave revolts. Specific provisions for substitute service in the patrols, detailing how replacements could be hired and who was liable for defaults of service, were clearly aimed at nonresidents, whether they lived in Charles Town or farther afield.[16] Critiques of absenteeism were also a subtext within South Carolina's culture of celebrating the "active" or "attentive" planter. The laudatory rhetoric of letters and articles in this vein printed in the *South Carolina Gazette,* the foundation of such clubs as the Winyah Indigo Society with their prizes for high crop yields and technological innovations, and the circulating literature of agricultural "improvement"— exemplified in a transatlantic context by James Crokatt's self-compiled pamphlets and models of machinery—were all emblematic of this culture. For its part, the South Carolina Assembly adjourned at vital points in the annual cycle of rice cultivation so that its members could supervise sowing, harvesting, and other key tasks on their lands.[17] Hailing activism had an inverse of implied criticism of the nonattentive, nonresident planter whether he or, exceptionally, she was in Charles Town or abroad.

Until the 1770s, however, distinctions between the different forms that absenteeism took were not a matter of public debate. The prevalence of absenteeism was recognized in South Carolina's laws, which stipulated the specific means for collecting taxes on the lands of "any person or persons living or residing out of the limits of this Province." No additional rates, however, were levied on such lands, and they were to be taxed "rateably and proportionably, according to the quantity of acres, and as if the same were in the actual possession of some person or persons living or residing within this Province."[18] In neighboring Georgia statutes observed the commonness of landownership by nonresidents, noting that "there are Sundry Tracts of Land, Lots, houses and monies the Proprietors whereof are not resident in this Province" without placing any extra taxes or penalties on them.[19] Nor did overseas absenteeism register as being politically deleterious. When Henry Laurens complained that when land monopolies "happen to fall into the hands of Non residents they are most pernicious to a Young Colony," he referred not to absenteeism in South Carolina but to his fellow South Carolinians land banking in Georgia. "I have never been afraid to declare my sentiments freely to my friends in this place who hold idle Lands in our Neighborhood yonder," he declared.[20]

Only in the early 1770s, as political fissures between Britain and its American colonies widened, did absenteeism register as a political issue in South Carolina. British residents' ownership of property in the colony had earlier suggested the depth of their stake in the colony's development and prosperity as well as a consonance of interests with its resident merchant-planter elites. As political-economic divisions between Charles Town and London grew, however, this absentee ownership acquired a more sinister dimension. Staying in London in 1771, Laurens was struck by the political quietude of London's Carolina merchants in the face of harsh ministerial policy toward America: "America has many powerful Enemies here, and not a few among them who triumph in Coaches raised by Spoils drawn from that Quarter. Such think themselves Friends to America, if they encourage Trade from thence, for their own Emoluments, but have no Idea of opposing Ministerial Attempts to deprive her of her most valuable priveleges. Others are Friends, because they wish Success to their Plantations and Estates there, but regard them as being only in a distant County of the Kingdom. Such are Enemies to our truest Interests, without knowing themselves to be so."[21]

Still, the potentially malign consequences of transatlantic absenteeism were not recognized formally until conflict was imminent. Nonresidence, it was then concluded, was a strong guide to political loyalties. The Provincial Congress, which first met in January 1775 as the successor to the colonial assembly, called on absentee landowners to return to South Carolina in June 1775 "for the better defence of our liberties and properties," linking residence in South Carolina with the defense of the colony. The call was formalized by a congressional resolution, though those who had left the colony on grounds of health or were over sixty or under twenty-one years of age were exempted.[22] In Georgia moves in 1777 to strip absentees of uncultivated lands were more insidiously motivated—promoted by residents eager to get the land themselves. An act passed by the Georgia Assembly in June 1777 decreed that absentees had six months to settle or cultivate their land, after which time that land would be declared vacant, a move that would have allowed the state to profit by reselling the confiscated tracts. The confiscations would have hit residents of neighboring South Carolina hardest, as they were the most numerous absentee landowners in Georgia, and the act's offending section was consequently repealed after three months.[23]

Conversely, in South Carolina a proposal for a double tax on land, urban lots, and slaves owned by absentees was rejected by the Provincial Congress in

June 1775, and it was not until March 1778, more than two years into the Revolutionary War, that this fiscal disincentive was finally imposed. News of the tax caused understandable alarm among absentee landowners in Britain. "I have been a good deal alarmed at a report which has prevailed here, that the Proprietors of Estates in Carolina without distinction are required to appear there, within a given time upon pain of confiscation of their Property, or some other grievous Penalty," wrote Margaret Colleton, who lived in London and owned two lowcountry plantations, to her agents in Charles Town. She continued, "I firmly trust that a helpless woman in the 76th year of her age, not native, nor even an Inhabitant, and therefore certainly as little obnoxious, as she can be serviceable, will [not] be exposed to the loss of the whole, or any part of her Property, or to any Penalty whatever, for not performing a voyage, which the Infirmities of her time of life would render impossible, even in a Season of profound tranquility."[24] The terms of the law's renewal the following year might have eased Colleton's fears. It specified that the double tax applied to all males over the age of twenty-two who held land in South Carolina but did not live in the by-then United States; the earlier statute had applied regardless of gender to "all persons" over twenty-two who lived abroad. With both statutes noting that "there are divers tracts of land, slaves and monies at interest in this State, held, owned, or claimed by persons not residents here, who pay no taxes or other charges toward the support of the Government of this State," the double tax was a device to bolster the war effort and tease out absentees' true loyalties. Failure to pay within two years incurred confiscation of lands by the state. Georgia followed suit with a nearly identical law in May 1778.[25]

Acquiring Lands in South Carolina

Across the eighteenth century British residents came to own property in South Carolina in four principal ways, though these differed in importance over time. First, property was bought in Charles Town by merchants, imperial officials, and naval personnel who later relocated to Britain. Second, it was acquired in lieu of debts. Third, it was received through marriage and inheritance. Fourth, British residents bought plantation land and urban properties in South Carolina either to augment existing holdings in the colony or as new speculative ventures.

Absentee landholding in South Carolina was closely connected to patterns of movement within the British Empire. Commercial mobility, with merchants relocating from Charles Town to London, predominantly for business reasons, was the largest single factor behind transatlantic absenteeism. The largest and most politically active group of absentee landowners was made up of merchants who had accrued real estate in South Carolina before transferring their businesses from Charles Town to Britain. Settling mostly in London, where they became the city's principal traders to South Carolina in the middle quarters of the eighteenth century, these included the likes of John Watkinson, Samuel Wragg,

James Crokatt, John Beswicke, and Richard Shubrick. Each had spent several years in Charles Town honing their business acumen and building a network of contacts in South Carolina. Watkinson invested in several residential and commercial plots during his time in Charles Town in the 1720s. Having returned to London about 1729, he became a prominent merchant in the Carolina trade and regularly petitioned the British government on issues concerning the colony. He retained "messuages, lands and tenements . . . lying and being in Charles Town" until his death in 1742, when Richard and Thomas Shubrick were appointed his attorneys in the town. They were entrusted to claim the rents from Watkinson's Charles Town properties and then dispose of his estate in South Carolina.[26] Richard Shubrick too held on to his Charles Town and lowcountry landholdings after returning to London in 1747. He retained the four town lots he had bought in 1746 in Ansonborough, on Charles Town's northern fringe, eventually selling them in December 1759. He also kept Quenby, his plantation on the Cooper River, along with a stake in five hundred acres of land on the Port Royal River, southwest of Charles Town.[27] John Beswicke, who had been "Considerably Concern'd in Trade" in Charles Town, held on to a house in Charles Town after he moved to London in 1747.[28]

Imperial officials and military and naval personnel were another group who acquired land while stationed in South Carolina and retained it after returning to Britain. James Glen, South Carolina's governor between 1743 and 1756, invested in land in the colony, buying a small plantation and nineteen African slaves. He retained the plantation and slaves after leaving the colony for Britain in 1761.[29] Thomas Boone, governor between 1761 and 1764, retained some 8,815 acres in South Carolina after his departure and by the American Revolution had as many as 184 slaves on his plantations in the colony.[30] The naval careers of British admirals George Anson and Peter Warren took them to Charles Town, where they accumulated landholdings in the colony. Warren received two grants in 1733 and 1736 of nearly 2,000 acres of undeveloped land to the north and west of Charles Town. Anson, later famous for circumnavigating the world, had accrued 12,000 acres of land by the time he left South Carolina in 1735. These included a Charles Town lot and valuable land to the north of the town that took his name in becoming its first suburb, Ansonborough. A further six British naval or military officers would have their lands confiscated by the state in 1782.[31]

Not all absentee landholdings in South Carolina were acquired deliberately. With commercial debts often secured through mortgages, defaults led to the securities—plantations or urban property—passing to the creditor, as frequently happened in the West Indies.[32] James Crokatt acquired two plantations in this way as he settled his affairs in the colony before returning to Britain.[33] He then augmented his landholdings by assuming joint ownership of two other plantations in the 1740s with his commercial partners in Charles Town, in both cases apparently through mortgage foreclosures. In January 1742, the partners took ownership of some four hundred acres in Berkeley County and in June 1745 came into possession of one hundred acres on Wadmalaw Island, Colleton County.[34] London merchants Joseph and Henry Guinand similarly took control of a plantation in South Carolina, Walnut Hill, in 1763 following the bankruptcy of correspondents in Charles Town. Uninterested in keeping "an old worn out Plantation," they instructed their attorneys to sell it and its resident slaves within two years.[35] Charles Ogilvie acquired a house in Savannah valued at £552 in payment for debts from a failed merchant partnership in the town.[36]

Marriages and inheritances were other common ways for land to fall into the hands of nonresidents. By the Revolutionary War, Ogilvie had a diversified land empire in South Carolina and Georgia that he reckoned to be worth some forty thousand pounds. His first and most valuable holdings came through his wife, Mary, whom he had married in London in November 1762 after transferring his business from Charles Town the year before. She had inherited two plantations, Richfield and Mount Alexander, each of around one thousand acres on the Combahee River near the border with Georgia, in 1761 from her father, James Michie, formerly chief justice of South Carolina.[37] Members of the Colleton family living in Britain, having inherited their lands in South Carolina from the original proprietors, maintained estates in the colony throughout the colonial era.

Such was the appeal of property in South Carolina that absentee landowners continued to add to their assets there after relocating to Britain. They were attracted by the availability of land, its remunerative potential, and the economies of efficiency and scale to be derived from augmenting existing holdings. Familial—often fraternal—ties facilitated such ventures and made for reassuring supervision of existing land. Having moved to London, Samuel Wragg coordinated his acquisitions through his brother Joseph, who remained in Charles Town; Henry Middleton performed the same role for his brother William. For his part, Thomas Shubrick kept an eye on his brother Richard's Quenby plantation, while former governor James Glen entrusted his brother-in-law, John Drayton, with supervising the running of his lowcountry plantation, reciprocating in England by overseeing the education of Drayton's sons. Just as blood connections built trust into transatlantic commercial partnerships, they also offered security in buying and owning land four thousand miles away. They mitigated the risks inherent in long-distance management, particularly of fraud and of inefficient or incompetent oversight.[38]

As the zone of rice production expanded north and south through South Carolina and Georgia's coastal lowcountry and, from mid-century, as grain farming became established further inland, opportunities abounded for buying land and emulating the diversified and integrated "plantation empires" developed most elaborately by Henry Laurens and Jonathan Bryan, one of Georgia's leading planter-statesmen.[39] Absentees in Britain joined the rush to seek grants of newly surveyed land on the agricultural frontiers from South Carolina's governor and council. Samuel Wragg was an early exponent. After returning to London, he augmented his already extensive landholdings in South Carolina during the 1730s, including grants of three thousand acres in Granville County in 1734 and fifty-five hundred acres in Craven County four years later. The Granville County grant, at least, neighbored lands already owned by his brother, signaling how Wragg understood the practical benefits of fraternal oversight. Thirty years later William Middleton and former governor Thomas Boone, both of whom had relocated permanently to Britain, extended their plantation interests in the region, recognizing the potential returns on offer as the pace of expansionism quickened and risiculture took off across Georgia's coastal plain in the 1760s. Boone acquired new lands that his local agent judged would "make a good plantation for about thirty-five hands" and spent some £5,200 currency on slaves to labor on it.[40] Middleton capitalized on his brother's presence in South Carolina and his ability to extend and supervise their landholdings in the region. A local agent was deputed to get a survey made of lands that Middleton had recently purchased and he agreed to make visits to Middleton's plantation in Georgia once or twice a year. Eager to join the land bonanza taking place across South Carolina's southern border, the brothers instructed their agent to make a list of the "taskable Hands at the Euhaws and the River May," two of their South Carolina plantations, so that Henry Middleton—controlling his and his brother's land interests in the region—might "be able to judge how many [slaves] can be spared from these Plantations in order to make another settlement or two in Georgia."[41]

No British resident took advantage of the dramatic speed of expansion across South Carolina and Georgia—and the investment opportunities it provided—more prodigiously than Charles Ogilvie. Making periodic visits from London, he installed his nephew George as itinerant manager of his many land ventures located from one end of South Carolina to the other. For a further degree of oversight, he made his friend Alexander Garden his attorney and agent in Charles Town, where he was charged with the "care and direction" of Ogilvie's estates. Ogilvie's portfolio had begun with the two Combahee River plantations that his wife had inherited, Richfield and Mount Alexander. To these he added an isolated tidal rice plantation, Myrtle Grove, on an island in the mouth of the Santee River fifty miles northeast of Charles Town. Near Camden in the fast-developing backcountry, some one hundred miles inland from Charles Town, he bought Belmont, an 813-acre grain-producing plantation on the Wateree River that was notable for the "extream fertility of its Soil which often times produced fifty, sixty and seventy Bushels of Grain per acre," together with an adjoining tract, Camden Mead. Among Camden Mead's 7,359 acres were 1,350 acres of "River Swamp of very superior Quality." Unlike the desolate Myrtle Grove, Belmont had "a good dwelling House and all other necessary Buildings."[42]

Besides these, Ogilvie acquired multiple and mostly undeveloped tracts across South Carolina's agricultural frontiers in a speculative land-buying spree of huge ambition. It was a clear vote of confidence in the colony's productive capacity. In the western backcountry, he bought a further 360 acres near Belmont and a 100-acre tract near Camden Mead along with "a Tract on Colonel's Creek, Wateree River," which he let out for a term of seven years at seventy pounds currency annually, together with "five other Tracts on Wateree River containing 1,435 acres" and a 500-acre grant "on the South Side of Wateree River near Cockey Mount." Scattered on the frontier northwest of Charles Town were "Two Tracts on Peedee River containing 885 acres . . . One Valuable Tract on the High Hills of Santee . . . 697 acres . . . Half of 800 acres St. Steven's Parish, Santee," and one tract of unspecified size "in Amelia Township adjoining Santee River near McCords Ferry supposed to contain Mines." In addition, well to the south on the Savannah River were two tracts "containing 1,890 acres Swamp in St. Peter's Parish." That Ogilvie acquired several of these tracts during the early 1770s suggests that he, for one, did not foresee an imminent threat to the current imperial polity and consequently to his tenure on his lands. As late as April or May 1775 he further added to his landholdings by purchasing, sight unseen, tracts in Georgia, which his nephew bought on his behalf at a Savannah auction.[43]

While the potential returns offered by plantations on the frontiers of the region's expanding cultivated zone tempted some investors, another favored means by which absentees in Britain extended their planting concerns was by securing land that adjoined their existing properties. As a relatively "known commodity" with which the absentee owner might be familiar or whose "fit" with the owner's current landholdings an agent in South Carolina could easily assess, contiguous land carried a lower risk than did remoter acquisitions. Contiguity also promised economies of scale in commodity production, particularly in the tasking and oversight of an enlarged slave workforce on a single site, though this might be tempered by concerns about the risks of greater congregations of slaves. A further advantage of adding adjoining lands lay in their potential for agricultural complementarity. John Colleton, who lived in London, inherited town lots and buildings in Charles Town and three plantations in the South Carolina lowcountry: Mepkin, a tract of some three thousand acres on the Cooper River; Mepshew, a two-thousand-acre tract on the Cooper River; and Watboo, a vast barony of some twelve thousand acres at the headwaters of the same river. Colleton, who appears never to have set foot in South Carolina, employed Robert Raper as a local agent to oversee his property holdings in the colony. Raper sought to improve the lands' agricultural yield and in 1761 acquired fifty acres of rice swamp adjoining Colleton's Mepshew plantation on his employer's behalf. It was, he explained to Colleton, a good bargain: "I have exchanged 50 acres of dry land at Mepshew with one Singleton for 50 acres of Swamp tideland which is worth near Twenty pounds an acre, & the other is not worth more than Three or Four pounds. The reason of this good Exchange is that Mr. Singleton has no dry land to put a house on near his Swamp."[44] It took nearly six years to integrate the new swampland into the operations at Mepshew, during which time John Colleton died and bequeathed the plantation to his wife, Margaret, but by 1767 Raper could confidently report that the additional fifty acres were ready to clear and plant for the next rice crop. The new acreage, he told his employer, would make Mepshew "a Compleat Plantation in 2 years time," indicating the higher revenues it should yield as a result of scale and complementarity.[45]

More ambitious absentees in Britain bought entire established plantations, further testament to the returns anticipated from lowcountry South Carolina. Peter Taylor, a merchant in Whitehaven on England's northwest coast, had inherited land in South Carolina from his uncle and relied on trusted family connections in the colony to supervise his plantation affairs. He added to his landholdings by buying another plantation, Charleywood, on the Wando River, about twenty miles northeast of Charles Town. His cousins, who lived in South Carolina, posted a bond of £24,000 in provincial currency—about £3,430 sterling—as security. The plantation contained, his overseer reported, "good Negroe houses, a good Dwelling house . . . a good corn House, Kitchen & Sick House . . . [and] two good river Dambs." The arrangement Taylor struck with his cousins points to the mutual advantages to be derived from absentee land management. In return for their financial brokerage and four or five annual visits to check on his plantation, Taylor employed the Charles Town firm run by his cousins' sons to export his plantation's rice.[46]

Land also attracted more speculative investments in South Carolina. Because all land in the colony was taxed at the same rate, there were no acquisitions in South Carolina on the scale of some in North Carolina and Virginia, such as by John Carteret, Earl of Granville, who received some twenty million acres of northern North Carolina, or Lord Fairfax, who received five million acres in Virginia's Northern Neck in 1745, both on the basis of inherited claims. Instead most landholdings in the undeveloped backcountry were smaller than three hundred acres.[47] Nor was there anything comparable to the land grab that took place in Florida during the 1760s. After Britain was ceded East and West Florida by Spain in 1763, absentee investors bought hundreds of thousands of acres in the new provinces, though most attempts at settling the land failed.[48] But acquisitions of this type did take place in South Carolina, albeit on a less dramatic scale, and shared a common motive with the larger and more publicized ventures. Speculative investors bought land in the colony, as elsewhere in North America, in the hope of making huge profits. Most investors of this type had only a limited or no direct connection to South Carolina; nor did most ever intend to reside on or actively manage their lands. The partnership of Sir William Baker, Nicholas Linwood, and Brice Fisher, three MPs who clubbed together to buy large tracts of land in South Carolina, is illustrative. All three were important London merchants, though only Baker had an interest in trade to South Carolina. Rather than actively manage their forty thousand acres of land themselves or through appointed agents, the partners instead hired two local agents to subdivide and sell the land in smaller tracts. In an advertisement for their lands in April 1767, the three partners noted that "we have received information that several persons have committed trespass on the said Barony, by making Settlements thereon," further suggesting that the lands were not under management but were being land banked for windfall profits on resale.[49]

Retaining Assets in South Carolina

Merchants in Charles Town had many different reasons for buying town lots and properties. Owning a town house that doubled as commercial premises and living space saved rent payments to a landlord, though capital was needed to buy the property in the first place. For some, buying additional urban properties had greater appeal than purchasing agricultural land. In owning nearby premises, a merchant could keep a close eye on his urban assets, unlike more distant and inaccessible plantation landholdings. He could more easily bring his commercial judgment to bear in urban property management, observing market conditions firsthand and either collecting rent himself or deputing a clerk to do so. For other merchants, the greater financial rewards of plantation ownership—not to mention the status and political authority it brought—compensated for the greater risks involved and the different skills required, as the number of Charles Town traders who moved from commerce into planting made evident. The intrinsic but differing appeals of owning urban property and plantation lands were significant as well to merchants who left the colony for Great Britain.

Once back in London, these merchants had compelling financial reasons to hold on to fixed assets in South Carolina. Part of the appeal of urban lots and properties was the steady and reliable yield they offered through rents that could be collected and regularly remitted by agents based in Charles Town. In its consistency, this rental income contrasted with the inherently unpredictable returns generated by the transatlantic trading ventures that formed the basis and the greatest share of their revenues. Rental returns also contrasted with plantation revenues, which, though potentially more remunerative, carried higher risk through their greater exposure to the vicissitudes of climate, harvests, slave welfare, and elastic and exogenous—mostly European—demand for produce. Some absentees may have preferred town property assets as those seem to have been more easily liquidated than agricultural lands, sales of which were complicated by hard-to-monetize factors such as the value of crops growing on a plantation and of the slaves working on it.

In this financial basis for their property investments in South Carolina, British merchant absentees differed from their counterparts in the Chesapeake tobacco trade, in which it was common for British—mostly Scottish—trading firms to own country stores in Virginia tobacco country. In the tobacco trade, these premises were commercially integral to operations, serving as a base from which the firms' representatives on the ground bought tobacco directly from producers and stocked European goods for part or whole exchange.[50] In contrast, it was not necessary for purely commercial reasons for British merchants trading to South Carolina to maintain fixed assets in the colony. The London merchants who dominated Britain's export trade to South Carolina sold goods on commission to local traders or sent their wares to formal commercial partners. These Charles Town–based merchants kept the goods in their own stores for sale to consumers. Warehousing for rice, naval stores, deerskins, and indigo for shipment to Europe was similarly locally owned. Urban properties in Charles Town were stand-alone financial investments for British owners, rather than being integral to their owners' commercial operations. Having bought properties during early-career spells in Charles Town, merchants who relocated to Britain retained them for the predictability of the income those properties delivered.

Property in Charles Town was a steady and lucrative investment. By the 1750s the town had been largely rebuilt following a devastating fire in November 1740 that had destroyed many properties and an estimated £200,000 worth of merchandise. With a population of about nine thousand, Charles Town was the fourth largest settlement in British North America, and visitors were struck by the grandeur of its buildings.[51] "Houses are all neat and fine, handsome and large and built of brick," observed the Swiss immigrant Johannes Tobler in 1753, "but the plots for them, especially on the side of the street toward the sea, are very expensive, since one of them, 50 feet wide and 100 feet long, costs over five thousand Gulden [about £750]."[52] In extolling South Carolina's productivity and value in a report to the Board of Trade two years earlier, Governor James Glen had noted the "many houses that have cost a thousand and twelve hundred pounds sterling," leaving aside the most desirable properties "on the Bay" that were closest to the Cooper River and its wharves.[53]

Rental income from these urban properties was at the heart of their appeal. "The houses are very lucrative, since some bring in up to one thousand Gulden [about £150] annually in rent," Tobler noted. In surveying rents on one hundred houses and lots "fronting the River on the Bay of Charlestown," Glen found that annual rents of £700 in currency—about £100 sterling—were common. To put these rents in a transatlantic context, Charles Pinckney, a wealthy Charles Town lawyer, paid only a little more in annual rent—£120—for a furnished house in London's fashionable West End while living in the capital in the early 1750s, a sum another Carolinian visitor to London judged a "Tip-Top Rent."[54] Located on a prime commercial thoroughfare and within touching distance of the town's wharves, the properties commanding the highest rents in Glen's sample were most often occupied by merchants. The rental yields that British absentees made from their Charles Town properties bear out Tobler's impressions and Glen's assessment, and they support a recent analysis of the profitability and dynamism of Charles Town's property rental market that suggests that during the 1750s and 1760s urban rental returns could rival the profits from most plantations.[55] Moreover, arguably the greatest appeal of urban property compared to plantation lands was not the absolute return to be made from town rents but the lower capital barriers to entry. For example, a Charles Town house bought for £100 could deliver a regular income starting within a month of tenants taking residence there. For every £100 invested in *developed* plantation land producing rice and indigo, much more would have to be spent on buying slaves and equipment to work it; the costs of improving *undeveloped* land—of clearing woods, building dwellings, and setting up irrigation—were far higher. No agricultural land could pay such a quick return on capital invested.

The two Charles Town properties belonging to London resident John Colleton illustrated the good yields that urban property could deliver. Each was being let for £75 a year when they were sold for £1,000 apiece in 1762, a rise from £71.8s.9d. annually three years earlier. The purchaser then raised the rent to £80 a year, eight percent of the property's sale price.[56] Robert Raper, agent in Charles Town for several absentee property owners and the port's deputy naval officer, was himself a tenant to an absentee who lived in Middlesex, England. His landlord, Joseph Stephenson, was also his boss—Charles Town's naval officer, despite his permanent residence in Britain—who thus profited doubly from South Carolina, drawing a salary for his commission and rent from his locum tenens and deputy. Raper paid Stephenson an annual rent of £100 for his Charles Town house, which was prestigiously located next to the governor's residence, remitting the money twice a year.[57] James Crokatt's annual rental returns on his several Charles Town properties amounted in 1767 to £1,390 in currency, or some £180 sterling, while Walter Mansell, a merchant who relocated to London in 1770, estimated the returns on the land and property he retained in Charles Town at "upwards of £500 sterling pr. an." in 1773.[58]

Rental returns did not translate into pure profit for property owners, however. Fire insurance at around one percent of the property's value, legal fees at the beginning and end of contracts, and maintenance costs were all outlays to be reckoned with.[59] Landlords also incurred property taxes. Rates fluctuated annually according to the colonial government's revenue needs; in the mid-1760s, for example, tax ranged between 3s.6d. and 20s. for every £100 of a property's assessed value.[60] In 1762 property tax amounted to £10.9s. on each of Colleton's bay houses, some 14 percent of the rent they produced annually, while Crokatt's tax assessment was a "very large" £204.8s.2d. currency, or about £29 sterling, around 16 percent of their rent. Unsurprisingly, Crokatt was keen for his agent in Charles Town to find tenants who would pay his property taxes as well as their rent.[61]

For absentees, employing a Charles Town–based agent to arrange essential maintenance, find tenants, collect rent, and arrange the sale of properties was an extra cost. The wear and tear caused by tenants was a further unpredictable expense. Landlords who lived in Charles Town found this a problem, but non-residents, and especially those without a reliable agent on the ground, were at greater risk through being less able to monitor disorderly tenants. Such occupants could prove more trouble than they were worth, as another absentee in Britain, Benjamin Bushnell, discovered to his cost. Having tried to manage his rental property in Charles Town without a local agent, he found that his tenants had—ostensibly to his benefit—"paid for many Repairs without Charging and often caused their own Negroes to do something to the House & kept no Account thereof." On closer inspection, the tenants' attempts at home renovation had done more harm than good: Bushnell's failure to employ an agent had been a false economy. He eventually appointed as his agent Robert Raper, who found the house "in a bad Condition in want of Repair," because of which he could charge the next tenant only £250 currency, or about £36 sterling, a year.[62]

Returns on Absentee-Owned Plantations

If urban properties were easier in theory for absentee owners to manage from afar and through rents could provide regular and predictable revenue, plantations in South Carolina offered absentees riskier but potentially more lucrative sources of income. Successful returns depended on a greater number of variables: principally astute management by local agents; the reliability and judgment of resident overseers; technological investment; and the productivity of the slave labor force.[63] Plantation profits were also more subject to the vagaries of climate, with its implications for crop yields and prices, while absentees had to reckon with the expense of paying agents to make periodic visits to their estates. Robert Raper received five hundred pounds currency a year from Margaret Colleton to organize provisions and maintenance for the two lowcountry plantations she inherited on the death of her husband, John, in 1766.[64] Compared to even the good income to be made from urban properties, however, a well-managed and productive plantation could yield greater returns on capital invested. During the 1750s and 1760s resident planters considered an annual return of between 10 and 15 percent on invested capital—in slaves, land, equipment, and provisions—to be a good profit. Henry Laurens's 3,100 acre Mepkin plantation, which he bought from John Colleton in 1762, was the jewel of his plantation empire. When Laurens acquired it, Mepkin was a monocultural rice plantation delivering an annual return of about 10 percent; after diversifying into corn, firewood, and lumber to meet growing demand in Charles Town, it realized annual profits of more than 20 percent from the mid-1760s.[65]

The historian Max Edelson has argued that estates in South Carolina run by absentee planters in Britain were less profitable than those closely attended by their owners, echoing an assessment long made, though recently challenged, with respect to the British West Indies.[66] It has been assumed that in both regions the extended lines of oversight and decision making inherent in absenteeism diminished plantation efficiency, though planters who spent most of their time in Charles Town—the domestic or seasonal absentees—were able to attend to plantation affairs at crucial moments in the agricultural cycle, such as personally overseeing planting or harvesting, making immediate decisions on the marketing of crops or the next season's planting, and enforcing their personal authority.

Contemporaries certainly believed that absentee-owned estates were less productive. Henry Laurens predicted a "great prospect of success" at his newly bought Broughton Island rice plantation in Georgia in 1768, "if my affairs would admit of residence upon the spot." Had he been in residence, he would have expected annual returns of at least £2,000, clear of charges, on invested capital of £7,500, "but under the management of Hirelings the Lord knows what I may make."[67] It was a view shared by his brother James, one of several agents whom Laurens entrusted to keep an eye on his plantations during his sojourn in Europe from 1771 to 1774. "You might easily put that Plantation on better footing were you on the Spott," James Laurens told him as he reported on his underperforming Wright's Savannah plantation in Georgia.[68]

Whether or not absentee-owned plantations had lower productivity and delivered smaller profits than those owned by South Carolina residents—and insufficient evidence survives to make a clear judgment—such plantations clearly still delivered enough profits to make them desirable investments. Laurens relied on the income from his South Carolina and Georgia plantations in the early 1770s while living in Europe, where he oversaw his sons' education.[69] The willingness of absentees to retain lands after leaving the colony permanently and the fact that some absentees amassed further lands in South Carolina after they had left testify to the appeal of a diversified landholding portfolio. The plantation empires that Samuel Wragg and Charles Ogilvie constructed in South Carolina and then retained after leaving the colony are cases in point. George Austin too falls into this category. After a merchant career in Charles Town, he retired to his native England in 1763. Though he never returned to South Carolina, he kept his plantations, which on his death in 1774 totaled 6,305 acres and 176 slaves.[70]

Evidence from plantations owned by British residents confirms their profitability. Watboo and Mepshew, John and Margaret Colleton's two remaining lowcountry plantations after the sale of Mepkin, were some twenty-five miles north of Charles Town in South Carolina's core planting zone. Originally part of the twelve-thousand-acre Watboo Barony granted to the Colleton family in the late seventeenth century, both plantations by the 1760s were agriculturally diversified, producing rice, indigo, and lumber. They also benefited from a navigable river connection to Charles Town, which reduced transportation costs. Mepshew had about thirty working slaves and produced about one hundred barrels of rice a year in the early 1760s. Though its estimated value then is not known, a decade later it was reckoned to be worth more than six thousand pounds.[71] Together Watboo and Mepshew delivered a profit of about one thousand pounds in 1764–65, a sum that would have been higher but for several unusually large deductions. These included a doctor's bill for three years, two years' worth of taxes, "several charges for Accidents that may not happen again," and repairs to a boat that took rice and lumber from the plantation for sale in Charles Town.

Margaret Colleton later told her Charles Town attorneys that she had been bequeathed Watboo and Mepshew, "together with all the Negroes, Stock &c . . . for my support and maintenance." The revenue they produced was such that she had been persuaded to divest her property holdings in Britain. "Relying upon the income of these Estates [Watboo and Mepshew], which by the Care of my Attorneys for some years I duly received," she informed her attorneys, "I have been liberal with my property in this Country to my Relations and Connexions."[72] Charles Ogilvie estimated that between 1763 and 1774 his two Combahee River plantations yielded "Crops to the annual value of £1,100 Sterling or thereabouts, clear of all deductions," and he reckoned that his more remote Myrtle Grove plantation, settled in 1774, "would have been exceedingly profitable in a few years." Myrtle Grove had, Ogilvie later reported, broken even just a year after being established, in 1775 producing "189 Barrels or Tierces of Rice . . . besides Indico and Corn more than sufficient to pay all charges."[73] Absentees either sold their plantation rice to traders in Charles Town or shipped it to Britain on their own account, according to which they believed would be most profitable.[74]

Besides regular returns on invested capital, two other incentives encouraged British residents to own land and property in South Carolina. Both were based on the embedded value of the assets. In observing how some of the wealthiest residents of the plantation colonies combined landowning and trade, the historian Jacob Price noted that "undeveloped land held for appreciation might still be valuable enough to support some credit and thus indirectly be productive."[75] If this were true for absentee owners of land in South Carolina, it would connect their landholdings, particularly in the case of merchant absentees, to their commercial concerns. Regardless of whether their tracts were developed and produced revenue or were undeveloped, they might have been used to bolster their owners' credit. As such, they could increase their owners' ability to raise capital for other ventures and investments. Investors also bought plantation land and urban properties because these were expected to rise in value over time. This was the case in the more explicitly speculative ventures, such as those of the London merchants Baker, Linwood, and Fisher, who purchased undeveloped land because it had development and resale value. Windfall gains were also possible on land with potential for urban development. Anticipating Charles Town's expansion, the South Carolina Society, a gentlemen's club in the town, bought Richard Shubrick's four Ansonborough lots on its northern edge for five hundred pounds in 1759. As Charles Town grew and Ansonborough became one of its most desirable residential quarters, the land rose in value to an estimated five thousand pounds in 1768.[76]

Drawing conclusions from the values of specific urban properties is harder. On inheriting an established plantation, undeveloped tracts, and town lots in Georgetown after the war, British resident John Martin chose to sell the land but retain the lots, since "they might improve [in value] in time."[77] It is unclear whether Martin's hope was realistic. While deeds of sale and newspaper advertisements often recorded the sale prices of lots and buildings, it is impossible to know how they were altered over time. For example, John Watkinson bought part of a Charles Town lot in 1726 for £1,500 currency. After he moved to London and then died, it was sold in 1743 for £1,800 currency.[78] James Crokatt sold a plot of ground and a brick house in Charles Town for £1,260 currency in 1765, exactly double the price he had paid for them in 1731. Nothing is known of how either Watkinson's or Crokatt's property changed between purchase and sale—whether improvements were made or whether years of tenant occupation took their toll. Even with this caveat, rises in value of 20 percent over seventeen years in Watkinson's case—just over one percent annually—and three percent annually in Crokatt's seem meager, particularly when set against expected yields from commerce and planting and when interest on loans contracted in Charles Town delivered returns at between eight and ten percent.[79] Given the evidence on rental returns, it seems likely that the annual yields delivered by urban properties were a stronger motivation for absentees to retain them than was the hope of long-term appreciation and windfalls.

How did all these returns—agricultural, rental, and appreciative—compare with what absentee owners could get on investments in Britain? If Henry Laurens's comments on fellow planter Henry Gray's relocation to Britain in 1764 are typical, South Carolina's merchant-planters held the more pedestrian returns made in Britain in a certain disdain. Noting Gray's plan to "fix in some cheap country in the West of England & to do a great many fine things in the farming way & dabble a little now & then in commerce," Laurens compared Gray's annual returns of ten to twelve percent on his South Carolina lands, which were advertised for sale before Gray left, with the three to four percent he expected him to make yearly in England. To Laurens, this equated to "leaving good Wheat Bread to take up with Rye," and he predicted that Gray would "probably return to us after a year or two of fruitless & vexatious toil."[80] Annual returns on British securities supported Laurens's estimates: during the 1750s yields on East Indies stock and bonds and on government stock hovered around three percent—well below the profits on staple agriculture that might be expected in the South Carolina lowcountry.[81] The commercial profits of London's overseas merchants were higher, sometimes reaching the levels associated with plantation returns. Adam Smith considered a return of double the interest rate—between six and ten percent—as a "good, moderate reasonable profit"; well-established merchants counted on a return of ten to fifteen percent from a successful year's trading.[82]

London's Carolina merchants also bought estate land in Britain, though social considerations were a stronger motivation than the land's productive capacity or its long-term investment value. Several acquired sizable estates within twenty miles of London, in keeping with the many other City of London merchants who acquired country properties on the capital's fringes: John Beswicke in Hillingdon; John and Sarah Nickleson in Stanmore; Richard Shubrick in Greenwich and his son, also Richard Shubrick, in Enfield. William Baker bought the Bayfordbury estate in Hertfordshire, which totaled around 3,900 acres, for £21,000 in 1756.[83] Like his colleagues, James Crokatt similarly diverted commercial capital into land. He bought Luxborough Hall in Essex, a grand country estate about eleven miles northeast of London, for £19,500 in 1750 and spent a further £10,000 repairing and furnishing the house. "I think he has Grandour enough for his Money," one visitor from South Carolina drily observed.[84] As well as the neoclassical mansion and 18 acres of garden, the estate included the freehold of six farms, two meadows, and glebe lands covering some 520 acres, which together generated an estimated annual return of £870.[85]

Absenteeism and Agency

James Crokatt exemplified the political consequences of absenteeism for the relationship between South Carolina and Great Britain. The land and property he bought while living and working in Charles Town were important both to his commercial rise and to his assiduous service to South Carolina in London, whether officially as the colony's agent in the capital or in his private advocacy for South Carolina in political circles and his encouragement of its agriculture and commerce. His real estate purchases can be grouped into three categories: those for immediate personal use; short-term speculations; and longer-term investments. In February 1731 he paid Joseph Wragg £2,450 currency for part of two Charles Town lots on the north side of Broad Street.[86] Here, on Charles Town's main thoroughfare, Crokatt had his countinghouse and store. In October 1731 he bought an adjoining "brick messuage"—perhaps another store—for £630 currency from Samuel Wragg, who was by then living in London.[87] Crokatt expanded his facilities as his business grew, and these sites were central to his commercial operations in the town. Other purchases bore the hallmarks of short- and medium-term speculation. These included commercial property in Charles Town and two tracts of land on Charles Town Neck, on the peninsula north of the town. In one deal Crokatt bought part of a town lot for £1,535 currency before selling it two weeks later for £1,750—a quick profit of £215.[88] Covering just seventy and forty-six acres respectively, the two tracts on Charles Town Neck were relatively small and were probably country retreats rather than working plantations: one contained a "good Dwelling-House, Kitchen, Garden and Orchard of Fruit Trees," with no mention made of crops or resident slaves. He sold both a little over three years after buying them, the smaller tract having appreciated in value by some 45 percent.[89]

Some of Crokatt's other acquisitions were longer-term investments. Shortly before his long-planned departure from the colony in June 1739, he bought two tracts of land from colleagues on the Royal Council. Both were adjacent to land in the colony's interior that had been set aside for the development of townships—new, planned settlements designed to attract white settlers into inland areas in a government-backed plan to ameliorate South Carolina's worrying racial imbalance and to buffer the lowcountry from French, Spanish, and Indian threats. Crokatt's purchase of these tracts so close to the time of his departure suggests that he hoped they would yield long-term windfall gains. They consisted of twelve hundred acres in Granville County, to the north of Purrysburgh Township, and one thousand acres in Craven County, part of the land set aside for Queensborough Township.[90] Though South Carolina's projected townships ultimately failed to attract settlers in the numbers hoped for, in the late 1730s they were seen to offer strong financial prospects for investors, whose land was expected to increase in value as the townships expanded. That Crokatt retained property in Charles Town after returning to Britain further suggests a long-term investment strategy, as well as the appeal of urban rental yields. He retained three houses and a "low water lot" in Unity Alley and five tenement houses "on the Bay," which he had bought for £4,000 in 1732. These properties brought in some £1,390 currency, or about £180 sterling, in rent annually by 1767, when they were finally sold, and included both retail and residential space.[91]

Crokatt's property holdings in South Carolina reinforced his commercial connections with the colony. In his advocacy for South Carolina during his time in London before, during, and after being official agent, his efforts reflected broad personal interest in the colony. Whether giving evidence on salt imports to South Carolina, on indigo growing, or on sericulture, Crokatt was informed by an interest that went beyond his trading concerns, extensive though they were. The commercial, economic, social, familial, and territorial interconnections of his motives made him an assiduous appellant for the colony. His concern for South Carolina's economic vitality and its inhabitants' well-being was a product of his deep personal links to the colony and his commercial interest in South Carolina's trade: more than ten years spent living there; a wife and two children born in South Carolina; and extensive property and landholdings there. Becoming the colony's agent in London in 1749 simply formalized the representative role that Crokatt had already been playing. He can hardly have been motivated by the post's salary; the two-hundred-pound annual wage constituted loose change for a man who spent nearly thirty thousand pounds buying and renovating a country estate. This multiplicity of interests in South Carolina, in which landholdings played a significant part, was embodied as well in the Carolina lobby in London in which Crokatt played the leading mid-century role but whose advocacy for the colony stretched back twenty-five years before his return to Britain in 1739. Between its first sustained activity in 1715 and the early 1770s, the British merchants trading to South Carolina who were at the forefront of the lobby were also the largest group of absentee owners of land and property in South Carolina. Within Parliament MPs with landholding connections in South Carolina helped usher favorable bills through their legislative stages. James Edward Colleton, the elder brother of absentee estate-owner John Colleton, introduced the legislation to assist colonial silk production in 1750, and Sir Peter Warren, the former admiral with tracts north and west of Charles Town, helped to steer the potash legislation through parliamentary waters the following year.[92]

Absentee owners of property and land in South Carolina formed the core of the colony's most regular advocates in London: John Watkinson, Samuel Wragg, John Beswicke, Richard Shubrick, Sir William Baker, and Charles Ogilvie. The intersection of landowning and political advocacy was apparent throughout their lobbying campaigns across the middle decades of the eighteenth century. In February 1748 the Board of Trade received a delegation of nine merchants trading to South Carolina who appealed against the issuance of currency in South Carolina, which they feared would depreciate debts owed to them and harm the colony's economic health. At least six of them owned land or property in the colony.[93] In 1756 seven London residents petitioned to urge Edmund Atkin, a long-serving member of South Carolina's Royal Council and head of the council's committee on Indian affairs, to accept the post of "Agent & Superintendant for Indian Affairs in the Southern parts of North America," the Crown's official diplomat with the region's Native American tribes. His expertise in Indian negotiations, they argued, was essential, as Anglo-French hostilities in North America threatened to unleash warfare on South Carolina's frontiers and endanger the whole colony. All seven petitioners on this matter of strategic, rather than specifically commercial, importance to South Carolina had territorial investments in the colony.[94] Similarly, when nine London merchants petitioned the Board of Trade in March 1772 to approve a cession of land made to Georgia by local Indians, they made their ownership of land in that colony central to their appeal. "Your Memorialists are considerably interested in the welfare and prosperity of the Province of Georgia," they argued, "having large sums of Money and great Property there, not only as Merchants, but also from having purchased valuable Tracts of Land and settled many Plantations."[95] Land and property holdings deepened British residents' interests in the region and strengthened their advocacy on its behalf. The absentees also used their landholdings to convey a symbolic message, suggesting to their correspondents in South Carolina a continuing loyalty to the colony that went deeper than commerce or profit.

Philanthropic gestures signaled absentees' ongoing commitment to South Carolina alongside their property investments. The historian Peter Marshall has suggested that studying British philanthropy toward American causes helps to answer the question of "who cared about the thirteen colonies" in Britain by showing the breadth of interest in America among residents of mid-eighteenth-century Britain.[96] Charitable giving was certainly used by London merchants to demonstrate personal interest in and attachment to Carolinian causes. In April 1741 James Crokatt donated £1,000 currency, or about £140 sterling, to be given to residents of Charles Town who had lost homes and goods in the fire that had wracked the town the previous November. During the 1760s Carolina traders in London gave to causes in South Carolina ranging from a subscription to resettle German Protestants in the colony to a fund-raising effort organized by Charles Crokatt to pay for a peal of bells for St. Michael's Church in Charles Town. The bells appeal achieved a "very Liberal" subscription from the capital's Carolina merchants.[97]

In looking at lobbying in Britain for North American causes, historians have emphasized lobbyists' commercial interests as the motivating force in their advocacy. Thus "leading merchants might work disproportionately hard to get bounties for particular colonial exports but then they stood to gain disproportionately by transporting the goods involved."[98] While commercial interests were certainly vital, London's Carolina merchants' interests in the colony did not begin and end with its trade. The breadth and depth of their connections to South Carolina—personal, familial, commercial, financial, territorial, and philanthropic—explain the particular activism that distinguished London's Carolina lobby from other North American lobbies in the capital during much of the eighteenth century. These connections made the Carolina lobby closer in form to the capital's West Indies lobby, many of whose members had also lived, worked, married into, and owned land in the colonies whose interests they sought to represent. Whether they were deliberately or inadvertently acquired, property and landholdings in Charles Town and across its fertile hinterland entrenched the merchants' interest in South Carolina's economic, demographic, and social well-being. Non-merchant absentees—those who did not have explicitly *commercial* links with South Carolina—were active too in signing petitions and lobbying Parliament on the colony's behalf. A petition to the British Treasury in February 1763 that appealed for liberty to export rice directly from South Carolina to foreign colonies in the Americas and to Madeira and the Canary Isles specifically distinguished its signatories—all British residents—as "several Merchants in London, Planters of So. Carolina, and owners of Ships trading to his Majesty's said Province in America."[99] When a consequent proposal came before a Commons committee, William Middleton—not a merchant but a major landowner on both sides of the Atlantic—was one of the main witnesses to give evidence, telling MPs of his birth and longtime residence in South Carolina, and describing how plantations in the colony were managed.[100]

For London's leading Carolina merchants, at least until the 1760s, the ownership and remote management of plantations, urban properties, or both were central to the intricate bonds that connected them to South Carolina, entwined with their commercial, personal, and familial connections spanning the Atlantic.

That British residents came to own lands in South Carolina and Georgia was a function of the Carolina trade's distinct features. Chief among these was the high proportion of London's Carolina merchants, relative to their counterparts in other branches of North American trade in the capital, who had spent the early part of their careers in South Carolina before transferring their businesses across the Atlantic. In Charles Town they had acquired land and property, which was often augmented in lieu of debts owed to them in the colony. As astute merchants, they grasped the economic logic of having a diversified portfolio of investments. Reliable rental returns and the potential for high profits on plantation enterprises encouraged them to retain these holdings when living in Britain, even if these investments were subsidiary, rather than integral, to their commercial operations. These investments also had symbolic value, publicly signaling an ongoing commitment to the land that furnished the bulk of their trade and where friends and family remained.

In contemporary British discourse, absentee land and property ownership in South Carolina attracted little of the public attention and none of the abuse that were heaped on its "cankerous" guises in Ireland and the West Indies. This was partly a consequence of scale, with fewer absentee owners of property in South Carolina than of property in Ireland or the West Indies living in Britain, and partly a result of the South Carolina absentees' lower profile in British society. While a number bought large estates in Britain, chiefly within a short distance of London, none of these matched the size or opulence of some of the lavish country estates of absentee West Indian planter dynasties, such as Fonthill in Wiltshire or Harewood House in Yorkshire, which became bywords for nouveau riche ostentation. In addition, for all their significance for relations between Great Britain and South Carolina, no owners of property in South Carolina matched the political influence in Britain of leading West Indian absentees such as William Beckford, lord mayor of London, a leading supporter of John Wilkes, and one of some seventy West Indies merchants who were MPs in the second half of the eighteenth century.[101] This helps explain why the importance of the South Carolina absentees has been overlooked from a "metropolitan" perspective: absentee owners of land in South Carolina did not make the splash or court the controversy in British society that their West Indian counterparts did.

Just as Carolinian absentees slipped under the radar of mainstream political, social, and satirical attention in Britain, absentee landowners living overseas were small enough in number relative to the total number of landowners in South Carolina and had small enough landholdings that they escaped the kind of attention in the colony that their counterparts in the Caribbean received in the West Indies as well as in Britain. Additionally, plantation owners' custom of relocating seasonally to Charles Town to escape the worst of the lowcountry's heat and fevers meant that nonresidence on a plantation was an established cultural and economic norm in South Carolina. Critiques of absenteeism in the colony were more subtle than those in the West Indies, though fear of slave rebellion and dereliction of civic duty were present in both. Until the 1770s at least, such critiques did not distinguish between absenteeism's different domestic/seasonal and transatlantic/permanent forms in South Carolina. Only when political relations between Britain and America reached a crisis point were distinctions drawn between the different forms that absenteeism took. It was at this point that British owners of property in South Carolina became, in Henry Laurens's words, "Enemies to our truest Interests, without knowing themselves to be so."[102] Ironically, the political agency of absentees in Britain had worked largely to South Carolina's benefit, their landholdings reinforcing their commercial, familial, and social ties to the colony and strengthening their activism. The importance of absenteeism and its political consequences to South Carolina accentuates the colony's developmental parallels with the West Indies. As with the Caribbean, absenteeism helped construct and maintain an assertive lobby in London on South Carolina's behalf: far from being "cankers" to the colony's riches, absentees helped amplify its voice in the metropolitan corridors of power.

CHAPTER FOUR

"FROM HUMBLE & MODERATE FORTUNES TO GREAT AFFLUENCE"

The Transatlantic Carolina Trade and Imperial Crises

"The success of a Crokatt, a Shubrick, or a Beswicke, but a few Years here in the Mercantile Way, or of a Lynch, or Huger, or a Serre, in the Planting Way, with many other such Instances, proves more in Favour of South Carolina, than all the Pamphlets that were ever wrote about."[1] In 1749 London's three principal Carolina merchants—James Crokatt, Richard Shubrick, and John Beswicke—were held up in Charles Town as paragons of commercial achievement. All three had begun their careers in South Carolina, where their commercial training, as the correspondent to the *South Carolina Gazette* implied, had furnished them with the skills and resources that formed the basis for their efflorescence in business in the imperial capital. South Carolina could bask in their reflected glory; their accomplishments were testament to the potential of a place where "but a few Years" could turn a colonial trader into a major metropolitan merchant. Two years, three years, and ten years respectively after they had relocated from Charles Town to London, Beswicke, Shubrick, and Crokatt were still synonymous with commercial success. For the *Gazette*'s anonymous correspondent, it was three merchants who had left the colony, rather than their counterparts, who continued to prosper in trade in Charles Town, who best epitomized the transformative power of commerce. These three pillars of London's Carolina trade continued to be held in high regard, even at four thousand miles' remove. Rather than diminishing their relevance, being at the center of imperial commerce and politics increased their appeal.

By the mid-1760s attitudes among Charles Town merchants toward their London counterparts had begun to shift. Commercially the capital's share of South Carolina's overseas trade was as great as ever. London continued to dominate the export trade to the colony. The capital accounted for some 85–90 percent of Britain's exports to South Carolina between 1760 and 1775—a function largely of the superior credit London's merchants could offer their Charles Town counterparts compared to merchants in Britain's regional ports as well as the capital's better access to European and Asian textiles.[2] In the slave trade too London continued to play a major organizational and financial role. Of the 103 slave ships from Britain that arrived in Charles Town between 1769 and 1774, 25 were from London—more than from Bristol and second only to Liverpool.[3] The capital also remained the principal hub for South Carolina's agricultural exports. In 1763, for example, London handled 93 percent of South Carolina's indigo exports and received 24 percent of its rice exports to Britain, mostly for reexport to northern Europe. This was second only to Cowes, an important transshipment port on the Isle of Wight. Cowes's share of the rice reexport trade is deceptive, however, since a high proportion of the port's rice trade was controlled by merchants in London.[4]

At the same time, the Carolina "interest" in London reached its zenith. Collectively, London's Carolina merchants were wealthier and more prominent in the city's commercial life during the 1760s than ever before. Their political lobbying reached new heights at a time when other North American lobbies in London were lapsing into inactivity. While the Virginia "interest" in the capital declined, perhaps as a result of the consolidation of the capital's tobacco trade into fewer hands, London's Carolina trade continued—as had long been the case—to be dominated by a small number of firms and individuals.[5] Far from reducing its vigor, this concentration of power seems to have made the Carolina lobby more coherent and responsive. Lobbying remained central to the activities and identities of these wealthy London merchants. Carolinians visiting London joined them in signing petitions and attending parliamentary committees considering colonial trade.

In South Carolina politicians and merchants also continued to regard lobbying in London as essential. This long-established approach had paid dividends in the past, representing Carolinian grievances and facilitating the colony's trade. In the mid-1760s this lobbying reached the high point of its influence, led assiduously by Charles Garth, who had been made the colony's official agent in London in 1762. London's Carolina merchants, acting in concert with Garth as commercial interlocutors with the British state, were at the forefront of campaigns to liberalize and incentivize colonial exports. Although not always successful, the lobby could congratulate itself on significant legislative accomplishments: securing the renewal of the bounty for Carolinian indigo that had been introduced in 1748; gaining permission to export rice from South Carolina to new markets; and coordinating a campaign for a bounty on exports of hemp from the colonies. London's Carolina merchants also lobbied strenuously on the colony's behalf against the Stamp Act.

Lobbying was especially vital for South Carolina compared to the other American colonies, authorities in Charles Town believed, because of the particular legal impediments that constrained the colony. While the Navigation Acts allowed Britain's more northerly North American colonies to export their grain and fish freely to European markets, exports of South Carolina's two staples, rice and indigo, remained strongly circumscribed by the laws. "The laws of trade lay greater restrictions on this province than on many of her sister colonies," the South Carolina Assembly's Committee of Correspondence complained to Garth in September 1764. "Almost all our commodities are enumerated, whereas few or none of theirs are so, notwithstanding ours are such as tend wholly to improve, and by no means interfere with those of the mother country."[6] The discrepancy was clearest in the relative treatment of South Carolina's rice and northern colonies' corn. Urging Garth to press the case in London for the lifting of restrictions on the direct export of rice to northern Europe, the committee failed to see "any reason why ships from America loaded with Rice should not be excepted from touching any Ports of England in the Passage to and from America, to or from any Ports North of Cape Finisterre as well as those loaded with Corn."[7] It also singled out the different regulations governing the importation of salt. As well as the restrictions on exports, the committee noted that "our imports [are] much more confined [than other colonies'], particularly that of salt—an article of the greater consequence, which most of the other colonies are prepared to import directly from Portugal, but we are not allowed that privilege."[8] Public critiques in South Carolina of the mercantilist strictures that governed British trade policy were articulated on grounds of competitive disadvantage: the laws were unfair because they treated other colonies more favorably. The assembly's complaints, however, were the thin end of the wedge. Although in 1764 the intersection of free trade economic theory and republican ideology was yet to be articulated, more systematic—though still largely tacit—condemnations of how British mercantilism subordinated South Carolina's economic interests would emerge alongside ideological critiques of British political authority in the years that followed.[9]

The idea that advocacy in London was an effective conduit for South Carolina's grievances rested on the assumption that the interests of London's Carolina traders were fundamentally aligned with those of the colony. As the 1760s progressed, this notion was increasingly challenged. Growing political disputes between South Carolina and Great Britain were mirrored by increasing mistrust between Charles Town's merchants and their London counterparts. London's Carolina merchants came under growing criticism in South Carolina for their business practices, their conspicuous wealth, and their purported political orientation as political tension between Britain and its North American colonies mounted. This paralleled changes in the composition of London's Carolina trading community. Before the mid-1760s London's principal Carolina merchants had each spent time in Charles Town learning and building their trade, accumulating networks of trusted correspondents, participating in the civic life of the town, and often investing in land and property in South Carolina and Georgia. The merchants who from the mid-1760s replaced them at the forefront of London's Carolina trade lacked these personal experiences in or connections to South Carolina.

Changes in personnel and loss of trust eroded the assumed mutuality of interests between South Carolinians and their correspondents in London. Despite their lobbying accomplishments, London's Carolina merchants came to be viewed with growing skepticism by their Charles Town counterparts. Commercial disagreements arose, centering on suspicions of profiteering, sharp business practices, and outright fraud. By the eve of the American Revolution, London's Carolina merchants were viewed by many in South Carolina as being implacably hostile to the colony. This undercut connections between the colony and the mother country: South Carolina's interests could no longer be adequately served by a system that required distant agents to represent the colony by proxy, especially when the agents' actual commitment to the colony's interests was increasingly questionable. Interpersonal grievances laid bare deeper systemic inequalities. Reliance on far-flung advocacy symbolized a commercial system tilted against the colony, highlighting the constraints imposed by British law that ensured South Carolina's commercial subordination to Great Britain. Grievances about metropolitan commerce were not articulated as direct challenges to the British Empire's mercantilist orthodoxy but represented implicit critiques of it. These grievances permeated the colony's shifting political and ideological environment: the political, economic, and commercial motivations behind South Carolinians' growing resistance to British government were interrelated.

South Carolina's elites, a group that was among the chief beneficiaries of the British Empire, turned against the system from which it had so greatly profited. The self-confident, even self-congratulatory, mind-set that by the 1760s had developed among South Carolina's merchant-planter elites shaped their attitudes toward Atlantic trade, toward commercial advocacy in London, and through these toward British authority.[10] Within the colony politics continued to be defined by the assembly's self-confidence and assertiveness in challenging council and gubernatorial authority. In a classic exposition of South Carolina's colonial politics, Robert Weir made the case that, driven by their republican "country ideology" and self-conception as independent country gentlemen, elite Carolinians' political opposition to British government overrode material economic arguments for maintaining the imperial status quo. Responses to the conjoined commercial practices and political advocacy of London's Carolina merchants suggest how Carolinians' conceptions of political and commercial subjugation were interrelated. These subjugations represented two sides of the same coin—entwined and mutually reinforcing. A growing sense of commercial subordination to metropolitan traders mimicked political experiences, such as the sense of political subordination within the colony to British placemen whose appointments to positions in South Carolina restricted native Carolinians' access to high office. Commercial experiences and the system of trade that governed these experiences both drew upon and informed ideological resistance to British control.[11] Anglo-American trade became both a crucible for and a mirror on broader political controversies.

"Supported by the Whole Body of Merchants in London"

Charles Garth was appointed South Carolina's agent in London in May 1762. A cousin of the colony's governor Thomas Boone, he was "fixed upon tho' personally unknown" to his employers "as a Gentleman of Ability, Address, of Assiduity." The Committee of Correspondence further hoped, it told him, that it would "have sufficient cause to be satisfied with your faithful & diligent discharges of the duties of your station."[12] Garth proved an inspired choice at an apposite moment. Like James Crokatt's appointment in 1749, Garth's selection coincided with a revival in the British government's attention toward the country's Atlantic trade. An assiduous, well-connected, and newly appointed agent was well placed to galvanize South Carolina's lobby in Britain and exploit a favorable political agenda. The following three years would be the lobby's apogee.

A decade earlier the end of the War of the Austrian Succession in 1748 had heralded close parliamentary scrutiny of Britain's colonial commerce and a flurry of legislation. This included three acts directly affecting South Carolina: the 1750 Silk Act; the 1751 Potash Act; and most significantly, the 1748 Indigo Bounty Act. Driven by the same political-economic rationale, Prime Minister George Grenville's administration, in power between April 1763 and July 1765, introduced measures similarly designed to boost colonial prosperity and channel it back toward the mother country, thus augmenting Britain's own economy and its strategic power. Stimulating the production of nationally important commodities in the colonies was one element of this. Commodities that strengthened Britain's navy and merchant marine—the cornerstones of the nation's defenses and its ability to project power overseas—were especially favored: naval stores, hemp, and flax. South Carolina was well placed to capitalize on this stimulation. Further underpinning the drive to enhance colonial prosperity was the belief that colonial wealth would translate into greater prosperity for Britain through increased demand for the mother country's goods. The South Carolina lobby would take advantage of this, using the rationale of economic feedback to good effect when it resumed the long-running campaign for permission to export rice directly from South Carolina to other parts of the Americas in 1764.[13] The government's measures for economic stimulation would be overshadowed by its attendant efforts to make the American colonies more fiscally remunerative through the Stamp Act and to clamp down on the highly profitable smuggling of foreign wines and molasses through the Sugar Act, as well as the fierce resistance these aroused. The government's desire to incentivize commodity production would, however, have more subtle political ramifications within the Carolina trade in once again signaling the potential efficacy of the Carolina lobby in London.

Garth's first achievement as agent was getting the indigo bounty renewed. Having originally been set for a term of seven years, the bounty had been extended by Parliament in 1755; three years later London's Carolina merchants had defeated an attempt by one of the capital's West Indies merchants to open a trade exporting slaves into the French West Indies in exchange for French indigo. After hearing evidence against the application from "several merchants . . . trading to the province of South Carolina," the Board of Trade dismissed the application on the grounds that "the supply of the French colonies with negroes as well as the taking from them indigo in return would be impolitick and attended with dangerous and destructive consequences to the commercial interests of this country and of its colonies."[14] The privileged status of South Carolina's and Georgia's indigo was maintained. With the indigo bounty due to expire once more in March 1763, Garth lobbied the board with William Knox, agent for Georgia, for it to be extended for another seven years. Discovering that the customs commissioners had advised the British Treasury to end the bounty on the grounds that it had been fraudulently claimed on imports of French indigo, Garth called on sympathetic connections in Parliament for aid. He asked his two cousins who were MPs, James Edward Colleton and Charles Boone, both of whom had strong family connections to South Carolina, to attend the Commons committee on expiring laws to make South Carolina's case. With support from the Board of Trade the bounty was duly extended, albeit at a reduced rate of fourpence per pound of indigo.[15]

Since getting the indigo bounty extended was essentially a procedural victory that did not require any fundamental adjustments to government policy, Garth had no need to co-opt other interest groups. In contrast, simultaneous efforts to allow rice to be exported directly to Madeira, the Canaries, and other islands off the coast of Africa and to any part of the Americas required a much broader campaign. Direct rice exports to new markets had been an objective for South Carolina's planters and traders since the 1720s. Appeals to this end in 1745–46 had been rejected by the customs commissioners on the grounds that while the measure might benefit the colony, it would have unpredictable consequences for Britain's overall trade; a further attempt in 1758 for direct rice exports to any port in mainland Europe had been similarly rebuffed.[16]

Garth's campaigns for direct rice exports in 1763 reiterated how effective lobbying could be. He assembled a broader and more persuasive coalition of merchant support than in the two prior attempts, first securing the collective backing of London's Carolina traders by circulating a petition that was, as he told the Committee of Correspondence, "signed by every merchant of London in the Carolina trade."[17] The petition, which was heard by the Commons in March 1763, emphasized the breadth of its support, coming from "several Merchants in London, Planters of So. Carolina, and Owners of Ships, trading to His Majesty's said Province in America." It recapitulated the claims long made in support of freer rice exports: that present laws compelled two voyages, first to England and then on to the ultimate destination of the islands off Africa or in the Caribbean, raising transport costs and making the rice more vulnerable to pests during the long journey. This made it economically unviable against rice supplied by Genovese, Leghornese, and Levant merchants. Besides the specifics of rice shipping, the petition's patriotic economic rhetoric was calculated to appeal to wider political concerns, restating the arguments offered to great effect in the late 1740s and early 1750s. Not only would the deenumeration of rice promote South Carolina's economy; it would also "greatly redound to the Benefit of Great Britain" by increasing the demand for shipping, expanding the merchant marine, and strengthening demand for British goods, since the greater prosperity of South Carolina would filter back to manufacturers and suppliers in the mother country.[18]

"I am supported by the Whole Body of Merchants in London," Garth told his employers in South Carolina, "& have good reason to hope from Bristol." Support from traders in Britain's regional ports would be vital in demonstrating the commercial consensus behind the proposal. Garth solicited the aid of Robert Nugent and William Meredith, MPs for Bristol and Liverpool respectively, to galvanize the support of their commercial constituents. He also printed copies of a petition that he and Knox had given the Board of Trade on the matter in January and distributed them to merchants in both cities. A week after hearing the London petition, the Commons received a nearly identical petition from merchants of Bristol in support of the proposal, while William Meredith chaired a parliamentary committee examining the proposals.[19] James Crokatt, John Nutt, and William Greenwood each gave supporting evidence to Parliament on behalf of London's Carolina merchants, together with the former resident and major South Carolina landowner William Middleton. Crokatt explained the centrality of risiculture in South Carolina's economy; Nutt reported "the great spirit of Planting now arising in that Colony" but warned that "the Planters cannot reap the Fruits of their Spirit and Industry, unless new Markets are opened to them."[20]

The parliamentary committee resolved in favor of the rice petitions, concluding that direct exports of the grain from South Carolina to the African islands and the Americas would "greatly tend to increase the Culture and Commerce of the said Province."[21] This overrode objections raised in Parliament to the proposal, which Garth reported to the Committee of Correspondence. These included the protests that there was insufficient benefit to Great Britain to justify amending the Navigation Acts; that Britain would be bypassed in the reexport trade in rice to valuable northern European markets since both Madeira and the Caribbean island of St. Eustatius could be used as entrepôts for onward shipment; and ironically, that the boost given to the rice economy in South Carolina "would interfere with and reduce the cultivation of indigo." One objection was strikingly prescient: that by allowing trade to bypass Britain, the proposed measure "carried with it strong Symptoms & Wishes in design in a colony to become Independent of the Mother Country." It was pressure on parliamentary time, however, rather than any of these specific complaints,

that meant scrutiny of the proposal was repeatedly adjourned, and the parliamentary session ended in mid-April before legislation on the matter could
be passed.[22]

Undeterred when the rice proposal was rejected in 1763, Garth and Knox
reintroduced it to Parliament in March 1764. Their new petition appealed directly
to domestic British interests. Alongside regularly heard arguments for British
manufacturing and government income, it asserted the benefits of the slave trade
to the country. Growing rice in South Carolina and Georgia had, it argued, "been
productive of great Advantages to Great Britain, by increasing the Consumption
of British Manufactures in the said Colonies, increasing the Demand for Negroes, and augmenting the Freights of British Shipping, besides contributing to
the Increase of the public Revenue."[23] The application also explicitly linked rice to
contemporary geopolitics. It emphasized how trade with the Caribbean islands
captured from France and Spain during the Seven Years' War—Guadeloupe and
Martinique, and Havana in Cuba—had stimulated risiculture in South Carolina
and Georgia. Since these islands had been returned to France and Spain after
the war, this profitable market had been lost. The proposal seized too upon
South Carolina and Georgia's disadvantages compared to Britain's more northerly North American colonies, since exports of rice to foreign colonies in the
West Indies were forbidden while northern colonies' lumber, fish, and corn could
all be sent directly.

Evidence from the previous year's efforts was resubmitted, and Nutt and
Greenwood again spoke to the committee considering the application. In asserting their credentials as expert witnesses, they indicated their dominance of
the export trade to the region, avowing that between them they had exported
goods—"chiefly British manufactures"—worth around two hundred thousand
pounds to South Carolina and Georgia the previous year. If true, this amounted
to nearly two-thirds of total British exports to these colonies. Again, their testimony carefully fused specifically Carolinian concerns with a nod to domestic political-economic preoccupations, proposing the increased demand for
British manufactures that would come from a more prosperous rice-growing
region. Evidence from customhouses in South Carolina and Georgia revealed
that the 120,000 barrels of rice exported in 1763 had yielded twenty-two thousand pounds in revenues to the British Treasury.[24] This time the arguments won
the day. A bill specifically permitting direct rice exports to foreign colonies in
the West Indies and South America, but not the African islands, passed through
Parliament and received royal assent in April 1764.[25]

Merchant agency was instrumental again in securing a bounty on colonial
hemp the same year. Reflecting their particular activism among London's North
American lobbies, the capital's Carolina traders were once more to the fore.
Hemp was essential for rope making for the Royal Navy and merchant fleet,
and getting government support for its cultivation in the colonies had been a

long-standing ambition for American agents and merchants.[26] Taking advantage of the favorable political-economic climate that followed the end of the Seven Years' War, colonial agents and London's American traders mounted a concerted campaign for a bounty on North American hemp exports. The petition was unprecedented in the scale and breadth of its commercial support. Nearly all the American merchants in London backed the petition, Garth explained, "except those who have seats in Parliament, and who are going to be Judges, could not with Decency make themselves Parties to signing it."[27] In total, around one hundred merchants and agents, representing all the colonies from Massachusetts to Georgia, signed a petition to Parliament in November 1763 seeking "proper Encouragement for the Importation of Hemp and Flax from His Majesty's Colonies in America." As with the simultaneous petitioning on rice exports, all of London's principal Carolina traders were signatories, together with—and further suggesting Garth's influence in the campaign—two Carolinians temporarily resident in London.[28] In March 1764 Parliament approved a bounty on hemp and flax imported from the American colonies, to run for twenty-one years and worth eight pounds per ton for the first seven years. American hemp imports, Parliament concluded, would reduce Britain's dependence on Russian sources, encourage settlement of newly acquired lands in North America that were ideal for its cultivation, and encourage Virginia and South Carolina to diversify into a new commodity for an alternative source of income.[29]

"The important services they have done to America in General"

Effective commercial lobbying bred expectations that London's Carolina merchants would press similarly hard on more explicitly political issues. Their responses in 1765–66 to the Stamp Act and Mutiny Act would test these expectations. In November 1765 James Crokatt's Charles Town agent, Robert Raper, reported to him the hostility and disruption that the Stamp Act had brought about in South Carolina. Passed by Parliament in March 1765 and requiring that printed material in the colonies ranging from attorneys' licenses to newspapers bear official and often expensive stamps produced in Britain, the act amounted to a direct tax on the colonies. Riots erupted in Charles Town in October 1765. An effigy of a stamp official was publicly hanged, people suspected of supporting the act were harassed, and the house of a man rumored to be involved with the distributing of stamps was attacked and ransacked. The mob violence was effective in preventing the distribution of the stamps, meaning that the town's courts, which under the terms of the act could not function without stamped paper, closed at the beginning of November. In consequence, no commercial debts owed to London merchants could be recovered by legal process. Worse still, Charles Town's port was closed to shipping, since vessels too were required to have their paperwork stamped. Raper told Crokatt of "the Stagnation of Trade here and all along the Continent occasioned by the Stamp Act which is very disagreeable to this part of America. I dare say you have heard very fully about it & will endeavour to get it repealed."[30] Personal interest, Raper believed, would stir Crokatt and his fellow merchants in the capital into action. With popular resistance to the Stamp Act preventing the pursuit of debts, Raper warned another London client, William Greenwood, bluntly that unless the courts reopened, "many of you will suffer and several be ruined." A month later he reiterated his concerns, alerting his client to personal repercussions. "I have received no money this long time for your account and as we have no law to compel people to pay I cannot help you," he warned.[31]

Raper's confidence that the closure of Charles Town's courts and port would galvanize London's Carolina traders was not misplaced. Together with London's other Carolina merchants, Crokatt was to the fore in pressing for the Stamp Act to be repealed. Facing financial losses from the protests and deadlock in Charles Town, Crokatt and Greenwood represented the capital's Carolina trade in a delegation of twenty-eight London merchants to the British government in December 1765. Charles Ogilvie and John Clark, both significant traders to South Carolina, represented Georgia.[32] Raper and others in Charles Town could hardly have been unaware of the traders' efforts. North American newspapers carried reports from London of a "very numerous meeting of the merchants of this city, trading to North-America" on 4 December, from which the delegation that included Crokatt and Greenwood was selected. The reports made clear that the traders' goal was "to solicit some effectual remedy in the present distressed state of trade to the colonies." The newspapers, among them the *South Carolina Gazette and Country Journal*—launched in December 1765 and printed on unstamped paper in defiance of the new regulations—identified the "principal merchants trading to each colony" who took part in the delegation, including Crokatt, Greenwood, Ogilvie, and Clark.[33]

Long before the colonial press had publicized the London merchants' efforts to repeal the Stamp Act, Charles Garth had kept South Carolina's politicians informed of their behind-the-scenes lobbying. Garth had been elected as an MP in 1764, enabling him to report firsthand on government policies on American administration and revenue and on the opposition to the policies. Anticipating the hostility that the 1765 Mutiny Bill would arouse in South Carolina, in particular its stipulation that British troops in America might be billeted in private houses if no barracks were available, Garth alerted London merchants to the bill's introduction in Parliament. "I have sent to the merchants to acquaint them with the purport of it [the bill]," he told the assembly's Committee of Correspondence in April 1765, "leaving it to their discretion what steps they will choose to take but not without a hint what I think their friends in America have a right to expect from them." Suitably alarmed, London merchants in the various branches of American trade invited Garth to explain the Mutiny Bill and its likely implications to them. After the meeting, Garth informed the Committee of Correspondence that the merchants "appointed a Select Committee to meet every evening to consider of the most effectual method to avoid a measure so oppressive in its tendency" and that they had asked him and another MP to press the government to alter the bill.[34]

The eventual Mutiny Act, or Quartering Act, passed by Parliament in May 1765 exempted private houses from billeting troops, instead substituting empty houses, stables, alehouses, and barns in their place. The act remained a source of controversy, especially in New York, but Garth's letters ensured that his employers in South Carolina's government were fully informed of the merchants' role in watering down its most contested element. On the Stamp Act too Garth's reports supplemented newspaper reports in South Carolina of the London merchants' activism. In December 1765 Garth reported that the Committee of London Merchants—the group of twenty-eight traders including Crokatt, Greenwood, Ogilvie, and Nutt that headed the campaign—had urged British boroughs with manufacturing industries to alert their MPs to dire consequences if the Stamp Act continued. Describing the parliamentary debates for the repeal of the act in January 1766, he highlighted the merchants' petitions against it.[35] Aside from Garth's testimony and press reports, London's Carolina traders sought to impress upon their colonial correspondents their activism in overturning the Stamp Act. On 22 February 1766, the same day that the Commons voted for repeal, they "very becomingly chartered a Vessel," the optimistically named *Speedwell*, to carry the good news to South Carolina. As it turned out, news of the repeal of the Stamp Act arrived in Charles Town via a ship from Barbados on 3 May. A day later the *Speedwell* ran aground at the entrance to Charles Town harbor, though its passengers arrived safely. The *Speedwell*'s clumsy arrival and the preemption of the news it was carrying could not obscure, however, the gesture of support that London's Carolina merchants aimed to convey by chartering and dispatching the vessel.[36]

Like their counterparts in other branches of trade to America, who were reluctant to intervene in explicitly political matters, London's Carolina merchants acted on commercial expediency rather than political principle in lobbying against the Stamp Act. Robert Raper's letters to stir his London correspondents into action had emphasized the impact that the closure of Charles Town's courts would have on their businesses. The preeminence of commercial factors in motivating London's North America merchants was evident in their own appeals for action, appeals which were reproduced in the colonial press. A letter from the Committee of London Merchants asking manufacturing towns and ports across England to oppose the act appeared in the *South Carolina Gazette and Country Journal*. "The present state of the British trade to North America, and the prospect of increasing embarrassment, which threatens the loss of our depending property there; and even to annihilate the trade itself" compelled concerted action, the letter began. There was no mention of the justice or injustice of internal taxation, or of any of the other constitutional questions that were vexing their correspondents in South Carolina and elsewhere in North America. Another letter from a London merchant that was reproduced in the *Country Journal* noted that "nothing less than an ample importation of the produce of the foreign islands, and an unrestrain'd exportation of the produce of North-America, could enable the people to pay their debts in England."[37] Property and debts, it was made clear to Carolinians, were at the forefront of their advocates' minds.

Regardless of their motivations, the London merchants' efforts against the Stamp Act were commended in South Carolina. Gratitude was directed principally toward the leading political agitators for repeal: the Committee of Correspondence asked Garth to pass on the assembly's thanks to "such of the members of both Houses of Parliament as have generously distinguished themselves in procuring the repeal." The assembly prepared an address of thanks to King George III; most publicly it commissioned a statue of William Pitt to stand in Charles Town in thanks for his powerful eloquence in Parliament against the act.[38] Although the London merchants' intervention in the Stamp Act debates did not garner comparable public celebration in South Carolina, their role in the repeal campaign was not ignored. The *Country Journal* noted how a procession of London's North American merchants, numbering some fifty coaches, had visited the king "to expression their Satisfaction at his signing the Bill for repealing the American Stamp Act."[39] The Committee of Correspondence also noted the merchants' assiduous lobbying. "We also think ourselves exceedingly obliged to the London Committee and the several Corporations, Merchants &c. that exerted themselves upon this trying Occasion," it told Garth, "and desire you will make known to them the grateful sense we retain of the important services they have done to America in General."[40]

"Commissions & profits arising from such Trade"

In their campaigns against the Mutiny and Stamp Acts, London's Carolina merchants had seemingly confirmed the efficacy of lobbying as a means of representing and redressing colonial grievances. Beneath the rhetoric in South Carolina that lauded their intervention, however, lurked a growing undercurrent of suspicion toward their business methods. Changing attitudes in South Carolina reflected a shift in commercial mind-sets in the colony, where merchants were increasingly reluctant to play the role of junior partners in Atlantic commerce. Despite their lobbying, London's Carolina traders came to be regarded with increasing mistrust, as their interests and motives for lobbying were seen to diverge from those of their colonial correspondents. The charges against them included conspiracy to disparage Carolinian output, manipulating prices in London and thereby defrauding their Charles Town correspondents, and excessive profiteering in the trade.

The controversy resulting from London merchants' attempts to compel their Charles Town correspondents to post bonds as guarantees of payment exemplified the growing divide. For Henry Laurens, efforts by two of London's principal Carolina trading houses, John Beswicke & Co. and Sarah Nickleson & Co., to force their Charles Town correspondents to post bonds were both a novelty and a deep affront. The dispute had arisen in late 1763. James Poyas, a Charles Town merchant regarded by Laurens as an "honest punctual dealer" with a good capital foundation, sought to switch his custom from Beswicke & Co. to Nickleson & Co., importing goods on credit from the latter rather than the former. Beswicke had offended Poyas by asking him to post bond for his debts, a legal guarantee that his firm would rank first among Poyas's creditors, above those owed money in the form of promissory notes or debts on account. The request reflected the mounting problems that London's merchants faced in recovering debts in South Carolina. Changes in the composition of London's community of Carolina traders and structural impediments to the collection of debts in the colony eroded trust on both sides of the Atlantic. During the 1760s the volume and value of South Carolina's exports hit new heights, and the number of trading houses in Charles Town was greater than ever before. However, evidence from London trade directories, merchants' petitioning, and later claims for prewar debts reveals that the number of trading houses in the capital's Carolina trade did not grow accordingly. London's end of the trade continued to be controlled by a handful of specialists who came to supply increasing numbers of Charles Town merchants and relied on trusted friends, family, and attorneys to chase up and secure repayment from their counterparties.

At the same time as networks of credit grew and spread, the personal links to Charles Town that had defined an earlier generation of London Carolina merchants became less pronounced. London's leading Carolina traders between the 1730s and the 1750s—men such as Samuel Wragg, James Crokatt, John Nickleson, and John Beswicke—had all spent the early part of their careers in Charles Town, building expertise and, crucially, personal connections in the trade. In contrast, the merchants at the forefront of London's Carolina trade in the 1760s appear not to have had comparable early commercial training in Charles Town. In the face of ever denser and more impersonal networks of credit and greater reliance on the law to reclaim debts, London's Carolina merchants became increasingly frustrated by the obstacles they faced in calling in debts in the colony. John Beswicke's attorney in Charles Town notified him of the advice from one lawyer in the town to a client not to pay debts to British merchants from any estates of which he was executor. If such debts were remitted in produce, the lawyer had explained, his client would find himself personally accountable to the other heirs and creditors for any loss on the consignments. "To prevent this practice of Correspondents or their Exors. paying English debts here," the attorney advised, "I would advise every Merchant in London to take a Bond from them to bind themselves, their Heirs, Exors. & c. to pay in London."[41] Residents of Charles Town were, moreover, better placed than their London counterparts to receive advance warning of an impending default or insolvency in the town, allowing them to head the queue in pressing their claims. The same Charles Town attorney advised Greenwood & Higginson that "if any Merchant breaks here & delivers up, his Debts in this place [Charles Town] will always be paid & the creditors in England will in such cases suffer by taking what is left."[42] It was rational, then, for London principals to seek to push their debtors in South Carolina into contracts that provided them with greater security as creditors. What was to London's Carolina traders a reasonable commercial arrangement had, however, more sinister connotations to their Charles Town correspondents.

Writing to Isaac King, a partner in Nickleson & Co., Henry Laurens unveiled a litany of Charlestonian grievances against London's merchants. First, the demand to post bond was intrinsically an "Affront to the Character of a Merchant." By implying doubt about a merchant's ability or willingness to repay a debt, it impugned both his honor and his credit—the two essential characteristics of any worthy trader. Second, that such a demand was made after a debt had been contracted, rather than "at the commencement of their correspondence," represented an abuse of the creditor's power—and a sign of the systemic commercial "hold" that London's principal traders had over their Charles Town correspondents to whom they exported goods on credit. Third, King had demanded that Poyas post bond, repeating Beswicke's earlier demand—the reason that Poyas had moved his account from Beswicke to Nickleson & Co. in the first place. This savored, according to Laurens, "too much of combination."[43]

London's leading Carolina merchants were in effect charged with exploiting structural conditions that allowed them to wield undue power over their correspondents: since the trade was concentrated among a small number of individuals and firms in London, the capital's traders were able to act as a cabal in collaborating and fixing their terms. At a time when residents on both sides of the Atlantic were increasingly alert to the menace of monopoly in trade and clique in politics, "combination" was a powerful charge.[44] The charge hinted at the deeper structural forces that permitted such a concentration—and "combination"—to occur: the compulsion through the Navigation Laws for South Carolinians, like other colonists, to send the bulk of their output to and to receive all their manufactured or processed goods from Great Britain. The requirement to post bond represented a fundamental shift in the contract between creditor and debtor, putting "more power into the hands of the Obligor than a Man ought to trust himself or another with & more than is intended to be countenanced by the Laws of the Land." By locating the contract of the debt in London, the bond permitted the creditor to compound interest, a "modern mode of calculations & accumulations of Interest & Interest upon Interest" that Laurens judged "Illegal."[45]

Traders in South Carolina were, Laurens believed, suffering not just at the hands of avaricious individuals in London. They were as well inherently disadvantaged by their peripheral location in a legal-commercial system that promoted metropolitan over colonial interests. "Is not the advantage of proving your debts upon Oath before the Lord Mayor of London which is to be received in our American Courts as ample testimonials of the Sums due to you without canvassing of Books & examination of Witnesses, enough?" he complained. Here he pointed to the stipulations of the 1732 Colonial Debt Recovery Act, which in seeking to facilitate the recovery of debts owed to British merchants in the American colonies, reduced the burden of proof required in pursuing such claims. British traders could swear to their local mayors or magistrates to the value of the debts due to them, "as if the Person or Persons making the same Oath or solemn Affirmation . . . had appeared and sworn or affirmed the Matters contained in such Affadvit or Affirmation viva voce in open Court."[46] Intended as a means of placing British creditors on an equal footing with their colonial counterparts by freeing them of the requirement to cross the Atlantic to present their claims in court, by the 1760s the Debt Act had come to be construed in a different guise: that of reducing the evidentiary burden on British creditors and further tilting the rules of trade in their favor.

For Laurens, the inequities that London merchants were trying to introduce to the Carolina trade were made even more obnoxious given the great riches they had derived from their business. The egregious wealth of London's Carolina merchants obviated the need for bonded security, he complained. "The Carolina Agents or Factors to a Man have sustained as few Losses by their Trade to this Colony as have been felt or known in any trade whatever to America & also because they have in general & almost to a Man by means of their Commissions & profits arising from such Trade, risen from humble & moderate Fortunes to great affluence, from walking upon foot to the command of Conveniences which render their legs and feet almost useless. These are facts very notorious and on which I need not enlarge."[47] Laurens's caustic remarks on the "great affluence" of London's Carolina traders are borne out by their grand lifestyles as they profited handsomely on the back of South Carolina's economic growth. The trappings of the principal partners in the six firms identified as "Carolina Merchant" in *Mortimer's Directory* in 1763—James & Charles Crokatt, John Beswicke, Richard Shubrick, John Nutt, Sarah Nickleson, and Grubb & Watson—are illustrative. Besides his lordly Luxborough Hall estate in rural Essex, James Crokatt was able to bestow ten thousand pounds on his son Charles at his marriage, a union portrayed by no less an artist than Thomas Gainsborough.[48] London's principal Carolina traders, such as Crokatt, acquired grand mansions in England's home counties, within easy reach of London. In so doing, they followed a path—from countinghouse to landed estate—that was well trodden in South Carolina but one achieved only by the most successful of London's overseas traders, most often by the wealthiest West Indies merchants.

With the proceeds from trading careers begun in Charles Town reinvested and augmented in London, traders such as John Beswicke, John and Sarah Nickleson, and Richard Shubrick embarked on the path to landed gentility. John Nickleson was reckoned at his death to be worth some £20,000, with assets including a country retreat fifteen miles northwest of London at Great Stanmore, Middlesex.[49] A few miles to the south, John Beswicke invested his proceeds from the Carolina trade in a large country mansion in Hillingdon. Conveniently placed near the highway from London to the fashionable spa resorts of Bath and Cheltenham, the appropriately named Little London was styled by Beswicke as his "Country Seat." Besides his estate land and property, Beswicke had at least £20,000 in liquid assets at his death, including the £500 he left "to my Negroe Manservant, Anthony," perhaps a former household slave brought from Charles Town.[50] When Beswicke died in 1764, Little London and its adjacent estate passed to his nephew and business partner, William Greenwood. They were later auctioned at Christie's, Pall Mall, and the sale advertisement revealed the estate's desirability. Little London was an "Elegant Villa . . . with roomy Stabling, Coach-house, Offices of every description, attached and detached; excellent walled Garden; Lawn, Shrubbery, containing about 31 Acres, and sundry rich Enclosures, comprising about 64 Acres . . . forming in the whole a desirable residence." Also for sale was the freehold of "several substantial houses with their gardens, offices and land, in the whole about 200 acres," which at the time was let to twelve tenants and produced an annual income of £550. In addition to his Middlesex estates, Greenwood amassed large landholdings in Yorkshire.[51] For his part, Richard Shubrick owned properties east of London at Mile End and Greenwich, areas known for their mansions, gentility, and popularity with affluent merchants and mariners.[52] On his death he left his widow and children several thousand pounds in government stock and cash along with his coach, chariot, and horses—abundant evidence of his elite lifestyle. His son, also Richard, owned a "very pleasant and desirable Villa" with gardens, orchards, and eighteen acres of land in Enfield, ten miles north of London.[53]

This was wealth to put even their richest counterparts in South Carolina in the shade. In a sample of eighty-four residents of Charles Town District who died in 1774, the mean net worth of the ten richest was £11,078—a figure comprising the value of their land, slaves, and goods. Take out the richest, Peter Manigault—who had a net worth at death of £32,737—and the mean drops to £8,672.[54] These Charlestonians were among the richest men anywhere in North America, but their wealth was modest in comparison to the capital's leading Carolina merchants with their English country estates and City of London countinghouses. In the context of London commerce, the Carolina merchants' city addresses denoted their elite status. Cannon Street had been the core locale for London's Carolina traders during the 1740s and 1750s but was eclipsed by still more prestigious commercial locations during the 1760s. Aldgate ward, on the city's eastern fringe, became a particular nexus for Carolina merchants, as did Broad Street and Bishopsgate wards, east of St. Paul's Cathedral.

At the heart of the city, a short walk from the Royal Exchange and the Carolina Coffee House, the streets and squares where the Carolina merchants congregated, such as Billiter Square and New Broad Street, offered some of London's top business addresses, suggesting that the trade became increasingly lucrative during the 1760s. At his Cloak Lane premises, James Crokatt was the second highest rate payer in the precinct and employed at least four apprentices as clerks and bookkeepers at one time. By 1763 Crokatt had effectively retired from the Carolina trade and was only in nominal partnership with his son, but he still paid a very high £84 in personal tax and £14 in tax on his property. The same year Richard Shubrick paid £16.8s. in tax on his Barge Yard premises. The same year—and at the same time that he tried to make James Poyas post bond— John Beswicke paid rates of £20 on his Queen Street premises and £100 in personal tax. These tax returns placed both Beswicke and Crokatt easily among the wealthiest London merchants in overseas trade; only forty-three London merchants across all branches of trade paid £100 or more in personal tax in 1763.[55]

Descriptions of the merchants' London houses shed further light on their wealth. Countinghouses also served as homes, at least during the working week, blurring the boundaries between merchants' professional and personal lives. They commonly lived above their working quarters and shared living space with their families and with their clerks and apprentices. While London merchants were generally restrained in their displays of wealth, at least in their premises in the city, the capital's leading Carolina merchants defied convention. William Greenwood's countinghouse on Budge Row rivaled any City of London dwelling and marked him as a merchant of the highest rank. His was "a commodious, substantial brick dwelling house and offices, court yard, counting houses, and cold bath, [with] standing for two carriages and stabling for five horses." Its grand interior included "fourteen bedchambers and dressing rooms; a genteel dressing room; breakfast and dining parlours; noble hall; principle and back stairs; a convenient kitchen, laundry and suitable connected offices and cellarage."[56] Charles Ogilvie's house on Fludyer Street, Westminster, epitomized metropolitan gentility. On a fashionable residential street that linked Whitehall with St. James's Park, it was richly decorated with "pea-green silk taboray curtains, sopha chairs and stools, elegant pier glasses and girandoles, a needlework carpet, fashionable sideboard of plate containing 800 ounces, fine household linen, china, a small library of modern books, wines, a large iron repository, and other valuable effects."[57] While he also kept premises at Billiter Square in the heart of the city, Ogilvie's Fludyer Street house gave him easy access to the pleasures of London's West End and to Parliament, where he was briefly an MP in the early 1770s.[58]

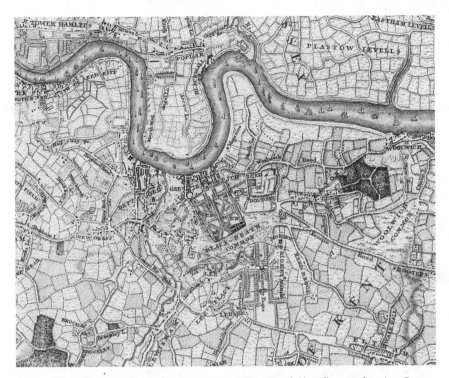

A Map of London and the Adjacent Country 10 Miles Round, (detail) 1748, showing Greenwich. Richard Parr (fl. 1723–51) after John Rocque (d. 1762). Yale Center for British Art, Paul Mellon Collection.

As London's Carolina merchants lived more and more extravagantly on the back of their commerce, some in South Carolina began to harbor suspicions about the practices that generated their profits. The alleged treatment of Carolinian commodities in London was a particular grievance—and a challenge to the probity of London's merchants, accentuating suspicions of metropolitan bias against South Carolina's producers and exporters. The capital's indigo traders were widely imagined to be bilking Carolinian producers through a cabal to disparage the quality of the product. "To the very great discouragement of the planters," a report claimed in the *Gentleman's Magazine,* "the dealers in that commodity [Carolina indigo] have combined to lessen and run down the value of it, till they get it at a very low rate, into their hands, and then sell it for French indigo; which they set a much higher value upon."[59] The charge was made publicly in Charles Town. As pronounced in the *South Carolina Gazette* by Moses Lindo, appointed by the colony as inspector general of indigo in an effort to raise the quality of exports of the dye, "It is beyond dispute that a Cabal has been formed in London, united with some who are obliged to this province for a great part of what they enjoy, to *depreciate Carolina* Indico."[60] Historians have shown that the poor reputation of Carolinian indigo, and the lower price it fetched compared to French and Spanish indigo, was for the most part deserved: it was the "serviceability" of South Carolina's crop as a low-cost dyestuff for Europe's textile sector that underlay the strong growth of South Carolina's indigo production and exports in the third quarter of the eighteenth century.[61] Nonetheless the perception of malign practices was real. London dealers' "tricks of the trade" were more than simply economic slights.

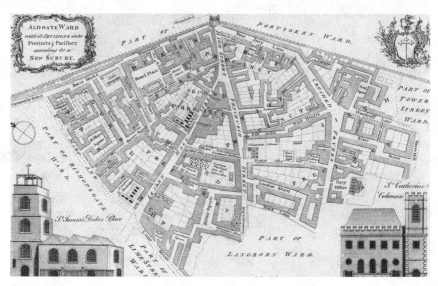

Aldgate Ward, 1760s. Benjamin Cole, 1697–1783, after unknown artist. Yale Center for British Art, Paul Mellon Collection.

For South Carolina's indigo producers, used to the high esteem their rice garnered in overseas markets, the poor reputation of their dye represented a powerful challenge to their skills as planters.[62] Conspiracy theories served subconsciously to absolve indigo planters from the imputations about their product's low standing. London traders made an easy but genuinely held target. Claims of metropolitan sharp practice explicitly contrasted commodity markets in London with those in Britain's regional ports. Henry Laurens complained of a "most extraordinary loss" of about nine percent in weight in the indigo he had shipped to Sarah Nickleson & Co. in April 1763. As the indigo had been in a "remarkably dry" parcel that he had packed himself, Laurens was convinced that the lost weight could only have been due to fraud in London. "Such a loss," he lamented, "was unknown upon Indigo some Six or Seven years ago & thank God is still unknown (except where it has really been tampered with) in Bristol & Liverpoole." Indigo was falling prey, Laurens feared, to the swindles long suspected of London importers of other colonial products, such as naval stores. Again a distinction was drawn between the markets for pitch and tar in London and those in the regional ports. "A fact not to be denied," he told Isaac King, "[is] that if you divide a parcel of pitch weighing in Average 360lbs. Grose per Barrell or thereabouts when Shiped send one half to Bristol and the other half to London the former will hold its weight & produce a full Credit in your Account Sale & the latter will fall short at least 15 per Cent often 20." Similarly, Laurens noted, "Purchase the very same barrel & transport it to Poole & it will be there as ponderous as it was in Carolina."[63]

Claims of fraud at the hands of London dealers were not unique to the 1760s, for either Carolinian or other colonial commodities. As with naval stores, systematic fraud was also held to be commonplace within the capital's deerskins trade. Laurens had been on the receiving end of the machinations of London deerskin traders at the start of his career in the 1740s, a cautionary experience he would remember for the rest of his life.[64] By the 1760s, however, sharp practices in the naval stores and deerskins markets paled in comparison to suspected malfeasance in the indigo trade. Naval stores and deerskins accounted for a decreasing share of South Carolina's exports, and their economic importance to the colony had shrunk proportionately (tables 4 and 5). Indigo, in contrast, represented a growing and increasingly vital commodity for South Carolina, and was well established as the colony's second most valuable export.[65] Metropolitan conspiracy against Carolinian indigo therefore represented a far greater affront to South Carolinians. Depreciations of the character of Carolinian indigo simultaneously challenged planters' self-conceived expertise and judgment. Neither planters nor merchants in South Carolina felt an equivalent personal pride in the naval stores or deerskins they sent to Britain. In economic terms, the greater value of indigo to the colony by the 1760s meant that falls in its price were—and were recognized to be—of much graver consequence.

Table 4: Exports of Naval Stores from South Carolina, 1740–72

	Total exported (barrels)		
	Tar	Pitch	Combined
Mean yrs. 1740–44	5,424	11,290	16,714
Mean yrs. 1745–49	2,813	10,779	13,592
Mean yrs. 1750–54	3,976	13,865	17,841
Mean yrs. 1755–57	3,141	4,630	7,771
Mean yrs. 1758–61	1,891	5,696	7,587
Mean yrs. 1762–66*	2,894	8,393	11,287
Mean yrs. 1768–72	4,363	6,158	10,521

Source: Clowse, *Measuring Charleston's Overseas Commerce*, 65–66, table B-31.

*no data available for 1767

Table 5: Exports of Deerskins from Charles Town, 1730–75

		Destinations								
	Skins exported	London		Bristol		Other British		All others		All points
		Hogs-heads	% of total exports	Hogs-heads	% of total exports	Hogs-heads	% of total exports	Hogs-heads	% of total exports	Hogs-heads
Mean yrs. 1730–34	84,000									
Mean yrs. 1735–39	112,000									
Mean yrs. 1740–44	125,000									
Mean yrs. 1745–49	147,000									
Mean yrs. 1750–54	134,000									
Mean yrs. 1755–59	137,000									
Mean yrs. 1760–64	112,000									
Mean yrs. 1765–69	82,000									
Mean yrs. 1770–75	52,000									
1758		313		146		13		31		503
1759		263		307		42		2		614
1760		416		119		8		3		546
Mean yrs. 1758–60			60		34		4		2	
1762		224		180		9		25		448
1763		534		266		1		0		801
Mean yrs. 1762–63			61		36		1		3	
1766		332	73	70	15	17	4	37	8	

Source: Converse D. Clowse, *Measuring Charleston's Overseas Commerce, 1717–1767* (Washington, D.C.: University Press of America, 1981), 54–55, table B-11.

London's dominance of the indigo market further aggravated the supposedly sharp practices in the trade. Unlike the rice trade, in which South Carolina's planters generally sold their grain to commission merchants in Charles Town, larger indigo growers sent their produce on their own account and risk to London. This reflected the long-standing expertise in indigo dealing in the capital and the city's preeminence as a center for distributing dyestuffs in Britain and to continental Europe. The first pamphlets to encourage indigo culture in South Carolina had asserted the primacy of the London market, trumpeting the capital's standing as "the greatest and best Market for it [indigo] in the World" and advising that "the Buyers are mostly rich men."[66] In sending their indigo to London, planters hoped to achieve the good prices they felt their produce deserved, and the city became by far the largest destination for Carolinian indigo, receiving around nine-tenths of the colony's indigo exports during the 1760s (table 6).[67] Opportunities for South Carolina's producers to divert their indigo exports to Britain's regional ports were limited, and as an enumerated commodity, direct indigo exports to foreign markets were forbidden. The comparative advantages London possessed in the marketing of indigo left producers with little choice but to live with the supposed sharp practices of the capital's dealers and traders.[68]

In parallel to London's overall control of the indigo trade in the British Empire, the trade in the dye within the capital was controlled by a handful of merchants. This further curtailed colonial sellers' ability to circumvent unfair practices in London by sending their indigo to other buyers. Table 7 shows the dominance of a small number of London indigo importers. It draws upon the only surviving ships' manifests from Britain's eighteenth-century Carolina trade, collected by Charles Town's naval office between January and March 1764 and sent to the Board of Trade in London. The forty-one manifests record the cargo carried by each ship, by whom in South Carolina it was sent, and to whom in London it was conveyed. They record eighteen ships embarking for Cowes, almost exclusively carrying rice for reexportation to northern Europe; fifteen for London; six for Gosport, another transshipment port for rice; three for Bristol; and one each for Falmouth, Liverpool, and Portsmouth.[69] While the sample is small, these ships carried more than three-quarters of the indigo imported into England from South Carolina that year. Eleven of the London-bound ships carried indigo, in ninety-four separate consignments from Carolinian planters and merchants containing 293,828 pounds of the dye—79 percent of the total 372,900 pounds imported into England from South Carolina in 1764.[70] Of the total indigo captured in the manifests, some 93 percent was consigned to just six firms: John Beswicke & Co., 37.5 percent of the total; Sarah Nickleson & Co., 15.6 percent; Charles Ogilvie, 10.8 percent; John Nutt, 10.2 percent; Grubb & Watson, 9.7 percent; and Charles Crokatt, 7.1 percent. These importers sold it in London to specialist dyers or to wholesale grocers in exchange for cash and exportable goods.[71]

The domination of London's indigo imports by a small number of merchants is further evidence that London's Carolina trade was concentrated in fewer hands than other branches of London's Atlantic trade were.

Suspicions in South Carolina of London business practices were echoed by verdicts on the character traits of the capital's principal Carolina merchants. John Nutt was regarded by one Charles Town correspondent as "a right down London merchant" who had "as much religion in him as merchants of London in general have."[72] Even trusted correspondents were felt to pose corrupting influences to the many Carolinian youths sent for education in England. Henry Laurens declined to ask his London "trading Friends" to receive his seven-year-old son Henry Jr. when he went to be schooled in London in 1771: "I dread their Kindness to our Youth, because of the Effects of such Kindness, which are commonly loose manners and morals, waste of Time and very idle Expences."[73] He repeated the point in several letters to friends, associating the "superabundant Kindnesses" of "City Friends and Acquaintances" with the laxity and immorality that had "so often proved pernicious to our Carolina Youth."[74]

"Join to quench the growing Evil"

Ongoing commercial activism by London's Carolina merchants during the late 1760s and early 1770s did little to mitigate the growing skepticism of their business practices. With support from a number of the traders, Charles Garth asked Parliament in 1767 to lift temporarily the duty on rice imported into Britain. Duties on imported foodstuffs were designed to protect domestic cereal producers, but a poor harvest in Britain the previous year had raised cereal prices and made rice a valuable dietary substitute. To increase supplies of provisions and to lower their cost, Parliament agreed to suspend the duty in May 1767 and extended the suspension the following year.[75] In February 1770 eighteen of the capital's Carolina traders petitioned Parliament to reduce the rice import duty permanently. Their appeal again carefully fused domestic and colonial interests with fiscal, commercial, and strategic concerns. The increase in rice imports and consumption in Britain that would result from the measure would, they argued, compensate for the lower duties, while the greater availability and lower price of the grain would help the poor. The petitioners further emphasized the benefits of an expanded trade to British shipping, the economic benefits for the colonies, and the greater demand for British manufactures this would therefore bring.[76] The same month fifteen of London's Carolina traders joined Charles Garth in successfully appealing for another seven-year extension to the indigo bounty.[77] In both cases Garth relayed the merchant activism to the Committee of Correspondence.[78]

London's Carolina traders were continuing to prove assiduous lobbyists on commercial issues where metropolitan and colonial interests were closely aligned. Higher exports of rice from South Carolina resulting from the liberalization

Table 6: Destinations of Indigo Exported from Charleston, 1758–72

Destinations

	London		Bristol		#3 British port			Other British ports		All others		All points	Total exported from SC
	lbs. (000s)	% of exports	lbs. (000s)	% of exports	name	lbs. (000s)	% of exports	lbs. (000s)	% of exports	lbs. (000s)	% of exports	lbs. (000s)	lbs. (000s)
1758	397.1	71	56.7	10	L'pool	75.1	13	33.9	6	-	-	562.9	
1759	508.1	73	123.6	18	Chester	43.1	6	19.8	3	-	-	694.7	
1760	439.7	88	32.1	6	L'pool	7.9	2	18.4	4	-	-	498.2	
1762	252.1	96	7.7	3	Dundee	1.7	1	0.8	-	-	-	262.3	
1763	426.8	93	25.0	5	Cowes	5.5	1	1.7	-	0	0	459.0	
Mean yrs. 1760–64													423.0
1766	404.4	81	53.4	11	Leith	9.1	2	15.5	3	18.4	4	500.8	
1768												478.0	
1769												361.6	
Mean yrs. 1765–69													432.1
1770												528.4	
1771												434.8	
1772												662.7	
Mean yrs. 1770–72													639.9

Source: Clowse, *Measuring Charleston's Overseas Commerce*, 70–71, table B-41.

Note: The table shows the proportionate share of Carolina indigo imports between British ports in the four years during the 1760s—1760, 1762, 1763, and 1766—for which statistics survive. In these years 88 percent of South Carolina's indigo exports went to London in 1760, 96 percent in 1762, 93 percent in 1763, and 81 percent in 1766.

Table 7: London Traders' Share of Indigo Exports, January–March 1764

Ship	Date of clearing Charles Town (1764)	No. of consignments	Trader to whom indigo consigned (lbs.)							
			John Beswicke	Sarah Nickleson	Charles Ogilvie	John Nutt	Grubb & Watson	Charles Crokatt	Others	TOTAL
Union	6 Jan.	12	15,902	1,590	-	379	-	1,454	4,144	23,469
Prince of Wales	7 Jan.	3	15,763	-	-	1,698	-	-	-	17,461
Little Carpenter	24 Jan.	12	8,224	-	-	2,631	14,991	676	4,225	30,747
Minerva	31 Jan.	9	-	19,752	-	1,539	-	2,362	-	23,653
Prince George	13 Feb.	3	1,903	-	-	-	-	6,764	-	8,667
Fortune	[undated] Feb.	6	12,495	-	-	892	-	3,238	566	17,191
America	18 Feb.	16	51,630	-	1,232	4,422	-	2,873	1,153	61,310
Nancy	24 Feb.	12	-	-	29,889	12,094	9,115	2,566	2,902	56,566
Little William	10 Mar.	4	1,083	-	630	-	-	2,997	1,562	6,272
Heart of Oak	29 Mar.	16	844	24,401	-	6,406	4,272	3,864	6,243	46,030
Black Prince	31 Mar.	1	2,462	-	-	-	-	-	-	2,462
Total consignments		94								
Individual total (lbs.)			110,306	45,743	31,751	30,061	28,378	26,794	20,795	293,828
% of total indigo imported			37.54	15.57	10.8	10.23	9.66	9.12	7.08	100

Source: Charles Town Naval Office, ships' manifests, January–March 1764, CO5/511/2–58, National Archives, London.

of the British market, for example, promised financial rewards for planters and for traders on either side of the Atlantic, as well as dietary benefits for Britain's hungry poor. As Laurens foresaw the suspension of the rice import duty in 1767, "the Carolina Planter will get an advanced price of all the saving of Duty, upon his Rice" while, taking a rather idealistic and romantic view of English attitudes toward the American colonies, he wrote that the "English Farmer & Labourer will not get a grain of Rice extraordinary nor one farthing the cheaper, but he will have the satisfaction of paying to America, what otherwise he would have contributed to the Revenue."[79]

In their hopes that London merchants would take action on more contentious political issues—hopes perhaps raised by the merchants' responses to the Stamp and Mutiny Acts—Carolinians would be disappointed, however. The London merchants' ambivalence in the face of the British government's clampdown on South Carolina's coastal shipping is a case in point. Historians have long identified the tightening of customs administration in Charles Town in the mid-1760s as a signal moment in radicalizing the town's merchants and planters.[80] Customs officials had earlier turned a blind eye when coastal vessels moved between Charles Town and lowcountry plantations without having completed all the necessary paperwork. From 1765 they began prosecuting this technical breach of the Navigation Acts, seizing vessels and fining their owners. This represented a direct challenge to the autonomy of the colony's planters and traders—an imperial intrusion into hitherto routine local practice. Although Charles Garth raised the matter with the Board of Trade and the British Treasury, British merchants failed to back up his protests, suggesting a lack of interest in essentially internal Carolinian matters and a growing divergence with their counterparts in Charles Town. Had London traders sought to persuade the government to intervene, they might have again demonstrated the efficacy of merchant lobbying as a means of representing and addressing colonial grievances and sent a renewed signal of their own commitment to South Carolina; the absence of such efforts compounded their correspondents' grievances.[81]

Amid widespread fury in Charles Town over alleged racketeering and venality by customs collectors in applying the laws, Henry Laurens felt particularly victimized. Three of his coastal vessels were impounded in 1767 and 1768 by the vice admiralty court, first introduced to America in 1764 to render verdicts on alleged breaches of customs regulations and, most controversially, presided over by a judge without a jury. Besides attacking British officialdom in the town's courts and press and in pamphlets that were distributed throughout the colonies, Laurens tried to galvanize transatlantic unity among merchants in both Charles Town and Britain. He stressed that not only did the onerous regulations and their zealous enforcement put his own business concerns at stake, but so too they threatened cross-sectional interests within South Carolina and in its transatlantic trade, including the local merchants whose costs were raised and exchanges interrupted, the planters whose crops were hindered from reaching markets, the tradesmen whose services oiled the wheels of commerce, and by implication, the Carolina merchants in Britain who would suffer higher knock-on costs.

Laurens's efforts show again how Carolinians understood the role of their metropolitan correspondents. Besides their commercial activity, London's Carolina merchants had particular access to and influence with government. Using this access and influence was both their responsibility to their colonial partners and in their own personal interest. After the seizure of his vessel *Ann* in June 1768, Laurens encouraged his connections in London to pursue his case through political and legal avenues. Spelling out his aspirations for their advocacy, he hoped the case would "not be call'd Mr. Laurens's but the Case of the British Merchants trading to America in the Case of the Ship *Ann*."[82] To galvanize the support of Britain's American traders, Laurens sent copies of the vice admiralty court's proceedings to merchants in London and Bristol, "& to many great Personages at the West End of that Great City [Westminster]." He explained, "We hope that the Merchants in England in general will stir up their Friends in Parliament to reconsider some Measures lately established for the Regulation of the American Trade, which otherwise will in all probability become the Ruin and destruction of that Trade. When I say We, I mean the principal Merchants as well as almost every individual sensible Person in this Town."[83]

Laurens devoted much time in 1769 to orchestrating a British lobby against both the cause and the effect of the abuses by Charles Town's customs officials and the vice admiralty court. Sending copies of the court proceedings against him to the London merchant Richard Grubb, he was sure that Grubb would agree that "such proceedings of Tyrannical, Insidious, Perjured, and Temporizing Officers ought to be made Public. I make no doubt of your consulting with some of your Brother Merchants upon the most effectual means to make them so; and that you will at least put one or both the papers into the hands of some of Your *honest* acquaintance at t'other end of the Town [MPs at Westminster]."[84] His letters repeatedly stressed the consonance of Carolinian and British commercial interests in opposing the courts and their corruption, and he urged coordinated action. "Wise and prudent therefore (in my humble opinion) would it be for Merchants on both sides of the Water to exert their utmost abilities to bring some Amendments in, if not a total abolition of, the modern Jurisdiction of that Court [vice admiralty court] before it be so well established as to stare them in the face with prescription," Laurens proposed to the slave traders Ross & Mill.[85] Writing to the Liverpool slave trader John Tarleton, he highlighted the danger posed to British traders of overpowerful officialdom in the colonies: "the danger of Vesting any one Man with exorbitant Powers, which danger I think you Gentlemen in Great Britain trading to this part of the World are as much exposed to as we who reside here." Again the lobbying of British merchants—not just those in London but also those in regional ports—would be pivotal: "We shall feel the dreadful effects of it, if you do not join to quench the growing Evil."[86] Laurens's calls for British merchants to make a concerted campaign against the depredations of the vice admiralty court fell on deaf ears, however. There is no evidence that Carolina traders, whether in London, Bristol, or Liverpool, petitioned on the matter. Their passivity stood in stark contrast to the unanimous resolve among Charles Town's merchants, 111 of whom signed a letter to Charles Garth protesting against the behavior of the port's customs collector.[87]

The failure of British merchants to agitate against the vice admiralty court's abuses was matched by their relative quietude on the Townshend Duties. Introduced by the British government in 1767 alongside changes to American customs and courts, the Revenue Act imposed new duties on colonial imports of tea, glass, lead, paints, and paper. London's Carolina merchants reacted passively to the new duties—known as the Townshend Duties because of their introduction by Chancellor of the Exchequer Charles Townshend—as did their counterparts in other branches of North American trade. The contrast with the merchants' earlier activism against the Stamp Act was pronounced. Not until 1770, when a coordinated effort in the colonies to force the government to withdraw the duties had led to a campaign for the nonimportation of British goods, did London's North America merchants petition Parliament for the Townshend Duties to be revoked. Even then they made it clear that the merchants were motivated by commercial factors, rather than any constitutional opposition to Parliament taxing the colonies. Charles Garth reported to the Committee of Correspondence in February 1770 that a merchant petition against the duties was in the offing, and a month later he described how it was presented to Parliament. By this point, however, Lord North's government had already made clear its intention to repeal the duties, with the exception of the duty on tea, highlighting the belatedness and timidity of the London merchants' petitioning efforts.[88]

Without pressing economic grounds to intervene in the disputes surrounding the customs and the vice admiralty courts or, until nonimportation began to bite, against the Townshend Duties, British merchants showed their reluctance to jeopardize their access to government by protesting on matters of political principle and colonial rights. They had cultivated their relations with government over time, facilitating lobbying on the economic issues that did matter greatly to them, such as the regulation of the rice and indigo trades. In his letters to the Committee of Correspondence in early 1770, Garth signaled where the merchants' foremost concerns lay by devoting far more words to their commercial lobbying than to their involvement in the petitioning against the Townshend Duties. For the London merchants, the storm over the vice admiralty courts presented no immediate or direct threat to their commercial interests; for all Laurens's apocalyptic rhetoric, it was hard for them to envisage closer regulation of intercoastal shipping and spats between Charles Town traders and imperial officialdom seriously threatening Atlantic trade as a whole. Moreover, the vice admiralty courts dispute was rooted in political controversy. It had its basis in the British government's attempts to enforce the Navigation Acts more stringently and raise revenue in the colonies—attempts that in Charles Town had become suffused with personal intrigue and charges of corruption, venality, and scapegoating. If Britain's merchants had lobbied the government on the matter, it would have implied a critique of imperial policy and unwarranted interference beyond their business interests. They were not willing to risk their role and influence as commercial interlocutors on matters of political principle, especially where these matters seemed to have little bearing on their own trade.

Despite their advocacy on commercial matters such as rice import duties and the indigo bounty, Britain's Carolina merchants were consistently reluctant to intervene in the political disputes of the late 1760s and early 1770s. Their resistance to the Stamp Act had been motivated by the direct threat that it, or rather the Carolinian response of boycotts and obstructionism, posed to their trade. Though their opposition was welcomed in Charles Town, it implicitly revealed the causal link between commercial interest and political mobilization. The contrast between the British merchants' willingness to lobby on commercial issues and their hesitancy on political issues as Anglo-American relations deteriorated emphasized this link. British traders' slowness to take up the cudgels on the Townshend Duties until threatened by the economic sanction of nonimportation, together with their apparent ambivalence toward the alleged abuses of the customs commissioners and vice admiralty courts, suggested a divergence of political interest with their Charles Town trading partners. Growing suspicion of London business practices and resentment at the egregious profits the capital's merchants were seen to be making from the trade, at the same time that they were exerting ever greater credit-based control over their trading partners in South Carolina, fed Carolinians' burgeoning sense of inequality within the trade and revealed to them a divergence of interest with their counterparts in Britain. The escalating political tensions of 1773 and 1774 would expose these fault lines.

"I don't know that we have a Zealous friend or Advocate among the Merchants"

By 1774 nearly all of London's Carolina merchants were regarded as politically hostile toward the American colonies. Living in London as he oversaw his sons' European education, Henry Laurens assessed those merchants' politics firsthand. He reflected to his brother, "I don't know that we have a Zealous friend or Advocate among the Merchants in our Walk [Carolina walk of the Royal Exchange], one or two excepted."[89] Laurens was not alone: his words were echoed by other Americans in London. In February 1775 Josiah Quincy Jr., a young Bostonian whose travels took him to both Charles Town and London in the early 1770s, noted just eleven London merchants whom he did not consider "bitter enemies" of America. The capital's Carolina merchants were implicated by their absence: none figured among the eleven non-enemies on Quincy's list.[90] The same month the radical Virginian William Lee, then living in London, identified the leading Carolina merchants John Nutt and Christopher Rolleston as particular foes to the colonies. They were men, he wrote, who "should be stigmatized in America."[91]

The Carolina merchants in the capital who were identified as enemies of the colonies did not have the direct personal connections to South Carolina that a previous generation of London's Carolina traders had. Up to the early 1760s the likes of James Crokatt, John Beswicke, John Nickleson, Richard Shubrick, and Samuel Wragg had spent formative spells in South Carolina, building their businesses and immersing themselves in the colony's commercial and public life. As former residents, they could claim a natural sympathy with South Carolina, with their landholdings in the colony reinforcing their personal and commercial attachments. By the mid-1760s all these figures had left the trade. Wragg died in 1749 and Nickleson in 1754, leaving his commerce to be continued by his wife, Sarah, and her new business partner, Isaac King. John Beswicke died in 1764 and was succeeded in trade by his nephews, William Greenwood and William Higginson. Richard Shubrick seems to have left his trade in the hands of his son, also Richard, after his death in 1765. James Crokatt retired from trade in about 1760. His son Charles and son-in-law John Nutt took on much of his trade, and he allowed his son to call his firm James & Charles Crokatt to lend it his personal prestige. Charles Crokatt lacked his father's commercial acumen, however. Amid a number of misguided commercial ventures and a disastrous attempt to run for Parliament, his business foundered. Nutt would be Crokatt's principal legatee in trade, inheriting many of his father-in-law's connections in Charles Town.[92]

James Crokatt retired largely to Luxborough, his country estate in Essex, spending just Wednesdays and Thursdays in London by the mid-1760s. With the same "improving" spirit with which he had promoted diversification in South Carolina, at Luxborough he adopted the lifestyle and interests of an English gentleman farmer, growing wheat, beans, potatoes, and fodder for his horses and cattle; building dams on the local river for irrigation canals; and encouraging like-minded agricultural innovators to visit his estate to see his trials of a new drill plough.[93] As his focus on domestic agriculture increased, Crokatt began to wind down his investments in South Carolina as he sought to simplify his portfolio of investments. He did so with customary assiduity, castigating his agent in the colony for minor errors in his accounts and taking the unusual step of bypassing him altogether to harass his debtors in Charles Town personally. "You should have left this Affair intirely to myself, or any other," the agent replied in exasperation, "as you cannot be a judge of people's circumstances here so well as me."[94] Some of his Charles Town properties sold quickly; intractable tenants and the extensive repairs needed in several houses made it harder to dispose of others.

South Carolina continued to figure in Crokatt's thoughts. As late as 1770 he joined fellow London Carolina merchants in donating to a fund for the bells at St. Michael's Church in Charles Town. Coming after his retirement from commerce, it seems to have been a donation motivated by altruism rather than commercial expedience.[95] In 1772 he was visited by Henry Laurens, his former apprentice, who was by then largely retired from Atlantic trade and visiting Europe to supervise his sons' education.[96] Two men who had been at the forefront of South Carolina's mid-century transatlantic trade, had grown rich on it, and had epitomized the colony's mid-century Atlantic connections once again came face-to-face. Any resentment from Crokatt's failure to offer Laurens a place in his business twenty-five years earlier had long since passed. For his part, Laurens reflected that Crokatt had been "misguided" by the other apprentices also seeking partnership. His former mentor was contrite: "with great affection pressing my hand in his, [Crokatt] declared he was Sensible he had used me very Ill," Laurens recalled, "& that he Should never forgive himself."[97] Laurens's moving report of the encounter suggested a mellowing in Crokatt's notoriously brusque demeanor. More symbolically, their meeting embodied the personal and commercial bonds that had yoked the colony and the mother country together but which by the early 1770s were being increasingly tested by political and ideological divergences. Crokatt would not live to see the final rupture between South Carolina and Great Britain. His death in March 1777, "in the 76th year of his age," was reported widely in the London press.[98] Perhaps more than any other figure, he had cultivated and capitalized on the commercial potential of the mid-century Carolina trade. His commercial acuity had propelled him to the forefront of trade, first in Charles Town and then in London.

For the most part, the leading Carolina merchants in London from the mid-1760s had not cut their teeth in South Carolina in the same way as had their forebears in business such as Crokatt. The capital, not Charles Town, had been their commercial proving ground. Cousins William Greenwood and William Higginson had trained in London with their uncle John Beswicke. Originally from Yorkshire in northern England, John Nutt had not had a colonial apprenticeship; instead his trade advanced through his family connection in the capital to James Crokatt. The younger Richard Shubrick and Charles Crokatt had both been born in South Carolina but had moved to London before the age of ten and spent their adult lives in and around the capital.

There were exceptions. Benjamin Stead had relocated his business from Charles Town in 1759 and continued as an export-import merchant in London's Carolina trade until the American Revolution. He was noted for his pro-American sympathies and was regarded by Laurens as "without Exception" one of the "best men in our Carolina Trade."[99] Charles Ogilvie, with his peripatetic trading and plantation-building career, was in London in the early 1770s. Though he would suffer after 1783 for his wavering political affiliations during the Revolutionary

War, before the outbreak of war he was not singled out as being notably hostile to America. Instead, and showing a further link between commercial experience in South Carolina and pro-American sympathies, Ogilvie was one of only four London merchants involved in trade to South Carolina to petition the king in October 1775 urging conciliation with the American colonies. The others were Benjamin Stead; Edward Bridgen, well known for his pro-American views; and Joseph Nicholson, a former Charles Town merchant who had relocated to London in 1764.[100] But traders such as Stead and Ogilvie were in a minority. Overall, by the eve of the Revolutionary War, London's Carolina merchants matched their counterparts in other branches of the capital's North American trade more closely than ever before—merchants who had been trained and spent their whole careers in the capital. As such they lacked the personal bonds, experiences, and sympathies toward South Carolina that had been the hallmark of their leading predecessors' careers.

John Nutt was one of the new generation of London's Carolina traders to be identified as both a profiteer from the trade and an implacable opponent to America. Although he sat on merchant committees that drafted pro-American petitions before the war, this contradiction was less paradoxical than it seems.[101] London's largest Carolina merchants, having proffered the most liberal credit to South Carolina before the war—both a mark of their commercial scale and a means of cementing their share of the market—were the most overextended in the colony. They were well aware of this. Typifying the unease, Nutt complained in January 1774 to a Savannah partnership indebted to him for goods imported on credit that their "two Store accounts are now very large and embarrassing."[102] His fellow London traders Graham & Clark sought to confine their trade to Georgia to a smaller and more reliable circle, having been similar victims of overexposure. Writing to acknowledge their reluctance to take on any business with his new partnership, the Savannah merchant James Habersham observed that they were "contracting until you have wound up your Affairs to a Narrower Compass, and got them in the hands of punctual Correspondents."[103] With extensive monies owed them in South Carolina and Georgia, Nutt and his counterparts had good reason to urge conciliation: they foresaw that a breakdown of Anglo-American relations would leave them with uncollectible and crippling debts in South Carolina. But among Charlestonians increasingly quick to perceive conspiracy between British merchants and the British government, the merchants' actions spoke louder than their conciliatory words. Once-routine transactions took on new, pernicious dimensions.

"Parties in the attempt against us"

Nutt's involvement in the arrival of East India Company tea in Charles Town in December 1773 earned him particular and widespread obloquy in South Carolina. Together with Greenwood & Higginson, Nutt had written to the East India

Company earlier in the year to propose merchants in Charles Town who might receive and market the company's tea and for whom he would be guarantor. Nutt nominated Roger Smith, a major trader in the town; Greenwood & Higginson put forward their associates Andrew Lord and William & George Ancrum and even provided a ship to carry the tea to Charles Town. For those in the colony seeking confirmation of metropolitan conspiracy, the ship, the *London*, was appropriately named.[104] The tea arrived in Charles Town on 2 December to a reception that echoed the conflagrations in New York, in Philadelphia, and most momentously, in Boston. With tea invoked across the colonies as a symbol of unwarranted British taxation, Parliament's legislative tyranny, and the East India Company's pernicious influence, Charles Town residents were encouraged to make an example of the consignment. Newspapers reprinted anti-tea polemics from the Philadelphia and Boston press and, two days before the tea's arrival, ominously relayed reports from New York of the vilification and burning in effigy of the city's tea commissioner William Kelley.

New York's example gave the words of "Junius Brutus," writing in the *South Carolina Gazette*, extra weight: "As to the gentlemen who, it is said are appointed *commissioners* to receive and distribute the *Stampt Tea*, they are so well known among us," he warned, "that scarce a single inhabitant can be persuaded to believe, they will descend to an acceptance of the detestable consequences."[105] After widespread debate in Charles Town as to how best to respond, the town's residents behaved with more restraint than their counterparts further north. The nominated tea commissioners required little persuasion in deciding to decline the consignments. The *London* was prevented from unloading its cargo. "In imitation of the northern towns, declarations were made that it should not be landed" was Governor William Bull's measured report on the dispute to the Earl of Dartmouth, secretary of state for the colonies. Later in December the 257 chests of tea on board were taken ashore without public affray and impounded in the basement of the town's Exchange. "There never was an instance here," the *Gazette* observed proudly of Charles Town's considered and peaceful resolution of the problem, "of so great a Number of Packages, being taken out of any Vessel, and thus disposed of, in so short a Time . . . the People, though not pleased with seeing it landed at all, were perfectly quiet."[106]

For Ralph Izard, a scion of one of the lowcountry's oldest and wealthiest planter families, the consignment of the tea to Charles Town demonstrated how commerce and politics were indivisible in Britain's oppression of her American colonies. Writing from Europe, where he spent much of the 1770s, to Thomas Lynch, who was representing South Carolina at the Continental Congress in Philadelphia, Izard charged that "the tea, which has occasioned so much trouble, would never have been sent to America, had not many of these gentlemen [London's American traders] offered themselves as security for it . . . the merchants, who ought to have been the natural guardians of the interests of America, submitted to the infamy of becoming parties in the attempt against us."[107] The yoking of trade and politics as combined instruments in oppressing America legitimated commercial boycotts in return as means of political resistance. Izard advocated targeted boycotts of individual merchants in London. These would serve as a powerful demonstration of Carolinian grievances and a means of punishing those felt to be particularly responsible for the commercial-political oppression of the colony. He explained that "every friend to America, ought solemnly to engage to have no more dealings with them [the consigners of the tea]. There is no doubt, but our present unhappy situation, is in a great measure owing to them. One of them [Nutt], I know, owes his existence to the gentlemen of Carolina; and when a man repays favors, with such infamous ingratitude, it is not only weak, but criminal to support him. There is a ridiculous notion prop-agated, that he sells indigo better than other people. This I cannot believe; but were it true, it is a very insufficient reason why he should be placed in a state of princely magnificence, and by that means, be the better enabled to exercise with credit and authority, his enmity against us."[108]

Made in October 1774, Izard's demand for a special boycott of Nutt and Greenwood & Higginson for their role in exporting the tea to Charles Town was overtaken by events. Within weeks of his call, a nonimportation campaign came into effect across the colonies, reviving the strategy adopted in response to the Stamp Act in 1765–66 and the Townshend Duties in 1768–70. Nonimportation placed a blanket ban on imports from British merchants, affecting all traders equally, regardless of whether they were perceived to be sympathetic or im-placably hostile to the colonies. Selective retaliation would be deferred until af-ter American independence.[109] Besides his far-sightedness in regard to targeted boycotts, Izard's critique of London's Carolina trade is revealing in its analysis of the terms of trade and the political connotations that the trade had assumed. Credit—the lifeblood of Anglo-Carolinian commerce—had come to represent commercial repression and, through it, colonial subservience. According to Izard, who was hardly a political radical, Nutt's "princely magnificence," the com-mercial standing he owed entirely to Carolinian customers, and his extension of credit were entwined, allowing him to retain a mercantile "hold" over the colony. By the eve of the American Revolution, commercial subservience had come to represent in microcosm the imperial control against which Charlestonians in-creasingly chafed. London's traders became associated with hostile government policy and were seen as agents in delivering it. Moreover, for the many residents in South Carolina—from Atlantic traders to urban artisans—who were tied into the webs of credit emanating from London traders such as Nutt, this control was not a matter of abstract political philosophy but a personal daily experience.

There is little evidence that London's Carolina merchants actively took po-litical stances that merited the censure directed toward them. Instead, and in marked contrast to their commercial activity, which was viewed by Carolinian observers as inherently oppressive by the mid-1770s, it was the traders' political inactivity until at least late 1774 that heightened Carolinian suspicions.[110] Quietude was interpreted as acquiescence in or tacit approval of ministerial policy, particularly given the stark contrast with the vigorous Stamp Act repeal campaign mounted by London merchants in 1765–66. When the British government responded to the Boston Tea Party and other colonial resistance by proposing the Coercive Acts—or "Intolerable Acts" to many in America—in the first months of 1774, it was London's community of expatriate Americans, rather than the capital's American traders, who stepped up to campaign against the proposals. Most controversially, the punitive acts set out to close the port of Boston until recompense was made for the destroyed tea, to subject Massachusetts to the direct control of the British government, and to transfer the trials of British officials from Massachusetts to Great Britain or elsewhere. Henry Laurens attended a large meeting at London's Thatched House tavern—a regular haunt of the government's opponents—on 24 March 1774. Laurens expected it to be "a large Meating of Merchants & other[s] . . . to petition Parliament to forbear or at least Suspend Such dangerous Severity until the Supposed offenders have been called to answer for their Conduct." British merchants trading to New England would support the petition, he believed, since they stood to lose the one hundred thousand to two hundred thousand pounds they had advanced in credit to Bostonians, "for when all the priveledges of Trade are taken from that Town & Country, there will be no means . . . for paying old Debts, & all America will take the Alarm."[111]

Laurens was prescient, but in a different way than he imagined. After the war many British merchants would be forced to write off thousands of pounds of debts in America. In the immediate term, however, the threat of the losses that would be incurred by the closure of Boston's port did not trigger any concerted response from London merchants against the coercive legislation. How many merchants attended the Thatched House tavern meeting is unknown, but the petitions to Parliament that emerged from the meeting gave an indication. Rather than being drawn up by the merchants whom Laurens had expected to be in the vanguard, the petitions were instead composed by "several Natives of North America." Reflecting the profound disquiet that the Boston Tea Party had caused within London's commercial sector, city merchants were conspicuously reluctant even to sign the petitions.[112] While South Carolina was more heavily represented among the petitions' signatories than any other colony, this was largely because of the number of young Carolinians being educated in London. The *South Carolina Gazette* proudly reported that "of the Twenty-nine Gentlemen who dared to inscribe their Names to the Petitions presented to both Houses of Parliament, against *the Boston Port Bill*, there are no less than *eleven* Natives of *this* Province," whom it went on to name.[113] Sixteen of the thirty-one signatories to a petition to the king protesting against the coercive legislation, drawn up on 31 March 1774, were South Carolinians.[114] Having failed in their opposition to the Boston Port Act in March, "several Natives of North America" petitioned the House of Lords on 11 May against the Massachusetts government and administration of justice bills then before Parliament. Numbering fifteen of the thirty signatories, South Carolinians were once more to the fore in a petition that again conspicuously lacked the support of British merchants.[115] At the moment when merchant advocacy and interaction with the British state were most wanted, they failed to materialize.

Behind the British merchants' ambivalence was an unwillingness to take a stand against the Coercive Acts while American resistance was couched in ideological or constitutional terms. Before the onset of nonimportation later in 1774 and in the absence of targeted boycotts against specific merchants, there were simply no sufficiently compelling economic grounds for them to oppose government policy.[116] The quietude of London's Carolina merchants, none of whom either signed any of the petitions or participated in the campaigning in 1774, confirmed the earlier suspicions that Laurens and others had about their true loyalties. Ralph Izard typified the views of many when he summed up merchants' complaisance or—more sinisterly—their acquiescence in British government policy. "The merchants, notwithstanding the situation of affairs in America, dreadfully alarming as they are," he complained, "sit perfectly satisfied and contented."[117]

Only six months later, in January 1775, with the looming threat of a total dislocation of Anglo-American trade, did London's North America merchants meet to discuss a collective response to the Coercive Acts. Nonimportation in the thirteen colonies had begun the previous month. Nonexportation, a far more worrying prospect for British traders with sizable debts in America since it would prevent them from receiving produce in payment for debts owed to them, was due to take effect in September 1775. A committee was formed, comprising the leading merchants in each branch of London's American trade, to prepare a petition alerting Parliament to the "alarming State" of the trade. Including merchants with a spectrum of views on the American crisis, the committee was ostensibly a remarkable cross-sectional grouping. South Carolina's representatives appeared to epitomize this. The colony's five members were William Greenwood, John Nutt, and Christopher Rolleston—each reputedly hostile to colonial interests; the moderate William Baker Jr.; and incongruously, the Virginia native and pro-American firebrand William Lee.[118]

To Carolinians, however, the four petitions addressed by London's merchants to Parliament and then to the king between January and March 1775 were too little too late. The merchant petitioning, Izard told Thomas Lynch, was incoherent, "ill-timed and will prove ineffectual."[119] The merchants' failure to make common cause with the protests of expatriate Americans in London reflected their divergent interests: while the expatriates saw profound ideological and political issues at stake, most merchants would protest government policy only on economic grounds.[120] For Izard, the lack of solidarity not only undermined the effectiveness of any petitioning—which was necessarily weakened when undertaken by separate groups—but also once again revealed that merchant criticism of government policy was guided purely by self-interest. "The truth is," he reported to Lynch, "they are, in general, puffed up with pride and unmindful of the interest of their employers."[121] His choice of words betrayed a deeper conception of merchant agency and Atlantic political economy: the "employers" were American colonists. It was to this group that London's Carolina merchants—and by implication their peers in all the North American trades—owed their eminence and their fortunes; because of this, they should also owe them their allegiance. For Izard and other Carolinian observers, however, the reverse had been true. London's Carolina traders had profited unduly from their trade, finagled their correspondents with sharp business practices, and lured and then oppressed them with credit. When their agency was most required, they treated their "employers" with contempt. As Carolinians took increasing pride in their ability to harness their environment to productive ends, supplying the commodities on which London's traders relied, their understanding of their relationship to their metropolitan counterparts changed. No longer was South Carolina an outpost in the Atlantic wilderness, and Carolinians no longer were nor should be the dependent partners in the imperial-colonial relationship. Their reliance on the agency of merchants in Britain was invalidated. A system of representing colonial interests and grievances that had served their purposes in a time of political tranquillity was exposed by imperial crisis as being fundamentally untenable and counterproductive.

CHAPTER FIVE

THE VOYAGE OF THE *LORD NORTH*

American Independence, Anglo-Carolinian Trade, and Unfinished Business

In December 1782 the final British troops withdrew from Charleston at the end of the Revolutionary War.[1] The evacuation brought to an end the British forces' two-and-a-half-year-long and increasingly beleaguered hold on the town. Memories of the occupation and the savage fighting that characterized the war in South Carolina were still fresh in April 1783 when the five-hundred-ton ship *Lord North* arrived at the entrance to Charleston harbor. One of the largest vessels in Atlantic trade and named after the British prime minister whose policies had led Britain and America to war, its nomenclature could almost have been calculated to inflame tension in the port. It duly did. "Any idea of our present Secretary of State was so obnoxious to the Americans," a London newspaper reported, "that they insisted the ship should either change its name or depart without breaking bulk." Commercial priorities won out. "The captain was obliged to new christen his ship before he was suffered to land his cargo," the report went on. The *Lord North* duly became the *Financier*. Thus renamed, it unloaded its goods and took on a cargo of rice, indigo, and tobacco for its return voyage to London.[2]

The *Lord North* incident represents postwar Anglo-American rapprochement in microcosm. First, the ship's arrival in Charleston so soon after American independence highlights the rapid resumption of trade between the newly independent United States and Great Britain. Second, for many in Charleston the vessel's unsubtle nomenclature revealed a deeper truth: the persistence of American subservience in Atlantic commerce. For them, the *Lord North* encapsulated British arrogance, its name a symbolic reassertion of commercial control. Third, the forced renaming of the ship reflects an aspect of postwar Anglo-Carolinian commerce that is often overlooked. British shipping and merchants continued to dominate South Carolina's overseas trade, but Charlestonians found subtle ways to reshape their commerce. If through the 1780s the structural conditions of trade could not be overturned, the individual decisions Charlestonians made in their choice of trading partners reveal their greater influence in postwar trade than they appreciated or historians have credited them with. Based on prewar and wartime interactions, these choices also cast light back onto Anglo-Carolinian commerce and politics before the American Revolution.[3]

After the war Britain once again became the biggest market for South Carolina's exports and the largest supplier of its imports. British merchants satisfied the postwar surge in consumer demand, in particular for tools, machinery, and African slaves, as Carolinians rushed to restock plantations ravaged by war and restart agricultural production. South Carolina had witnessed some of the most vicious fighting in the whole of America, with estates destroyed and some thirty thousand slaves leaving the state between 1775 and 1782. As planters sought to rebuild their plantation labor forces, in the four years after 1783 the slave trade to Charleston exceeded even its former levels. Some 8,200 slaves were brought into Charleston between 1783 and 1787, most on British ships. French and Dutch merchants—although in theory well-placed to capitalize on their countries' wartime alliances with the United States—were unable to compete with the liberal credit extended by their British rivals or, in consumable goods, with the quality and low prices the British could offer. The swift resumption of trade with Britain and the volume it reached within half a decade of the end of the war are striking. In London the Carolina trade remained a specialist field of commerce, and there remained a dedicated Carolina "walk" at the Royal Exchange until at least the mid-1790s.[4]

Despite the ravages of war and South Carolina's much-diminished capacity to produce rice and indigo, its prewar mainstays, trade between the new state and Britain soon reached impressive volumes (table 8). Between 1784 and 1791 the value of goods imported into South Carolina from England averaged £328,253 per year, against £363,037 between 1768 and 1774, excluding the nonimportation year of 1770.[5] However, the apparent return of South Carolina's overseas trade to levels approaching the antebellum status quo disguised major upheavals within the trade. Structural continuities in the types of products exported and the goods imported, in their origins and destinations, and in their approximate volumes masked pronounced discontinuities in the personnel who conducted the trade. The wartime hiatus in trade led several of London's Carolina merchants to withdraw from Atlantic commerce. Retirements, terminations of partnerships, and the loss of trusted correspondents on the other side of the Atlantic proved powerful deterrents to resuming trade. Huge commercial losses forced others to quit and to concentrate on pursuing their debts in South Carolina. As important, the creation or renewal of trading connections between Charleston and London was also powerfully influenced by political factors. London trading houses were alternatively spurned or rewarded for their wartime political loyalties.

"The usual intercourse of Commerce be again resumed": London Merchants and Wartime Lobbying

British government in South Carolina had ended—in practice, if not yet formally in name—in September 1775. The last governor, Lord William Campbell, fled from Charleston to a British warship in the harbor, taking with him the last vestiges of royal authority. For nearly five years, until British forces under Sir Henry Clinton recaptured it in May 1780, Charleston would be in American hands. Lawful trade between South Carolina and Great Britain came to an end. Although illicit cargoes made it through to Charleston, often routed through the Caribbean, regular trade was curtailed on both sides of the Atlantic: by American boycotts and embargoes; and by the American Prohibitory Act, passed by Parliament in December 1775 to forbid all trade with the rebellious colonies.

With normal commerce stopped, London's Carolina merchants turned to the British state for remediation. Throughout the Revolutionary War they kept up the political lobbying that had been integral to their prewar business. In particular, they were haunted by the specters of having property in South Carolina seized and being denied the debts owed to them in South Carolina. Those who had extended the greatest credit to the colony before the war—those held by Carolinians as most implacably hostile to America—naturally stood to lose the most and led the way in pressing the government for help. William Greenwood and John Nutt had attempted to forestall the Prohibitory Act that would outlaw trade with the colonies, addressing the Board of Trade in November 1775 on behalf of "the Merchants of London trading to South Carolina and Georgia." Carolinian and Georgian rice imports should, they argued, be excluded from the forthcoming act.[6] An exemption would in theory—and had they been able to circumvent the embargoes by then adopted in America—have enabled them to recoup debts in the region by importing rice in payment. No exemption was made, however. The Prohibitory Act, which not only forbade trade with the colonies but also made American exports legitimate prizes of war, confirmed the Carolina merchants' worst fears.[7]

The merchants were discovering that the power of British political institutions to mediate Anglo-American trade was, for the time being at least, much diminished. London's Carolina traders would confront this new reality time and again in a tireless campaign over the next twenty years to recover their prewar debts. In the immediate term, however, the traders concentrated their efforts on ensuring that these debts received due legal recognition in Britain. Greenwood & Higginson, John Nutt, Richard Shubrick, and Christopher Rolleston were among eighteen signatories to a petition to the secretary of state Lord George Germain in January 1778 urging that American adherence to prewar debts be a stipulation of any reconciliation with the rebellious colonies. The same men, forming a distinct grouping of metropolitan North America merchants, followed this up with a similar petition to the king.[8]

A shift in British military strategy in 1778 offered hope. With a deadlock in the fighting in the northern colonies, British politicians and commanders pinned their hopes for success in the war on what they saw as untapped reservoirs of loyalism in the South. Retaking Georgia and the Carolinas, it was felt, would unleash Loyalist passions and propel the British army victoriously northward.

Table 8: South Carolina–Value of Exports to and Imports from England (£ Sterling), 1768–91

	Exports	Imports	Exports as % of imports	Value of exports to England per capita (£ st.)	Value of imports from England per capita (£ st.)
1768	508,108	289,868	175.3		
1769	387,114	306,600	126.3		
1770	278,907	146,273 [a]	190.1		
1771	420,311	409,169	102.7	3.38 (£3.7s.6d.) [b]	3.29 (£3.5s.8d.) [b]
1772	425,923	449,610	94.7		
1773	456,513	344,859	132.3		
1774	432,302	378,116	114.3		
Total 1768–69, 1771–74	2,630,271	2,178,222		120.8	
Average 1768–69, 1771–74 [c]	438,379	363,037		120.8	
1775	579,549	6,245	n/a		
Total 1768–75	3,488,727	2,330,740	-	149.7	
Average 1768–75	436,091	291,343	-	149.7	
1776	13,668	0	-		
1777	2,234	0	-		
1778	1,074	0	-		

Year				
1779	3,732	0	-	1.44 (£1.8s.8d.)
1780	708	236,941	-	
1781	94,368	330,847	28.5	
1782	14,182	69,743	20.3	
1783	74,589	226,737	32.9	
1784	163,540	442,465	36.9	
1785	212,229	278,389	76.2	
1786	198,454	181,410	109.4	
1787	229,086	281,647	81.3	
1788	258,029	291,429	88.5	
1789	215,890	359,214	60.1	
1790	253,022	359,592	70.4	1.02 (£1.0s.4d.)
1791	230,879	431,880	53.4	
Average 1784–91	220,141	328,253	67.1	
Average 1784–91 as % of average 1768–69, 1771–74	50.2	90.4		

Source: Carter et al., *Historical Statistics*, V, 710–13.

Notes: [a] year of nonimportation agreement
[b] calculated using population figures for 1770
[c] years of nonimportation excluded (average for six years—1768–69, 1771–74)

As British troops prepared for their southern campaign, to begin with the recon-
quest and pacification of Georgia, Lord Germain received a letter from Greenwood & Higginson, Clark & Milligan, and John Nutt. The traders applauded the
plan to "reduce the disaffected people of that Province to a just Sense of their
Duty and Allegiance." They appealed that once Georgia was pacified, they should
be exempted from the Prohibitory Act and allowed to receive produce—albeit,
in deference to political considerations, only from estates owned by British residents or American Loyalists—as recompense for prewar debts in South Carolina
and Georgia.[9] Further petitioning reflected the ebb and flow of the war. The success of British arms in Georgia in 1779 prompted the merchants to send congratu-
lations and express hope that order would be quickly restored as the colony was
brought back into the imperial fold. The traders' basic demand, that prewar debts
be made a condition of the reestablishment of civil government in colonies and
in any peace settlement, did not vary.[10] The recapture of Savannah in December
1778 and Charleston in May 1780 by Sir Henry Clinton's troops and the prospect
of renewed trade with Georgia or South Carolina gave the petitioning further
impetus. British authorities were generally sympathetic. Parliament legislated in
1780 to permit trade between Britain and the "Towns, Ports, or Places, in North
America, which are or may be under the Protection of his Majesty's Arms."[11]
London's Carolina traders complained in a July 1780 petition to the king about
the seizure of account books, indigo, and other property by Clinton's forces in
Charleston, since these items could be "applied to the discharge of British Debts."
Lord Germain forwarded the petition to Clinton in Charleston.[12]

With the military situation in the southern theater changing fast and with
their links to South Carolina severed by war, the merchants were, however,
deprived of the reliable and timely information that had been central to their
peacetime business. As such, much of their petitioning was superseded by events
before the government could consider their demands, let alone transmit them
to South Carolina. By the time London's Carolina and Georgia merchants expressed hope to the Board of Trade in July 1781 that "the usual intercourse of
Commerce be again resumed," British military fortunes in the region had gone
into reverse. The expected Loyalist upsurge had never properly materialized,
and Patriot militias had driven the British back to the confines of Savannah,
Charleston, and a few isolated backcountry outposts. Calls made in the summer
of 1781 for the restoration of civil government in South Carolina and the hope of
"bringing back the People of Carolina to a true sense of the blessings of being
once again Reunited with the Parent Country" reflected the aspirations, and de-
lusions, of a year before. They bore little resemblance to the rapidly deteriorating
situation for British forces on the ground.[13]

The reopening of direct trade between England and South Carolina and
Georgia after a four-year hiatus in 1780 had actually exacerbated British debts
in the colonies (table 9).[14] Some £637,531 of goods were imported into South

Carolina while Charleston was in British hands between May 1780 and December 1782. Agricultural output was severely reduced as a result of marauding troops, who destroyed crops and equipment, the loss of slave labor, as slaves took the opportunity to escape the plantations, and the disruption of transport links. South Carolina's exports to England in the entire war between 1776 and 1782 were valued at only £129,966, or just over 20 percent of the value of the imported goods. The proportion of imports to exports between England and Georgia was similar, though the volumes were much smaller. Since the overwhelming volume of goods exported to the colonies would have been on credit, British merchants not only failed to reduce their debt exposure in the region during the war but also saw the total debts owed to them increase significantly.

Table 9: South Carolina and Georgia—Value of
Imports from and Exports to England, 1776–82 (£ Sterling)

	South Carolina			Georgia		
	Imports	Exports	Exports as % of imports	Imports	Exports	Exports as % of imports
1776	0	13,668	-	0	12,569	-
1777	0	2,234	-	0	0	-
1778	0	1,074	-	0	0	-
1779	0	3,732	-	85	607	-
1780	236,941	708	-	91,888	2,251	2.4
1781	330,847	94,368	28.5	14,059	506	3.6
1782	69,743	14,182	20.3	340	6,804	-
Total	637,531	129,966	20.4	106,372	22,737	21.4

Source: Carter et al., *Historical Statistics,* V, 710–13.

Once news of the British surrender at Yorktown in October 1781 arrived in London, revealing the inevitability of Britain's defeat in the war, the capital's North American merchants turned their efforts to ensuring that their debts would be fully recompensed in the peace settlement. London's Carolina traders were once more to the fore. A committee of merchants "trading to the Provinces of South Carolina and Georgia previous to the year 1776" was formed and headed by William Greenwood, John Nutt, and John Clark. In petitions in August and October 1782 to the new government led by the Earl of Shelburne, the committee sought "clear & solid Stipulations . . . for the complete Security of the legal demands of the British merchants and those they represent previous to the year 1776."[15] Carolina and Georgia traders were also prominent in a lobbying effort comprising traders from across London's prewar American trades. Their leading role reflected the scale of their trade and their losses, and their significance within London's American trade. Of the twenty traders who petitioned Shelburne on North American debts in April 1782, seven would claim a total of £646,857 in debts in South Carolina and Georgia—more than a quarter of the total debts of £2,324,889 that London merchants would later claim across all the former American colonies.[16]

The merchants' petitioning to the government in 1782 was marked by a self-exculpatory approach as they sought to absolve themselves of responsibility for their losses. Like the committee of Carolina merchants, they identified themselves as having been interested in the American trade "previous to the year 1776." This was an attempt to distinguish the legitimacy of their debts "contracted under the Faith and Sanction of the British Laws before the unhappy Dispute commenced" from the wartime losses run up by "adventurers" who had attempted to continue trading during the war, in defiance of the Prohibitory Act. Such adventurers had placed themselves outside the protection of British law and could therefore have no claim for redress. Further attempting to bolster the legitimacy of their claims, the prewar traders spuriously sought to transfer the blame for their losses to the British government. They wrote to Shelburne in April 1782 that it was "by the operation of the Prohibitory and other Laws [that] your Memorialists have been prevented by receiving Payments of their just Debts and have thereby been plunged into the utmost Difficulty and Distress": but for the Prohibitory Act, they implied, trade would have continued as normal.[17]

Pursuing prewar debts impelled new organizational coherence among London's North America merchants. Coordinated lobbying among merchants in different geographic branches of American trade had been rare before the war. Differences in how various American exports were treated in the Navigation Acts had served more often to divide than to unite the American traders, with rare exceptions such as the Stamp Act lobbying. Paralleling the divergent sectional interests within the American colonies, and postwar states, Carolina merchants had sought to influence policy on South Carolina, Chesapeake merchants had done so on Virginia and Maryland, and New England merchants had tried to influence policy on New England. In contrast, the issue of prewar debts affected merchants across the branches of American trade. Securing favorable government policy on these losses accordingly required concerted action. A committee of London's prewar American merchants was established in mid-1782. This resurrected an ad hoc grouping convened in 1765 to coordinate merchant appeals against the Stamp Act but which had been active only intermittently in the next ten years, for instance in its belated calls for the repeal of the Townshend Duties in 1770 and for reconciliation in 1775.[18] It comprised the leading prewar merchants and—signifying the status of London's leading Carolina traders—was led by William Greenwood and John Nutt alongside the Maryland trader William Molleson.

In six petitions between August and November 1782, the committee pressed the government to ensure that full payment of prewar debts would be enshrined in the peace treaty with the United States. Their efforts did not go unnoticed: Shelburne advised peace commissioner Richard Oswald of the "daily applications" of "some of our most considerable merchants."[19] As details of the proposed treaty emerged—specifically that prewar debts would be judged in American courts—the committee's tone became more desperate. By late November 1782 the American traders were demanding that their claims be heard in British courts. As they saw it, "any System for their Security and Satisfaction would be . . . of little importance if it is not fixed on a Solid Basis here, for if they are compelled to seek redress from their Debtors in North America by having recourse to the Courts there, it would . . . be an absolute mockery of their Sufferings." No courts in America could be impartial, since the debt claims would be determined by "Judges and Jurors composed of those very People many of whom have been the Chief Authors and Instruments of their misfortunes."[20] To the merchants' frustration, however, this was exactly the agreement that would be reached in Article IV of the Treaty of Paris, signed in September 1783.

"Enjoyment on one side, and Restrictions on the other": The Restoration of Anglo-American Trade

Establishing the conditions for revived Anglo-American trade had been among the top priorities as the peace talks dragged on in Paris during 1783. The British Parliament turned its attention to trade with America early in the year against a backdrop of increasingly bitter party politics. Prime Minister Shelburne's resignation at the end of February precipitated a six-week "inter-ministerium" before an unlikely coalition government led by the rivals Charles James Fox and Lord North took office in April. Reflecting Shelburne's desire for commercial reciprocity and his philosophy of "trade over dominion" toward the former colonies, the chancellor William Pitt the Younger introduced the American Intercourse Bill to the Commons at the beginning of March. Though strikingly liberal in its trade policy toward America, specifically in its proposal to grant American and British merchants the same status in British and West Indian ports, hardened American observers saw ministerial duplicity even in this conciliatory approach. Reporting to Congress from London, Henry Laurens regarded the bill as "speciously conducive to the mutual Interests of Great Britain and America"—hardly a ringing endorsement of a major shift in British commercial policy.[21]

Opposition within Parliament was more concrete. Shelburne's opponents condemned the bill's generosity toward America. Fox feared that it would fuel jealousy from Britain's commercial rivals, and MPs resisted any significant trade concessions to the United States, particularly regarding the lucrative West Indies markets. The American Intercourse Bill was progressively amended and never came to a vote.[22] Its next iteration was even more reactionary. While it stipulated that British goods be exported to the United States exactly as before the war, American vessels were to be limited to carrying only American produce in their trade to Britain. This was to be done directly, meaning that the produce could not be transshipped through foreign ports. Even this failed to satisfy Parliament's protectionist hawks. A third version introduced was still more hard-line, banning American ships from trading with British colonies, a move aimed principally at excluding them from the West Indies. Other clauses sought to hinder the United States from developing trade with other European powers. MPs had comprehensively rejected Shelburne's vision of an ongoing commercial union between Britain and the independent United States.[23]

The radical overhaul of the bill overtook merchants' lobbying efforts. Pitt had solicited the opinions of the Committee of London Merchants trading to North America, which after several meetings presented him with a report on the bill.[24] As the draft legislation became progressively more restrictive, London's American traders upped their efforts. On 5 April some 150 London merchants "interested in the Commerce with North America" petitioned the king asking for measures "likely to revive the Commercial Intercourse between this Country and North America." In particular, they sought "Liberality" in the "Laws which may be made for the Regulation" of the trade, so as to "re-establish and perpetuate perfect Harmony and Friendship between the Two Countries." This would effectively restore the prewar system of trade. Although some of the petitioners had interests in the Carolina trade, major prewar Carolina traders such as John Nutt, Greenwood & Higginson, Christopher Rolleston, and James Poyas were conspicuously absent.[25]

As negotiations limped on in Paris in May and June, British attitudes hardened further against free trade. Mercantilists—"elements of the old Leaven among us, [of the] disposition of monopolizing the Trade and Navigation of the World to ourselves," complained James Bourdieu, later to become one of London's leading postwar Carolina traders—made the case for British ships to monopolize trade with Britain's remaining colonies. Tracts such as the Earl of Sheffield's best-selling *Observations on the Commerce of the American States* maintained the mercantilist dogma that now that the United States was a foreign power it should lose its prewar, imperial right to trade with the British West Indies. Underpinning Sheffield's and other mercantilist thinking was the preservation of British naval power: direct commerce with the islands would allow the United States to build up its marine strength and through this threaten British supremacy at sea. This preoccupation was recognized in South Carolina, where the following year the legislature judged that the object of British trade policy was not only "to prejudice the commerce" but also "to suppress the maritime progress of the United States."[26]

Henry Laurens, engraving, 1784. John
Norman, 1748?–1817, engraver.
Library of Congress.

"Reciprocity appears now to mean, Enjoyment on one side, and Restrictions on the other," Henry Laurens caustically characterized the hardening of
British policy. Having gone to London from the negotiations in Paris, where he
had been one of the U.S. peace commissioners, Laurens followed the shifting
political climate in Britain closely. He attributed the toughening of attitudes to
the "sudden and unexpected arrival [in London] of divers Ships and Cargoes
from different Ports in the United States." The first American ships had arrived
in the River Thames as early as February 1783, an event widely reported in London newspapers. The *Bedford,* carrying whale oil from Nantucket, led the way.
Ships from the island off New England had in fact continued to sail to Britain
throughout the war, but to the press this technicality was far outweighed by the
symbolism of the new arrival. As the *London Chronicle* reported, the *Bedford* was
"the first vessel that has entered the River belonging to the United States." The
Bedford was not alone: the newspaper also noted that "three American vessels,
which were lying at Ostend when the Preliminaries were signed, are now in the
river, off the Tower, with the 13 stripes flying." The news was repeated verbatim
in the Charleston press as soon as it had crossed the Atlantic. Alongside was a
report that in London "a great number of vessels are already getting ready for
Virginia, Maryland and Carolina States," giving further impetus to traders in the
port who were preparing to resume business with Britain. In their eagerness
to get back into transatlantic trade, Laurens believed, his countrymen gave the
impression that they were willing to do so on any terms.[27]

Legislatures across the new states were confused about how to receive British ships that arrived in American ports before peace was formally declared.
As individual states resumed trade with Britain, there was a snowball effect as
states vied for competitive advantage. A Pennsylvanian delegate to Congress,

Thomas FitzSimons, reported in April 1783 that "the Commercial people of this City [Philadelphia] are Anxious to Know whether Vessels or Goods Comeing into this state from Great Britain, or any of her ports or Colonys can be admitted to entry at the Custom house." With no satisfactory answer from Congress, Philadelphia merchants turned to the state's courts, where judges permitted British vessels to enter. Word soon spread to other states. Virginia delegates to Congress asserted in May that a "commercial intercourse is under present circumstances carried freely from other States with our late Enemy, and as far as an advantage can be drawn from it, Virginia must certainly be entitled to share in it." Over the course of 1783, British shipping was readmitted across the United States: as North Carolina delegates complained in September, "other states found other excuses for opening their ports and the disease soon became general."[28]

Across the Atlantic, evolving British policy enshrined the revival of antebellum mercantilism. In May an Order in Council declared that only unmanufactured American goods could be imported into Britain, applying the same restrictions as to Britain's colonies; in June the prewar "Old Subsidy" of five percent import duty was reimposed on imported Virginian tobacco. Exports from South Carolina were similarly treated along colonial lines. American indigo and naval stores could be freely imported into Britain, though the prewar bounties no longer applied; rice could be imported duty free so long as it was shipped on to continental Europe as most of the grain had been before the war.[29] Yet for South Carolinians the reopening of the key British export market for the state's produce was outweighed by other restrictions. The hardening of British commercial policy toward the United States reached its apogee with an Order in Council in July 1783 that limited trade between the United States and Britain's West Indies colonies to vessels owned and built in Britain. With this lucrative trade for South Carolina's shipping cut off, the state stood to lose heavily. Laurens considered the restrictions "an Insult upon a free People," and South Carolina was one of the states to seek united action. In March 1784 it passed an act authorizing Congress to prohibit any British-owned ships carrying West Indian produce from landing in American ports. Requiring interstate legislation and enforcement, however, the proposed boycott never materialized, stifled by the states' inability to act in concert.[30]

"Commerce again shall lift her drooping head": The Resumption of Anglo-Carolinian Trade

In a still highly charged political atmosphere—where politics, economics, and commerce were closely entwined—and before the peace treaty had been signed, trade resumed between Britain and South Carolina. As Britain's politicians and theorists debated the terms of the country's postwar trade and with negotiations between Great Britain and the United States continuing in Paris, merchants on both sides of the Atlantic wasted little time in getting back to business. Trade between Britain and South Carolina was no exception. Despite extensive damage to the town during the war, the harbor, wharves, and warehousing in Charleston were in good enough repair. Merchant ships left London for Charleston as early as February 1783. They arrived in early May, when the first notices advertising goods from London appeared in the Charleston press. The appropriately named copper-bottomed brigantine *Lightening* was apparently the first to arrive. It was then among the earliest ships to make the return journey from Charleston, along with the patriotically named *Washington,* the *Charlestown Packet,* and the newly christened *Financier.* A contemporary poem captured the enthusiasm generated by the prospect of renewed commerce. Britain's diminished status meant that future trade would operate among more equal lines: "Britannia now her haughty claims foregoes / With open arms her commerce now she sues / And greets as friends whom late she fought as foes." Freed from the imperial restrictions of prewar trade, diverse foreign markets would be open to the fruits of the United States' land and labor. Many nations would clamor for America's trade. The poem continued,

> Columbia hail, thy toils now happy o'er,
> Thy fertile fields no more defil'd with gore
> Shall yield large harvests to thy rustic swains,
> And Peace and Plenty glad thy happy plains;
> Commerce again shall lift her drooping head,
> And the Atlantic scarce sustain thy trade;
> While different nations shall thy harbours croud,
> And the produce of every land afford.[31]

Across the Atlantic, from August 1783 London newspapers advertised the arrival of ships from Charleston carrying rice, indigo, and passengers.[32] South Carolinians were among the many Americans who traveled to Britain soon after the peace to establish trading connections, restoring a pattern of commercial visits that had taken place in the decade before the Revolutionary War. The visitors also called on manufacturers supplying export goods for the American market to observe production personally and select merchandise. The Charleston merchant John Edwards Jr. was one such visitor in summer 1783, meeting James Bourdieu and other London merchants as he sought to forge commercial links in the city. A fellow Charleston trader, Thomas Corbett, visited England's manufacturing towns to buy "a very large and compleat Assortment of GOODS suitable for the approaching season."[33] For Henry Laurens, his countrymen's eagerness to reenter trade with Britain showed their dependence on the British market and undermined America's negotiating position in Paris at a critical juncture. Witnessing American desperation, British politicians could take a harder line and pander to domestic sentiment. "The moment the sound of Peace reached her

[America]," Laurens observed, "she poured her Ships & Merchandize into British ports and received without ceremony or decent Solemnity the Ships & Merchandize of Britain, the Enemies of our Country & such there are, took advantage of her comingness, clamoured against permitting American Ships to be Carriers of West India produce, [and] the Ministers whose seats were not very firm, took the alarm [and] grew coy."[34]

In Britain newspapers were quick to trumpet postwar preferences in Charleston for British trade. When South Carolina's governor Benjamin Guerard gave a cordial reception to the first British ship to arrive in Charleston after news of the peace, London's *Public Advertiser* took it as evidence that it "affords the pleasing Prospect of a Trade being once more opened between Great Britain and America, to the mutual Benefit of both Countries."[35] To newspapers' delight, Britain's continental rivals were by contrast being spurned. "A letter from Havre de Grace [Le Havre]," the *Public Advertiser* reported in September 1783, "says that a vessel is arrived there from Charles Town in South Carolina; in which they learn, that several French Ships lie there, but cannot get half their Lading, whilst the ships bound to England have all full Cargoes; and the Merchants there seem more inclined to ship their Goods for England, than for any other Parts."[36] Beneath the patriotic bombast, such reports accurately conveyed the turn that South Carolina's postwar Atlantic trade had taken. Nowhere was the upsurge in commercial activity more visible than in Charleston. "The genius of our people is entirely turned from war to commerce. Schemes of business & partnerships for extending commerce are daily forming," reported local resident David Ramsay.[37]

Besides these local partnerships, merchants in Charleston also forged formal transatlantic connections. Brothers-in-law William Freeman Jr. and Robert Pringle Jr., son of the major Charleston merchant of the same name, made one such partnership. Pringle Jr. was a former doctor who had developed "an inclination for merchandize," and his willingness to sell part of his landholdings to release capital to invest in the firm illustrated the widespread expectation of the money to be made in postwar trade.[38] The pair went into partnership in Charleston in June 1783, each investing two thousand pounds in joint stock. Under their agreement, Pringle was to remain in Charleston and Freeman was to represent the firm in Bristol, for which he departed in July. Freeman's uncle William Freeman Sr. had been a major transatlantic trader in Bristol before the war. Freeman Sr. had sensibly invested "the greater part" of his trading capital in British real estate "for want of Employ of it during the American war." Hard to liquidate, his landed assets constrained his ability to invest capital in the new firm. The firm was, though, able to draw heavily on Freeman Sr.'s expertise on all aspects of transatlantic commerce: which commodities to trade; to whom to offer credit and for how long; and what the first cargo of merchandise from England should include.[39]

British merchants such as Freeman benefited from long-standing personal connections to South Carolina and the networks of credit and knowledge that

stemmed from them. Familial links persisted or were established. Most important was the liberal credit that British merchants, unlike their European counterparts, were willing to extend to South Carolina's traders and planters. British
merchants therefore retained a strong—and to many locals, dominant—presence
in Charleston. British traders had flocked to the town after it was recaptured in
1780. Some were returnees, having left South Carolina with the onset of hostilities four years earlier but now looking to resume their businesses; others
were first-time arrivals, attracted by the potential profits on offer. Charleston's
wartime Loyalist press recorded how numerous new partnerships were founded
in the port in the wake of the British reoccupation.[40] After British forces left
Charleston in December 1782, many of these traders applied successfully to remain while they ran down their inventories. From 1783 many others crossed the
Atlantic to set up in trade or to make trading connections in Charleston, paralleling similar movements to Boston, New York, and Philadelphia.[41]

At the end of the war, the individual states controlled who could or could
not become a citizen and adopted different laws and qualifications for citizenship
and naturalization.[42] In South Carolina the legislature assured British traders the
right to enter and establish themselves in the state in August 1783 in accordance
with the preliminary terms of peace. The state would go on to grant citizenship of South Carolina to many British merchants, whether they had come to
Charleston during the war and remained or were newly arrived. Particularly
galling to many of the town's residents was the fact that even Loyalist merchants
who had been expelled from South Carolina found ways to continue trading.
Two Charleston traders, John Hopton and Robert Powell, who were expelled
from the state in 1783 on account of their loyalism, continued in business by
swapping locations with their partner, Samuel Brailsford: they went to trade in
Britain and were replaced in Charleston by Brailsford, who had been based in
Britain before the war.[43] Another expelled merchant, John Tunno, took up trade
in London, corresponding with his brother Adam, who replaced him in Charleston and took citizenship in 1784.[44]

New British entrants to the market arrived with large quantities of goods and
offered generous credit to South Carolinian consumers, principally to plantation
owners keen to rebuild and restock their estates and who, in a cash-poor economy, required extensive credit until they could market their crops. Merchants
in Charleston were offered imported goods on twelve months' credit by their
counterparts in Britain: Robert Pringle Jr. was proposed such terms by "several
merchants of note in London & other cities in Gt. Britain" but declined them
because of his existing connection with Freeman Sr. in Bristol.[45] For South Carolina's planters and the British entrants to business in Charleston, the new arrangements were mutually beneficial. Competition among merchants and high
levels of imports suppressed the price of imported goods. At the same time, this
competition and the large number of ships entering Charleston helped raise rice

prices, since planters could drive a hard bargain when selling their rice to traders in the port. These considerations also lowered freight costs. In a number of decisions in 1783 and early 1784, South Carolina's planter-dominated legislature reflected this mutuality of interest with decisions that favored the British merchants. In February 1783 British merchants who had stayed in Charleston during the war were granted leave to remain while they sold off their stocks. Next, this grace period was extended to cover the months when most rice was exported, January and February. Further legislation attempted to combat legal discrimination against British merchants by obliging any trials involving foreigners to be heard before a jury in which half the members were themselves foreign. A final series of decisions granted citizenship to most of the merchants who applied. Only those most closely implicated in the British wartime occupation were denied.[46]

Combined with the British merchants' widely observed "adventuring spirit," the accommodating legal environment allowed the traders—both those who had operated in occupied Charleston and been allowed to remain and their newly arrived compatriots—to acquire a large share of South Carolina's overseas trade. For cultural, linguistic, and economic reasons, European rivals were unable to compete. A report drawn up at the end of the decade for Secretary of State Thomas Jefferson attributed British merchants' dominance of the Carolinas' and Georgia's overseas trade to their understanding of and responsiveness to American customers: "The American Merchant is very explicit in his demands for Goods, he details every thing with the greatest care: and his Correspondent in Great Britain complies with his orders with the most pointed exactness. It rarely ever happens but that the English Merchant sends the kind, quality and quantity of Goods, and the exact proportion as they are ordered." Setting out the long-established terms of credit between British merchants and their counterparts in the southern states, the report concluded that "it will be difficult if not impracticable to form any Houses here, French or Dutch, which will be able to divert the present channel of Trade, unless they go on the same or a plan similar to it. Credit the Planters must have, and consequently those who can give to them will be called upon to supply their demands. . . . French or Dutch Houses for want of this necessary knowledge, and being unacquainted with the English Language, will long labour under difficulties surmountable only by their forming connections with the most respectable families in this Country who will be a constant match over the debtors, their abilities and prospects."[47]

Continental European merchants most importantly lacked either the local expertise or the generous credit that distinguished their British counterparts. Notoriously unwilling to extend credit to buyers in the newly independent United States, continental merchants preferred to minimize the risk of losses by demanding cash payment on delivery—cash which South Carolinians, like their compatriots in the other states, did not have. "Tales of want of faith and of bankruptcies in America, which are disseminated by the English papers, deter them

[French merchants] from thinking in that way," Thomas Jefferson lamented from Paris.[48] The European merchants' competitive disadvantage was compounded by the poorer value of their goods. Complaints about the quality and price of French merchandise were rife. "Since the Peace, we have never had a single French House, that commanded Respect, or that has been intitled to it," Charleston traders Brailsford & Morris complained as late as 1787. "We have only been troubled by a set of needy Adventurers, without Fortune or Character, who by importing the refuse of the French manufactures, have effectually strengthened our prejudices in favour of the British. There are a few Dutch, and Germans, who are honest, industrious, and enjoy a pretty good Credit, but they are limited in their resources, and are too phlegmatic for adventure." By contrast, "the British Merchant, being ready to make larger advances on Consignments than we have hitherto been able to obtain from those of any other Country, necessity has compelled us to accept their offers, and against our wishes, establish a preference in their favour."[49] Charleston's customs collector concurred. "The United Netherlands, Hamburgh, and Sweden have had several Ships here, but from their not being acquainted with the Trade have imported such Articles as are not saleable; Time and experience will teach them the proper Goods for this Country," he reported.[50] British merchants already had the benefit of both time and experience.

In satisfying planter-led consumer demand and by undercutting European rivals, the new British traders upset Charleston's commercial equilibrium. Goods—often sold at auction for cash and at a loss—flooded the market, undercutting the port's established merchants. Auctions in particular "very much injured the sales by the regular merchants," Robert Pringle Jr. complained in early 1784. Fortunately they were decreasing so that "Trade must shortly revert to its former regular channels—much to the benefit of the resident merchants who have constant customers."[51] Charleston continued to attract new British entrants and returnees throughout the decade. George Ogilvie, a young Scot who had managed his uncle's estates in South Carolina before the war before fleeing on account of his loyalism, had hoped to return to South Carolina in August 1783. However, having had his property in the state confiscated, he perhaps wisely decided that "the temper of the People is such that it would be madness to attempt going out until the ferment subsides."[52] Nonetheless by 1788, "having met with some losses in trade" in Britain, he was back in Charleston to seek a change of commercial fortune, with his wife and children planning to follow him if his venture succeeded.[53]

"Members and heads of a British faction": Anti-British Sentiment in Charleston

Perceptions of British commercial dominance unleashed powerful anti-British feeling in Charleston. "Has Britain signed the Definitive Treaty? Has she, according to the preliminaries agreed upon, withdrawn her troops from New York and St. Augustine? No, my Countrymen, she has not; she is deceitful, and there is no truth in her. Be ye therefore watchful over whom you suffer to come among you," "A Columbian" warned fellow Charleston residents in the *South Carolina Weekly Gazette* in July 1783. With Britain stalling over the definitive terms of peace, British merchants and former Loyalists were seeking to undermine America's fragile political and commercial independence. Only reliable patriots and merchants from the United States' wartime European allies should be favored with business: "Give encouragement to your faithful Allies that have rendered you such essential service in the hour of danger. It is such men you ought to receive, for they only are to be depended upon. They have fought and bled for you, and will again, to all faithful subjects. Let us also encourage every other Nation. Then our land will be filled with men, who come not from motives of avarice and disaffection, but to support and maintain the most wonderful revolution, purchased with blood and treasure, since Noah's Flood."[54]

Against a backdrop of inflammatory rhetoric and renewed grievances, riots targeting the Loyalist merchants who had been allowed to remain and the new arrivals from Britain shook Charleston in July 1783. Governor Guerard's blithe assurance to British merchants that they were "entirely safe both in person and property from any mobs, riots &c. as there will be none" epitomized the authorities' lack of control. The *Lord North* incident represented a symbolic tip of the iceberg.[55] Twenty years earlier the town's artisans had been in the vanguard of the Stamp Act protests; after the war the same sections reprised their anti-British activism. Many of the foremost agitators, from the bluntly named Marine Anti-Britannic Society led by Alexander Gillon, had been members of Charleston's prewar Sons of Liberty. British merchants were physically assaulted in the riots— in contemporary parlance, given a "pumping"—and their premises vandalized.

The authorities' condemnations revealed a more nuanced view of the British traders' role in South Carolina's commercial rehabilitation. Not only were the riots "disgraceful to good government," Guerard fulminated, but in addition, "ill impressions may be made on the minds of the numerous foreigners amongst us, prejudicial to our rising commerce."[56] In a widely circulated pamphlet, "A Patriot" articulated the interplay between overseas trade, foreign traders' investment in South Carolina, and the state's general economic health. "This country is evidently formed for commerce, and nothing can be more ruinous to its interest, than riot and disorder," he argued, "for no man in his senses will trust his property in a country where, in one hour, his fortune may be laid in ruins." At a time when the state was poised to return to its prewar trading prosperity, small-minded hostility toward the British traders risked derailing this renaissance: "Our ports begin to be crouded with shipping, our stores to be filled with goods, agriculture will soon flourish, and on these the Wealth and Grandeur of the State must inevitably grow, if Liberty and Good Policy prevail; but if PRIVATE RESENTMENT can with impunity distract the Tranquillity of Government, Trade will forsake our shores, and Contempt and Reproach must of consequence take place." The consequence of forcing merchants to flee the port, "A Patriot" warned in a follow-up piece, would be that those who remained would monopolize the marketplace, harming the interests of planters and artisans alike: "If the people are once blindly led into measures which shall confine the trade of the country in a few hands, they, too late, will find the merchants imposing what terms they may think proper. The planter may make an abundance to sell, and foreign markets may pay high prices for his produce, but the griping hand of a monopolizer at home may leave him but a poor compensation for his trouble. The mechanic may apply with industry to his business, but the languor into which his country will fall, will soon reduce him to poverty and contempt: but, let the channels of commerce be open and safe, and let her be led into your ports by as many hands as may chuse to come, and then trade will flourish in all its branches and amongst all order, and happiness and plenty will cheer every heart."[57]

Government action, notably incorporating Charleston as a city to make law and order easier to maintain, applying the rule of law, and appealing to economic self-interest, succeeded for the most part in quelling popular tumult. As Anglo-American relations remained tense throughout the 1780s, however, over issues such as Britain's retention of forts on the United States' northern frontier, the debts owed to prewar British traders, American planters' losses on slaves who had left with the British evacuation, and Americans' right to trade with the West Indies, popular resentment of British merchants' supposedly privileged position in the port persisted. Renewed violence occasionally erupted, notably in July 1784. The South Carolina legislature's decisions to restore confiscated estates to thirty-five wartime Loyalists and to amerce—impose a fine—rather than confiscate the estates of ninety-five others were irritants no doubt compounded by high prices, shortages, and the stifling heat of a lowcountry summer.

The possibility that communal discord would discourage foreign trade and thereby retard South Carolina's commercial resurgence was particularly concerning to the state's government. Writing to the *South Carolina Gazette & General Advertiser,* "Another Patriot" felt compelled to set the record straight "for the information . . . of the people in Europe." He sent word via a ship heading to Europe of a "*simple* fact: There are three of four artful, designing and turbulent men, who govern and influence a few weak and deluded persons. They call themselves Whigs, but on whom the best Friends of the State bestow the appellation of WHIG-DEVILS." These men, he avowed, stirred up the trouble by rousing drunken sailors to do their bidding: "And how do these Whigs (O what a prostitution of the name!) effect their purpose. They hire a very considerable number of poor sailors, coop them up in a Long Room, charge and prime them for several hours with pure spirit, and in the dusk of evening they sally. They are instantly opposed, their leaders taken, and their feeble supporters dispersed."[58] Press reports in Britain suggested that "Another Patriot" and others of a like mind were right to be worried about perceptions abroad. In stark contrast to the optimistic reports of renewed Anglo-Carolinian trade that had immediately followed the peace, London newspapers painted an apocalyptic scene. A series of lurid reports attributed the Charleston riots to "republicans . . . intoxicated with their darling independence" and relayed the general "anarchy and confusion" in the southern states. The situation was reported to be particularly chaotic in Charleston, "where the appellation of Tory is more fatal to individuals than conviction for the worst of felonies in England."[59] Despite the well-publicized disorder, commercial calculations appear to have outweighed safety concerns, as trade between England and South Carolina grew steadily throughout the 1780s.

Suspicion of British commercial motives in Charleston spanned the broadening divide between those who favored and those who opposed closer federal union in the United States. The judge and ardent anti-Federalist Aedanus Burke charged in an anonymous 1786 pamphlet that Britain had planted "a standing army of merchants, factors, clerks, agents, and emissaries, who out-manoeuvre, undersell and frighten away the French and Dutch who came here, monopolized our trade, speculated on our necessities and . . . plunged us into a debt." This was evidence, he claimed, of a British plot to recapture America through commerce rather than by arms. Explicitly yoking British traders to ministerial policy, he asked, "Can you deny, that you are not mere merchants, than members and heads of a British faction, to sow discontent and promote the views of your ministry?"[60] In the later 1780s resistance to opening state courts to lawsuits from prewar British creditors, as compelled by the federal Constitution, was influential in generating opposition to the Constitution in South Carolina and other major debtor states.[61]

Conversely, advocates of the new national Constitution saw federal union, with the power to regulate commerce vested in the national government, as vital to curtailing British dominance of South Carolina's trade. The Charleston merchants William Brailsford and Thomas Morris summed up this aspiration. Writing to Thomas Jefferson in October 1787, they expressed hope that "the Federal System, as recommended by the Convention, will be acknowledged here and adopted by our Sister States. Our commerce will then experience the fruits of Order and Energy, and those Nations, who now view us with Contempt, who ridicule our Folly and Disunion, and who are enriching themselves on our Spoils, will gladly court our rising Consequence."[62] If they differed from anti-Federalists in their prescription for the problem, they accorded in their diagnosis of its cause. Like Aedanus Burke, Brailsford & Morris saw insidious British policy lurking within individual British merchants' trading strategies. Resurrecting a language of bondage and subservience, they saw South Carolina's trade as "fettered by British policy" and were "anxious to emancipate our Country from the restraints imposed on her by the policy of England." At the same time, they also attributed British preeminence in the state's trade to specific structural factors: the debts due to merchants in Britain; the presence of so many British traders in Charleston, among whom, ironically, was William Brailsford's father, Samuel; and the liberal credit offered by the British. Trading strategies, they believed, were an instrument of British government policy. British policy "shackled" Charleston's overseas trade through its merchants "sending out fresh Goods and of the first quality, which supports those favourable impressions of their superiority."[63]

Table 10: Rice Exports from South Carolina and Georgia (Barrels), 1768–89

	South Carolina			Georgia	Total (barrels)	Total (lbs. 000s)*
	Charleston	Beaufort and Georgetown	Total			
1768	118,493	7,045	125,538	17,733	143,271	75,238
1769	108,682	6,900	115,582	16,740	132,322	69,469
1770	126,237	5,568	131,805	22,129	153,934	80,815
1771	119,942	5,209	125,151	25,232	150,383	78,951
Average 1768–71	118,339	6,181	124,520	20,459	144,979	76,118
1772	100,745	4,076	104,821	23,540	128,361	67,390
1773	126,940	8,103	135,043	29,661	164,704	86,469
1774	118,482	7,563	126,045	27,684	153,729	80,708
Average 1772–74	115,389	6,581	121,970	26,692	148,662	78,189
1784	61,974	-	61,974	-	61,974	-
1785	63,732	-	63,732	-	63,732	-
1786	66,557	-	66,557	-	66,557	-
1787	65,195	-	65,195	-	65,195	-
1788	82,400	-	82,400	-	82,400	-
1789	100,000	-	100,000	-	100,000	-
Average 1784–89	73,310	-	73,310	-	73,310	-

Source: Carter et al., *Historical Statistics*, V, 764–66.

* Number of pounds per barrel varied from year to year.

"Manifestly far from being cordial Friends": Echoes of Prewar Trade

In the decade after independence, it seemed to many in South Carolina that the old rules of the game had been firmly reestablished. This extended to conceptions of the British end of the trade, with British merchants widely held to hold the upper hand in transatlantic commerce once more. In a charge list strikingly reminiscent of the prewar disputes, London merchants were again accused of conspiring to defraud American correspondents, profiteering from the trade, overstocking American markets, and drowning Charleston traders in easy credit. Suspicions of sharp business practices among London's Carolina traders persisted. Echoing the distrust that continued to pervade diplomatic relations between the two nations and the commercial inferiority complex emerging across American seaports, Carolinians continued to believe that they were being exploited by their London counterparts. Before the war London merchants and brokers had been widely suspected of conniving against Carolinian indigo, deprecating its quality to reduce its price.[64] London's skinners—an "adroit Fraternity"—were similarly held to be systematically defrauding deerskin exporters.[65] Perhaps reinforced by the inequalities still enshrined in Britain's economic policy toward the United States, this persecution complex persisted in South Carolina after the war. Charleston merchants still felt themselves to be unequal partners in Atlantic trade with Britain. Having returned to South Carolina in 1785, Laurens sent the London merchants Bridgen & Waller a cargo of deerskins and warned them that "this may be a New Article for you, but I don't know one in which the Brokers practice more fraud." Purchasers were also apt to find "imaginary faults" in rice.[66] Laurens advised the same correspondents at length on how to judge and market indigo, "as you have not had much Experience in that Branch," and warned them how the "artful Buyer" and the "tricks of your tradesmen" in London conspired to defraud producers and importers of deerskins, indigo, and rice alike.[67]

Systemic indebtedness to British traders was another—and perhaps still more distressing—throwback to the prewar polity, resurrecting a sense of commercial inequality. David Ramsay recalled popular angst in the 1780s in his *History of South Carolina*, published two decades later. "The people of Carolina had been but a short time in the possession of peace and independence," he reflected, "when they were brought under a new species of dependence . . . so universally were they in debt beyond their ability to pay."[68] Despite connoting ongoing domination by the former mother country, liberal British credit was an addictive stimulant in the state, lubricating the rebuilding of plantations and resumption of trade. Overstocking was a feature of the Charleston market as early as 1783. South Carolina was not unique: easy credit and overstocking swiftly became common in port towns and cities across the United States. Surpluses of imported goods were widely reported in the British press.[69] In June 1783 Henry Laurens counseled one British merchant seeking to trade to America to "forbear your adventures for a little time until things are settled in America [as] every market there is at present fully supplied with Merchandize of every kind and probably overloaded. The great number of Ships gone with cargoes to America from France, Flanders, Holland, England, Ireland &c. must supply the Country with more goods than can be sold in three Years and more perhaps than will be paid for in ten . . . I would recommend to you Sir to avoid the Rock which many others are at this moment running their heads against, who will come home by and by with empty Pockets cursing America for their own Folly."[70]

A glut of consumer goods brought down businesses in ports across the United States after the war, but local factors—and in particular the devastation of its agricultural base—made South Carolina's debt crisis especially severe.[71] Besides acquiring more merchandise than they could profitably sell, planters and merchants racked up debts to British merchants through massive credit-backed imports of enslaved Africans to replace the slaves who had left South Carolina between 1775 and 1782. "During the course of the War upwards of 20,000 Negroes were carried away by the British or died of the Small pox, Camp Fevers &ca. within their Lines, which Number must again be supplied before the produce of this Country will be equal to what it was formerly," Charleston's collector of the customs opined in December 1784, voicing a common assumption.[72] Timothy Hall, a newcomer to Charleston from New Jersey, observed the planters' rush to rebuild their slave labor forces: "Having been stripped of their stock [plantations] could yield no relief unless they [planters] could fall on some mode of procuring negroes . . . when the British merchants threw out the bait they took it as their only resource . . . it was no wonder their necessities got the better of their judgment."[73]

Robert Pringle Jr. was one of many merchants keen to get a slice of the slave trade. Among his first requests to his partner in Bristol in September 1783 was that he should "endeavour if possible to get some consignments of Negroes here."[74] South Carolina's demand for slaves reconnected the state not only to prewar transatlantic channels of trade but also to British West Indies markets, despite the ban that forbade American vessels from trading with the sugar islands. The islands were able to supply surplus or newly arrived slaves to satisfy burgeoning demand in South Carolina; in return they once again provided a market for the state's rice and lumber exports, if these products were shipped in British boats.[75] The resumption of the slave trade further exposed the commercial paradoxes—not to mention the moral hypocrisies—within renewed Anglo-American trade. Henry Laurens was happy to advise London merchants on which Charleston firms would receive cargoes of African slaves, despite beginning to express qualms about the traffic in human cargo and growing indebtedness in South Carolina. "Respecting the African Trade I have only to repeat [that] Many Men in this State I apprehend will be ruined by its continuance," he advised a London correspondent. "My private sentiments of the morality of the traffic entirely aside, this

Country already overwhelmed with debt will sink deeper & deeper by excessive importations until the evil shall purge itself off."[76] Between 1783 and 1787, the year when South Carolina's legislature temporarily banned further slave imports in an attempt to reduce planter indebtedness, the number of slaves brought into Charleston reached record high levels. Four slave ships arrived in South Carolina in 1783, followed by seventeen in 1784, nineteen in 1785, five in 1786, and three in 1787. Most were British. Together they brought more than 8,300 slaves.[77]

Table 11: Indigo Exports from South Carolina and Georgia (lbs.), 1768–88

	South Carolina	Georgia	Total
1768	566,600	19,700	586,300
1769	402,700	13,900	416,600
1770	550,800	22,300	573,100
1771	434,200	19,900	454,100
Average 1768–71	488,575	18,950	507,525
1772	853,700	11,900	865,600
1773	720,600	-	720,600
1774	815,100	-	815,000
1775	1,122,200	-	1,122,200
Average 1772–75	877,900	11,900	880,875
1784	713,700	-	713,700
1785	654,800	-	654,800
1786	840,600	-	840,600
1787	974,100 *	-	974,100 *
1788	833,600 *	-	833,600 *
Average 1784–88*	803,360	-	803,360

Source: Carter et al., *Historical Statistics*, V, 749–50; Nash,
"South Carolina Indigo," 371, table 3.
*For Charleston only.

South Carolina's reduced capacity to produce rice and indigo exacerbated the growing debt crisis by limiting its ability to offset imports through staple exports. Merchants and planters were caught in a classic investor's paradox. They needed to import slaves, plantation hardware, and machinery to restore the state's productive base. However, their plantations could not in the short term—until rebuilt and restocked—generate the returns to service or repay the debts incurred. A run of three poor rice harvests between 1783 and 1785 exacerbated the problem. A structural deficit that began when Atlantic trade resumed persisted throughout the first decade of independence. In 1784 South Carolina imported English goods to the value of £442,465 and exported just £163,540 in produce to England. Average annual exports to England between 1784 and 1789 were two-thirds of the value of imports from England, a reversal of the state's prewar trade bilateral trade surplus, when exports had in most years well exceeded imports.[78] Throughout the 1780s South Carolina's rice exports lagged well below prewar levels. On average 73,310 barrels were exported each year between 1784 and 1789, just 60 percent of the 121,970 barrels shipped on average between 1772 and 1774 (table 10). Indigo exports were healthier, at only just below prewar levels. The loss of the prewar bounty did not deter production, and South Carolina exported on average approximately 803,000 pounds of the dye each year between 1784 and 1788, compared with an average of around 878,000 pounds annually between 1772 and 1775 (table 11). Only from the mid-1790s did indigo production cease to be cost-effective, as Carolinian indigo was supplanted in European markets by plentiful low-cost, high-quality produce from India, and planters turned instead to cotton.[79]

By the mid-1780s South Carolina's political instability and its growing debt crisis—and the trading imbalances that underlay it—were causing growing alarm in the state. "This country wants nothing but industry & honesty to make it one of the most flourishing States in the world; but the madness of speculation & the weakness of government have made it at present a theatre of discontent & confusion," David Ramsay wrote to a friend at the Confederation Congress in 1785.[80] Looking back on Carolinians' rush to repair and restock their estates, Ramsay would identify excessive borrowing as the principal cause of the state's economic hardships during the 1780s. Planters "did not always content themselves with moderate supplies for necessary purposes; but in too many cases embarrassed themselves with pecuniary engagements for the discharge of which the most favourable seasons, largest crops, and highest prices for the same would have been scarcely sufficient."[81] The assembly's moratorium on overseas slave imports in 1787 reflected official concern over the state's debt burden; originally designed to run for three years, it would be repeatedly renewed until 1803.[82] As the debt crisis extended into 1787, Henry Laurens's rhetoric increasingly stressed the values of self-reliance and self-denial: "It would be one of the greatest blessings that could light on this Country were it to be for three or four years wholly restrained from Credit. We should get out of debt & then become honest again; in the mean time We should find ready money enough to pay for the common necessaries of Life which are all We need and all We are entitled to, except from our own exertions, in our present circumstances."[83]

Table 12: British Share of Foreign Shipping in Charleston, 1786–88

Outbound	British ships	Total ships	British ships as % of total	British tonnage	Total tonnage	British tonnage as % of total
1786	168	234	71.8	16,855	21,933	76.8
1787	150	212	70.8	17,106	20,587	83.1
Total	**318**	**446**	**71.3**	**33,961**	**42,520**	**79.9**

Inbound	British ships	Total ships	British ships as % of total	British tonnage	Total tonnage	British tonnage as % of total
1787	92	141	65.2	7,080	8,644	81.9
1788	158	231	68.4	19,199	25,063	76.6
Total	**250**	**372**	**67.2**	**26,279**	**33,707**	**78.0**

Source: British consular reports on foreign shipping in U.S. ports in
Charles R. Ritcheson, *Aftermath of Revolution: British Policy towards the United
States, 1783–1795* (Dallas: Southern Methodist University Press, 1969), 369–71.
Note: Data covers November of previous year to November of year specified

Laurens was rare in his reflective detachment. More radical voices such as Christopher Gadsden, before the war the leading voice of Charleston's radical Sons of Liberty, and Aedanus Burke reflected more prevalent anti-British feeling. Commercial logic and continuing geopolitical disputes with Britain seemed to encourage the diversion of trade away from the former mother country. American toleration of British commercial restrictions smacked of continuing subservience. "All the States may be said to be Shopkeepers," Gadsden complained to Thomas Jefferson, "and what Folly for any, to give the Preference to that Nation which is the least important to them, that consumes the smallest Quantity of their Produce, which with regard to our chief Staple Rice, is the Case of Gt. Britn. who tho' they have made Peace, are manifestly far from being cordial Friends with us." Others, however, saw the British as the victims of their own success, with the competitiveness of the Charleston market suppressing profits and the unreliability of consumers leaving many in the red. One Charlestonian correspondent to a London newspaper was "amazed at the credulity of the English merchants" who persisted in sending goods to South Carolina long after European competitors had given up, despite the diminishing returns, losses, and "the knavery and bad payments they have met with."[84]

Regardless of British merchants' motivations, however, and the profitability or otherwise of their businesses, statistics compiled by the official consul that Great Britain employed in Charleston supported contentions of renewed British dominance. British ships were calculated to represent about 71 percent of the total foreign shipping and 80 percent of the total foreign tonnage clearing Charleston between November 1785 and November 1787, and approximately 67 percent of the foreign shipping and 78 percent of the foreign tonnage entering the port between November 1786 and November 1788 (table 12). Statistically, at least, Britain's share of the trade of newly independent South Carolina was nearly as great as it had been of colonial South Carolina before the war.

"After a Storm at Sea is over":
British Merchants and the Postwar Carolina Trade

The apparent return of South Carolina's overseas trade to the antebellum status quo disguised major upheavals within it. A more nuanced picture emerges from a focus on the British end of the trade and the interpersonal rapprochements within it, challenging contemporary jeremiads in Charleston of renewed commercial subservience to a monolithic cadre of British merchants. As Anglo-American relations had worsened spasmodically in the decade before the war, Charleston's merchants had by and large continued trading with their regular British correspondents, regardless of the British merchants' responses to American grievances—for example whether they had or had not petitioned the British government for redress. The calls made by South Carolinians on the eve of the war for selective boycotts of supposedly hostile British merchants had been overtaken by blanket embargoes. However, by focusing on the run-up to the American Revolution, studies of British merchants' responses to the Anglo-American crises of the 1760s and 1770s have missed the longer-term implications of these calls for selective boycotts.[85] The real impact of these calls was felt only after 1783.

The resumption of trade with Britain brought dividends for supporters of the American cause. Samuel Brailsford, the merchant who had replaced his Loyalist partners John Hopton and Robert Powell in Charleston in 1783 after their expulsion from the state, had been based in Bristol before the war. He sought to reestablish the firm's trade and seek compensation for its losses. Brailsford's prewar politics explain why he was more acceptable in Charleston's postwar political ferment and also reveal the political heterodoxy possible in Anglo-American partnerships before the war. In contrast to his Loyalist partners, Brailsford had moved in pro-American circles in Bristol, where he had associated with the New York–born radical and MP Henry Cruger, welcomed the antiestablishment firebrand John Wilkes to the city in 1772, and had corresponded with the keen American patriot William Lee. Together with Richard Champion, a major local merchant, Brailsford had led the city's "American Merchants, Traders, and Well-wishers to American Commerce" in petitioning the king in September 1775 to urge conciliation with America. More significant still was his practical assistance to the state of South Carolina during the war, when through his Charleston lawyer he had lent more than two thousand pounds to the state's treasury to support its war effort.[86]

Political orientation was just as important for merchants in London seeking to enter or reenter the Carolina trade. The partners in Bird, Savage & Bird, the capital's leading recipients of Carolinian rice after the war had all received their training with William Manning, a merchant known for his wartime support for the American cause.[87] When Henry Laurens resumed trading to London after the war, exporting produce for sale on commission, it was chiefly to three firms, Manning & Vaughan, Bourdieu & Chollet, and Bridgen & Waller.[88] All three had traded to South Carolina before the war, but not as Carolina specialists. Their commerce with the then colony had been part of broader American trading portfolios. Bourdieu and Chollet were listed in London directories before the war as being French and St. Eustatius merchants, illustrating the territorial breadth of their trade. A former merchant-planter on St. Kitts, Manning had become one of London's largest West Indies merchants after moving to the capital in the late 1760s. Bridgen & Waller had principally traded to North Carolina.[89] Laurens's postwar connections with the three firms reflected their sympathy toward America and his personal links to the principal merchants in each business: William Manning, James Bourdieu, and Edward Bridgen. During Laurens's imprisonment in the Tower of London between October 1780 and December 1781, after he had been captured at sea by the British while en route to Holland, each had visited him regularly and lobbied the British government for his release.[90]

That these merchants campaigned for Laurens was symptomatic of their advocacy for the American cause before, during, and after the war. Manning had sympathized with American grievances during the early 1770s and with fellow West Indies traders had petitioned Parliament in February 1775 against the trade restrictions they blamed for the Anglo-American crisis.[91] His partner and son-in-law, Benjamin Vaughan, was a leading figure in British pro-American circles before the war, counting Benjamin Franklin among his friends and publishing an edition of Franklin's writings in London in 1780. Vaughan's connections to Lord Shelburne and advocacy of a constructive approach to Anglo-American relations earned him a place at the Paris peace negotiations in 1782–83.[92] For his part, Bourdieu was regarded as "a great stickler for American independence" and attempted to intercede in America's favor at the peace talks. Probably un-beknown to his admirers in South Carolina, however, Bourdieu and his part-ner, Samuel Chollet, had in 1773 offered to transact the East India Company's shipments of tea to both Charleston and New York. The firm had withdrawn their offer only because of a dispute over the exchange rate to be applied on the shipments.[93] Bridgen's strong pro-American sympathies before, during, and after the war were more constant. In October 1775 he had signed a petition to George III that called for a total cessation of hostilities in America, and like Vaughan, he formed a close friendship with Franklin and mixed with Britain's leading pro-American advocates.[94]

Vaughan and Bridgen had put their sympathy into practice during the war by serving on a committee established in December 1777 to raise money for American prisoners of war in Britain. British merchants had long used philan-thropy to show their personal commitment to America. With the outbreak of war, however, donations to explicitly American causes assumed far greater political resonance, particularly after news arrived of the British defeat at Saratoga in Oc-tober 1777 and American independence first appeared to be a real prospect. De-signed to supply the prisoners with clothing and other necessities, the prisoners-of-war fund was the most prominent of these causes. Its donors were a roll call of opponents to the government's war policies. Like Vaughan and Bridgen, William Manning was another donor to the fund, alongside the leading London radicals John Sawbridge and Richard Oliver and more moderate conciliators such as Lord Shelburne and the Marquess of Rockingham.[95] Bridgen maintained his support for the United States after independence. He reflected that during the war he had "spent not a small sum in behalf of the right of America and Mankind," partly in a scheme that he proposed to Benjamin Franklin in which he would supply Con-gress with copper blanks for coins or arrange for the coins to be minted to any chosen design. Despite failing to make any headway with the coinage scheme and losing money on it, Bridgen looked back with satisfaction that "this great and Important revolution will be of general good to the world."[96]

Pro-American sympathizers found that their public support for American causes during the war was helpful when they sought to recover landholdings that had been seized amid blanket confiscations from Loyalists and British ab-sentees. Because of Bridgen's pro-American initiatives, Franklin personally lobbied the North Carolina legislature to return lands and slaves on the Cape Fear River that had been seized from him in 1779.[97] Franklin wrote to the state's governor to identify Bridgen as "a particular Friend of mine and a zealous one of the American Cause" and a man who "from the beginning of our Difference with England, uniformly, openly & firmly, espoused the Interests of our Coun-try." Bridgen's lands were eventually restored to him in 1785.[98] Attributing North Carolina's confiscation of his lands to certain legislators who coveted them, he was charitably stoic. "After a Storm at Sea is over," he reflected, "it takes some time before the waves subside, and why will you expect that every thing should immediately be smooth, after so great a Conflict?"[99] Another public subscriber to the prisoners-of-war fund, William Baker Jr., had led London merchants in their lobbying for conciliation with America in 1775. A confiscation order on his extensive South Carolina landholdings was downgraded in 1784 and lifted in 1786. In evidence to the state's senate and assembly, Baker's lawyer swore that "ever Since the Commencement of the War [he] has been a warm advocate for the Rights of America" and that he had "always been foremost in liberal Contributions for the relief of American prisoners." The committee deciding his case returned his lands to him on the grounds that he had been "a warm friend to America since the commencement of the war."[100]

By contrast, British merchants who had actually or supposedly been hostile to the American cause found that their perceived political orientation returned to haunt them in peacetime. None of London's leading Carolina traders before the war had been regarded as sympathetic to the American cause, with Greenwood & Higginson, John Nutt, and Christopher Rolleston singled out as notable enemies of the colonies. Their wartime commercial strategies may have reinforced suspicions of anti-American bias. Many merchants in trade to North America followed William Freeman Sr.'s uncontroversial course and withdrew uncommitted capital from trade to buy British land instead as a more secure investment. Others diversified into branches of North American trade that were still open—a riskier but still politically neutral choice. London's leading Georgia merchants, Davis & Strachan, were involved during the war in the trade to the loyal colony of Quebec; so too was John Shoolbred, one of Britain's largest traffickers of slaves before the war.[101]

The investment strategy that London's leading prewar Carolina merchants chose was more controversial. They took advantage of the financial opportunities provided—albeit indirectly—by the war. Although London's Carolina traders did not directly supply the British war effort with arms and provisions during the war, they were large investors in government stock. As government expenditure rocketed in wartime, so too did its borrowings as it financed the war effort in large part by expanding the national debt. Loans funded some 40 percent of government expenditures during the war, and government stock was marketed heavily, with City of London merchants and financiers the largest subscribers.[102] Among these, individuals and firms in the Carolina trade were major purchasers, seeking a secure haven for trading capital that could no longer be safely invested in transatlantic cargoes. Their stakes were announced in the London press, appearing in the published lists of patriotic investors. John Nutt subscribed fifteen thousand pounds to the total of twelve million pounds loaned to the government in 1779–80. Investing the same amount the following year, he was joined by Greenwood & Higginson, who bought twelve thousand pounds, and by fellow traders to South Carolina and Georgia, including Davis, Strachan & Co., six thousand pounds; and Clark & Milligan, three thousand pounds.[103] Their subscriptions signaled the great sums of money at the firms' disposal and hinted at their overall capitalization; the amounts subscribed by Nutt and by Greenwood & Higginson, for example, comfortably exceeded the median average.

In subscribing to the loans, the merchants made a rational investment decision: the four percent interest on government stock represented a reliable return on capital at a time when other commercial investments were neither reliable nor secure. More symbolically, the merchants' subscriptions to the loans represented a twofold commitment to the government. First, they signaled a confidence in its capacity to raise the taxes and duties needed to fund its debt repayments. Second, they were a public commitment to its war effort, albeit one in which calculations of commercial self-interest were also at play. Their loans helped to make the government's military strategy in America possible, in effect financing military actions to restore the prewar status quo. The merchants expected returns on the capital invested in the loans and, by investing in this way, endorsed a return to the prewar trading arrangements through which they had prospered. While it is not certain that these subscriptions were known in South Carolina, as publicly advertised gestures they offered a pointer to the investors' political loyalties.

In particular, John Nutt's purported hostility toward America led him to be shunned in postwar commerce. Despite Nutt's expertise in the Carolina trade, particularly in marketing indigo, Henry Laurens avoided dealings with him after the war. Personal animosity between the two men and Nutt's political stance made him, Laurens believed, "an Enemy to my Country."[104] Besides the suggestiveness of their loan subscriptions, the merchants' anti-American reputations had been reinforced by their wartime conduct. One episode exemplified Nutt's apparent hostility to the American cause. Nutt—who supposedly had influence with Lord Hillsborough, Lord North's hard-line secretary of state—secured the release from British prison of his longtime correspondent Gideon Dupont Jr., and in so doing he converted Dupont from being an advocate of American independence at the start of the war into a Loyalist. Dupont, a merchant in Charleston before the war, had been sent by South Carolina's provisional government to France "for the purpose of purchasing . . . necessaries such as stores, ammunition & arms." However, when the vessel was seized by the Royal Navy, Dupont was taken as a prisoner to Portsmouth before being freed "in consequence of interest made for him by Mr. John Nutt." Dupont returned as a Loyalist to British-occupied Charleston, and the episode was later presented to the British government as evidence of Nutt's own staunch loyalism.[105]

James Poyas was spurned by prewar connections on similar grounds. Formerly a merchant in Charleston, Poyas had transferred to London in 1767 and before the war had maintained a transatlantic partnership with Daniel DeSaussure, who after the war became one of the partners in the new firm of Smiths,

DeSaussure & Darrell. Two of the firm's other partners, George Smith and Josiah Smith Jr., had been Poyas's attorneys in the colony. Poyas criticized the American cause and his associates' handling of his funds in South Carolina during the war, and as a result the new firm terminated its connection with him after the peace.[106] Meanwhile the ruse of former Charleston Loyalists Robert Powell and John Hopton to overcome their banishment from South Carolina by sending their British partner Samuel Brailsford to Charleston in their place was, though clever in theory, unsuccessful in practice. The ploy was scuppered by long memories in the port. The firm was shunned despite the fact that the two former Loyalists were in London, and it went bankrupt in 1786.[107]

Charles Ogilvie's attempt during the war to cut his cloth to changing political realities in South Carolina backfired.[108] For Ogilvie, the lure of profit, and perhaps a desperation to maintain links with South Carolina, had led him to circumvent legal impediments and continue trading with the colony before its recapture by British forces in 1780. Illicit trade to America through the Dutch Caribbean colony of St. Eustatius, long a site for contraband interimperial commerce, was a popular route for British merchants.[109] Trade through French ports, one of several avenues that Ogilvie tried, was another illegal option. With his extensive landholdings in South Carolina, Ogilvie had even more at stake in the war than did most of his trading counterparts in London. His wartime maneuverings illustrated the political tightrope that Atlantic merchants were willing to tread in order to secure their investments. Having signed the pro-American petition to the king in October 1775, he went to South Carolina in 1777. After a year in the colony, he joined several other American traders in Nantes, one of the main ports in France's war-time trade with the United States.

In Nantes, Ogilvie and several other American traders corresponded with the American commissioners in Paris between November 1778 and February 1779, seeking support and protection for a convoy they were trying to send to America. Ogilvie's association with this group—several of the other Nantes traders were Americans who had escaped from British prisons—in their attempt to send war supplies to the rebellious colonies might suggest he was strongly attached to the Patriot cause.[110] More likely Ogilvie was acting from self-interest, capitalizing on an opportunity to reenter trade, restore his finances, and show an ongoing commitment to South Carolina. A February 1779 letter to his nephew George spelled out these concerns. Preparing to return once again to Charleston but anxious lest his earlier departure from the colony might have led to his estates in the region being confiscated, he sought news of "all my Concerns in South Carolina & Georgia" and "the kind of reception I might expect to meet on my Arrival . . . my long Detention in England (though unavoidable by me) may have given room for Surmises to my disadvantage on the other side."[111] In early 1779 Ogilvie attempted to return to South Carolina, sailing from France, as he would later tell Britain's postwar Loyalist Claims Commission, in a small vessel in the hope that it would be seized by the British, since all prisoners of the British were exempted from the penalties of South Carolina's Confiscation Act. Initially his scheme went according to plan. The vessel was captured by a British privateer, and Ogilvie was held on parole in Bermuda for eight months. The British recapture of Charleston in May 1780 prompted him to make one last critical switch of allegiances. Permitted to leave Bermuda, he went back to South Carolina, where he became an enthusiastic supporter of British dominion and took office in its wartime administration as deputy commissioner for sequestered estates. His prominence in British-controlled Charleston would, however, soon count against him.[112]

When South Carolina's General Assembly met in February 1782 in Jacksonborough, a village some thirty-five miles south of Charleston, which remained in British hands, it identified Ogilvie as having been in the fifth and most heinous category of Loyalists: "those who have borne commissions, military or civil, under the British government since the conquest of South Carolina." As was prescribed in the "Act For Disposing of Certain Estates, and Banishing Certain Persons, Therein Mentioned," all of Ogilvie's estates were confiscated and he was banished from the state.[113] On his return to London, he lamented that he had been "stripped almost naked of property . . . there is not one single acre of Land, nor Negro or other Article as yet restored to my Children, or to any body for them." Even while in Charleston he had been powerless to prevent the sale of his "two most productive plantations," Richfield and Mount Alexander, in early 1782. In total, Ogilvie estimated the value of his lost American property at some forty thousand pounds.[114]

Ogilvie's perambulations around the war-torn Atlantic as he attempted to shore up his finances and secure his Carolinian properties may have been extreme, but they were not unique. Like Ogilvie—who had continued to acquire lands in the region as late as spring 1775—Samuel Carne, another former Charleston merchant and a medical doctor who had relocated to London during the 1760s, had evidently not foreseen the imminent Anglo-American rupture. He had invested in two South Carolina plantations in 1774, the 1,300-acre Haggatt Hall and the 1,440-acre Crowfield, both in St. James Goose Creek Parish to the north of Charleston. Realizing the prospect of war, Carne rushed to South Carolina in the autumn of 1775 to try to extricate his fortune and to call in the debts he was owed in the colony.[115] Anxious to return to Britain but finding that it was no longer possible to travel directly from Charleston to British ports, he left South Carolina on board a ship to Nantes. On the high seas Carne's travails continued. The vessel he was traveling on was intercepted by a British privateer and taken to Liverpool. Carne was arrested since he was unable to prove that while in Charleston he had refused to take an oath against the British. The indigo he had brought back from South Carolina was seized. In embarrassment, Carne left Britain for the West Indies in 1779, traveling first to St. Kitts and then to

St. Eustatius, where he supported himself by plying his former trade as a doctor and performing surgery. On hearing of British military successes in the southern colonies, Carne continued his odyssey, and like Charles Ogilvie, went back to South Carolina. He set about pursuing his outstanding debts of some £10,372 after the British retook Charleston in 1780 and tried to curry favor with the authorities by signing a letter to Lord Cornwallis congratulating him on his military victory at the Battle of Camden, in central South Carolina. The epistle came back to haunt him at the end of the war, when it was cited as evidence of his staunch loyalism. Unable to stay in Charleston, Carne sold off his stock of medicaments, property in the town, and household furniture and left with the British forces in December 1782. His estates were confiscated by the state.[116]

"No lawful impediments": Pursuing Prewar Debts in Britain and South Carolina in the 1780s

The Treaty of Paris made clear that the United States was responsible for repaying the bona fide prewar debts contracted in the former American colonies. Unlike the treaty's controversial Article V, which ambiguously stipulated that the U.S. Congress would "earnestly recommend" that the states restore property and rights to Loyalists, Article IV demanded that there be "no lawful impediments" to the collection of debts contracted on either side of the Atlantic before the war. With the states comprehensively ignoring Article V's "earnest recommendation," the British government was forced by public and political sympathy for the Loyalists' plight to take responsibility for covering Loyalist losses. It established the Loyalist Claims Commission, which met for the first time in August 1783 and over the next six years examined some 3,225 claims.[117] By excluding prewar commercial debts from the commission's remit—this was the United States' responsibility—the British government effectively decoupled Loyalist and merchant interests.

Within the United States, responsibility for compelling prewar commercial debts to be settled lay with state courts. This devolution had major ramifications for British claimants. Levels of prewar debts were highest in the plantation South, and it was here that opposition to Article IV of the treaty was greatest. Courts in South Carolina and Georgia were among the most intractable. According to one Carolinian, congressional recommendations were viewed "like the Pastoral Letters of a Bishop" and were treated with about as much reverence.[118] British merchants seeking prewar debts in South Carolina ran into a popular and legal backlash fueled by the arrival in Charleston of new British traders in Charleston, who had flooded the market with goods and credit. "The Power of the People having virtually superceded the Law," one Charleston attorney told a British creditor, his chances of recovering his client's debts were sorely limited.[119] Legislation gave formal vent to popular clamor. Explicitly contravening the Treaty of Paris, state law in South Carolina prohibited legal suits to recover debts contracted before February 1782. The notorious Pine Barren Act of 1785 allowed debtors to repay their creditors with land in place of cash: many chose to do so with nearly worthless tracts—pine barrens—giving rise to its name. By devaluing prewar commercial debts, it made them nearly impossible to reclaim.

Compensation claims to the British government complained of the "divers lawful impediments" to the collection of debts in South Carolina, directly breaking the peace treaty. Even after the Pine Barren Act was struck down by South Carolina's courts in January 1787, its replacement, the Act to Regulate the Recovery and Payment of Debts, allowed debtors to repay their creditors in three installments over three years. A revision to the law the following year gave debtors even more generous terms: five installments over five years.[120] In England, Isaac King attributed his debtors' evasions to the legal environment in South Carolina. "If your Assembly possessed any principle of honour," he complained to his Charleston attorney, "they would be ashamed to act so unjustly & directly contrary to Treaty; while they were considered as in a state of Rebellion such conduct was expected from them, but now their Independence is admitted they should pay some regard to Justice & the Law of Nations." He considered the state's assembly members who had passed South Carolina's debt laws "in a worse light than Highwaymen," a view no doubt compounded when one of his own debtors was able to avoid repayments by being elected to the assembly and claiming legislative privilege from arrest.[121]

Recovering debts in South Carolina was time consuming and dispiriting. The frustration felt by the family of one London merchant, Joseph Nicholson, typified that felt by many, amplified by straitened circumstances. Unpaid debts in the state had reduced Nicholson, they claimed, "from a Situation of comparative Elevation in which he and his Family enjoyed every comfort that affluence could afford to one of embarrassment and distress."[122] Other claimants confirmed reputations for avarice that they had earned before the war by dunning debtors for full and immediate payment and refusing to accept partial settlements. Their efforts bore little fruit.[123] Agents and attorneys in South Carolina were employed to pursue debtors through the courts, and British merchants regularly crossed the Atlantic to press in person for repayment. John Alexander Ogilvie did so on behalf of his father, Charles, during the 1780s; and Edward Neufville did so in the mid-1780s. William Greenwood Jr. went to South Carolina on behalf of Greenwood & Higginson in 1790, while as late as 1791 Richard Shubrick paid "his native Country a visit in order to settle sum of his oldest concerns."[124] John Nutt employed the Charleston lawyer William Loughton Smith, an old family connection whose London education Nutt had supervised during the 1770s, to pursue debtors in the state.

For Britain's merchant creditors, the fundamental weakness of the Articles of Confederation between the United States underlay the (il)legal impediments to claiming debts. Without a strong federal government to compel acquiescence, individual states could disregard international agreements, specifically on the question of debts. "However much I dislike the British Govt.," Isaac King reflected, "I detest republican Govt. or no Govt. still more."[125] Ratification of the federal Constitution in 1788 therefore prompted high hopes among some that treaty obligations would finally be honored and prewar debts repaid. The "abuse of Power" by South Carolina's Assembly would soon be curtailed, King's Charleston attorney informed him in January 1789, "as our Federal Government will soon be organized."[126] Other frustrated claimants were more skeptical, their faith in American justice tainted by bitter past experience. As John Nutt explained in a letter to William Grenville, the British foreign secretary, in 1792, "With respect to opening the Law Courts of America at this distant period of time, we have but too much reason to fear it will now avail us but little, such has been the devastation and change of property occasioned by deaths, insolvencies, removals and other attendant circumstances of delay."[127] Ultimately, Britain's prewar Carolina traders had mixed fortunes. William Higginson, who determinedly chased the debts owed to him and his late partner, William Greenwood, through the federal courts, was one beneficiary, winning several cases in 1793 against former Charleston correspondents.[128] Samuel Brailsford was less successful when he took the Loyalist claims of his former partners, John Hopton and Robert Powell, all the way to the U.S. Supreme Court: the court unanimously rejected them in 1794. In a paradoxical twist, by taking American citizenship in order to pursue the claims, Brailsford rendered himself ineligible to make comparable claims in Britain.[129]

Often frustrated in their efforts to reclaim their debts through South Carolina's courts during the 1780s, London's prewar Carolina traders looked increasingly to the British government for redress. They resurrected the lobbying tactics they had used before and during the war, putting their trust in tried and tested methods despite the geopolitical shifts that had dislocated their business activities. A specialist Committee of South Carolina Merchants and Traders was operating in the mid-1780s and met Prime Minister William Pitt in December 1786 to discuss "matters relating to the American trade."[130] Prewar debts were presumably on the agenda. A personal meeting with the prime minister indicated the group's influence and suggested top-level government interest in the matter; before and during the war, merchants had to be content with making their case to the Board of Trade or in letters and petitions to the secretaries of state. The Committee of London Merchants, with John Nutt at its helm, was prolific in telling the British government about its members' travails in pursuing prewar debts. It found a sympathetic ear. Suggesting that lobbying still worked, merchant reparations became one of the major contentions in Anglo-American diplomacy throughout the 1780s, with Pitt's administration pressing the United States on the matter.

Determined obstructionism in the states and South Carolina specifically—a function of the ineffectiveness of federal fiat—starkly illustrated the new geopolitical realities, however. Neither the Committee of London Merchants nor the British government acting on its behalf could force the states to make reparations. Nor, for all its compassionate noises, was the British government prepared to pay compensation itself. To a certain extent, this was a question of funds: grappling with the huge deficit left by the war, government finances could not stretch so far, particularly when the government was already compensating dispossessed Loyalists in land and money—a bill which eventually reached three million pounds.[131] More significantly, an important diplomatic point was at stake. If the British government had reimbursed the British merchants, it would have absolved the United States of one of its treaty commitments and surrendered an important bargaining chip. Commercial compensation was a critical element in a delicate balance of grievances that remained unresolved after the Treaty of Paris, alongside navigation rights on the Mississippi, Britain's forts on the United States' northern frontier, American rights to trade with the West Indies, and restitution for slaves freed and evacuated—or, to American complainants, "carried off"—when British forces left America at the end of the war; many of those slaves were from South Carolina. With the British government unwilling to give ground on prewar debts, British claimants were caught between American intransigence and British resolve to retain strong cards to play in future negotiations.[132]

Nor were the prewar traders—unlike the thousands of Loyalists who had fled America after the war—able to capitalize on public sympathy in Britain. A popular sense that the government was neglecting the Loyalists in the peace negotiations had helped bring down Shelburne's administration in March 1783, and much of the Loyalists' compensation was ultimately raised through public lotteries.[133] Compared to the sentiment that the exiles' plight aroused, Britain's merchant creditors were confronted by public and political indifference: Isaac King attributed the Commons being "so sanguine" on the matter to Britain's own "distressed state."[134] While Carolinian Loyalist exiles such as Elias Ball could look to public figures such as his "particular Friend" Lord Cornwallis to press their cases before the Loyalist Claims Commission, reimbursement of British traders for prewar debts was left squarely, and in keeping with the terms of the peace, to the American side.[135]

The divergence of Loyalist and merchant interests became most apparent in the mid-1780s, when the two groups came into direct opposition. The Loyalist lobby had powerful emotive appeal. With advocates such as Cornwallis—still a respected figure in Britain but a pariah among many in South Carolina for commanding British forces in the southern campaign during the war—it could wield strong influence in the halls of power. The Loyalist lobby tried repeatedly between 1785 and 1787 to persuade Pitt's government to block Americans from using British courts to claim prewar debts from Loyalists exiled in Britain. A bill that was introduced into Parliament to this effect would, had it become law, have contravened Article IV of the Treaty of Paris and matched the legal impediments in the United States that were stopping British merchants from recouping their prewar debts. The Committee of London Merchants opposed these attempts on the grounds that such a measure would make its own members' claims even harder to pursue. After vigorous debate in the press the bill was withdrawn.[136] The controversy highlighted the divergence between Loyalist and merchant factions; the Committee of London Merchants' successful opposition to the proposals also signaled its own traction in domestic politics, even though it was unable to translate this into legislative or financial achievement in the United States.

"Carolina disappointments": Assessing the Debts in the 1790s

Only with the ratification of the federal Constitution in 1790 did the United States government assume responsibility for state debts. Federal authority finally offered British traders the prospect of recovering prewar debts through American courts, although the passage of time and the inevitable deaths, insolvencies, and relocations of the intervening years dampened expectations. Together with two London merchants involved in the Chesapeake tobacco trade before the war, Duncan Campbell and William Molleson, John Nutt assembled the outstanding claims of prewar British traders. Their report to the British government in February 1791 calculated that British creditors were owed £412,000 in prewar debts in South Carolina, a figure that had swelled with interest to a total of £687,953. This was the second highest amount for any state, behind the £2,305,408 owed in Virginia.[137] The plantation states' overwhelming share of the overall debts owed in the United States to British merchants has been traced back to the unprecedented demand for northern colonies' cereal in 1774–75, when Britain suffered a dire harvest. Coupled with the boycott of British imports in 1775, bumper cereal exports in those years had allowed farmers and merchants in New England, New York, and Pennsylvania effectively to write off long-standing trade deficits with British merchants in a single year.[138]

Debts on account, in bond, and through outstanding loans were the most common claims connected to South Carolina. This again pointed to commercial overextension by British firms in the then colony by offering overgenerous credit and overstocking the market in Charleston, supporting the charges leveled against them in South Carolina before the Revolutionary War.[139] Debts incurred through wartime trade between Britain and America—such as when Charleston was in British hands between 1780 and 1782—were specifically excluded from inclusion, according to the terms agreed in 1790 for addressing debts in America. Only debts verifiably contracted before the war would be eligible for redress. Claimants such as Nutt and Greenwood & Higginson had specifically identified themselves as traders "previous to 1776" in their lobbying efforts throughout the 1780s, distinguishing themselves as respectable, legitimate merchants rather than the "adventurers" who had engaged in wartime commerce.

The vast majority of British debts claimed in South Carolina—some £596,289, or 87 percent of the total—were by London merchants (table 13). Some £562,538, or 94 percent, of these were claimed by just nine firms, a concentration made even more striking when the claims of one such firm, Powell & Hopton, which were rejected as fraudulent, are discounted.[140] The nature of the claims impels some caution in drawing conclusions. The claims were self-estimated and probably therefore erred on the high side, while individual claimants calculated interest over different periods and at different rates: some compounded interest; some did not.[141] Some London trading houses were more cautious in extending credit to colonial customers than others. Overall, however, British merchants both before and after the war used the length and generosity of their credit as one of their chief calling cards. Long and generous credit was key to competitive advantage and to attracting new correspondents. Higher volumes of trade and greater cash flow allowed merchants to offer more extensive credit, closely linking length of credit to commercial scale. As such, the British traders who had extended the most credit to customers in South Carolina, and who were consequently the most exposed when war broke out, were the largest participants in the Carolina trade. These were the trading houses hit hardest by the war and the largest claimants in 1790.

Despite the problems posed in interpreting the postwar debts, the claims are a good guide to London merchants' relative exposure in trade to South Carolina before the war. Greenwood & Higginson and John Nutt submitted the largest and fourth largest of all American claims by London merchants, for losses of £269,760 and £103,680 respectively. The firms had been the leading London trading houses to South Carolina and the most financially overextended in the colony before the war: their personal appeal to the Board of Trade in November 1775 for the rice trade from South Carolina and Georgia to be exempted from the Prohibitory Acts was made with good reason.[145] Both firms' claims were exclusively for debts in South Carolina and Georgia, confirming their geographic trading specialism: Greenwood & Higginson claimed £211,533 in South Carolina and £58,227 in Georgia; Nutt claimed £61,081 in South Carolina and £42,599 in Georgia.

What became of London's leading prewar Carolina traders, with their extensive debts in South Carolina and Georgia? While their debts and the opprobrium directed toward them by former correspondents explain why they withdrew from the Carolina trade after the war, they remained wealthy and would not have been held back from reinvesting in the Carolina trade by a lack of funds. Nor did the massive losses that Greenwood & Higginson and Nutt suffered in South Carolina diminish their status in the City of London. Despite complaining in 1778 that "the Carolina Gentlemen had got his whole Fortune, to a single Guinea," Nutt had been able to spare £30,000 to invest in government stock during the war, and Greenwood had invested £12,000.[146] On Greenwood's death in April 1786, his remaining fortune and diverse portfolio of lands were distributed among his family. He left one son his grand Little London estate in Middlesex and another his extensive landholdings in Yorkshire. The sons received his "plantations and negroes" in America jointly, while his daughter had to make do with £6,000 and a joint share of the rest of his unspecified estate in Britain.[147]

Other merchant claimants similarly prospered despite their uncollected debts in South Carolina. Richard Shubrick, who submitted claims in 1790 for debts of £30,049 in South Carolina and £18,064 in Georgia, left an estate of at least £20,000 on his death in 1797.[148] James Poyas, who had claimed losses of £15,656, continued to operate in business from prestigious locations in the heart of London—Broad Street, Throgmorton Street, and Lothbury—though his field of trade after the war is unclear. He left substantial bequests when he died in 1799, including a dowry of £5,000 for his daughter. Christopher Rolleston, who together with his partner Edward Neufville had claimed £81,600, continued in trade near Poyas and eventually retired to a country estate in his native Nottinghamshire, where he became the county's high sheriff.[149] The merchants' continuing wealth was matched by high status in the City of London. Greenwood remained one of the capital's most eminent commercial figures in the 1780s, his expertise and his standing reflected in his appointment as one of three arbitrators in a celebrated public dispute between the government and a major London merchant over wartime provisioning.[150] Shubrick's omission from London trade directories after 1783 suggests that he withdrew from trade, but he continued as a director of the London Assurance Company until his death.[151] Nutt too remained active in the city, both in business and on philanthropic committees.[152] Greenwood and Nutt continued to be members of the Committee of North American Merchants, which Nutt jointly chaired, and which took the lead in promoting traders' prewar debt claims.[153]

For the most part, London's leading prewar Carolina traders concentrated after the war not on trying to renew trading connections to South Carolina but instead on recouping their outstanding debts in the state. Lack of capital per se did not prevent them from reentering trade to South Carolina after the war. The greater obstacle lay in how their debts had been contracted. Prewar and wartime politics—or, specifically, *purported* political orientation—mattered in postwar trade. The liberality of credit offered by prewar London merchants and their dominance of the export trade to Charleston had given rise to suspicions in South Carolina that they were profiteering from the trade, financing extravagant lifestyles, and dominating their debtors. This credit was, moreover, conflated with political enmity to the American cause. The debts had been the source of what Ralph Izard had termed the London merchants' "princely magnificence"

Table 13: London trading houses claiming more than £10,000 in debts in South Carolina, 1790

	Claims in South Carolina	Claims in Georgia	Claims in other states	Total claims	Claim in S.C. as % of total debt claimed in S.C. by London merchants (£596,289)
Greenwood & Higginson	£211,533	£58,227	–	£269,760	35.5
Neufville & Rolleston	£81,600	–	–	£81,600	13.7
John Nutt	£61,081	£42,599	–	£103,680	10.2
Powell & Hopton	£59,500	£13,600	–	£73,100	10.0
Davis, Strahan & Co.[a]	£47,040	–	£1,849	£48,889	7.9
Robert Smyth[b]	£38,399	–	£1,476	£39,875	6.4
Richard Shubrick	£30,049	£18,064	–	£48,113	5.0
Graham, Johnson & Co.[c]	£17,680	£18,700	–	£36,380	3.0
James Poyas	£15,656	–	–	£15,656	2.6
Others (9 claimants)	£33,751				5.7
Total	**£596,289**				

Source: Katherine A. Kellock, "London Merchants and the Pre-1776 American Debts," *Guildhall Studies* 1 (1974): 114, 122–24, 126, 141–13, 145–56.

Notes: [a]Firm listed in London directories on Tower Hill in 1769 and Mincing Lane in 1783. William Davis and James Stra[c]han had been partners with James McKenzie in James McKenzie & Co., the major prewar Cowes reexporting house for Carolinian rice. See *PHL*, V, 313n; VI, 8on.
[b]Robert Smith had operated a "Carolina House" in Aldermanbury, London, before the war but had filed for bankruptcy in November 1774 (John Laurens to HL, 15 November 1774, *PHL*, IX, 645).
[c]Details of Graham, Johnson & Co.'s trade are obscure, but the firm appears to have been an offshoot of the major Georgia trading house of Graham, Clark & Co. (Kellock, "London Merchants and the Pre-1776 American Debts," 124).

and the instrument of their commercial hold on Carolinian correspondents.[154] It would be too simplistic to suggest that these debts were a principal factor in American resistance and rebellion. The debts nevertheless symbolized the systemic British constraints on the colonial economy that derived from the Navigation Acts and the mercantilist precepts that were enshrined in law and policy. After the war the debts symbolized the London firms' former dominance of South Carolina's Atlantic trade and impeded the firms from reentering the trade. Firms such as Greenwood & Higginson, John Nutt's, and Rolleston & Neufville— London's largest prewar Carolina houses, the biggest creditors to South Carolinians, and consequently the most financially exposed when war broke out— were too closely implicated in the prewar system. Their pursuit of their debts in South Carolina was a potent reminder of their prewar dominance and approach to trade, and it led them to be ostracized from resuming in trade to the state.

Credit strategies from before the war, which broadly reflected the relative scale of merchants' trade, thus came back to haunt London's Carolina traders. Those that had extended credit most liberally to their colonial correspondents— generally the largest London Carolina houses such as Greenwood & Higginson and John Nutt—lost the most. But these firms were best able to bear the losses. Individuals and firms that had been in tough financial straits even before the war or which had relied most on their assets in South Carolina were hit far harder. In Charleston, as local traders Brailsford & Morris claimed, it may have been "those Commercial Houses who enjoyed the first reputation prior to the Revolution" who were most affected by "the Calamities of War." In London the firms that were already struggling appear to have suffered most.[155] Samuel Carne, who had twice traveled to Charleston during the war in an attempt to call in the debts he was owed there, died bankrupt in 1786.[156] Charles Ogilvie and Isaac King, who had each run into financial difficulties in the early 1770s and had therefore become more dependent on fixed and liquid assets in South Carolina, found themselves in dire financial troubles.

King's experiences epitomize the travails of the prewar Carolina traders in London who relied most heavily on their assets in South Carolina, whether in the form of money owed to them or in their landholdings. Looking back in 1790 on seven years of fruitlessly pursuing his debtors in the state, he reflected that "patience is a necessary ingredient to pass thro' life with tolerable quiet, but very few [are] embued with a sufficiency of it to combat Carolina disappointments."[157] His counterparts from London's prewar Carolina trade would surely have concurred. The debts owed to King in South Carolina long predated the war, stretching back to his partnership in Nickleson & King during the 1760s. Few businesses had been hit harder by the spectacular collapse of the Charleston firm Middleton, Liston & Hope in 1766. Nickleson and King sued the firm in an attempt to recover some £26,000, and following a "bootless & disagreeable Voyage" to Charleston in 1767 to pursue the claim, King returned to the colony twice during the 1770s to the same end.[158] After the war King needed his assets in South Carolina in order to reestablish himself in commerce. "Want of [money] prevents me from fixing in any Business," he told one of his debtors in Charleston, "& keeps me wandering about in an unsettled state."[159]

Straitened circumstances forced King and other former London Carolina traders to start afresh in more humble locations. King found modest accommodation in Bristol, taking a room in, appropriately, King's Square, where he paid £35 a year in rent "including Board at a decent Table." A counterpart went to Lancaster in northern England "to see if he can fit in any Business there."[160] Another option was to leave Britain altogether to take up trade or planting in South Carolina: despite their rough legal treatment by the state and the stalling tactics of their debtors, for some former London Carolina traders it still held the prospect of economic opportunity. The Bristol merchant and manufacturer Richard Champion suffered the second largest losses of any British trader during the war. He calculated his firm's losses at £182,382, including interest, mostly in Massachusetts. With his trading and industrial concerns in Britain ruined, Champion moved with his family in 1784 to South Carolina, where his brother-in-law was a merchant. He established successful backcountry plantations near Camden.[161] Even Isaac King was tempted. He mused in 1785 that if he could not recover the Carolinian debts that would restore him to his former level in England, "I can see nothing else that I can do but go to Carolina in the Winter, purchase a plantation with a few Negroes upon Credit . . . & pass the remainder of my life in the Woods of America under a Govt. I most cordially detest."[162] King never acted on his whim. Remaining in England, he spent the rest of his days frustrated by the ongoing evasions of his debtors and by the laws that favored them.

The contrasting postwar fortunes of the merchants who had been at the forefront of the transatlantic Carolina trade before 1776 may seem self-explanatory. That Charleston's merchants selected their trading partners after the war on the basis of their correspondents' political orientation appears at first glance obvious: pro-American houses such as Manning & Vaughan, Bourdieu & Chollet, and Bridgen & Waller prospered; and those most tainted by prewar hostility, whether real or not, including Greenwood & Higginson, John Nutt, and others, found themselves excluded from the trade. But the influence of prewar politics on postwar commerce in restored Anglo-Carolinian trade was nonetheless significant. Trade did not simply resume in its former channels. Statistics showing how, overall, Britain came once again to dominate South Carolina's overseas trade by volume and national share disguise a more nuanced scenario on the ground. Jeremiads circulating in postwar Charleston lamented the renewed dominance of British traders. These merchants were variously said to have "monopolized" and "shackled" South Carolina's trade; their "cunning strategy" was designed to divert trade away from America's wartime allies, the French and the Dutch. A pervading discourse voiced by Federalists and anti-Federalists alike

told of the state's commercial subservience to a monolithic cadre of British traders. Evidence of the commercial choices made in postwar Charleston tempers
these lamentations. Individual business decisions belie the rhetoric of collective
impotence in the face of Britain's legal impediments, systemic advantages, and
the commercial guile of its merchants. The details of Charleston's postwar trade
and the travails of London's prewar Carolina traders reveal how American commercial agency was greater, and exercised more freely, than contemporaries and
historians have recognized.

The prewar political and commercial choices made by Britain's Carolina
traders had long-term consequences. Before the war South Carolinians lacked
the collective power to challenge the specific London traders whom they held
as agents of ministerial intrigue and hostility. Embargoes such as the nonimportation campaign in 1770 served as blunt instruments of commercial retaliation,
cutting off trade to both sympathizers and purported antagonists alike, rather
than precisely targeting the latter. However, after 1783—despite widely held perceptions that America's political independence had ushered in a new era of commercial servility, or a form of half-independence—merchants in Charleston were
able to exercise the selective discrimination that they had been unable to achieve
before the war.

Taking a more "intertemporal"' approach to eighteenth-century commerce
between Great Britain and America, its political subtexts, and its implications
by spanning the years on either side of the American Revolution allows such
insights. Too often the periods before and after American independence are
disconnected through preoccupations in American history with distinct "colonial," "revolutionary," "Federal," and "early republic" entities and in British history with a dichotomy between a "First" British Empire that looked westward
across the Atlantic and a "Second" British Empire centered on India and the
east. Histories that either conclude in 1783 or begin then omit the continuities
of the period and their potential in interpreting the past. Exposing how prewar
commercial strategies and decisions transcended the American Revolution but-
tresses interpretations of the revolution that emphasize the importance of social,
material, and economic forces. Showing how supposedly anti-American British
merchants were treated after the war accentuatuates the depth of the opprobrium that had been directed toward them before the war. Condemnations of
their acquiescence with or, worse, complicity in hostile ministerial policy during
the 1760s and 1770s were not simply rhetorical devices. These merchants were
accused of conspiring to deprecate Carolinian produce to defraud their suppliers
in the colony, of profiteering from their trade, of ensnaring correspondents in
webs of easy credit, and of failing in a duty in which they had once excelled: that
of representing South Carolina's interests and complaints to the British government. The intersection of these political and commercial grievances within

the transatlantic Carolina trade casts light on how one once powerful set of Anglo-American ties broke down.

Contemporary perceptions make this approach especially resonant. Looking at American independence from both sides of 1776 or of 1783 more closely reflects notions held at the time that the United States' break from Great Britain was a continuing process, rather than a done deal. For many in South Carolina—whether Federalists or anti-Federalists—formal separation from Great Britain amounted only to semi-independence. Nowhere was this more visible than in the state's Atlantic commerce. Responses in South Carolina to the state's postwar trade with Britain suggest how, for many in the 1780s, commerce and American independence were entwined, symbiotic, and—both figuratively and literally—"unfinished business."

CONCLUSION

"Let me have done with American lands"

After moving from London to Bristol in search of cheaper accommodations, Isaac King briefly considered setting up a plantation on the undeveloped tracts of land he still owned in South Carolina. As the 1780s progressed, however, his disillusionment with the recalcitrance of his debtors and South Carolina's courts mounted. "I can see no inclination in any of the people of the Land of Liberty to pay the Debts they owe to the subjects of a Monarch," he lamented.[1] Rather than move to South Carolina, he chose to stay in Britain and to sever his landholding ties with the state entirely. "I do not wish to possess Landed property anywhere but England," he told his attorney in 1788. Three years later, with his tracts in South Carolina still unsold, King instructed his attorney to "sell them for what you can get & let me have done with American lands."[2] King's frustrations were typical of the problems faced by many British residents who had owned land in South Carolina before the war. Some had escaped having their land confiscated only to encounter new legal obstacles.

Margaret Colleton, the London-dwelling owner of Mepshew and Watboo plantations on the Cooper River, did not live to see confirmation of her fears that her lowcountry plantations would be confiscated. In July 1778 she had been "a good deal alarmed" at a report in London of the law recently passed in South Carolina requiring absentee owners of land in South Carolina "to appear there, within a given time upon pain of confiscation of their Property, or some other grievous Penalty."[3] Colleton was among the 237 individuals stripped of their lands by the South Carolina General Assembly at Jacksonborough in February 1782. The forfeiture also applied to her heirs. Colleton died in 1780 and left her plantations to her brother-in-law, James Edward Colleton, from whom ownership was swiftly transferred to a cousin, James Nassau Colleton.[4] On inheriting the properties, Nassau Colleton began a three-year struggle to overturn their confiscation. In November 1782 he wrote to Benjamin Franklin, then serving as one of the U.S. peace commissioners in Paris, seeking Franklin's intercession with Congress and with authorities in South Carolina. Nassau Colleton emphasized to Franklin that he had "never been in any manner inimical to their [the American] Cause though he could be of no assist[ance] to it, not having had the actual Possession of any thing in that Country, and the moment he now has the prospect of it, entertains the greatest desire to become a Resident there."[5]

Taking matters into his own hands, Nassau Colleton left Britain for South Carolina in early 1783. He arrived to find that the war had left his plantations in disarray, like so many others in lowcountry South Carolina. During the war Watboo had "suffered much by the different Armies . . . from the Destruction of the Negroes, which they have been too much encouraged to."[6] Between thirty and forty slaves had fled Mepshew for British-occupied Charleston in the early months of 1783 in the hope of getting to St. Augustine, but they had been seized en route to Florida by an American privateer.[7] Worse for Nassau Colleton was that his estates had been divided up and sold. He appealed both to the state's commissioners of forfeited estates and the South Carolina General Assembly arguing that Margaret Colleton's age and infirmity had made it impossible for her to travel to South Carolina; moreover, she had paid the double tax on her estates, thereby supporting the state's government. After his initial pleas fell on deaf ears and Watboo was sold at public auction, Nassau Colleton further signaled his commitment to South Carolina by swearing an oath of allegiance to the state to become a citizen. The following year, in March 1784, he was among those whose confiscations were commuted to an obligation to pay an amercement of 12 percent of the value of their properties; in 1786 this final penalty was lifted. As Watboo had already been sold, however, Nassau Colleton received merely the purchase money for the plantation.[8] Other prewar absentees, including his cousin Thomas Boone, were even less fortunate. Even though he had paid the double tax on his property, such was the resentment toward Boone in South Carolina after his contentious spell as governor in the early 1760s that his appeals for clemency were flatly rejected. "The general opinion here," one observer in Charleston wrote, "is that he was so strongly attached to the British government as they would and ought to make him a confiscation . . . he certainly suffered very much, as all his valuable property here was sold."[9]

Another to pursue his losses doggedly was Charles Ogilvie, among the largest absentee owners of South Carolinian estates before the war. From London, where he lived until his death in 1788, he continued to stake his claim to his confiscated properties in South Carolina and Georgia. He petitioned the assembly for the return of Richfield and Mount Alexander, his two most valuable plantations, which had been seized and sold in 1782. Both were eventually returned to his sons and heirs, John Alexander Ogilvie and Charles Ogilvie Jr., though some of Mount Alexander's acreage had been sold to an American officer. Richfield remained in John Alexander Ogilvie's hands until 1802.[10] John Alexander Ogilvie also went to Georgia to investigate his father's affairs there. As late as 1803 Ogilvie's possessions in Georgia were still being scrutinized by Britain's debt and compensation commission.[11]

A resurrection of the transatlantic market in South Carolinian land after American independence suggested, as did Britain's renewed preeminence in South Carolina's transatlantic trade, a return to antebellum conditions. American independence and the ongoing legal wrangles over Loyalist confiscations and prewar debts did not deter some in Britain from buying lands or taking possession of inherited estates in South Carolina. For many, the new state still offered the hope of profits that were unachievable in Britain. John Martin, a resident of Cumberland in northern England, inherited an estate near Georgetown from his brother. After crossing the Atlantic to settle his new lands in 1788, he was enraptured by his new planter's lifestyle. "I have a very good house to live in," he wrote from his plantation, Belvoir, to his son in London, "and pretty near 60 negroes small and great about me to do what I order. Almost 30 are employ'd every day amongst the Rice . . . my Garden & Vineyard afford all sorts of Delicates, such as Peaches, Pomegranates, Figgs, Grapes . . . and all kinds of Vigatables." Martin made plans to send rice, indigo, and cotton to Britain in exchange for imported goods, believing that "most things sell for near one hundred per cent." A neighboring storekeeper was thought to make such a high margin even though he did not import his goods personally.[12] Martin was not alone in Britain in seeing the potential of South Carolinian land. The London merchants James Bourdieu and Samuel Chollet acquired five thousand acres of prime undeveloped land on the Edisto River in 1785, apparently with a plan to partition it into smaller tracts for resale. Reckoned by a surveyor to be "of the best quality," it was valued at two guineas per acre.[13] Transatlantic landholding, it seemed, might continue much as it had before the American Revolution.

With South Carolina in urgent need of capital to rebuild and restock, British investors such as Bourdieu & Chollet were obvious sources of investment. Sales of land in South Carolina and Georgia on the British market reflected British residents' continuing interest in the region's economic prospects. In 1787 Henry Laurens tried to sell his two Georgia plantations, Broughton Island and New Hope, in Britain. Though each had been ravaged during the war, Laurens hoped that together with two undeveloped tracts and lots in the planned town of Brunswick, the plantations would raise some eight thousand pounds. He advised his friend William Manning that the offer price was just half their actual value and persuaded him to advertise the lands in London, Bristol, and Liverpool newspapers. Recognizing the integration of the plantation economies of the American South and the West Indies, the advertisements emphasized the tracts' complementarity for a buyer with land in the West Indies. The South Carolina properties would make "an excellent Addition to an Estate in Jamaica, or other West India islands" on account of the lumber and provisions they might supply, given their number of "Cypress, Pine, Oak, Hickory, and Ash trees" and "Ranges for raising Horned Cattle, Horses, Hogs &c. in the greatest Abundance."[14]

Vast tracts in South Carolina's backcountry, its population growing fast with the arrival of new settlers, were also offered at auction in London, further indicating the hopes that Britain remained a fertile market for Carolinian land. Tracts on the Congaree and Wateree Rivers, near the state's new capital, Columbia, and totaling some 250,000 acres, were auctioned in London in 1789. Appearing alongside adverts for Jamaican plantations and English country estates, auction notices stressed that the lands were at least partially cultivated, including "several capital rice works, with houses and other buildings" and land "naturally adapted to the culture of indigo and tobacco," as well as being good cattle country. Potential owners need not fear having to eke a living out of the woods: the plantations were touted as equivalents to more familiar West Indies or British investments.[15] The same year a plantation sixty miles from Charleston and with navigable river access to the port was auctioned at Garraway's Coffee House in London, while a Charleston wharf with stores and five town lots was offered in the British capital for private sale.[16]

TO be SOLD, upon very moderate Terms, the undermentioned Tracts of Land, in the STATE of GEORGIA, in North-America.
I. That valuable Island called BROUGHTON, in the River Altamaha; containing Nine Hundred Acres, more or less, of the best planting Land for Rice, Indigo, Indian Corn, Cotton, &c. &c.
II. Also that valuable Tract, opposite and within a Quarter of a Mile of the Island, called NEW HOPE; containing Three Thousand Acres, more or less; from Seven to Nine Hundred Acres of which is the best River Swamp; the Remainder excellent Pine Land, with some Oak and Hiccory.
These two Tracts would make an excellent Addition to an Estate in Jamaica, or other West-India Islands; as the Swamp and High Land, together abound with Cyprefs, Pine, Oak, Hiccory, and Ash Trees, and have Ranges for raising Horned Cattle, Horfes, Hogs, &c. in the greatest Abundance. Four Hundred Acres on the Island, and about Two or Three Hundred on New Hope Swamp, have been well banked in; the Foundations of the Banks would make the Work of a new Settlement very eafy.
A Veffel of nine Feet Water Draught may load at the Landing of either Place; and one of fixteen Feet Draught, may proceed within nine Miles.

Notice for sale of Broughton and New Hope Plantations, *Public Advertiser*, September 1787

South Carolina's postwar land legislation was carefully constructed, however, to prevent an influx of foreign investors or long-term reliance on their capital. New laws designed to encourage settlement in the state tolerated temporary absenteeism while setting time limits on the practice. As such, the laws represented a marked hardening of South Carolina's prewar ambivalence toward absentee landownership. The tax act passed in March 1783—the first law enacted in the state after independence from Great Britain was formally secured—renewed the double tax first imposed in 1778 on land, town properties, and slaves owned by nonresidents.[17] A year later, in March 1784, the state repealed a law dating back to 1704 that had permitted newly arrived "aliens" to buy or inherit land in South Carolina. In its place, a new citizenship law was passed, making citizens of all "free white persons" who lived in the state for one year and swore allegiance. The law notionally sanctioned absenteeism, allowing nonresidents to retain lands in South Carolina unless they had been named in the 1782 Confiscation Acts. This was on the proviso, though, that they become citizens or sell their land to citizens within seven years; March 1791 was the cut-off point. "Whereas sundry real estates within this State are the property of persons not citizens thereof, and have not been confiscated by the Legislature," the statute declared, "Be it therefore enacted by the authority aforesaid, That nothing herein contained shall extend to deprive any such person or persons of their property in the said real estates; provided, they shall be admitted citizens of this State, or sell their said estate to a citizen thereof, within seven years from the passing of this Act."[18]

Notice for sale of Eveleigh's Wharf, Charleston, *Public Advertiser,* April 1789

For SALE by private Contract, ALL that valuable WHARF, known by the Name of EVELEIGH's WHARF, fituated in EAST BAY, in the City of CHARLES - TON, State of SOUTH CAROLINA, with the Stores and other Erections thereon; together with five Lots of Land adjoining thereto, lately granted by the Legislature of the faid State.

The Terms of Payment will be made eafy to a Purchafer, and may be known and a Plan of the Premifes viewed by applying to John Tunne, Efq America-fquare, London; or to Mr. William Saunders, in Briftol.

Similar legislation balanced incentives for foreigners to invest much-needed capital in South Carolina with safeguards to stop their influence from becoming too powerful. An aversion to the memory of indebtedness and "domination" by external powers, such as Britain's prewar Carolina traders, was clearly felt, as it was in other states as well. One of North Carolina's delegates to Congress put it explicitly: "*Aliens* cannot hold soil in the United States. . . . However the means of becoming a Citizen with us [North Carolina] is extremely easy. Was not this distinction held up British Merchants and others would try to hold us again in a species of Slavery by getting Mortgages & other holds on our Lands."[19] The precarious balance between investment and influence was made manifest in another act passed in South Carolina in 1784. Its boldly stated purpose was "to encourage subjects of Foreign States to lend money at interest on real estates within this state." The act allowed foreigners to lend money to individuals in the state and permitted South Carolinians to mortgage their land as security in these transactions. However, while foreigners were allowed to prosecute lawsuits to recover debts, they could not take possession of property in the state through mortgage foreclosures. Instead they could sell any property gained in this way and repatriate the proceeds.[20] An important channel through which British creditors had come to own land in South Carolina before the war was closed. Through the 1784 acts, South Carolina's state government sought to prevent the prewar Anglo-Carolinian polity from being reproduced. British capital might have an influential role to play in postwar development, but it would not be allowed to be a harbinger of a renewed metropolitan-colonial relationship.

Across the United States the right of foreigners to own land was formally legalized only in Pennsylvania.[21] For its part, Georgia followed South Carolina's lead. A law passed in Georgia in February 1785 allowed foreign lenders to pursue their debtors through the state's courts, but like South Carolina's legislation the previous year—on which it was clearly modeled—it denied the foreign lenders the right to enter or take possession of any premises that fell into their hands through defaults.[22] Other acts in Georgia went further and exceeded South Carolinian precedent. While foreigners who owned lands in South Carolina were given seven years' grace to become citizens and thereby keep their properties, Georgia's 1785 Citizenship Act gave noncitizens the right to own personal property, rent houses, and sue for debts but prevented them from suing to acquire real estate in lieu of debts owed them. The same year the state imposed a double tax on lands whose owners had been absent from the state for more than a year, resurrecting the charge imposed on nonresidents in 1778. With the aim of discouraging land banking and promoting settlement in Georgia, the double tax was imposed on uncultivated lands whether the owners lived abroad or elsewhere in the United States. Significantly, however, absentee owners who were citizens of and who lived in another American state were excused the double tax if they brought a portion of their lands into cultivation; for foreign owners, there was no such remission.[23]

For would-be British buyers, legal and political deterrents ultimately outweighed the investment potential of properties in South Carolina. The likes of John Martin and Chollet & Bourdieu were few and far between. Uncertainty clouded the political backdrop. Continuing diplomatic tensions between Britain and the United States were accompanied in Britain by the widespread expectation that the confederation between the states would soon fall apart. In South Carolina hostility toward exiled Loyalists persisted longer than perhaps anywhere else in the United States, reflecting the particular bitterness of the Revolutionary War across the South.[24] Not only did this hinder efforts to recover prewar debts, but in addition it also further deterred Carolinian refugees from returning to their estates. Together with the hostility toward British merchants in Charleston, widely reported in the British press, and the impending compulsion for those owning land in the state to take citizenship, many potential British buyers were put off. Exiled in Britain, the former lowcountry planter Elias Ball wrote in October 1788 to discourage his cousin in South Carolina from trying to sell land on the British market. The impending citizenship requirement, he advised, made British residents reluctant to buy lands in America: "Your states have taken the most effectual steps to prevent people purchasing estates. No man can hold an Estate in your country for any length of time without he becomes a Citizen &

resides among you & no man will chuse to risque himself a property in a country where the legislature interferes in private contracts & bargains made between man & man."[25]

Agricultural depression and falling land prices in South Carolina further dashed hopes of quick and easy profits. According to his cousin, Richard Shubrick "never Receiv'd a Farthing from his Estates he sold in Carolina."[26] Nor did John Martin's high hopes for his Carolinian estates materialize. After he died in 1790, his son discovered that Belvoir Plantation was worth just sixteen hundred pounds, against his father's estimate of four thousand pounds, and that his father had been deeply in debt. Visiting the plantation, his attorney reported "only eight shillings and ten pence found in money." Martin Jr. duly disposed of the plantation lands, keeping only two Georgetown plots since "they might improve in time."[27] Henry Laurens was similarly frustrated in his attempts to sell his Georgia plantations in Britain. No buyers were forthcoming, despite the plantations' supposedly bargain price, and Laurens retained the lands until his death in 1792. Likewise a 107,000-acre tract near Camden in the center of South Carolina that had been advertised in London newspapers in 1789 failed to attract a buyer. It was put up for auction the following year.[28]

The transatlantic marketing of lands in South Carolina and Georgia and the laws that governed these land sales epitomized the ambivalence that characterized relations between Britain and its former colonies after the war. Britain was an important source of capital and investment. South Carolinians recognized and sought to harness this. At the same time they feared the influence of the former imperial power, which portended a return to prewar control and restraint; hence the citizenship requirements written into land legislation. This ambivalence was mirrored in postwar trade. While British ships flocked once again to Charleston and British merchants again became the chief suppliers of slaves, goods, and equipment to the state, for many in South Carolina this was a marriage of necessity, not choice. The intertwined concerns of land and trade in South Carolina after 1783 signaled how individuals and the state alike struggled to reconcile divergent economic and political urges.

Transatlantic ownership of plantations lands and urban properties had been central to the Anglo-Carolinian polity over the previous sixty years. For all the negative connotations that the term aroused in Britain, absenteeism had been a powerful and beneficial connective force, underpinning the economic and commercial links that Britain's Carolina merchants had with the colony. It was integral to the special assiduity with which these merchants advocated for South Carolina and represented its needs and grievances in the imperial corridors of power. Later, as political tensions between Great Britain and its colonies in North America mounted, absentees' ownership of these lands and properties in South Carolina became to many in the colony a symbol of British control. Measures taken after the war to preclude absenteeism reflected how its political and economic significance was appreciated in the state. Preventing lands from falling into the hands of permanent nonresidents allowed South Carolina to exercise the autonomy and control that many residents felt it lacked in its postwar trade with Britain, despite the exclusion of the most objectionable prewar and wartime British merchants from business. British capital and goods were vital to South Carolina's economy: French, Spanish, and Dutch traders were unable to compete in either quality of goods or the credit they offered. For all the popular anger in South Carolina at Britain's renewed preeminence in its trade, suppressing it was neither practical nor wise. In contrast, curtailing British landownership within the state offered a means of asserting autonomy and signifying a different relationship with the former mother country without endangering economic redevelopment.

The postwar political connotations of trade and land reprised their prewar significance. Trade between Britain and South Carolina had long been shaped by politics; in the decade before the Revolutionary War, the trade had become increasingly politicized. As did merchants in other branches of Britain's overseas trade, but with special assiduity, London's Carolina merchants understood lobbying as a vital and regular aspect of their business. Within the transatlantic Carolina trade, this lobbying was for much of the eighteenth century a force for stability. Successes between the 1730s and the 1750s in securing bounties and stimuli or in opening new markets for South Carolina's produce, as London merchants capitalized on prevailing political sentiment and economic theory, signaled the merchants' commitment to the colony's agricultural diversification and economic growth. In the London Carolina lobby's effectiveness on commercial issues, however, the seeds of later disharmony were laid.

The quietude of London's Carolina merchants during the political controversies of the late 1760s and the 1770s contrasted with their earlier activism on more explicitly commercial matters. This political passivity coincided with changes within the group. London's Carolina trade was concentrated in relatively few hands throughout the eighteenth century. Between the 1730s and the early 1760s the capital's leading Carolina merchants were men who had spent their early careers in Charleston building experience and connections. As these men retired from trade in the 1760s, the merchants who replaced them as London's preeminent Carolina traders lacked the depth of their forerunners' connections to the colony. Against rising tensions within the British Empire, the trade's concentration among—or, to some Carolinians, domination by—a small group of London traders took on menacing dimensions. The group's apparent ambivalence toward the American policies of successive British governments was interpreted as signifying personal lack of interest in American grievances or, worse, outright hostility. Evidence of the traders' purported profiteering—achieved variously through their dominant share of Britain's Carolina trade, the credit through which they ensnared colonial correspondents, and their disparagement of Carolinian produce for personal gain—as manifested in grandiose mansions and opulent lifestyles, had confirmed that Carolinian and British interests were no longer aligned.

Not only in South Carolina was trade with Britain fundamental to conceptions of independence and identity after the war. Commercial issues would be central in the often fraught relationship between Great Britain and the United States throughout the decade after American independence. Not until the negotiations for the Jay Treaty in 1794 would the British and American governments formally attempt to resolve the commercial, territorial, and financial disputes that marked the two nations' uneasy postwar rapprochement. Within the United States, business connections with and attitudes toward Britain and its remaining colonies would influence individual and regional perspectives on the merits, nature, and limits of closer federal union. Atlantic reengagement—and specifically absorption into a commercial orbit where Great Britain remained the leading player—confounded Jeffersonian ideals of agrarianism and self-sufficiency. For Britain, exports to the United States grew to some 25–30 percent of the country's total exports in the years that followed American independence.[29] In return, the United States remained a vital supplier of Britain's commodity imports, notably the cotton that fueled British industrial growth and from the 1790s supplanted indigo and then rice as South Carolina's principal agricultural staple and the raison d'être of the state's slave economy.

Reaction to the Jay Treaty would reopen the lingering sores of restored Anglo-Carolinian trade. The treaty maintained restrictions on trade between the United States and the British West Indies, one of several clauses that, to the treaty's opponents in America, smacked of quasi-colonial subordination to Great Britain. Planters throughout the southern states condemned the Jay Treaty for its failure to compel Britain to pay compensation for slaves liberated during and after the war. A wave of protests in Charleston in July 1795, after ratification of the treaty, harked back to the anti-British rioting of 1783 and 1784.[30] For Britain's prewar Carolina traders—or their inheritors—who were still pursuing debts owed them in the former colony, there was a modicum of relief as the United States agreed to reimburse some of their claims. After more than a decade of pursuing the claims, however, this small victory for the merchants was largely pyrrhic. Compensation amounted to far less than the sums claimed, while further diplomatic and bureaucratic hurdles lay ahead. William Higginson and John Nutt would have to wait until 1803 to receive their compensation, fully twenty years after American independence and nearly thirty years since the debts had been contracted: Higginson received some £40,173 of the £211,533 that he and his late partner, William Greenwood, had claimed; Nutt got a paltry £10,978 of the £251,387 that, including interest, he had sought.[31] At the start of a new century in which Britain would continue to be central to South Carolina's commerce, residents on either side of the Atlantic were still coming to terms with the breakdown, reconstitution, and political entanglements of trade.

ABBREVIATIONS

CO	Colonial Office manuscripts, National Archives, London
IKL	Isaac King Letterbook, South Caroliniana Library, Columbia, S.C.
JHC	*Journals of the House of Commons.* London: His Majesty's Stationary Office, 1802
LRP	*The Letterbook of Robert Pringle, 1737–45,* ed. Walter B. Edgar. 2 vols. Columbia: University of South Carolina Press, 1972
LRR	Letterbook of Robert Raper, 1759–70, Bodleian Library, Oxford (microfilm)
OFP	Ogilvie-Forbes Papers, South Carolina Historical Society
PHL	*The Papers of Henry Laurens,* ed. David R. Chesnutt et al. 16 vols. Columbia: University of South Carolina Press, 1968–2003
Prob.	Records of the Prerogative Court of Canterbury (wills), National Archives, London
SCDAH	South Carolina Department of Archives and History, Columbia
SCG	*South Carolina Gazette*
SCHM	*South Carolina Historical Magazine*
SCHS	South Carolina Historical Society, Charleston
SCL	South Caroliniana Library, University of South Carolina, Columbia
T	Treasury manuscripts, National Archives, London
WMQ	*William and Mary Quarterly*

NOTES

INTRODUCTION

1. Isaac King to Joshua Ward, 9 October 1790, IKL.
2. Henry Laurens (hereafter HL) to Isaac King, 6 September 1764, *PHL*, IV, 400–401.
3. The classic analysis is Robert M. Weir, "'The Harmony We Were Famous For': An Interpretation of Pre-revolutionary South Carolina Politics," *WMQ* 26.4 (1969): 473–501.
4. Progressive historians in the early twentieth century saw a reaction against indebtedness as being a preeminent motivating force behind the American Revolution, most notably Arthur M. Schlesinger, *The Colonial Merchants and the American Revolution* (New York: Columbia University Press, 1918), esp. 359–60; Charles A. Beard, *Economic Origins of Jeffersonian Democracy*, 2nd ed. (New York: Macmillan, 1927), esp. 270–72. A more nuanced understanding of economic factors, in particular their role in informing and reinforcing ideological positions, is a feature of more recent scholarship. See, for example, Marc Egnal, *New World Economies: The Growth of the Thirteen Colonies and Canada* (Oxford: Oxford University Press, 1998); John J. McCusker and Russell R. Menard, *The Economy of British America, 1607–1789* (Chapel Hill: University of North Carolina Press, 1985), 351–77; Woody Holton, *Forced Founders: Indians, Debtors, Slaves and the Making of the American Revolution in Virginia* (Chapel Hill: University of North Carolina Press, 1999), 39–129.
5. Timothy H. Breen, "'Baubles of Britain': The American and Consumer Revolutions of the Eighteenth Century," *Past and Present* 119 (May, 1988): 88.
6. There is extensive literature on merchant "interest groups" or "lobbies" and the colonies' official agents in London, who often helped to coordinate the lobbying: Michael G. Kammen, *A Rope of Sand: The Colonial Agents, British Politics and the American Revolution* (Ithaca, N.Y.: Cornell University Press, 1968); Jack M. Sosin, *Agents and Merchants: British Colonial Policy and the Origins of the American Revolution, 1763–1775* (Lincoln: University of Nebraska Press, 1965). The interaction of colonial interest groups and the British state has been elaborated most fully in Alison Olson, *Making the Empire Work: London and American Interest Groups, 1690–1790* (Cambridge, Mass.: Harvard University Press, 1992), which highlighted the important connective role that semistructured interest groups such as merchant lobbies played in the British Empire and argued that mutual interest was a powerful force for stability: "in the heyday of empire substantial numbers of Americans identified with English interest groups and through them had an informal but effective voice in the making of English decisions that affected them; they co-operated with the British government because they were getting what they wanted out of it" (Olson, *Making the Empire Work*, xi). For sectoral studies of colonial interest groups and the British state, see Rebecca Starr, *A School for Politics: Commercial Lobbying and Political Culture in Early South Carolina* (Baltimore: Johns Hopkins University Press, 1998); Alison Olson, "The Virginia Merchants of London: A Study in Eighteenth Century Interest Group Politics," *WMQ* 40.3 (1983): 363–88; Andrew O'Shaughnessy, "The Formation of a Commercial Lobby: The West Indies Interest, British Colonial Policy and the American Revolution," *Historical Journal* 40.1 (1997): 71–95; O'Shaughnessy, "The West India Interest and the Crisis of American Independence," in Roderick A. McDonald, *West Indies Accounts: Essays in the History of the British Caribbean in Honour of Richard Sheridan* (Kingston: University of the West Indies Press, 1996), 126–48; William A. Pettigrew, "Free to Enslave: Politics and the Escalation of Britain's Transatlantic Slave Trade, 1688–1714," *WMQ* 64.1 (2007): 3–38.

7. Alexander Hewitt, *An Historical Account of the Rise and Progress of the Colonies of South Carolina and Georgia*, 2 vols. (London, 1779), I, 109.

8. 3 Geo. II c. 28, in Great Britain, *The Statutes at Large, from Magna Charta, to the Twenty Fifth Year of the Reign of King George the Third, Inclusive*, 14 vols. (London, 1786), V, 553–55. For a summary of the origins and impact of the Navigation Acts, see Nuala Zahedieh, *The Capital and the Colonies: London and the Atlantic Economy, 1660–1700* (Cambridge: Cambridge University Press, 2010), 36–38. The first Navigation Act in 1660 compelled all goods taken to and from the colonies to be carried in English or colonial ships, with the masters and three-quarters of the crews to be English or colonial subjects. It "enumerated" or specified a list of colonial-produced commodities that could be exported only to England or to another English colony, including sugar, tobacco, coffee, indigo, and cotton. Prohibitive duties were placed on foreign tobacco and sugar to reward colonists with a virtual monopoly of the home market for their produce. Further Navigation Acts in 1663, 1673, and 1696 codified and reinforced the legislation's "mercantilist" strictures. Rice was added to the enumerated list in 1704.

9. Nuala Zahedieh, "Economy," in *The British Atlantic World, 1500–1800*, ed. David Armitage and Michael J. Braddick (Basingstoke: Palgrave, 2002), 58.

10. In the extensive literature on South Carolina's Atlantic connections and the role of exogenous demand in its early economic history, see in particular Peter A. Coclanis, *The Shadow of a Dream: Economic Life and Death in the South Carolina Lowcountry, 1670–1920* (New York: Oxford University Press, 1989); Peter A. Coclanis, "Global Perspectives on the Early Economic History of South Carolina," *SCHM* 106.2 (2005): 130–46; R. C. Nash, "Urbanization in the Colonial South: Charleston, South Carolina, as a Case Study," *Journal of Urban History* 19.1 (1992): 3–29; R. C. Nash, "South Carolina and the Atlantic Economy in the Late 17th and Early 18th Centuries," *Economic History Review* 45.4 (1992): 677–702; Kenneth Morgan, "The Organization of the Colonial American Rice Trade," *WMQ* 52.3 (1995): 433–52. On the organization and structure of the Atlantic Carolina trade, see in particular R. C. Nash, "The Organization of Trade and Finance in the Atlantic Economy: Britain and South Carolina, 1670–1775," in *Money, Trade, and Power: The Evolution of Colonial South Carolina's Plantation Society*, ed. Jack P. Greene, Rosemary Brana-Shute, and Randy J. Sparks (Columbia: University of South Carolina Press, 2001), notably 74–107; R. C. Nash, "The Organization of Trade and Finance in the British Atlantic Economy, 1670–1830," in *The Atlantic Economy during the Seventeenth and Eighteenth Centuries: Organization, Operation, Practice, Personnel*, ed. Peter A. Coclanis (Columbia: University of South Carolina Press, 2005), 95–151. On the interrelation of Atlantic and inland Indian trades, see Eirlys M. Barker, "Indian Traders, Charles Town and London's Vital Link to the Interior of North America, 1715–1755," in *Money, Trade and Power*, ed. Greene et al., 141–65; Peter C. Mancall, Joshua L. Rosenbloom, and Thomas Weiss, "Indians and the Economy of Eighteenth-Century Carolina," in *Atlantic Economy*, ed. Coclanis, 297–322.

11. On the formative influence of the Caribbean in South Carolina's settlement and development, see Coclanis, *Shadow of a Dream*, 56–67; Converse D. Clowse, *Economic Beginnings in Colonial South Carolina, 1670–1730* (Columbia: University of South Carolina Press, 1971), 69–227; Peter H. Wood, *Black Majority: Negroes in Colonial South Carolina from 1670 through to the Stono Rebellion* (New York: Norton, 1974), 13–34; Richard S. Dunn, "The English Sugar Islands and the Founding of South Carolina," *SCHM* 72.2 (1971): 81–93; Jack P. Greene, "Colonial South Carolina and the Caribbean Connection," *SCHM* 88.4 (1987): 192–210; Richard Waterhouse, "England, the Caribbean, and the Settlement of South Carolina," *Journal of American Studies* 9.3 (1975): 259–81.

12. George Milligen Johnston, *A Short Description of the Province of South-Carolina, with an Account of the Air, Weather, and Diseases, at Charles-Town. Written in the year 1763* (London, 1770), 25.

13. Wood, *Black Majority*, 33.

14.   Important exceptions that emphasized the thirteen colonies' integration into a wider British American empire include Jack Greene, *Pursuits of Happiness: The Social Development of the Early Modern British Colonies and the Formation of American Culture* (Chapel Hill: University of North Carolina Press, 1988); Andrew J. O'Shaughnessy, *An Empire Divided: The American Revolution and the British Caribbean* (Philadelphia: University of Pennsylvania Press, 2000); McCusker and Menard, *Economy of British America.*

15.   "An Attempt towards an Estimate of the Value of South Carolina, for the Right Honourable the Lords Commissioners for Trade and Plantations, 1751," in *The Colonial South Carolina Scene: Contemporary Views, 1697–1774,* ed. H. Roy Merrens (Columbia: University of South Carolina Press, 1977), 178.

16.   Peter A. Coclanis, "The Hydra Head of Merchant Capital: Market and Merchants in Early South Carolina," in *The Meaning of South Carolina History: Essays in Honor of George C. Rogers, Jr.,* ed. David R. Chesnutt and Clyde N. Wilson (Columbia: University of South Carolina Press, 1991), 2; Nash, "Organization of Trade and Finance" (2001), 75.

17.   Jacob M. Price, "What Did Merchants Do? Reflections on British Overseas Trade, 1660–1790," *Journal of Economic History* 49.2 (1989): 267–84; Jacob Price, "Who Cared about the Colonies? The Impact of the Thirteen Colonies on British Society and Politics, c. 1714–1775," in *Strangers within the Realm: Cultural Margins of the First British Empire,* ed. Bernard Bailyn and Philip Morgan (Chapel Hill: University of North Carolina Press, 1991), 395–436.

18.   Robert Pringle (hereafter RP) to Richard Thompson, 2 September 1738, *LRP,* I, 30.

19.   London's primacy in Britain's overseas trade in the eighteenth century has been examined and reasserted in Perry L. Gauci, *The Politics of Trade: The Overseas Merchant in State and Society, 1660–1720* (Oxford: Oxford University Press, 2001); Perry Gauci, *Emporium of the World: The Merchants of London, 1660–1800* (London: Continuum, 2007); Zahedieh, *Capital and the Colonies.* These join important works on the overseas trade of Britain's regional "outports" such as Bristol and Glasgow, notably Kenneth Morgan, *Bristol and the Atlantic Trade in the Eighteenth Century* (Cambridge: Cambridge University Press, 1993); T. M. Devine, *The Tobacco Lords: A Study of the Tobacco Merchants of Glasgow and their Trading Activities, c. 1740–1790* (Edinburgh: Edinburgh University Press, 1975). Historians' greater focus on the outports has reflected the more extensive survival of commercial correspondence and administrative data from these locations. In contrast, London's eighteenth-century port books were destroyed by officials at the Public Record Office in the 1890s, and much other material on the capital's commerce was lost during the Blitz. On the destruction of the port books, see Jacob M. Price and Paul G. E. Clemens, "A Revolution of Scale in Overseas Trade: British Firms in the Chesapeake Trade, 1675–1775," *Journal of Economic History* 47.1 (1987): 2.

20.   Converse D. Clowse, *Measuring Charleston's Overseas Commerce, 1717–1767: Statistics from the Port's Naval Lists* (Washington, D.C.: University Press of America, 1981), 54–55, 59, 67, 81; Nash, "Organization of Trade and Finance" (2001), 74–107; David Richardson, "The British Slave Trade to Colonial South Carolina," *Slavery and Abolition* 12.3 (1991): 125–72; Daniel C. Littlefield, "The Slave Trade to Colonial South Carolina: A Profile," *SCHM* 91.2 (1990): 68–99.

21.   T79/37/289, National Archives, London.

CHAPTER ONE: "THE METROPOLIS OF SOUTH CAROLINA"

1.   Cape Finisterre is the westernmost point in Spain. See 3 Geo. II c. 28, in Great Britain, *Statutes at Large,* V, 553–55.

2.   Historians have debated the Rice Act's economic significance for South Carolina. For Eugene Sirmans, it "started a boom in the colony's rice production," and Kenneth Morgan noted that rice production and prices nearly doubled in its wake. John McCusker and Russell Menard, however, have suggested that its "effect was small." See M. Eugene Sirmans, *Colonial South Carolina: A Political History, 1663–1763* (Chapel Hill: University of North Carolina Press, 1966), 162; Morgan, "Colonial American Rice Trade," 439; McCusker and Menard, *Economy of*

British America, 179. Providing statistical ballast to McCusker and Menard's observation, Peter Coclanis demonstrated the exponential growth of South Carolina's rice industry during the 1720s, when exports grew more than threefold, implicitly downplaying the significance of the legislation; see Coclanis, "Rice Prices in the 1720s and the Evolution of the South Carolina Economy," *Journal of Southern History* 48.4 (1982): 531–44, esp. 532. For a discussion of the 1730 rice lobbying in the context of commercial lobbying in London, see Starr, *School for Politics,* esp. 24–43, which suggested how the tactics and style of London lobby politics influenced South Carolina's political culture.

3. *JHC,* XXI, 464, 470; Great Britain, *Calendar of Treasury Books and Papers, 1729–45,* 5 vols. (London: H.M.S.O, 1897–1903), I, 332. The petitions themselves appear not to have survived. On the MPs' interests and activities, see Romney Sedgwick, ed., *The House of Commons, 1715–1754,* 2 vols. (London: H.M.S.O, 1970).

4. Wood, *Black Majority,* 148–53; Richardson, "British Slave Trade," 170–72.

5. Coclanis, *Shadow of a Dream,* 64–65; Coclanis, "Rice Prices in the 1720s," 533.

6. On the revolt against and revocation of proprietorial government, see Robert M. Weir, *Colonial South Carolina: A History* (New York: KTO Press, 1983), 94–103; Walter B. Edgar, *South Carolina: A History* (Columbia: University of South Carolina Press, 1998), 102–7.

7. "The Metropolis of South Carolina": this epithet featured commonly in eighteenth-century descriptions of the town. For example, in 1709 the surveyor John Lawson "arriv'd at Charles Town, the Metropolis of South Carolina," while a visiting British officer, Lord Adam Gordon, noted his arrival in Charles Town, "the Metropolis of South Carolina," in 1764. Describing the British campaign in the southern colonies in 1779, James Madison observed Britain's "rapacious zeal for the rich and flourishing Metropolis of South Carolina." See John Lawson, *A New Voyage to South Carolina, containing the exact description and natural history of that country: together with the present state thereof* (London, 1709), 2; [Lord Adam Gordon], "Journal of an Officer who Travelled in America and the West Indies in 1764 and 1765," in *Travels in the American Colonies,* ed. N. D. Mereness (New York: Macmillan, 1916), 397; James Madison to William Bradford, 30 October–5 November 1779, in James Madison, *The Papers of James Madison, Congressional Series,* ed. William T. Hutchinson et al., 17 vols. (Chicago: University of Chicago Press; Charlottesville: University of Virginia Press, 1962–1991), I, 312.

8. On mercantilism and colonial policy, see Michael G. Kammen, *Empire and Interest: The American Colonies and the Politics of Mercantilism* (Philadelphia: Lippincott, 1970), esp. 40–42, 48–50; Menard and McCusker, *Economy of British America,* 35–38; Joyce E. Chaplin, *An Anxious Pursuit: Agricultural Innovation and Modernity in the Lower South, 1730–1815* (Chapel Hill: University of North Carolina Press, 1993), 27–29; Cathy D. Matson and Peter S. Onuf, *A Union of Interests: Political and Economic Thought in Revolutionary America* (Lawrence: University Press of Kansas, 1990), 15–20.

9. James Glen, "An Attempt towards an Estimate of the Value of South Carolina, for the Right Honourable the Lords Commissioners for Trade and Plantations, 1751," in *Colonial South Carolina Scene,* ed. Merrens, 183.

10. Francis Yonge, *View of the Trade of South Carolina, with Proposals Humbly Offer'd for improving the same* (London, c. 1722), 12–14.

11. Joshua Gee, *The Trade and Navigation of Great Britain Considered,* 3rd ed. (London, 1731), esp. iv (quote), 22–23, 48–53, 100–106.

12. Olson, *Making the Empire Work;* O'Shaughnessy, "Formation of a Commercial Lobby."

13. On parliamentary petitioning, see James Bradley, *Popular Politics and the American Revolution in England: Petitions, the Crown, and Public Opinion* (Macon, Ga.: Mercer, 1986), 17; Julian Hoppit, "Patterns of Parliamentary Legislation, 1600–1800," *Historical Journal* 39.1 (1996): 109–31. On the composition of eighteenth-century parliamentary committees, see Paul Langford, "Property and 'Virtual Representation,' in Eighteenth-Century England," *Historical Journal* 31.1 (1988): 102–3.

14.   Kammen, *Rope of Sand*, 3–15; Ella Lonn, *The Colonial Agents of the Southern Colonies* (Chapel Hill: University of North Carolina Press, 1945), 53–59.

15.   The 1704 Naval Stores Act had introduced a bounty of six pounds per ton on colonial hemp, four pounds per ton on tar, four pounds per ton on pitch, three pounds per ton on rosin and turpentine, and one pound per ton on masts. See 3 & 4 Anne c. 10, in Great Britain, *Statutes at Large*, 176; Thomas Cooper and David J. McCord, eds., *The Statutes at Large of South Carolina*, 10 vols. (Columbia: A. S. Johnson, 1836–41), II, 600–602; Lonn, *Colonial Agents*, 66–67.

16.   The petitions were CO5/1264/301; CO5/1265/11; CO5/1293/71–74; CO5/1293/75–77; CO5/867/117; CO5/358/50–51; CO5/358/146; CO5/358/244–47; CO5/358/284; CO5/359/233–50; CO323/9/11–13; CO5/361/48; CO5/361/105–6 (National Archives, London). A handful of names on the petitions are illegible and have been excluded from the subsequent analysis. One of the two lists was compiled by Stephen Godin in 1729, when he was acting as London agent for South Carolina's Council. The council at the time was at odds with the colony's assembly over the assembly's desire for more local currency to be issued, which the council—and many London merchants—feared would lead to inflation in South Carolina and the devaluation of debts contracted in the colony. Samuel Wragg was then acting as agent in London for the South Carolina Assembly—or as Godin termed it, "the Planters' pretended Parliament." Godin presented the Board of Trade with a list of "British Merchants Trading to Carolina who are no[t] Planters" (CO5/361/9–11). The other list was drawn up retrospectively by South Carolina's Assembly in 1737 and identified the "several Merchants and Traders in London" active in 1730 (CO5/367/116–39). On the analytical utility of petitions in assessing commercial organization, see Gauci, *Politics of Trade*, 129–34.

17.   Jacob Price and Paul Clemens identified some 111 firms that imported tobacco into London in 1719, using the sole surviving London port book from the eighteenth century (Price and Clemens, "Revolution of Scale," 19–21).

18.   The ten who appeared five or more times, with the number of times their names appeared and the inclusive dates within the period 1715–30, were Samuel Barons (eight, 1715–23), John Bell (five, 1715–30), James Crane (five, 1715–23), David Godin (nine, 1717–30), Stephen Godin (eleven, 1715–30), John Hewlett (five, 1719–30), John Lloyd (seven, 1715–29), Richard Shubrick (father of the Richard Shubrick discussed below; five, 1722–30), Samuel Wragg (five, 1719–30), and William Wragg (six, 1715–30). On the Wraggs and Godins, see Henry A. M. Smith, "Wragg of South Carolina," *South Carolina Historical and Genealogical Magazine* 19.3 (1918): 121–23; Edgar and Bailey, *Biographical Directory*, II, 283–85, 729–31.

19.   RP to Thomas Morson, 28 December 1738, *LRP*, I, 56–57.

20.   Instances of unsuitable merchandise sent for sale in Charles Town by ill-informed British merchants abound in Pringle's papers. One firm speculatively sent a cargo of buckram, a stiff cloth useful only for corset makers, of which there were none in Charles Town; a dozen fishing rods were part of another cargo, which was "Intirely unsaleable here & not at all proper for this Country" and which was eventually sent back to London. Woollens that arrived at the start of the summer and which the Charles Town storekeeper would have to keep in storage for several months were a regular bugbear. See RP to James Goodchild, 18 June 1739, 16 June 1740, and 31 March 1741; to Andrew Pringle, 29 March 1742; to Cookson & Wellfitt, 10 April and 2 September 1742, *LRP*, I, 99, 226–27, 306–7, 356–57, 361–62, 398–99.

21.   Great Britain, *Calendar of State Papers, Colonial Series*, 45 vols. (London: Longman, Green, Longman and Roberts, 1860–1994), XXXIV, 243–44.

22.   Records of shipownership corroborate the link between petitioning activity and scale of participation in London's Carolina trade. Samuel Barons and John Bell, both of whom signed more than five petitions, each had a stake in ten vessels that cleared Charles Town between 1717 and 1739. John Lloyd and Thomas Hyam, who signed five and four petitions respectively, had stakes in five vessels. See CO5/510, National Archives, London; Clowse, *Measuring Charleston's Overseas Commerce*, 141, table C-61.

23. CO5/510, National Archives, London; Transatlantic Slave Trade Database: http://slave voyages.org/voyages/mODR6HMW (accessed 31 October 2016).

24. George C. Rogers Jr., *Evolution of a Federalist: William Loughton Smith of Charleston, 1758–1812* (Columbia: University of South Carolina Press, 1962), 12; W. Robert Higgins, "Charles Town Merchants and Factors Dealing in the External Negro Trade, 1735–75," *SCHM* 65.4 (1964): 206.

25. Olson, "Virginia Merchants of London," 371, 378–80. Interaction with the Board of Trade fell correspondingly, with no Virginia merchants appearing before it between 1733 and 1751. Although Olson noted continuing interaction between London's Virginia merchants and the treasury, she observed a net decline in the Virginia merchant community's activity and impact. The capital's Virginia traders had been by far the most active North American commercial lobby in London before 1725: they had submitted thirty-six petitions to the king, Parliament, and other branches of government. London's New England merchants had petitioned sixteen times, and the capital's New York merchants had petitioned on six occasions.

26. CO5/538/50–51 (quote), National Archives, London.

27. Edgar, *South Carolina: A History*, 100.

28. CO5/1264/301, National Archives, London. The petition was signed by Samuel Barons, John Bell, Joseph Boone, Michael Cole, James Crane, Edward Cripps, Stephen Godin, David Guerard, Richard Higginson, Abel Kettleby, Robert Livingston, John Lloyd, John Metcalfe, William Newbury, John Payne, Samuel Pickering, Andre Poon, H. Wigginton, Philo Woodward, Joseph Wragg, and William Wragg. CO/5/1264/301, National Archives, London.

29. Weir, *Colonial South Carolina*, 83–85; Verner W. Crane, *The Southern Frontier, 1670–1732* (Ann Arbor: University of Michigan Press, 1956), 62–86.

30. CO5/1265/11, National Archives, London. Along with colonial agent Kettleby, fourteen merchants trading to South Carolina signed the petition against Virginia's arms trade with the Indians: Samuel Barons, Nathaniel Bradley, Michael Cole, Henry Daniels, James Deane, Stephen Godin, Richard Higginson, Robert Johnson, James Kinloch, John Lloyd, Andre Poon, William Rhett Jr., John Styleman, and William Wragg. In total there were twenty-nine signatories to the two petitions, of whom fifteen signed only the July petition, five signed only the September petition, and nine signed both.

31. *JHC*, XVIII, 262.

32. David Ramsay, *History of South Carolina from Its First Settlement in 1670, to the Year 1808*, 2 vols. (1809; repr., Spartanburg, S.C.: Reprint Co., 1959), II, 114.

33. On the legislative framework for South Carolina's commodity exports, including rice, two classic works remain useful starting points: Lewis C. Gray, *A History of Agriculture in the Southern United States to 1860* (Washington, D.C.: Carnegie, 1933), esp. 284–86; and Charles M. Andrews, *The Colonial Period of American History*. Vol. IV, *England's Commercial and Colonial Policy* (New Haven, Conn.: Yale University Press, 1938), esp. 96–97.

34. 3 & 4 Anne c. 5, in Great Britain, *Statutes at Large*, IV, 170.

35. Gee, *Trade and Navigation*, 23. The role of the enigmatic ship's captain in the enumeration was later invoked by both G. L. Beer and C. M. Andrews in their influential accounts of Britain's colonial trade (George Louis Beer, *The Commercial Policy of England towards the American Colonies* [New York: Columbia College, 1893], 53; Andrews, *Colonial Period of American History*, IV, 97).

36. Great Britain, *Journal of the Commissioners for Trade and Plantations, from April 1704 to May 1782*, 14 vols. (London: H.M.S.O., 1920–28), II, 617–18.

37. Great Britain, *Calendar of State Papers, Colonial*, XXXIII, 62.

38. CO5/358/146, National Archives, London; *JHC*, XX, 62–63.

39. The bill appears to have had support from both the government and regional trading interests. The three MPs who introduced it to Parliament are indicative: Martin Bladen, MP for Stockbridge in Hampshire, was a member of the Board of Trade, was an expert on trade

and colonial affairs, and owned a plantation in the West Indies; Sir Abraham Elton was a commercial magnate in and MP for Bristol; and Archibald Hutcheson, MP for Hastings in Sussex, was a well-connected former member of the Board of Trade. The most likely reason for the bill's failure is that it ran out of parliamentary time. Wragg's costs are revealed in a retrospective claim for a total of £500 he submitted to South Carolina's Assembly in 1742 for his efforts. However, the assembly found no evidence that he had spent more than the £183 it agreed to reimburse him. See *Commons Journals*, XX, 463–65; *Journal of the Commons House of Assembly, 1742–1744*, 225–26; Sedgwick, *House of Commons, 1715–1754*.

40. A. S. Salley, ed., *Journal of the Commons House of Assembly of South Carolina, February 23rd 1724/5 to 1st June 1725* (Columbia: Historical Commission of South Carolina, 1945), 23 March 1725, 66.

41. Earl John Perceval, *Manuscripts of the Earl of Egmont: Diary of Viscount Percival, afterwards First Earl of Egmont*, 3 vols. (London: H.M.S.O, 1920–23), 26 March 1735, II, 154. For their part, the Georgia Trustees recognized the reciprocal advantages of good relations with Fury and his employers. Agreeing to the South Carolinian authorities' request that Fury's salary be temporarily paid through a bill drawn on the trustees in London, Egmont recorded that the trustees considered that "it was a neighbourly action, and would engage Mr. Fury to be affectionate to our colony" (Perceval, *Manuscripts*, 16 January 1735, II, 221). Fury had been appointed as South Carolina's metropolitan agent in 1733.

42. 8 Geo. II c. 19, in Great Britain, *Statutes at Large*, V, 674–75; *Commons Journals*, XXII, 453, 464–65, 469, 473–75, 493. Some seventeen of the thirty-seven MPs named to the committee that considered the bill and proposed the law's extension to Georgia were members or trustees of the Georgia Society. On the Georgia interest in Parliament, see also Richard Dunn, "The Trustees of Georgia and the House of Commons, 1732–1752," *WMQ* 11.4 (1954): 551–65; Betty Wood, *Slavery in Colonial Georgia, 1730–1775* (Athens: University of Georgia Press, 1984), 2–11, 34–48.

43. Quoted in Kammen, *Empire and Interest*, 68.

44. Of nineteen merchant "associates" studied by David Hancock whose pre-London travels are known, for example, three had spent time in North America; see Hancock, *Citizens of the World: London Merchants and the Integration of the British Atlantic Community, 1735–1785* (Cambridge: Cambridge University Press, 1995), 41n. See also William I. Roberts III, "Samuel Storke: An Eighteenth-Century London Merchant Trading to the American Colonies," *Business History Review* 39.2 (1965): 149.

45. Richard Sheridan estimated that if Antigua was typical of the Caribbean islands as a whole, a majority of London's West Indies merchants had spent time in planting or trade on the islands (Sheridan, "Planters and Merchants: The Oliver Family of Antigua and London, 1716–84," *Business History* 13.2 [1971]: 113). For other examples of West Indies merchants' formative spells in the Caribbean islands, see Richard Pares, "A London West India Merchant House, 1740–69," in *The Historian's Business and Other Essays*, ed. R. A. Humphreys and Elizabeth Humphreys (Oxford: Clarendon, 1961), 225; D. W. Thoms, "The Mills Family: London Sugar Merchants of the Eighteenth Century," *Business History* 11.1 (1969): 3; Hancock, *Citizens of the World*, 46–51.

46. The earliest record of Crokatt in South Carolina is from 1728, when he was executor of the will of David Durham, a Berkeley County planter (*SCG*, 26 February 1732; Edgar and Bailey, *Biographical Directory*, II, 213).

47. Population statistics are from Coclanis, *Shadow of a Dream*, 114, table 4–3; Carter et al., *Historical Statistics*, V, 651–55. On South Carolina's economic development during the 1720s and 1730s and Charles Town's commercial dynamism, see Coclanis, "Rice Prices in the 1720s," 532–33; Coclanis, *Shadow of a Dream*, 72–76; Nash, "Urbanization in the Colonial South," 3–29; Emma Hart, *Building Charleston: Town and Society in the Eighteenth Century British Atlantic World* (Charlottesville: University of Virginia Press, 2010), 17–50; Jeanne A. Calhoun, Martha A. Zierden, and Elizabeth Paysinger, "The Geographic Spread of Charleston's Merchant Community, 1732–67," *SCHM* 86.3 (1985): 186.

48. Will of James Crokatt, Prob. 11/1029, National Archives, London; Will of John Crokatt, Prob. 11/703, National Archives, London; Lothrop Withington, ed., "South Carolina Gleanings in England," *South Carolina Historical and Genealogical Magazine* 6.3 (1905): 121–22. William Woodrop married Elizabeth Crokatt (b. 1708, Edinburgh), on 3 May 1737. See Mabel L. Webber, "The Mayrant Family," *South Carolina Historical and Genealogical Magazine* 27.2 (1926): 83; *PHL*, I, 46n, 130n; *LRP*, II, 699.

49. George C. Rogers, *Charleston in the Age of the Pinckneys* (Norman: University of Oklahoma Press, 1969), 13; Great Britain, *Calendar of State Papers, Colonial*, XLI, 133, 157; *SCG*, 20 September and 1 November 1735.

50. RP to Cookson & Wellfitt, 20 March 1742, *LRP*, I, 350.

51. RP to Andrew Pringle, 22 September 1740, *LRP*, I, 248–49.

52. Public Register, South Carolina, Conveyance books [Charleston Deeds], vols. A, 220; B, 153; E, 313; F, 153; South Carolina Court of Common Pleas, Judgement Rolls: 19A, 36A, SCDAH.

53. Thomas Colyer-Ferguson, ed., *The Marriage Registers of St. Dunstan's, Stepney, in the County of Middlesex, 1697–1719* (Canterbury, 1898), 74; *SCG*, 26 February, 30 September, and 16 December 1732; 7 July and 25 August 1733; 29 October 1737; 2 February and 15 April 1738; Charles Town Naval Office list, 1738, CO5/510, National Archives, London.

54. *SCG*, 16 February 1734, 5 April and 31 May 1735, 31 January 1736 (quote), 6 November 1740; Charles Town Naval Office list, 1736–37, CO5/510, National Archives, London.

55. HL to Thomas Lloyd, 7 September 1767, *PHL*, V, 299–300.

56. Several studies of Laurens relate the episode. See C. James Taylor, "A Member of the Family: Twenty-five Years with Henry Laurens," *SCHM* 106.2 (2005): 123–25; Joseph P. Kelly, "Henry Laurens: The Southern Man of Conscience in History," *SCHM* 107.2 (2006): 104–6; David D. Wallace, *The Life of Henry Laurens* (New York: Putnam, 1915), 15–18; Daniel McDonough, *Christopher Gadsden and Henry Laurens: The Parallel Lives of Two American Patriots* (London: Associated University Presses, 2000), 17–18. For Laurens's contemporary letters describing his disappointment, see *PHL*, I, 178–85.

57. HL to Thomas Lloyd, 7 September 1767, *PHL*, V, 299–300.

58. Robert Raper to John Beswicke, 11 January 1762, LRR.

59. Peter Taylor Sr. to Peter Taylor Jr., 21 August 1758, Taylor Family Papers, SCL.

60. HL to John Mill, 9 October 1767, *PHL*, V, 343.

61. RP to John Richards, 3 August 1739, *LRP*, I, 121–22; Walter B. Edgar, "Robert Pringle and His World," *SCHM* 76.1 (1975): 1.

62. RP to Andrew Pringle, 10 July and 7 September 1742, and to John Keith, 3 September 1742, *LRP*, I, 387–88, 404–5, 406–9.

63. James Ogilvie to Alexander Ogilvie, 17 March 1743, OFP; Calhoun et al., "Geographic Spread," 200.

64. RP to Andrew Pringle, 18 March and 4 April 1745, *LRP*, II, 827–30, 833–36; Edgar and Bailey, *Biographical Directory*, II, 542–44.

65. RP to Thomas Pringle, 21 October 1746, Pringle-Garden Papers, SCHS.

66. Alexander Cumine to Alexander Ogilvie, 1 and 22 April (quote) 1763 and 17 March 1770, OFP. Cumine's strategy failed to pay off. The barriers to entering trade in Charles Town were greater than he had expected, and after seven years of trying to enter business he instead took a job as a Latin teacher.

67. HL to Bright & Millward, 12 January 1770; to Jeremiah Meyler, 12 January 1770; to Stephenson, Holford & Co., 31 July 1770; and to Mayne & Co., 1 August 1770, *PHL*, VII, 214–15, 216–17, 315–16, 317.

68. James Habersham to John Nutt, 31 July 1772, in James Habersham, *Collections of the Georgia Historical Society*, vol. VI, *The Letters of the Hon. James Habersham, 1756–1775* (Savannah: Georgia Historical Society, 1906), 195.

69. HL to John Lewis Gervais, 23 January 1773, *PHL*, VIII, 539.

70. Charles Ogilvie to Alexander Ogilvie, 9 February 1751, OFP.

71. Charles Ogilvie to Alexander Ogilvie, 17 July 1752, OFP.

72. The mortality rate among slaves on board British ships in the Atlantic slave trade between 1701 and 1750 has been calculated at 15.6 percent per voyage. This does not include the deaths of slaves before leaving the coast of Africa or, once they had arrived in the Americas, before they had disembarked or been sold, which could be nearly as high. See Herbert S. Klein, Stanley L. Engerman, Robin Haines, and Ralph Shlomowitz, "Transoceanic Mortality: The Slave Trade in Comparative Perspective," *WMQ* 58.1 (2001): 105–6, tables II, V, XI. Stephen D. Behrendt has estimated that "each year in the slave trade about one in five crew members died" (Behrendt, "Markets, Transactions Cycles, and Profits: Merchant Decision Making in the British Slave Trade," *WMQ* 58.1 [2001]: 180).

73. Charles Ogilvie to Alexander Ogilvie, 17 July 1752, OFP.

74. Charles Ogilvie to Alexander Ogilvie, 20 August 1752 (postscript to 17 July letter), OFP.

75. For an overview of the organization and structure of Charles Town's colonial-era trade, see Nash, "Organization of Trade and Finance" (2001), 77–85; Morgan, "Colonial American Rice Trade," 441–47.

76. Rogers, *Charleston in the Age of the Pinckneys*, 56. Six of the other wharves were named after local merchant-planters: Rhett's Bridge, Elliott's Bridge, Motte's Bridge, Pinckney's Bridge, Lloyd's Bridge, and Brewton's Bridge; the largest, containing the city market, was simply Middle Bridge (Calhoun et al., "Geographic Spread," 188).

77. Miscellaneous Records, 1749–51, 292–301, SCDAH; *SCG*, 19 October–9 November 1738.

78. South Carolina Court of Common Pleas, Judgement Rolls: 23A/58A, 24A/1A, 2A, 26A; 24B/2A, 19A, SCDAH.

79. *SCG*, 17 April 1736, 30 April 1741.

80. *SCG*, 15 May 1736, 7 September 1734.

81. South Carolina Court of Common Pleas, Judgement Rolls: 27B, 19A; 33A/108A, SCDAH.

82. CO5/367/61, 80–81, 87a; CO5/365/37–40, National Archives, London; W. O. Moore Jr., "The Largest Exporters of Deerskins from Charles Town, 1735–1775," *SCHM* 74.3 (1973): 144–47; *SCG*, 18 September 1736; J. H. Easterby and R. Nicholas Olsberg, eds., *Journal of the Commons House of Assembly of South Carolina*, 14 vols., 1736–57 (Columbia: Historical Commission of South Carolina, 1951–89), 1736–39, 174. On the public provision of goods to native Indians, see Mancall et al., "Indians and the Economy of Eighteenth-Century Carolina," 304–6.

83. Easterby and Olsberg, *Journal of the Commons House*, 20 January 1742, 318.

84. Easterby and Olsberg, *Journal of the Commons House*, 12 January, 28 February, and 28 April 1743, 109, 249, 395, 403; 13 January 1744, 520. On the broader impact of the 1739–48 warfare for Charles Town's trade, see Stuart O. Stumpf, "Implications of King George's War for the Charleston Mercantile Community," *SCHM* 77.3 (1976): 161–88.

85. RP to Andrew Pringle, 17 April 1742, *LRP*, I, 371; Easterby and Olsberg, *Journal of the Commons House of Assembly*, 16 and 18 February 1742, 379, 395. On the Shubricks' naval connections, see also *SCG*, 20 December 1742, 21 February 1743, 21 September 1748; Stumpf, "Implications of King George's War," 165.

86. Higgins, "Charles Town Merchants," 205–17.

87. Littlefield, "Slave Trade to Colonial South Carolina," 69–70; Richardson, "British Slave Trade," 127–29. Richardson estimated that about eighty thousand slaves came directly from Africa, with about thirteen thousand imported into South Carolina from other British colonies, and that 87 percent of the slaves brought directly from Africa were carried on vessels owned in Britain.

88. Littlefield, "Slave Trade to Colonial South Carolina," 94–98.

89. Klein et al., "Transoceanic Mortality," tables II, V.

90. *SCG*, 19 April 1739.

91. *SCG*, 14 June 1735. The story was newsworthy enough to be reprinted in a Philadelphia newspaper the following month: *American Weekly Mercury*, 31 July 1735. Peter H. Wood cited this case as an example of "semi-organized crime" by black slaves (Wood, *Black Majority*, 215–16). No court records of criminal cases in Charles Town before 1769 have survived.

92. Edgar and Bailey, *Biographical Directory*, II, 265–68, 379–80.

93. Henry A. M. Smith, "The Baronies of South Carolina," *South Carolina Historical and Genealogical Magazine* 18.1 (1917): 8–9. On the Ball family, see Edward Ball, *Slaves in the Family* (London: Penguin, 1999).

94. *SCG*, 22 November 1742; RP to Andrew Pringle, 11 June 1744, *LRP*, II, 708; Edgar and Bailey, *Biographical Directory*, II, 326.

95. CO5/366/105–6; CO5/381/262; CO324/37/112, National Archives, London. The *Gazette* reported Crokatt's appointment on 1 June 1738.

96. *SCG*, 2 December 1732, 13 November 1736; Hennig Cohen, *The South Carolina Gazette, 1732–1775* (Columbia: University of South Carolina Press, 1953), 17–18. For other examples of Crokatt's links to Scottish causes, see *SCG*, 29 September 1738, 19 April 1739; Scots Hospital of King Charles II, *A Short Account of the Institution, Progress, and Present State of the Scottish Corporation in London* (London, 1777), 39.

97. *SCG*, 27 December 1735, 31 January 1736, 22 December 1737.

98. *SCG*, 9 April 1737, 3 August 1738 (quote).

99. St. Philip's Parish, Charleston, S.C., Vestry Minutes, 1732–74, 50, SCDAH.

100. *SCG*, 4 May 1738, 21 June 1742 (on Beswicke); 22 April 1745, 7 April 1746 (on Shubrick).

101. Nash, "Trade and Business," 13. Notable Charles Town merchants in the first category were Gabriel Manigault, John Guerard, and Henry Laurens. George Austin, Laurens's business partner and a native of Shropshire, England, was a notable member of the second group.

102. Kathryn Roe Coker, "Absentees as Loyalists in Revolutionary War South Carolina," *SCHM* 96.2 (1995): 125–26; Eugene M. Sirmans, "The South Carolina Royal Council, 1720–1763," *WMQ* 18.3 (1961): 392.

103. Sirmans, "South Carolina Royal Council," 392.

104. George Udney to William Middleton, 13 January 1753, Middleton Family Papers, HA93: 722/124, microfilm, SCDAH.

105. On bills of exchange and other instruments of commercial credit, see Gauci, *Emporium of the World*, 52, 145; Price, "What Did Merchants Do," 278, 280. On the evolution of merchant banking, see Niall Ferguson, *The Ascent of Money: A Financial History of the World*, 2nd ed. (London: Penguin, 2009), 42–48.

106. Charles Ogilvie to Alexander Ogilvie, 20 March 1760, OFP.

107. *SCG*, 25 February 1764.

108. On "backward integration" strategies in Atlantic trade and planting, see Hancock, *Citizens of the World*, 81, 143–71; S. D. Smith, "Gedney Clarke of Salem and Barbados: Transatlantic Super-Merchant," *New England Quarterly* 76.4 (2003): 510.

109. Charles Ogilvie to Alexander Ogilvie, 22 February 1761, OFP. Ogilvie had been in partnership with John Ward during the 1750s, which terminated in March 1759. He then went into partnership with John Forbes, with whom he continued after relocating to London. See *SCG*, 31 March 1759; Calhoun et al., "Geographic Spread," 203, 209.

110. Charles Ogilvie to Alexander Ogilvie, 22 February 1761, OFP.

111. *SCG*, 23 March 1747.

112. *SCG*, 1 February, 19 April, 2 June 1739.

113. *SCG*, 16 November 1738–16 June 1739. Crokatt's gift for advertising apparently rubbed off on his young partner, Benjamin Smith. Smith's three-column spread in the largest type to announce the formation of his new firm, Benjamin Smith & Co., in 1752 has been called "the boldest advertisement that had yet appeared in the *Gazette*" (Rogers, *Evolution of a Federalist*, 14).

114. *SCG*, 5–25 April and 22 November 1735, 5 March 1737.

115. *SCG*, 15 and 22 May, 5 June 1736. For further examples of his assertiveness in reclaiming debts, see *SCG*, 9 February and 15 April 1738.

116. *SCG*, 15 January 1737. See also Judgement Rolls: 23A/58A; 24A/1A, 2A; 26A/78A, SC-DAH; *SCG*, 12 May 1733, 26 May 1746, 21 January 1751.

117. *SCG*, 29 December 1739. Crokatt's relationship with his agent, Robert Raper, continued for nearly thirty years. When they settled their account in 1767, Raper expressed his hope that "we may finish our Concerns as amicably as we began which I think was in the year 1739" (Robert Raper to James Crokatt, 14 February 1767, LRR).

118. Miscellaneous Records, 1749–51, 292–301, SCDAH; *SCG*, 19 October–9 November 1738. Smith had been at Crokatt's trading house as early as June 1735, when he was identified in a newspaper advertisement (*SCG*, 21 June 1735).

CHAPTER TWO: "FRIENDS TO ASSIST AT HOME"

1. RP to Andrew Pringle, 30 May (quote) and 20 July 1744, *LRP*, II, 699–701, 728–30.

2. Scottish-born Robert Pringle still conceived of Britain as "Home" in the 1740s, an affective and linguistic trait shared by many Carolinians whether born in Britain or in the colony.

3. Price and Clemens, "Revolution of Scale," 21–24; Price, "What Did Merchants Do," 281.

4. HL to Francis Bremar, 27 March 1749, *PHL*, I, 232. Laurens's omission of John Beswicke from this list, despite the scale of Beswicke's involvement in London's Carolina trade, probably reflected the small amount of trade the two did with one another.

5. Great Britain, *Journal of the Commissioners for Trade*, VIII, 273; CO5/65/1–3; Charles Town Naval Office Lists: CO5/509–11, National Archives, London.

6. The concentration of London's Carolina trade in the early 1760s is further confirmed by ships' manifests detailing indigo exports from South Carolina in 1764 (Charles Town Naval Office, ships' manifests, January–April 1764, CO5/511/2–63, National Archives, London).

7. Thomas Mortimer, *The Universal Director . . .* [*Mortimer's Directory*] (London, 1763). As the only London directory published before 1788 that was classified by field, *Mortimer's* is an invaluable source for the study of the city's merchants in the 1760s. The largest group is general merchants, without a defined field of trade. However, the directory has some limitations as a source. Containing around 2,900 names and addresses, including 1,252 individuals and firms listed as merchants, it was less comprehensive than contemporary directories such as the rival but unclassified *Complete Guide*. The *Complete Guide* contained around 4,200 entries in its 1760 edition and around 6,000 in 1765. After *Mortimer's* was published in 1763 no further classified London directories were published before 1788, making it hard to track participation in each trade over time. See Peter J. Atkins, *The Directories of London, 1677–1977* (London: Mansell, 1990), 22. *Sketchley's Bristol Directory* was the first classified directory in Bristol, in 1775. Among the 168 merchants listed, it categorized just one specialist Carolina trader, Samuel Brailsford. Formerly a prominent merchant in Charles Town, he had relocated to Britain in the late 1760s. See James Sketchley, *Sketchley's Bristol Directory; including Clifton, Bedminster, and the out-parishes of St. James and St. Philip* (Bristol, 1775).

8. His children's "disobedience" included his eldest daughter's elopement with an unsuitable husband, which had resulted in John Nickleson "raging like a Madman" and his wife "drowned in Tears"; and the conduct of his "Brutal Son" Jack, of whom Peter Manigault, visiting from Charles Town, remarked that "for sure a greater Mixture of Fool & Villain never met together in one Man." See Peter Manigault to Gabriel Manigault, 26 February 1754, Peter Manigault Papers, SCHS.

9. For example, the linen drapers Pomeroys & Streatfield and the woollen drapers Rogers & Dyson, who traded to South Carolina between the 1740s and the 1770s, and the textile wholesaler Nathaniel Newberry (*PHL*, I, 15n, 232; VIII, 261; Kellock, "London Merchants and the Pre-1776 American Debts"; City of London Land Tax Assessments, MS.11316/132–34, Guildhall Library, London; *London Directories*).

10. Major London overseas traders whose diverse portfolios included some interests in the Carolina trade included Sir William Baker, Richard Oswald, and Samuel Touchett.

11. Peter Guillery, *The Small House in Eighteenth-Century London: A Social and Architectural History* (New Haven, Conn.: Yale University Press, 2004), 7.

12. On London's dominance of British overseas trade, see Christopher J. French, "Crowded with Traders and a Great Commerce: London's Domination of English Overseas Trade, 1700–1775," *London Journal* 17 (1992): 29–32; Patrick K. O'Brien, "Inseparable Connections: Trade, Economy, Fiscal State, and the Expansion of Empire, 1688–1815," in *The Oxford History of the British Empire: The Eighteenth Century*, ed. Peter J. Marshall (Oxford: Oxford University Press, 1998), 61.

13. Morgan, "Colonial American Rice Trade," 436–38.

14. No data on the destination of Charles Town rice exports survive for the 1740s, but London's average annual share of the port's rice exports to Britain between 1734 and 1738 was 42 percent and between 1758 and 1760, 30 percent; see Clowse, *Measuring Charleston's Overseas Commerce*, 63, table B-26. A lawsuit brought by Richard Shubrick against a Capt. Salmond, whom Shubrick had chartered to collect a cargo of rice in Winyaw (Georgetown) in 1762–63, is an illuminating account of how the transatlantic rice trade was organized and the principal role of London merchants in it. Salmond was contracted to take a cargo to Madeira and then sail to Winyaw, where he would stay for forty days, unless loaded and dispatched earlier. In Winyaw, he was to "load his ship with such rice and other goods as the plaintiff's agents & c. should tender to be laden." If the ship failed to arrive in Winyaw by 1 March 1763, Shubrick's "factors or assigns" could choose either to load the ship as specified or refuse it altogether. Shubrick brought the case since Salmond never sailed from Madeira to Winyaw, and it was decided in Shubrick's favor. See Thomas Parker, *The laws of shipping and insurance, with a digest of adjudged cases; containing the acts of parliament relative to shipping, insurance and navigation . . . from Trinity term 1693, to Michaelmas term 1774* (London, 1775).

15. As with rice, there are no data on the destinations of Carolinian deerskins or naval stores between 1738 and 1758. However, between 1734 and 1738 London received an annual average of 50 percent of the colony's deerskin exports, 57 percent of its tar, and 53 percent of its pitch; and between 1758 and 1760 an annual average of 60 percent of its deerskins, 18 percent of its tar (second to Poole), and 31 percent of its pitch. See Clowse, *Measuring Charleston's Overseas Commerce*, 54–55, 67, tables B-11, B-32; Nash, "Organization of Trade and Finance" (2001), 88–89.

16. For more detail on the economic organization of South Carolina's Atlantic trades, see Nash, "Organization of Trade and Finance" (2001), 74–107; Nash, "Organization of Trade and Finance" (2005), 95–151, which elaborates on the comparative context of South Carolina's trade; Nash, "South Carolina Indigo," 362–92; Morgan, "Colonial American Rice Trade," 433–52. The Rawlinson, Davison & Newman Account Books (Guildhall Library, London) are underused sources on the marketing of rice and indigo, and a variety of other imported colonial produce, in London.

17. S. D. Smith and T. R. Wheeley, "'Requisites of a Considerable Trade': The Letters of Robert Plumsted, Atlantic Merchant, 1752–8," *English Historical Review* 124 (2009): 556; Roberts, "Samuel Storke," 155; Zahedieh, *Capital and the Colonies*, 69, 252–79.

18. Richardson, "British Slave Trade," 137–39; Littlefield, "Slave Trade to Colonial South Carolina," 84–94.

19. On London's share of the Atlantic slave trade to South Carolina, see Richardson, "British Slave Trade," 139. For evidence that the principal London Carolina merchants of the 1740s and 1750s had had limited direct participation in the slave trade when they had been based in Charles Town, see Higgins, "Charles Town Merchants," 205–17.

20. HL to James Crokatt, 2 January 1749; and to Isaac Hobhouse, 21 March 1749, *PHL*, I, 200–201, 226–27.

21. Among the other merchants who specialized in London's goods export trade to South Carolina between 1749 and the American Revolution, during which time sixty-three ships departed on slaving voyages from London and completed their journeys in South Carolina, only Benjamin Stead was active in the slave trade. He was a prominent slave trader in Charles Town before relocating to London in 1759, and his participation in the slave trade in London was concentrated in three years, when he had a stake in five slave voyages between 1764 and 1766. See Transatlantic Slave Trade Database: http://slavevoyages.org/voyages/oxw15R6C (accessed 31 October 2016). See also Richardson, "British Slave Trade," 125–72; Higgins, "Charles Town Merchants," 208, 210–11; *SCG*, 17 July 1755.

22. In this, the Carolina merchants appear to have more closely matched the commercial strategies of London's largest colonial merchants in the late seventeenth century, among whom Zahedieh observed "very high levels of regional specialization," than the merchants profiled by David Hancock, who participated in several different branches of trade. See Zahedieh, *Capital and the Colonies*, 103 (quote), 286; Hancock, *Citizens of the World*.

23. South Carolina Court of Common Pleas, Judgement Rolls: 45A/153A, SCDAH; Crokatt v. Muilman [1770], C12/540/24; CO5/65/27–29, 30–34, 37–39, 40–42, National Archives, London.

24. Charles Town Naval Office Lists: CO5/509–11, National Archives, London.

25. *Read's Weekly Journal or British Gazetteer*, 14 July 1750; [J. Osborn], *A Complete Guide to All Persons who have any Trade or Concern with the City of London, and Parts Adjacent*, 2nd–16th eds. (London, 1740–83), 1749–55, 4th–6th eds.; Trinity House, *The royal charter of confirmation granted by His most excellent Majesty King James II. To the Trinity-House of Deptford-Strond; for the government and increase of the navigation of England . . .* (London, 1763), 180.

26. Jonas Hanway, *An Account of the Marine Society [List of subscribers to the Marine Society], recommending the piety and policy of the institution, and pointing out the advantages accruing to the nation . . .*, 6th ed. (London, 1759), 13; *Court and City Register. For the year 1755 . . .*, 19th ed. (London, 1755), 207; *Public Advertiser*, 19 January 1754; *Lloyd's Evening Post*, 21 December 1764. On the culture of charity in mid-century London, see Donna Andrew, *Philanthropy and Police: London Charity in the Eighteenth Century* (Princeton, N.J.: Princeton University Press, 1989).

27. Bob Harris, "Patriotic Commerce and National Revival: The Free British Fishery Society and British Politics, c. 1749–58," *English Historical Review* 114 (1999): 285–313.

28. James Habersham to Graham, Clark & Co., 15 February and 15 June(?) 1771, in Habersham, *Collections of the Georgia Historical Society*, 121, 142–43.

29. South Carolina Court of Common Pleas, Judgement Rolls: 24B/32A, 26A/72A, 26A/75A, 27B/15A, SCDAH. These record the lawsuits through which Crokatt pursued debtors in Charles Town.

30. The turnover in personnel in these partnerships indicates the fluidity of Charles Town's commercial scene, in contrast to the relative stasis of London's Carolina trade. Beswicke's partnerships were with, successively, John Crokatt and Alexander Livie (1752–53), then with Livie and John McQueen (1753–54), with McQueen alone (1754–58), and with McQueen and Maurice Harvey (1758–62). See South Carolina Court of Common Pleas, Judgement Rolls: 33A/87A; 37A/12A; 45B/20A, SCDAH.

31. Miscellaneous Records, 1749–51, 92–94, 292–301, SCDAH.

32. Crokatt's business with Charles Town trading houses in this period was recorded in the first volume of the Laurens papers. See HL to Richard Grubb, 16 March 1748; to James Crokatt, 16 April 1748; to Savage & Pickering, 26 December 1748, *PHL*, I, 121–22, 130–31, 191–92. On Crokatt's shipping interests, see Charles Town Naval Office lists, CO5/510, National Archives, London; HL to James Crokatt, 13 April 1748, *PHL*, I, 126–27; Clowse, *Measuring Charleston's Overseas Commerce*, 151; R. Nicholas Olsberg, "Ship Registers in the South Carolina Archives, 1734–1780," *SCHM* 74.4 (1973): 212, 225.

33. Judgement Rolls: 32A/65A; 43A/50A, 139A/171A, SCDAH.

34. Robert Raper to Charles Crokatt, 13 January 1764; to Greenwood & Higginson, 6 March 1765, LRR.

35. HL to Rawlinson & Davison, 24 September 1755, *PHL*, I, 344.

36. HL to John Hopton, 4 September 1771, *PHL*, VII, 559.

37. Crokatt v. Barclay (1748), C12/2203/55; Watson v. Crokatt (1760), C12/907/77; Crokatt v. Muilman (1770), C12/540/23, National Archives, London.

38. On the different sectoral locales within London, see Gauci, *Emporium of the World*, 32, 43, 96.

39. Evidence on the Carolina merchants' locations was derived from [Osborn], *Complete Guide to . . . London*, 1740–83, 2nd–16th eds.; *Kent's Directory*, 1742, 1754, 1762; Mortimer, *Universal Director* [*Mortimer's Directory*]; *London Evening Post*, 24 January 1753; *Public Advertiser*, 13 June 1758; *Morning Chronicle and London Advertiser*, 31 January 1774. On the Royal Exchange, see Gauci, *Emporium of the World*, 39–56.

40. Bryant Lillywhite, *London Coffee Houses: A Reference Book of Coffee Houses of the Seventeenth, Eighteenth, and Nineteenth Centuries* (London: Allen and Unwin, 1963), 147–49. On coffeehouses as a specific locus for mercantile petitioning, see Alison Olson, "Coffee House Lobbying," *History Today* 41.1 (1991): 35–41.

41. RP to Andrew Pringle, 21 January 1743, *LRP*, II, 487–88.

42. RP to Andrew Pringle, 9 March 1744, *LRP*, II, 662.

43. Nicholas Rogers, *The Press Gang: Naval Impressment and its Opponents in Georgian Britain* (London: Continuum, 2007), 85–90; Dora Mae Clark, "The Impressment of Seamen in the American Colonies," in *Essays in Colonial History Presented to Charles McLean Andrews by His Students* (New Haven, Conn.: Yale University Press, 1931), 205–12.

44. RP to James Hunter & Co., 2 April 1737, *LRP*, I, 11.

45. RP to John Erving, 17 May 1740, *LRP*, I, 207. Crew members of another merchant vessel, the *Caesar*, were less fortunate in their attempts to avoid impressment by a gang from the *Tartar*, with one killed while resisting (*SCG*, 17 and 24 May 1740).

46. RP to Andrew Pringle, 27 January and 5 February 1743, and to Richard Partridge, 29 January 1743, *LRP*, II, 491–92, 497. On shortages of manpower caused by naval impressments, see also RP to Andrew Pringle, 31 December 1742, *LRP*, II, 471. The Royal Navy's impact on shipping was probably the reason that Charles Town's merchants, as Robert Pringle reported, were not too concerned about the lack of naval protection against Spanish vessels off the Carolina coast during the war: "we have had no King's ships on a Cruize for these Ten Months past, so badly is this coast taken care of & yet the Merchants here won't be Unanimous to Complain of Same."

47. The failure of London's Carolina lobby to press for the 1708 law to be enforced or for impressment in Charles Town to be otherwise curbed contrasted with the activity of the capital's West Indies lobby on the matter. The agents for the Caribbean sugar colonies, planters on the islands, and merchants trading to the islands petitioned the king and Parliament to complain about the effects of impressment on the West Indies. Thanks to their efforts, an act "for the better Encouragement of the Trade of his Majesty's Sugar Colonies in America" was passed in 1746 to prohibit impressment in the West Indies, making a distinction between the Caribbean and the North American mainland colonies. See Clark, "Impressment of Seamen," 212–15.

48. RP to Pringle & Scott, 15 May 1742, *LRP*, I, 374.

49. *JHC*, XXIII, 284. Permission was granted for direct exports of sugar to European points south of Cape Finisterre but not for the other commodities (12 Geo. II c. 30, in Great Britain, *Statutes at Large*, VI, 115–20). However, the act had little effect since unlike rice, sugar exports to southern Europe remained very small (O'Shaughnessy, *Empire Divided*, 61–62).

50. RP to Andrew Pringle, 5 July 1743, *LRP*, II, 577–78; Easterby, *Journal of the Commons House of Assembly*, vol. 1746–47, 251, 336, 380–81; *Parker's Penny Post*, 7 May 1725; *Whitehall Evening Post or London Intelligencer*, 20 October 1759.

51.   Britain did not automatically prohibit wartime trade with countries with which it was at war in the eighteenth century. On the theory and practicalities of trade with the enemy, see Richard Pares, *War and Trade in the West Indies, 1739–1763* (Oxford: Oxford University Press, 1936), 394–468.

52.   *JHC*, XXIII, 538–39, 542–43, 547, 551–52; "An Act to prohibit, for a Time therein limited, the Exportation of Corn, Grain, (Rice excepted), Meal, Malt, Flour, Bread, Biscuit, Starch, Beef, Pork, and Bacon" (14 Geo. II c. 3, in Great Britain, *Statutes at Large*, VI, 148).

53.   *The Gentleman's Magazine, and Historical Chronicle* XII (1742): 233–35. See also Marion B. Smith, "South Carolina and the *Gentleman's Magazine*," *SCHM* 95.2 (1994): 119–20; Sedgwick, *House of Commons*, I.

54.   15 Geo. II c. 33, in Great Britain, *Statutes at Large*, VI, 196.

55.   Among the extensive literature on the empire in mid-century British culture and political debate, see in particular on Britain's conjoined imperial-maritime-commercial policies, Daniel A. Baugh, "Maritime Strength and Atlantic Commerce: The Uses of 'A Grand Marine Empire,'" in *An Imperial State at War: Britain from 1689 to 1815*, ed. Lawrence Stone (London: Routledge, 1994), 185–223; and on the commercial legislation of the late 1740s and early 1750s, Bob Harris, *Politics and the Nation: Britain in the Mid-Eighteenth Century* (Oxford: Oxford University Press, 2002), 240–65. Other works have placed differing emphases on the emergence of an imperial consciousness in Britain: Kathleen Wilson, *The Sense of the People: Politics, Culture and Imperialism in England, 1715–1785* (Cambridge: Cambridge University Press, 1995); Kathleen Wilson, "Empire, Trade and Popular Politics in Mid-Hanoverian Britain: The Case of Admiral Vernon," *Past and Present* 212 (1988): 74–109; Kathleen Wilson, "Empire of Virtue: The Imperial Project and Hanoverian Culture, c. 1720–1785," in *An Imperial State at War*, ed. Stone, 128–64; Eliga H. Gould, *The Persistence of Empire: British Political Culture in the Age of the American Revolution* (Chapel Hill: University of North Carolina Press, 2000), 53–71; Bob Harris, "'American Idols': Empire, War and the Middling Ranks in Mid-Eighteenth Century Britain," *Past and Present* 150 (1996): 111–41; Bob Harris, "War, Empire and the 'National Interest' in Mid-Eighteenth Century Britain," in *Britain and America Go to War: The Impact of War and Warfare in Anglo-America, 1754–1815*, ed. Stephen Conway and Julie Flavell (Gainesville: University Press of Florida, 2004), 13–40; Marie Peters, "Early Hanoverian Consciousness: Empire or Europe?," *English Historical Review* 122 (2007): 632–68.

56.   Harris, "Patriotic Commerce and National Revival," 297; [Sir Matthew Decker], *An Essay on the Causes of the Decline in Foreign Trade, consequently of the Value of the Lands in Britain, and on the Means to Restore both*, 2nd ed. (London, 1750), 65.

57.   Ralph Davis, "The Rise of Protection in England, 1689–1786," *Economic History Review* 19.2 (1966): 313; John Brewer, *The Sinews of Power: War, Money and the English State, 1688–1783* (London: Routledge, 1989), 95–99, 211–17.

58.   *JHC*, XXIII, 682; XXV, 997–98, 1032–35; XXVI, 239–41, 267; Perceval, *Manuscripts*, III, 200.

59.   HL to George Austin, 17 December 1748, *PHL*, I, 185. The petition itself has apparently not survived.

60.   *SCG*, 5 and 19 February 1737.

61.   [James Crokatt, ed.], *Further observations intended for improving the culture and curing of indigo, &c. in South-Carolina* (London, 1747), 10.

62.   *SCG*, 23 March 1747, 15 August 1748. On proposals for agricultural diversification in the lower South, see also Chaplin, *Anxious Pursuit*, 134–59.

63.   Easterby, *Journal of the Commons House of Assembly*, 1749–50, 18.

64.   Gee, *Trade and Navigation*, 21.

65.   Easterby, *Journal of the Commons House of Assembly*, 1749–50, 99. On the production of indigo, see John J. Winberry, "Indigo in South Carolina: A Historical Geography," *Southeastern Geographer* 19.2 (1979): 91–102; Chaplin, *Anxious Pursuit*, 190–99.

66.   In assessing the short- and long-term economic consequences of the indigo bounty, R. C. Nash has pointed out that it had an important immediate effect, giving enough of a price stimulus to sustain South Carolina's fledgling indigo culture during the early 1750s, when its low price relative to that of rice led many planters to revert their entire operations to rice cultivation. He suggested that in the long term, however, the flat rate of the bounty had negative consequences, by encouraging the production of low-quality indigo: at a flat rate, the bounty was proportionately greater on low-grade than it was on higher-grade, more-expensive indigo. See Nash, "South Carolina Indigo," 375–76.

67.   [James Crokatt], *Observations concerning indigo and cochineal* (London, 1746); [Crokatt], *Further Observations*, 25. It is probable that Crokatt was also the anonymous London correspondent whose letter appeared in the *Gazette* in April 1745 informing Carolinians, "When you can in some measure supply the British Demand, we are persuaded, that on proper Application to Parliament, a Duty will be laid on Foreign Growth, for I am informed, that we pay for INDIGO to the French £200,000 per annum" (*SCG*, 1 April 1745).

68.   [James Crokatt], *Reasons for laying a Duty on French and Spanish Indico, and granting a Bounty on what is made in the British Plantations* (London, 1748), CO5/372/15–18, National Archives, London.

69.   As recorded in the *Journal of the House of Commons*, petitions were received from London's Carolina traders; Bristol's Carolina traders; "Merchants, Manufacturers and Traders of all Kinds" from Liverpool; South Carolinian planters; London dyers; and Southwark dyers; and other petitions came from dyers, clothiers, and dealers in the main textile-producing regions of England—Yorkshire, Lancashire, and the West Country: Exeter (Devon); Poole (Dorset); Manchester and Rochdale (Lancashire); Norwich (Norfolk); Nottingham (Nottinghamshire); Witney (Oxfordshire); Frome (Somerset); Bradford-on-Avon, Calne, Chippenham and surrounding villages, Heytesbury and Warminster, New Sarum and Trowbridge (all Wiltshire); and Halifax, Leeds, and Wakefield (Yorkshire). See *JHC*, XXV, 632–38, 643. The text of the petitions was summarized in the *Journal of the House of Commons*; the petitions themselves have not survived.

70.   *JHC*, XXV, 634–35.

71.   In deference to textile interests, a levy proposed on imported French and Spanish indigo was dropped (*JHC*, XXV, 658; 21 Geo. II c. 30, in Great Britain, *Statutes at Large*, VI, 411–13). Interestingly, the sole tract to be published against the proposed indigo bounty condemned it on grounds of patriotic commercialism. The bounty's generosity, the tract argued, would incentivize South Carolina's planters to concentrate exclusively on indigo production, drawing them all away from growing rice. Since rice required "fifty Times the Shipping and . . . twenty times the People than Indico can maintain," the consequence of this would be to decimate Britain's trading fleet with the colony, impoverishing merchants and, by implication, weakening the country's marine defenses. See [Anon.], *Ill-Judged Bounties tend to Beggary on both Sides or, Observations on a Paper intituled Reasons for laying a Duty on French and Spanish Indico, and granting a Bounty on what is made in the British Plantations* (London, 1748), 6–7 (quote).

72.   Easterby, *Journal of the Commons House of Assembly*, vol. 1749–50, 18–20, 52–54.

73.   HL to Richard Grubb, 15 June 1748, *PHL*, I, 148. Laurens evidently bore Crokatt no ill will for failing to offer him partnership in his trading house.

74.   Easterby, *Journal of the Commons House of Assembly*, vol. 1749–50, 276.

75.   On the repeated efforts to encourage sericulture, see Chaplin, *Anxious Pursuit*, 158–65; Gray, *History of Agriculture*, I, 184–88; and, specifically on silk cultivation in Georgia, Ben Marsh, *Georgia's Frontier Women: Female Fortunes in a Southern Colony* (Athens: University of Georgia Press, 2007), 53–61.

76.   *JHC*, XXV, 933, 996–97, 1024 (quote), 1063, 1114; 23 Geo. II c. 20, in Great Britain, *Statutes at Large*, VI, 469–70.

77.   *JHC*, XXVI, 215–16.

78. *JHC*, XXVI, 239–41, 267 (quote), 278, 288–92; 24 Geo. II c. 51, in Great Britain, *Statutes at Large*, VI, 577–79.

79. Easterby, *Journal of the Commons House of Assembly*, vol. 1751–52, 18–20, 52–54.

80. Easterby, *Journal of the Commons House of Assembly*, vol. 1749–50, 318–19. Fury's attempts to secure direct salt imports were recorded in Great Britain, *Calendar of Treasury Books*, V, 38. Charles II had allowed the New England colonies and Newfoundland to import salt directly from continental Europe because it was vital in the curing of fish. The rights were extended to Pennsylvania and New York in 1726 and 1730 respectively. See 13 Geo. I c. 5 and 3 Geo. II c. 12, in Great Britain, *Statutes at Large*, V, 442, 530–31.

81. CO5/372/162, National Archives, London.

82. *JHC*, XXV, 942.

83. *JHC*, XXV, 1033.

84. *JHC*, XXV, 1032–35; J. C. Van Horne and G. Reese, eds., *The Letterbook of James Abercromby, Colonial Agent, 1751–1773* (Richmond: Virginia State Library and Archives, 1991), 234n.

85. Easterby, *Journal of the Commons House of Assembly*, vol. 1752–54, 92.

86. Great Britain, *Journal of the Commissioners for Trade*, VIII, 273. The other appellants were William Baker, John Beswicke, Charles Crokatt (just seventeen years old at the time), Nathaniel Newberry, John Nickleson, Andrew Pringle, Richard Shubrick, and William Stone.

87. James Abercromby to James Glen, 6 April 1752, in Van Horne and Reese, *Letterbook of James Abercromby*, 32–34; Sirmans, *Colonial South Carolina*, 301; Mercantini, *Who Shall Rule at Home*, 80, 91. For a thorough account of McNair and the so-called "Sphinx Company" controversy, see Edward J. Cashin, *Guardians of the Valleys: Chickasaws in Colonial South Carolina and Georgia* (Columbia: University of South Carolina Press, 2009), 73–77. Glen's hostility to Crokatt has typically been explained in reference to Crokatt's stance on currency issuance and his intervention in the McNair case. Crokatt's intervention in the case of the *Vrow Dorothea* no doubt compounded Glen's antipathy. This Dutch ship was impounded in Charles Town in 1748 by the vice admiralty court on a charge of illegal trading in Jamaica. Crokatt pressed the case of the ship's owners—the Hopes, a leading Amsterdam banking house—at the High Court of the Admiralty in London. It reversed the vice admiralty court's decision, as a consequence of which Governor Glen lost the share of the ship's cargo to which he would have been entitled. See HL to William Hopton and to George Austin, 27 December 1748, *PHL*, I, 198–200.

88. HL to Rawlinson & Davison, 24 September 1755, *PHL*, I, 344.

89. Jack P. Greene, *The Quest for Power: The Lower Houses of Assembly in the Southern Royal Colonies, 1689–1776* (Chapel Hill: University of North Carolina Press, 1963), 61–65, 268–71; Sirmans, *Colonial South Carolina*, 303–9; Mercantini, *Who Shall Rule at Home*, 92–117.

CHAPTER THREE: "CANKERS TO THE RICHES OF A COUNTRY"?

1. [Decker], *Essay on the Causes of the Decline of the Foreign Trade*, 65.

2. On absenteeism in Ireland, see A. P. W. Malcomson, "Absenteeism in Eighteenth Century Ireland," *Irish Economic and Social History* 1 (1974): 15–35; articles in T. W. Moody, ed., *A New History of Ireland: Eighteenth Century Ireland, 1691–1800* (Oxford: Clarendon, 1986), 172–74, 210–13. These argue that absentee landlordism was less prevalent in Ireland than many contemporaries assumed. Malcomson also identified owners of Irish lands who lived elsewhere in Ireland, either in or around Dublin or at other estates elsewhere in the country, as "internal absentees." As many as half the absentee proprietors of Irish estates were estimated to fall into this group. See Malcomson, "Absenteeism," 23–24, 35.

3. Samuel Johnson, *A Dictionary of the English Language* . . . (London, 1755).

4. Sir Josiah Child, *A New Discourse on Trade* . . . (1693; 3rd ed., London, 1719), 157.

5. Gee, *Trade and Navigation*, 102.

6. Trevor Burnard, "Passengers Only: The Extent and Significance of Absenteeism in Eighteenth-Century Jamaica," *Atlantic Studies* 1.2 (2004): 178–95. Burnard has stressed the

more limited extent and more variable nature of Jamaican absenteeism than has been traditionally portrayed and has observed the benefits the West Indies derived from absentees' political agency in Britain. Likewise, B. W. Higman, *Plantation Jamaica, 1750–1850: Capital and Control in a Colonial Economy* (Kingston: University of the West Indies Press, 2008), has demonstrated the economic efficiency of absentee-owned plantations in Jamaica. For overviews of the historiography of absenteeism in its West Indian and Irish guises, see Higman, *Plantation Jamaica*, 22–29; Burnard, "Passengers Only," 179–80.

7.   Historians have long connected the concerted and often influential advocacy on behalf of the Caribbean sugar colonies in eighteenth-century London with the prevalence of West Indian absenteeism, but no such linkage has been observed for either South Carolina or any other North American colony (Burnard, "Passengers Only," passim; O'Shaughnessy, "Formation of a Commercial Lobby," 71–95). The literature on lobbying by merchants in North American trade in Britain has overlooked the role of absenteeism, instead conceiving claimants' interests primarily through their commercial, religious, ethnic, and kinship affiliations. See, for example, Olson, *Making the Empire Work*, 94–125; Price, "Who Cared about the Colonies," 395–436. Jack Greene is alone in having explored the political implications of transatlantic absenteeism for South Carolina, linking the lower rate of absenteeism in South Carolina than that in the West Indies to the formation of an indigenous political elite in the colony and, ultimately, to its rejection of British imperial authority, though his analysis does not examine the absentees' political role in London (Greene, "Colonial South Carolina and the Caribbean Connection," 209–10).

8.   Waterhouse, "England, the Caribbean, and the Settlement of South Carolina," 276; Henry A. M. Smith, "The Colleton Family in South Carolina," *South Carolina Historical and Genealogical Magazine* 1.4 (1900): 325–27. See also Russell R. Menard, "Financing the Lowcountry Export Boom: Capital and Growth in Early South Carolina," *WMQ* 51.4 (1994): 664. The Colletons were among a number of families to settle in South Carolina from Barbados and who, by owning estates in the Caribbean, brought another dimension of absenteeism to the colony. Others included the Middletons and the Bulls. On South Carolina's early connections with the West Indies, and in particular Barbados, see Dunn, "English Sugar Islands," 81–89; Greene, "Colonial South Carolina and the Caribbean Connection," 192–210. On the absentee ownership of Caribbean estates by South Carolina residents, see O'Shaughnessy, *Empire Divided*, 17.

9.   CO5/1264/301, National Archives, London.

10.   On residency on Virginia's tobacco plantations, see T. H. Breen, *Tobacco Culture: The Mentality of the Great Tidewater Planters on the Eve of the Revolution*, 2nd ed. (Princeton, N.J.: Princeton University Press, 2001), esp. 40–46.

11.   H. Roy Merrens and George D. Terry, "Dying in Paradise: Malaria, Mortality and the Perceptual Environment in Colonial South Carolina," *Journal of Southern History* 50.4 (1984): 533–50.

12.   Most influentially, Robert Weir identified the congregation of South Carolina's landowning planters and merchants in Charles Town as a principal factor in their coalescence as a powerful and self-conscious indigenous political elite. Sharing common interests and values, the group's harmoniousness characterized the colony's pre-revolutionary politics. See Weir, "Harmony We Were Famous For," 473–501. Inter alia, see also Richard Waterhouse, "The Development of Elite Culture in the Colonial American South: A Study of Charles Town, 1670–1770," *Australian Journal of Politics and History* 28 (1982): 391–404; Richard Waterhouse, "Merchants, Planters and Lawyers: Political Culture and Leadership in Colonial South Carolina, 1721–1775," in *Power and Status: Officeholding in Colonial America*, ed. Bruce C. Daniels (Middletown, Conn.: Wesleyan University Press, 1986), 146–72. On how nonresidency influenced agricultural productivity and shaped plantation labor regimes, see Laura Sandy, "Between Planter and Slave: The Social and Economic Role of Plantation Overseers in Colonial Virginia and South Carolina" (Ph.D. thesis, University of Manchester, 2006).

13. This group has largely escaped historians' attention, though for exceptions, see—on the experiences of South Carolinian visitors to Britain and how these influenced identity formation among the colonial elites—Max Edelson, "Carolinians Abroad: Cultivating English Identities from the Colonial Lower South," in *Britain and the American South: From Colonialism to Rock and Roll*, ed. Joseph P. Ward (Jackson: University Press of Mississippi, 2003), 81–105; Greene, "Colonial South Carolina and the Caribbean Connection," 209–10; Roe Coker, "Absentees as Loyalists," 119–34. Roe Coker offered a partial listing of Loyalist absentees whose assets were seized by the state of South Carolina after the war.

14. In 1782 South Carolina's General Assembly passed Confiscation Acts that identified some sixty British subjects as owners of land in South Carolina in absentia: "Confiscated Estates belonging to British Subjects Lying and being in the State of South Carolina" (Cooper and McCord, *Statutes at Large of South Carolina*, IV, 516–23). The list was printed in the *Royal Gazette*, 20 March 1782.

15. Frank W. Pitman, *The Development of the British West Indies, 1700–1763* (New Haven, Conn.: Yale University Press, 1917), 35–38; O'Shaughnessy, *Empire Divided*, 34. If absenteeism did indeed increase the risk of slave revolts in the Caribbean, it is perhaps ironic since many estate owners left precisely because of this anxiety; B. W. Higman has observed that "fear for their [planters'] own lives was a vital driver of absenteeism" in Jamaica (Higman, *Plantation Jamaica*, 7, 22). Conversely, despite constant anxiety of slave rebellion in South Carolina, particularly after the Stono Rebellion in September 1739, this does not seem to have been an important factor in motivating relocations from Carolina to Britain.

16. "An Act for the better establishing and regulating patrols" (1740), in Sally Hadden, *Slave Patrols: Law and Violence in Virginia and the Carolinas* (Cambridge, Mass.: Harvard University Press, 2001), 23–24, 73 (quote).

17. Chaplin, *Anxious Pursuit*, esp. 134–57; S. Max Edelson, *Plantation Enterprise in Colonial South Carolina* (Cambridge, Mass.: Harvard University Press, 2006), esp. 172–76, 196–99.

18. 1758 Tax Act (South Carolina), in Cooper and McCord, *Statutes at Large of South Carolina*, IV, 56.

19. 1769 Tax Act (Georgia), in Allen D. Candler and Lucian Lamar Knights, eds., *Colonial Records of the State of Georgia*, 26 vols. (Atlanta, 1904–16), XIX, pt. I, 109.

20. HL to Jonathan Bryan, 4 September 1767, *PHL*, V, 291. On South Carolinians' landownership in Georgia, see David R. Chesnutt, "South Carolina's Penetration of Georgia in the 1760s: Henry Laurens as a Case Study," *SCHM* 73.4 (1972): 194–208; Marsh, *Georgia's Frontier Women*, 99–102; Wood, *Slavery in Colonial Georgia*, 91–93.

21. HL to James Laurens, 26 December 1771, *PHL*, VIII, 130.

22. R. W. Gibbes, ed., *Documentary History of the American Revolution . . . , 1764–1776* (New York, 1855), 110; William E. Hemphill and Wylma A. Wates, eds., *Extracts from the Journals of the Provincial Congresses of South Carolina, 1775–1776* (Columbia: South Carolina Archives Department, 1960), 67.

23. "An Act for opening a land-office, and for better settling and strengthening this state" and "An Act to amend and repeal part of 'An Act for opening a land-office, and for better settling and strengthening this state,'" 7 June and 16 September 1777, in Candler and Knights, *Colonial Records of the State of Georgia*, XIX, pt. II, 53–58, 70–72; Lachlan McIntosh to HL and Joseph Clay to HL, 15 July and 16 October 1777, *PHL*, XI, 396–97, 557–58.

24. Margaret Colleton to Robert Raper and Francis Kinloch, 13 July 1778, Margaret Colleton Papers, SCL.

25. On the unsuccessful attempt to introduce a double tax on absentees in June 1775, see HL to John Laurens, 23 June 1775 and 22 March 1777; HL to John Lloyd, 11 February 1777, *PHL*, X, 192; XI, 299, 313. On its imposition in 1778 and its renewal in 1779, see Cooper and McCord, *Statutes at Large of South Carolina*, IV, 414–16, 487–88; Candler and Knights, *Colonial Records of the State of Georgia*, XIX, pt. II, 96.

26. Public Register, South Carolina, Conveyance books [Charleston Deeds], vols. A, 220; B, 153; E, 313; F, 153; Y, 379, 386, SCDAH; Miscellaneous Records, vol. EE, 30 June 1742, SCDAH.

27. Public Register, South Carolina, Conveyance books [Charleston Deeds], vol. VV, 510, 512, SCDAH; Memorials of South Carolina Land Titles, 1731–75, vi, 455, SCDAH; South Carolina Society, *The Rules of the South Carolina Society: Established at Charlestown A.D. 1736, chartered 17th May 1751* (Baltimore, 1937), 36.

28. RP to Andrew Pringle, 30 May 1744, *LRP*, II, 708; Robert Raper to John Beswicke, 24 July 1759, LRR.

29. James Glen Papers, 1738–77, SCL; E. Stanly Godbold Jr., "James Glen (1701–1777)," in *Oxford Dictionary of National Biography* (Oxford: Oxford University Press, September 2004).

30. Roe Coker, "Absentees as Loyalists," 131–32.

31. Glyn Williams, *The Prize of All the Oceans: The Triumph and Tragedy of Anson's Round the World Voyage* (London: HarperCollins, 2000), 9; Julian Gwyn, *The Enterprising Admiral: The Personal Fortune of Sir Peter Warren* (Montreal: McGill-Queen's University Press, 1974), 119–26; Mabel L. Webber, ed., "Josiah Smith's Diary," *South Carolina Historical and Genealogical Magazine* 34.4 (1933): 194–95. On land grants across the North American colonies to British military officers, see John Shy, *Toward Lexington: The Role of the British Army in the Coming of the American Revolution* (Princeton, N.J.: Princeton University Press, 1965), 357–58.

32. Historians have long been aware of absentee acquisition of estates in the West Indies through mortgage foreclosure. See notably work on the Lascelles family: Pares, "London West India Merchant House," 221; S. D. Smith, "Merchants and Planters Revisited," *Economic History Review* 55.3 (2002): 441–42, 450; Hancock, *Citizens of the World*, 146. Smith, "Merchants and Planters Revisited," 434–65, has argued that mortgage-backed credit was more significant in the West Indies trade than Pares allows. For an analysis of South Carolina's mortgage market in the first four decades of the eighteenth century, see Menard, "Financing the Lowcountry Export Boom," 659–76.

33. Public Register, South Carolina, Conveyance books [Charleston Deeds], vol. T, 113, 117, SCDAH. These were 540 acres on the Stono River, held against a payment of £763.5s. sterling by William Wilkins, a planter of James Island, and 200 acres in Christ Church Parish, held against a payment of £409 sterling by Daniel Crawford, a planter of that parish. After Wilkins's death in c. 1744, without having repaid the debt, Crokatt appointed Simmons and Smith, and George Seaman, George Austin, and Robert Raper, all in Charles Town, as his attorneys, "giving unto them or any two of them full power & authority" to foreclose and dispose of the property, including "any lands, houses, tenements & Negroes whatsoever." The land was sold in July 1747. See Public Register, South Carolina, Conveyance books [Charleston Deeds], vol. CC, 507, SCDAH.

34. Public Register, South Carolina, Conveyance books [Charleston Deeds], vols. BB, 120; X, 314, SCDAH.

35. Robert Raper to Joseph & Henry Guinand, 7 July 1763 and 15 April 1765, LRR.

36. T79/43/172–78, National Archives, London.

37. "Certificate by William Bull, Lt-Gov. of South Carolina of the lands owned by Charles Ogilvie and his losses," 25 November 1782; Charles Ogilvie to Alexander Ogilvie, 17 September 1783, OFP. See also http://south-Carolina-plantations.com/beaufort/richfield.html; http://south-Carolina-plantations.com/beaufort/mount-alexander.html (accessed 7 November 2016).

38. Sometimes, however, the tensions inherent in the devolved management of family landholdings led to the breakdown of fraternal relations: Samuel Wragg revoked his brother's power of attorney in the colony in 1742 after a dispute; Drayton's apparent tardiness with remittances from his brother-in-law's plantation led to his falling out with Glen, who charged him with having "ruined my credit both here [London] and Scotland" (James Glen to John Drayton, May 1775, James Glen Papers, SCL).

39.   Edelson, *Plantation Enterprise*, 200–254; Alan Gallay, *The Formation of a Planter Elite: Jonathan Bryan and the Southern Colonial Frontier* (Athens: University of Georgia Press, 1989), 84–108.

40.   Robert Raper to Thomas Boone, 2 July 1769, LRR.

41.   Henry Middleton to William Middleton, 8 February 1770, Middleton Family Papers, HA93: 722/121, microfilm, SCDAH. Henry Middleton's acquisition and development of lands in Georgia south of the Altamaha River—the so-called Altamaha Grants, which caused a long-running dispute between authorities in South Carolina and Georgia—has been discussed in Chesnutt, "South Carolina's Penetration of Georgia," 194–208.

42.   "Certificate by William Bull, Lt-Gov. of South Carolina of the lands owned by Charles Ogilvie and his losses," 25 November 1782, OFP; AO12/48/32–47, National Archives, London. George Ogilvie recounted his miserable experience at Myrtle Grove in letters to his sister (George Ogilvie to Margaret "Peggy' Ogilvie, 25 June 1774 and 22 November 1774, OFP). See also Edelson, "Plantation Enterprise," 144–46.

43.   "Certificate by William Bull, Lt-Gov. of South Carolina of the lands owned by Charles Ogilvie and his losses," 25 November 1782, OFP; AO12/48/32–47, National Archives, London.

44.   Robert Raper to John Colleton, 27 April 1761, LRR.

45.   Robert Raper to Margaret Colleton, 24 February 1767, LRR. Henry Laurens also acquired land contiguous to his existing holdings while away from South Carolina; see HL to James Laurens, 27 November 1773, *PHL*, IX, 177.

46.   Thomas Smith to Peter Taylor, 16 December 1769 and 14 July 1773; Matthias Rast to Taylor, 12 March 1773 (quote), Taylor Family Papers, SCL.

47.   Bernard Bailyn, *Voyagers to the West: A Passage in the Peopling of America on the Eve of the American Revolution* (New York: Vintage, 1986), 356; Rachel N. Klein, *Unification of a Slave State: The Rise of the Planter Class in the South Carolina Backcountry, 1760–1808* (Chapel Hill: University of North Carolina Press, 1990), 179.

48.   Bailyn, *Voyagers to the West*, 430–74; Hancock, *Citizens of the World*, 153–71. At least two London merchants with interests in the Carolina trade, George Udney and Samuel Touchet, joined this land rush (*PHL*, V, 166n).

49.   *SCG*, 27 April 1767. Despite the sale of some lands, Baker and Linwood retained vast landholdings in the colony until the American Revolution. When the lands were confiscated by the state of South Carolina in 1782, Baker's son and heir, William Baker Jr., and Linwood's widow, Jane, in 1782 together owned at least 47,000 acres in South Carolina, including Purrysburgh Barony of 12,600 acres, Black River Barony of 11,528 acres, Saltcatchers Barony of 11,679 acres, and Peedee Barony of 12,000 acres. See also Roe Coker, "Absentees as Loyalists," 123.

50.   Devine, *Tobacco Lords*, 83–87; Price and Clemens, "Revolution of Scale," 7–8.

51.   Kenneth Scott, "Sufferers in the Charleston Fire of 1740," *SCHM* 64.4 (1963): 203–11. Population estimate is from Coclanis, *Shadow of a Dream*, 113–14, table 4–3.

52.   Walter L. Robins, trans. and ed., "John Tobler's Description of South Carolina (1753)," *SCHM* 71.3 (1970): 145. Tobler's comments featured in his promotional pamphlet *Beschreibung von Carolina* (Description of Carolina). Although designed to encourage others from Switzerland to settle in South Carolina, it avoids the hyperbole and excessive "boosting" often found in the genre.

53.   Glen, "Attempt towards an Estimate of the Value of South Carolina," 180.

54.   Robins, "John Tobler's Description of South Carolina," 145; Glen, "Attempt towards an Estimate of the Value of South Carolina," 189–91; Peter Manigault to Anne Manigault, 8 December 1753, Manigault Family Papers, SCHS.

55.   Hart, *Building Charleston*, 84–88.

56.   Robert Raper to John Colleton, 10 May 1759; to James Crokatt, 20 April 1762, LRR.

57.   Robert Raper to Charles Crokatt, 23 January 1768; to Joseph Stephenson, 11 September 1768; to William Greenwood, 12 September 1768, LRR. Like other imperial officials who were

absentee property owners in South Carolina, Stephenson had probably bought the property while living in the colony.

58. Robert Raper to James Crokatt, 17 January 1767, LRR; *SCG*, 23 March 1767; Walter Mansell to the Committee of Warehouses of the East India Company, undated, 1773, in Francis S. Drake, ed., *Tea Leaves: Being a Collection of Letters and Documents Relating to the Shipment of Tea to the American Colonies in the Year 1773, by the East India Company* (Boston, 1884), 229–30.

59. Henry Laurens's letters from London to his brother James in Charles Town in 1772–73 offer valuable insights into the levels and arrangement of insurance premiums on Charles Town properties and, more broadly, on the development of insurance brokerage among the capital's merchants. "Every Man at the Coffee House writes policies now a days," Laurens reported, but he advised that "you may think it better to give 25/ per Cent 1¼ at the Royal Exchange than 20/ at the Carolina or Lloyd's Coffee House." Given the "precarious state of Commercial Fortunes in this City"—a reference to the credit crisis that had brought down many London firms—he suggested paying the higher premium, 1.25 percent, brokered by the specialist insurance companies, rather than the lower 1 percent premium commonly offered by individual traders, who were more likely to go out of business. See HL to James Laurens, 19 August, 26 September, and 5 October 1772; 11 March 1773, *PHL*, VIII, 422–29, 478–79, 490–96, 605–13.

60. Cooper and McCord, *Statutes at Large of South Carolina*, IV, 190, 214, 239.

61. Miscellaneous Records, 1749–51, 92–94, SCDAH; Robert Raper to James Crokatt, 20 April 1762; 2 March and 18 August 1763, LRR.

62. Robert Raper to Benjamin Bushnell, 28 March and 23 May 1760 (quotes), 29 April 1761, 30 March 1766, LRR; Elizabeth Bushnell account, 1777, Robert Raper Account Book, SCL.

63. On the relationship between planter and overseer, and in particular the importance of overseers' managerial and commercial acumen, see Sandy, "Between Planter and Slave," 65–66. On the recruitment of and responsibility vested in local agents, see also Hancock, *Citizens of the World*, 150–52.

64. Margaret Colleton account, 29 October 1779, Robert Raper Account Book, SCL.

65. *SCG*, 28 March 1761; Robert Raper to John Colleton, 27 February 1762, LRR; HL to Richard Oswald, 27 October 1768, *PHL*, V, 668; Edelson, *Plantation Enterprise*, 203–4, 240–44.

66. Edelson, *Plantation Enterprise*, 173–74; Burnard, "Passengers Only," 178–95; Higman, *Plantation Jamaica*, 22–29.

67. HL to Richard Oswald, 27 April 1768, *PHL*, V, 668.

68. James Laurens to HL, 6 January 1773, *PHL*, VIII, 523.

69. *PHL*, VIII, xiii, 106.

70. Edgar and Bailey, *Biographical Directory*, II, 44–45.

71. Robert Raper to John Colleton, 25 March 1759, 16 December 1760, 23 May 1761, LRR; Thomas Boone to Margaret Colleton, 29 September 1773, Margaret Colleton Papers, SCL. If Mepshew had thirty working slaves, it would also have had a number of enslaved residents who were not able to work—the very young, the infirm, and the elderly.

72. Margaret Colleton to Robert Raper and Francis Kinloch, 13 July 1778, Margaret Colleton Papers, SCL.

73. AO12/48/32–47, National Archives, London; "Certificate by William Bull, Lt-Gov. of South Carolina of the lands owned by Charles Ogilvie and his losses," 25 November 1782, OFP.

74. HL to William Cowles, 29 October 1771; to James Laurens, 5 December 1771, *PHL*, VIII, 22, 70.

75. Price, "Transatlantic Economy," 26.

76. HL to Benjamin Addison, 26 May 1768, *PHL*, V, 702.

77. John Martin to John Bold, 20 June 1791, John Martin Papers, SCHS.

78. Public Register, South Carolina, Conveyance books [Charleston Deeds], vols. E, 313; Y, 379, 386, SCDAH.

79.   South Carolina interest rates were legally set at 10 percent until 1748, when they were reduced to 8 percent. They remained at this level until 1777, when they were cut to 7 percent. See Coclanis, *Shadow of a Dream*, 105–6.

80.   *PHL*, IV, 343–45. Laurens's forecast that Gray would soon come back to South Carolina was prescient, since by late 1767 the Grays had returned to live on a plantation in St. James Goose Creek Parish. See Edgar and Bailey, *Biographical Directory*, II, 291–92.

81.   Peter G. M. Dickson, *The Financial Revolution in England, 1688–1756* (London: Macmillan, 1967), 471; Coclanis, *Shadow of a Dream*, 266n.

82.   John Habakkuk, *Marriage, Debt, and the Estates System: English Landownership 1650–1950* (Oxford: Clarendon, 1994), 420; Gauci, *Emporium of the World*, 86.

83.   Habakkuk, *Marriage, Debt, and the Estates System*, 422.

84.   Peter Manigault to Anne Manigault, 20 February 1751, Manigault Family Papers, SCHS.

85.   *Public Advertiser*, 9 March 1767.

86.   Public Register, South Carolina, Conveyance books [Charleston Deeds], vol. HH, 87, SCDAH.

87.   Public Register, South Carolina, Conveyance books [Charleston Deeds], vol. K, 361, SCDAH.

88.   Crokatt sold the land to Governor Robert Johnson, who already owned land abutting it. As such it was presumably more valuable to him than to Crokatt, explaining the price differential. See Public Register, South Carolina, Conveyance books [Charleston Deeds], vol. M, 163–81, SCDAH.

89.   Crokatt had bought the forty-six-acre tract on Charles Town Neck for £1,380 in July 1732 and sold it for £2,000 in September 1735, an annualized increase of just over 13 percent. What, if any, improvements he had made to the land or its buildings is unknown, however. See Public Register, South Carolina, Conveyance books [Charleston Deeds], vols. I, 640; K, 223; Q, 102; Memorial Books, 1731–78, III, 175, 13 March 1733, SCDAH; *SCG*, 14 October 1732 (quote), 14 June 1735.

90.   Public Register, South Carolina, Conveyance books [Charleston Deeds], vol. T, 110, 119, SCDAH.

91.   See, inter alia, *SCG*, 16 July 1763, 10 August 1765, 16 June 1766, 8 December 1766, 23 March 1767; Public Register, South Carolina, Conveyance books [Charleston Deeds], vol. GGG, 178. Collection of rents from these properties was entrusted to Crokatt's Charles Town attorney, Robert Raper. See Miscellaneous Records, 1749–51, 92–94, SCDAH.

92.   *JHC*, XXV, 933–1114; XXVI, 215–92.

93.   Great Britain, *Journal of the Commissioners for Trade*, VIII, 273. The nine appellants were James Crokatt, Charles Crokatt, Sir William Baker, John Beswicke, John Nickleson, Richard Shubrick, Andrew Pringle, Nathaniel Newberry, and William Stone.

94.   "Petition from the Agents for the Council & Assembly of South Carolina, other gentlemen & principal merchants to Edmond Atkin asking him to accept the post of Indian Agent." The petition was signed by James Crokatt, John Beswicke, Richard Shubrick, and John Watsone, all merchants who had relocated from Charles Town to London; and by William Middleton, Charles Pinckney, and Thomas Drayton, all former residents of South Carolina, though not directly involved in trade in London. See LO 893, Loudon Papers, Huntington Library, San Marino, Calif.; Mercantini, *Who Shall Rule at Home*, 74, 78.

95.   CO5/651/22, National Archives, London. Illustrating the overlap between London's Carolina and Georgia trades, the nine signatories all had interests in or were primarily involved in trade to South Carolina.

96.   Peter J. Marshall, "Who Cared about the Thirteen Colonies? Some Evidence from Philanthropy," *Journal of Imperial and Commonwealth Studies* 27.2 (1999): 54.

97.   *SCG*, 7 April 1741; Committee Appointed for Relieving the Poor Germans, *Proceedings of the committee appointed for relieving the poor Germans, who were brought to London and*

there left destitute in the month of August 1764 (London, 1765), 35; George W. Williams, *St. Michael's, Charleston, 1751–1951* (Columbia: University of South Carolina Press, 1951), 234–48. A parallel can be found in Gedney Clarke, a wealthy merchant in Barbados who used conspicuous acts of philanthropy to demonstrate his affiliations to New England, where he had begun in trade and with which he maintained an active commerce. These included donating a peal of bells to a Boston church and raising a fund for the widows and children of New England men killed in action against the French at Louisbourg. See Smith, "Gedney Clarke," 524–25.

98. Olson, *Making the Empire Work*, 104.
99. T1/425/215–16, National Archives, London.
100. *JHC*, XXIX, 605–6.
101. Lewis B. Namier and John Brooke, eds., *The House of Commons, 1754–1790*, 3 vols. (London: H.M.S.O, 1964), I, 154.
102. HL to James Laurens, 26 December 1771, *PHL*, VIII, 130.

CHAPTER FOUR: "FROM HUMBLE & MODERATE FORTUNES TO GREAT AFFLUENCE"

1. *SCG*, 21 November 1749, quoted in Rogers, *Charleston in the Age of the Pinckneys*, 14.
2. Clowse, *Measuring Charleston's Overseas Commerce*, 63, table B-26; 70, table B-41; Nash, "Organization of Trade and Finance" (2001), 88–89. On London's continued dominance of Britain's colonial trade during the third quarter of the eighteenth century, see French, "Crowded with Traders and a Great Commerce," 29–32.
3. Between 1769 and 1774 Liverpool ships made forty-seven slaving voyages to Charles Town and Bristol ships made twenty (Richardson, "British Slave Trade," 139, 161).
4. Evidence for this comes from the small collection of ships' manifests that recorded the identities of the exporters of rice on board seventeen vessels that cleared Charles Town for Cowes between January and April 1764 and the British merchants to whom it was sent. Nine of these ships contained cargoes of rice consigned to London firms, which presumably employed agents in Cowes: John Beswicke & Co.; Sarah Nickleson & Co.; Grubb & Watson; Charles Crokatt; Richard & Thomas Shubrick; John Watsone; and Benjamin Stead. See CO5/511/2–63, National Archives, London. On London merchants' activity in the reexport trade from south coast ports to northern European destinations, see also HL to John Nutt, 26 March and 9 April 1756, 15 February and 29 March 1763; to Grubb & Watson, 24 and 30 March 1763, *PHL*, II, 516–17; III, 259, 379–80, 368–67, 394. Ownership of transatlantic shipping further extended London merchants' commercial reach—their ships often carried rice between South Carolina and British outports, then on to continental markets. For details of London Carolina traders' extensive shipping interests, see Board of Trade and Secretaries of State: America and West Indies, Original Correspondence, Shipping Returns, South Carolina, 1721–65, CO5/509–11, National Archives, London.
5. Olson, "Virginia Merchants of London," 378–80. See also, on the West Indies interest in London during the 1760s and 1770s, O'Shaughnessy, "Formation of a Commercial Lobby," 71–95.
6. Committee of Correspondence (hereafter CoC) to Charles Garth, 4 September 1764, in Gibbes, *Documentary History of the American Revolution*, 4.
7. CoC to Charles Garth, 2 July 1766, Letterbook of Charles Garth, 1766–75, microfilm, SCDAH.
8. CoC to Charles Garth, 4 September 1764, in Gibbes, *Documentary History of the American Revolution*, 4.
9. For differing interpretations of attitudes toward the Navigation Acts in colonial America, see Matson and Onuf, *Union of Interests*, 3–25; John E. Crowley, *The Privileges of Independence: Neomercantilism and the American Revolution* (Baltimore: Johns Hopkins University Press, 1993), 29. Free trade and republican ideology evolved in tandem in late colonial America, Matson and Onuf argued, as Americans challenged the subordinateness and dependence

imposed by the imperial mercantile system. Conversely, John Crowley posited that Americans never really challenged mercantilist precepts: "right through to their declaration of independence, American patriots expressed a prevailing, and explicit, desire to maintain commercial dependence on Britain."

10. On the role of agricultural production, improvement, and exchange in shaping a confident self-image among South Carolina's late colonial elites as they transformed barren lands into profitable plantations and built multilocational, integrated enterprises, see Edelson, *Plantation Enterprise*, 166–99.

11. Weir, "Harmony We Were Famous For," esp. 498; Robert M. Weir, "Who Shall Rule at Home: The American Revolution as a Crisis for Legitimacy for the Colonial Elite," *Journal of Interdisciplinary History* 6.4 (1976): 679–80.

12. CoC to Charles Garth, 5 June 1762, Letterbook of James Wright and Charles Garth, 1758–66, microfilm, SCDAH. Garth replaced James Wright, a former attorney general of South Carolina and future governor of Georgia, who had replaced James Crokatt as agent.

13. On the measures introduced in 1763–64 to promote colonial commodity production, see Sosin, *Agents and Merchants*, 20–21. On the political economy of Grenville's legislative program, see Crowley, *Privileges of Independence*, 14–20.

14. Great Britain, *Journal of the Commissioners for Trade*, IX, 371.

15. Charles Garth to CoC, 29 October and 15 November 1762, 19 February and 30 April 1763, Letterbook of James Wright and Charles Garth, 1758–66, microfilm, SCDAH; CO5/377/161, National Archives, London; *JHC*, XXIX, 537.

16. CO5/371/78–83, 92, National Archives, London; Andrews, *Colonial Period of American History*, IV, 97.

17. Charles Garth to CoC, 19 February 1763, Letterbook of James Wright and Charles Garth, 1758–66, microfilm, SCDAH. Garth was not exaggerating: among the thirty-six signatories were James and Charles Crokatt, John Beswicke, John Nutt, Richard Shubrick and Richard Shubrick Jr., Greenwood & Higginson, Grubb & Watson, Charles Ogilvie, Benjamin Stead, Christopher Rolleston, and John Clark. The petition was also signed by several merchants associated with American trade more generally, including David Barclay & Sons, Mildred & Roberts, and Bartholomew Pomeroy, all linen drapers who exported principally to the middle colonies. See T1/425/215–16, National Archives, London.

18. T1/425/215–16, National Archives, London; *JHC*, XXIX, 526–27.

19. Charles Garth to CoC, 19 February 1763, Letterbook of James Wright and Charles Garth, 1758–66, microfilm, SCDAH; *JHC*, XXIX, 541.

20. *JHC*, XXIX, 605–6.

21. *JHC*, XXIX, 605–6.

22. Charles Garth to CoC, 30 April 1763, Letterbook of James Wright and Charles Garth, 1758–66, microfilm, SCDAH; CO323/17/57, National Archives, London.

23. *JHC*, XXIX, 958–59.

24. *JHC*, XXIX, 982. Customs records valued total British exports to South Carolina and Georgia in 1763 at £305,089, somewhat less than the £400,000 estimated by Greenwood and Nutt in their testimony to Parliament. Even if their estimation of their annual exports to the lower southern colonies was exaggerated, it was still indicative of their dominant share of the export trade to the region. See Carter et al., *Historical Statistics*, V, 710–13, 714–16.

25. *JHC*, XXIX, 1002, 1014, 1018, 1024, 1039, 1056; 4 Geo. III c. 27, Rice Act, in Great Britain, *Statutes at Large*, VII, 479–81. Permission was extended to North Carolina the following year (5 Geo. III c. 45, in Great Britain, *Statutes at Large*, VII, 543–44).

26. James Abercromby to John Blair, 15 December 1759, in Van Horne and Reese, *Letterbook of James Abercromby*, 327–29.

27. Charles Garth to CoC, 20 November 1763, Letterbook of James Wright and Charles Garth, 1758–66, microfilm, SCDAH.

28.   At least fourteen of the signatories were primarily involved in the Carolina trade. Their signatures feature near the top of the petition, suggesting their early involvement in the campaign and that the names were collected together, perhaps at the Carolina walk of the Royal Exchange or the Carolina Coffee House. They were James Crokatt, Charles Crokatt, John Beswicke, Richard Shubrick, John Nutt, William Greenwood, Sarah Nickleson & Isaac King, Christopher Rolleston, Alexander Watson, Richard Grubb, Charles Ogilvie, and William Thompson; the two visiting Carolinians were Arthur Middleton—later to sign the Declaration of Independence—and Alexander Peronneau. See Charles Garth to CoC, 20 November 1763, Letterbook of James Wright and Charles Garth, 1758–66, microfilm, SCDAH; CO323/17/54, 120, National Archives, London; *JHC*, XXIX, 995.

29.   CO65/201–10, National Archives, London; *JHC*, XXIX, 1011, 1025, 1035, 1040–41, 1056.

30.   Robert Raper to James Crokatt, 23 November 1765, LRR.

31.   Robert Raper to Greenwood & Higginson, 8 November and 18 December 1765, LRR. On resistance to the Stamp Act in South Carolina, see Maurice A. Crouse, "Cautious Rebellion: South Carolina's Opposition to the Stamp Act," *SCHM* 73.2 (1972): 59–71.

32.   London's Carolina traders also dominated the capital's trade to Georgia, as was made clear in contemporary petitions, in evidence to Parliament, and in postwar claims for debts in the two states. See, for example, the 1772 petition to the Board of Trade urging its approval of a cession of land to Georgia by local Indians; this was signed by nine "Merchants trading to Georgia," each of whom had interests in or was primarily involved in the Carolina trade: John Clark, Basil Cowper, James Graham, William Greenwood, William Higginson, John Nutt, Charles Ogilvie, William Thomson, and Alexander Watson (CO5/651/22, National Archives, London).

33.   *South Carolina Gazette and Country Journal*, 11 and 25 March 1765. The *South Carolina Gazette* had suspended publication in October 1765 in the absence of the stamped paper and with its "numerous subscribers," it reported, having declared "almost to a man, that they will not take ONE stampt news-paper, if stamps could be obtained" (*SCG*, 31 October 1765). Other colonial newspapers that named the London merchants in the anti–Stamp Act delegation included the *Newport Mercury* (Newport, Rhode Island), 17 February 1766; *New-York Gazette*, 18 February 1766; *Pennsylvania Gazette* (Philadelphia), 27 February 1766.

34.   Charles Garth to CoC, 5 April and 25 May 1765, Letterbook of James Wright and Charles Garth, 1758–66, microfilm, SCDAH; Lewis B. Namier, "Charles Garth and His Connexions," *English Historical Review* 54 (1939): 641–42; Sosin, *Agents and Merchants*, 33–36.

35.   Charles Garth to CoC, 23 December 1765, 19 January 1766, Letterbook of James Wright and Charles Garth, 1758–66, microfilm, SCDAH.

36.   Charles Garth to CoC, 22 February 1766, Letterbook of Charles Garth, 1766–75, microfilm, SCDAH; *PHL*, V, 50n. While London's merchants were the preeminent commercial force behind the repeal campaign, as befitted the scale of the capital's trade to America and their physical proximity to Westminster, Bristol's merchants too lobbied hard for repeal, as detailed in Starr, *School for Politics*, 51–57.

37.   *South Carolina Gazette and Country Journal*, 25 March and 8 April 1766.

38.   CoC to Charles Garth, 13 May 1766, Letterbook of Charles Garth, 1766–75, microfilm, SCDAH; *PHL*, IX, 128n; Mercantini, *Who Shall Rule at Home*, 229–33.

39.   *South Carolina Gazette and Country Journal*, 3 June 1766.

40.   CoC to Charles Garth, 2 July 1766, Letterbook of Charles Garth, 1766–75, microfilm, SCDAH. The assistance of British merchants in the repeal of the Stamp Act was also appreciated by Benjamin Franklin, who would have applauded the committee's expression of gratitude. As Pennsylvania's London agent, Franklin had informed his colonial employers that the "British Merchants trading to America have been extremely zealous and hearty in our cause; I hope they will receive the thanks of the several Assemblies"; see Benjamin Franklin to Joseph Fox, 24 February 1766 (quote); and to Pennsylvania Assembly Committee of Correspondence,

12 April 1766, in William B. Willcox, Leonard W. Labaree, et al., *The Papers of Benjamin Franklin*, 42 vols. (New Haven, Conn.: Yale University Press, 1959–2017, XII, 168, 239.

41.   Robert Raper to John Beswicke, 3 June (quote) and 18 July 1762, 15 February 1763; to Charles Crokatt, 16 February 1763, LRR.

42.   Robert Raper to Charles Crokatt, 8 November 1765; to Greenwood & Higginson, 1 August 1767 (quote), LRR.

43.   HL to Isaac King, 6 September 1764, *PHL*, IV, 399–400.

44.   On contemporary fears in Britain and America of political combination and conspiracy, particularly concerning the influence of Lord Bute in British politics, see Paul Langford, *A Polite and Commercial People: England, 1727–1783* (Oxford: Oxford University Press, 1989), 352–57; Bernard Bailyn, *The Ideological Origins of the American Revolution*, enlarged ed. (Cambridge, Mass.: Harvard University Press, 1992), esp. 144–48.

45.   HL to Isaac King, 6 September 1764, *PHL*, IV, 401.

46.   5 Geo. II c. 7, Colonial Debt Recovery Act, in Great Britain, *Statutes at Large*, V, 583.

47.   HL to Isaac King, 6 September 1764, *PHL*, IV, 400–401.

48.   Crokatt v. Hicks, C11/200/23, National Archives, London; Will of James Crokatt, Prob. 11/1029, National Archives, London; Maurie D. McInnes, ed., *In Pursuit of Refinement: Charlestonians Abroad, 1740–1860* (Columbia: University of South Carolina Press, 1999), 91–93. The original painting, *Portrait of Peter Darnell Muilman, Charles Crokatt and William Keable in a Landscape*, is jointly owned by the Gainsborough's House museum, Sudbury, Suffolk, and Tate Britain, London.

49.   Peter Manigault to Gabriel Manigault, 6 August 1754; to Anne Manigault, 30 August 1754, Peter Manigault Papers, SCHS; Will of John Nickleson, Prob. 11/810, National Archives, London; *Gazetteer and New Daily Advertiser*, 13 October 1770.

50.   Robert Raper to John Beswicke, 11 August 1760, 23 May 1761, LRR; J. S. Cockburn and T. F. T. Baker, eds., *The Victoria History of the County of Middlesex* (Oxford: Oxford University Press, 1971), 57, 62; Will of John Beswicke, Prob. 11/900, National Archives, London.

51.   *World*, 5 April 1792; Will of William Greenwood, Prob. 11/1142, National Archives, London.

52.   Guillery, *Small House in Eighteenth-Century London*, 161–77, 194–97.

53.   Peter Manigault to Ann Manigault, 20 February 1751, Peter Manigault Papers, SCHS; Will of Richard Shubrick, Prob. 11/912, National Archives, London; *St. James's Chronicle or the British Evening Post*, 3 September 1765; *Lloyd's Evening Post*, 4 September 1765; *Public Advertiser*, 6 April 1784.

54.   All figures are pounds sterling. In a sample of 919 decedents in 1774 across the North American colonies, 9 of the 10 wealthiest were South Carolinians. See Alice Hanson Jones, *Wealth of a Nation to Be: The American Colonies on the Eve of Revolution* (New York: Columbia University Press, 1980), 171, table 6.3; 176, table 6.6. Jones's probate data are not a perfect guide to wealth: the small sample size might easily miss the wealthiest individuals, while the data provide only a snapshot from a single given year and cannot reveal the fortunes of the richest living Carolinians. They nonetheless offer valuable indicative comparison. For detailed discussion of the merits of comparative probate data in socioeconomic analysis, see Coclanis, *Shadow of a Dream*, 83, which concludes that despite its limitations, it is a useful descriptive tool in assessing elites' wealth.

55.   City of London Land Tax Assessments, MS.11316/132–97, Guildhall Library, London.

56.   *Gazetteer and New Daily Advertiser*, 8 February 1787.

57.   *Morning Post and Daily Advertiser*, 2 September 1777. For a vivid description of Fludyer Street, where Henry Laurens was also a resident in the early 1770s, see Julie Flavell, *When London Was Capital of America* (New Haven, Conn.: Yale University Press, 2010), 16–17.

58.   Besides Ogilvie, the only other London Carolina trader to be an MP in the period was Sir William Baker, one of London's foremost merchants, who had interests across the North

American and West Indies trades. His sizable landholdings in South Carolina are discussed in chapter 3 of this book. Baker sat as MP for Plympton Erle in Devon between 1747 and 1768. Ogilvie's own spell as MP for West Looe in Cornwall between 1774 and 1775 was brief and undistinguished; he does not appear to have taken part in any of the important debates on America in this period. See Sedgwick, *House of Commons, 1715–1754*, I, 429; Namier and Brooke, *House of Commons*, III, 223–24.

59.　Quoted in John J. Winberry, "Reputation of Carolina Indigo," *SCHM* 80.3 (1979): 247.

60.　*SCG*, 29 November 1773.

61.　On the poor reputation and "serviceability" of Carolinian indigo, see Nash, "South Carolina Indigo," 383–84; S. Max Edelson, "The Character of Commodities: The Reputations of South Carolina Rice and Indigo in the Atlantic World," in *The Atlantic Economy during the Seventeenth and Eighteenth Centuries: Organization, Operation, Practice, Personnel*, ed. Peter A. Coclanis (Columbia: University of South Carolina Press, 2005), 349–55.

62.　On planters' self-identification with both rice and indigo, see Edelson, "Character of Commodities," 344–55; Edelson, *Plantation Enterprise*, esp. ch. 6. Edelson's characterization of the reputational connection between South Carolina's planters and their crops echoed T. H. Breen's analysis of Virginia's tobacco planters, whose crops were similarly evoked as being expressions of their character and skills. Breen termed the process "the expression of ego through a crop" (Breen, *Tobacco Culture*, 59).

63.　HL to Isaac King, 6 September 1764, *PHL*, IV, 268n, 398–99.

64.　As described in HL to Babut, Fils & Labouchère, 25 February 1786, *PHL*, XVI, 636.

65.　Between 1768 and 1772, for example, the average annual values of deerskin and naval stores exports from Charles Town were £15,000 and £5,000 respectively, against average annual exports of £284,000 of rice and £119,000 of indigo. Rice and indigo exports thus accounted for 65.3 percent and 27.4 percent respectively of South Carolina's total exports by value. See Nash, "Urbanization in the Colonial South," 7, table 1.

66.　[James Crokatt], *Observations concerning indigo and cochineal*; [Crokatt], *Further observations*, 4, 9.

67.　Some 40 percent of England's imports of British colonial indigo was reexported in the period 1756–76 with the remainder retained in England; see Nash, "South Carolina Indigo," 373, table 4.

68.　On the marketing of indigo and the organizational contrasts with the rice trade, see Nash, "Organization of Trade and Finance" (2005), 109–10; Nash, "South Carolina Indigo," 386. For examples of indigo being exported on its producers' account, see Greenwood & Higginson to Alexander Rose, 10 August 1768, Alexander Rose Papers, SCL; Austin & Laurens to John Nutt, 23 December 1755, and to Richard Shubrick, 17 January 1756; invoices, 22 March and 30 August 1760, *PHL*, II, 52–53, 72; III, 29, 44.

69.　Charles Town Naval Office, ships' manifests, January–April 1764, CO5/511/2–63, National Archives, London.

70.　Annual total from Nash, "South Carolina Indigo," 371, table 3.

71.　The sale and exchange of indigo, rice, and other imports by London's Carolina traders were documented in the ledgers of Rawlinson, Davison & Newman, leading London wholesale grocers. The ledgers covered the mid-1750s and contained accounts with, among others, the principal London Carolina trading houses: James Crokatt, John Nutt, John Beswicke, Sarah Nickleson, and Richard & Thomas Shubrick. They also revealed the firm's direct trade with independent Charles Town houses, including Austin & Laurens. See Rawlinson, Davison & Newman Account Book, esp. 77, 455, 498, Guildhall Library, London.

72.　Quoted in Rogers, *Evolution of a Federalist*, 60.

73.　HL to George Appleby, 2 April 1771, *PHL*, VII, 469.

74.　HL to Thomas Corbett, 4 April 1771; to John Hopton, 6 April 1771, *PHL*, VII, 475, 479.

75. The suspension of duty on rice was continued until May 1773. See *JHC*, XXXI, 337–74, 423–72; 7 Geo. III c. 30 and 8 Geo. III c. 2, in Great Britain, *Statutes at Large*, VIII, 12, 53; HL to James Grant, 11 February 1767, *PHL*, V, 233. On the role of the suspension in stimulating British demand for rice and Carolinian output, see Nash, "South Carolina and the Atlantic Economy," 692.

76. The eighteen London merchant petitioners were Edward Bridgen, Samuel Carne, William Davis, William Greenwood, Richard Grubb, Isaac King, James Mill, Joseph Nicholson, John Nutt, Joseph Nutt, Charles Ogilvie, James Poyas, William Roberts & Co., Christopher Rolleston, Gilbert Ross, Richard Shubrick, William Thompson, and Alexander Watson. Bristol merchants Basil Cowper and Edward Neufville too added their names. See T1/424/298–99, T1/480/354–55, National Archives, London.

77. Besides Garth, the petition was signed by London merchants Samuel Carne, John Clark, William Greenwood, Richard Grubb, William Higginson, Isaac King, Joseph Nicholson, John Nutt, Joseph Nutt, Charles Ogilvie, George Ogilvie, James Poyas, Christopher Rolleston, William Thompson, and Alexander Watson and by two Bristol-based traders, Basil Cowper and Edward Neufville (CO5/379/73, T1/424/298–99, National Archives, London).

78. Charles Garth to CoC, 5 February, 23 March, and 11 April 1770, Letterbook of Charles Garth, 1766–75, microfilm, SCDAH.

79. HL to James Grant, 11 February 1767, *PHL*, V, 233.

80. Weir, *Colonial South Carolina*, 299–301; Mercantini, *Who Shall Rule at Home*, 234–36; Edgar, *South Carolina: A History*, 216–18.

81. For Garth's unsuccessful petitions to the Treasury against the rigid enforcement of the Navigation Laws in respect of South Carolina's coastal trade, see T1/449/379–80, T1/453/127–33, National Archives, London.

82. HL to Ross & Mill, 2 September 1768, *PHL*, VI, 87.

83. HL to William Cowles & Co. and William Freeman, 2 March 1769, *PHL*, VI, 393–94.

84. HL to Richard Grubb, 4 March 1769, *PHL*, VI, 399.

85. HL to Ross & Mill, 10 March 1769, *PHL*, VI, 404–5.

86. HL to John Tarleton, 22 March 1769, *PHL*, VI, 417.

87. The Merchants of Charleston to Charles Garth, 8 October 1767, *PHL*, V, 341, 396–402.

88. Charles Garth to CoC, 5 February and 6 March 1770, Letterbook of Charles Garth, 1766–75, microfilm, SCDAH; Sosin, *Agents and Merchants*, 108–24.

89. HL to James Laurens, 5 February 1774, *PHL*, IX, 266.

90. Mark A. DeWolfe Howe, ed., "Josiah Quincy Jr., London Journal 1774–5," *Proceedings of the Massachusetts Historical Society* 50 (1916–17): 466–67; Paul Langford, "The British Business Community and the Later Nonimportation Movements, 1768–76," in *Resistance, Politics and the American Struggle for Independence*, ed. Walter H. Conser Jr. (Boulder: L. Rienner, 1986), 309–10.

91. William Lee to Richard Henry Lee, 25 February 1775, in Worthington C. Ford, ed., *Letters of William Lee: Sheriff and Alderman of London; Commercial Agent of the Continental Congress in France; and Minister to the Courts of Vienna and Berlin, 1766–1783*, 3 vols. (Brooklyn, 1891,), I, 130–31.

92. Watson v. Crokatt [1760], C12/907/77, Crokatt v. Muilman [1770], C12/540/24, National Archives, London; *Public Advertiser*, 2 January 1760; *SCG*, 3 May 1760. John Nutt married Crokatt's daughter, Mary, in 1755 (*London Evening Post*, 15 April 1755).

93. Royal Society of Arts, *Museum rusticum et commerciale: or Select papers on agriculture, commerce, arts and manufactures. Drawn from experience, and communicated by gentlemen engaged in these pursuits . . . Volume the Fifth* (London, 1765), 133–37, 281–88.

94. Robert Raper to James Crokatt, 11 June 1759, 8 July 1762 (quote), 2 March and 26 November 1763, *LRR*.

95. Rogers, *Evolution of a Federalist*, 60.

96.   HL to James Crokatt, and to William Cowles, 3 March, 26 March, and 20 April 1772, *PHL*, VIII, 208, 231, 277.

97.   HL to John Lewis Gervais, 4 March 1774, *PHL*, IX, 336.

98.   Inter alia, *Public Advertiser*, 8 March 1777.

99.   HL to Thomas Savage, 20 April 1772, *PHL*, VIII, 280.

100.   *London Evening Post*, 14 October 1775, cited in Sainsbury, *Disaffected Patriots*, 171–93; Will of Joseph Nicholson, Prob. 11/1105, National Archives, London; [Osborn], *Complete Guide to . . . London*, 1768–77, 11th–15th eds.; *London Directory*, 1776, 9th ed.; T79/37/250, 289 [Joseph Nicholson compensation claim], National Archives, London.

101.   Olson, "Virginia Merchants of London," 386; Alison G. Olson, "The London Mercantile Lobby and the Coming of the American Revolution," *Journal of American History* 69.1 (1982): 26–27, 31, 41n; Langford, "British Business Community," 309.

102.   John Nutt to John Jones, 8 January 1774, T79/5/35, National Archives, London.

103.   James Habersham to John Clark, 15 June 1771, in Habersham, *Collections of the Georgia Historical Society*, 141.

104.   Greenwood & Higginson to the East India Company (E.I.C.), 4 May and 22 December 1773; John Nutt to E.I.C., 14 July and 22 December 1773, in Drake, *Tea Leaves*, 208, 232–33, 267–68. Andrew Lord and William & George Ancrum apparently declined Greenwood & Higginson's nomination as tea commissioners, however, with the Charles Town trading house of Greenwood & Leger being appointed in their place.

105.   *SCG*, 29 November 1773 (quote); *South Carolina Gazette and Country Journal*, 30 November 1773.

106.   William Bull to the Earl of Dartmouth, 24 December 1773, in Drake, *Tea Leaves*, 339–41; *SCG*, 27 December 1773; George C. Rogers Jr., "The Charleston Tea Party: The Significance of December 3, 1773," *SCHM* 75.3 (1974): 153–68; Edgar, *South Carolina: A History*, 219. The tea was eventually auctioned off three years later to raise funds for the Patriot war effort.

107.   Ralph Izard to Thomas Lynch, 14 February 1775, in Anne Izard Deas, ed., *Correspondence of Mr. Ralph Izard, of South Carolina, from the Year 1774 to 1804; with a Short Memoir*, 3 vols. (New York, 1844), I, 47–48. Izard was also involved in attempts to broker conciliatory talks between leaders in the Continental Congress and the British government in 1774 and 1775. See Julie Flavell, "American Patriots in London and the Quest for Talks, 1774–1775," *Journal of Imperial and Commonwealth History* 20.3 (1992): 350–59.

108.   Ralph Izard to HL, 18 October 1774, *PHL*, IX, 593–94.

109.   On the prewar failure of traders in America to retaliate selectively against particularly resented British merchants, see Olson, "London Mercantile Lobby," 30–31. The article did not consider the postwar reaction, however.

110.   The London Carolina traders' political inactivity was typical of London's American merchants in general. See Kim, "Merchants, Politics and Imperial Crisis," 192. Only one London merchant with an interest in the Carolina trade, the slave trader John Shoolbred, publicly endorsed a policy of coercion toward America. He signed a progovernment petition to George III in October 1775 that expressed "Disapprobation and Abhorrence" toward the "unjustifiable Proceedings of some of your Majesty's Colonies in America" (*London Gazette*, 10 October 1775).

111.   HL to James Air, 21 March 1774, *PHL*, IX, 362.

112.   The merchants who did sign the petition were American natives: the noted radicals Stephen Sayre and William and Arthur Lee; Laurens, though he was no longer active in trade; former Boston merchant John Boylston; New England trader Thomas Bromfield; and Maryland trader Joshua Johnson (*PHL*, IX, 372n–74n).

113.   *SCG*, 6 June 1774. No original copy of the petition to the House of Commons, which was drawn up at the Thatched House Tavern on 24 March 1774, survives. It was, however, reprinted in the *Public Advertiser* on 26 March 1774, albeit without the names of the signatories. However, a petition to the House of Lords drawn up at the same venue two days later

has survived, and since the texts of the two petitions were virtually identical and both were signed by twenty-nine men, it seems probable that the same men signed both petitions. The eleven Carolinians to sign the Lords petition, and probably that to the Commons as well, were William Blake, Edward Fenwicke, William Hazell Gibbs, Ralph Izard, Henry Laurens, William Middleton, William Middleton Jr., Isaac Motte, Philip Neyle, John Peronneau, and Thomas Pinckney. See *PHL*, IX, 368–75; *JHC*, XXXIV, 595–96; *Lords Journals*, XXXIV, 98.

114.   *PHL*, IX, 375–77.

115.   *PHL*, IX, 445–49; *Lords Journals*, XXXIV, 182.

116.   Merchant quietude in response to the Coercive Acts has been discussed in Olson, "London Mercantile Lobby," 35; Langford, "British Business Community," 281–82; Sainsbury, *Disaffected Patriots*, 69–73.

117.   Ralph Izard to George Dempsey, 31 May 1775, in Deas, *Correspondence of Mr. Ralph Izard*, I, 79; *PHL*, IX, passim, esp. 435n.

118.   *Daily Advertiser*, 5 January 1775.

119.   Ralph Izard to Thomas Lynch, 14 February 1775, in Deas, *Correspondence of Mr. Ralph Izard*, I, 47.

120.   On the caution and commercial emphasis of the merchants' petitions, see Bradley, *Popular Politics*, 27–29; Sainsbury, *Disaffected Patriots*, 75.

121.   Ralph Izard to Thomas Lynch, 14 February 1775, in Deas, *Correspondence of Mr. Ralph Izard*, I, 47.

CHAPTER FIVE: THE VOYAGE OF THE *LORD NORTH*

1.   The town officially became Charleston in 1783 and is hereafter referred to by its new name.

2.   *South Carolina Gazette & General Advertiser*, 2 and 31 May, 3 and 7 June 1783. Reflecting the maritime superstition that to change the name of a ship courts disaster, the *Financier* was shipwrecked off the Scilly Isles on its way back. The ship, according to reports, "went to pieces in 15 minutes," with the loss of three members of its crew—its mate, one sailor, and a black servant—and its entire cargo. The story of the ship's travails was reported in the *Morning Herald and Daily Advertiser*, 19 September 1783, and news of its wreck appeared in the *General Evening Post*, 17 September 1783. On ship-naming practices in the prewar Carolina trade, see Rogers, *Charleston Tea Party*, 157.

3.   Historians have broadly construed the 1780s as a period of structural continuity in the American economy. For an overview of the literature, see David Hancock, "Transatlantic Trade in the Era of the American Revolution," in *Anglo-American Attitudes: From Revolution to Partnership*, ed. Fred M. Leventhal and Roland E. Quinault (Aldershot: Ashgate, 2000), 38–43. The most comprehensive study of early American economic history noted that, with Britain dominating its external trade, the American economy retained a colonial character and that the 1780s represented a pregnant pause in the new nation's economic development: "the decade immediately following the end of the war looked, economically, much the same as the decade preceding it, in basic structure if not in detail" (McCusker and Menard, *Economy of British America*, 367). Essential studies of Britain's postwar relations with the United States are Peter J. Marshall, *Remaking the British Atlantic: The United States and the British Empire after American Independence* (Oxford: Oxford University Press, 2012); Charles R. Ritcheson, *Aftermath of Revolution: British Policy towards the United States, 1783–1795* (Dallas: Southern Methodist University Press, 1969). See also the extensive recent literature on Loyalists in the postwar Atlantic: Maya Jasanoff, *Liberty's Exiles: How the Loss of America Made the British Empire* (London: Harper, 2011); Maya Jasanoff, "The Other Side of Revolution: Loyalists in the British Empire," *WMQ* 65.2 (2008): 205–32; Simon Schama, *Rough Crossings: Britain, the Slaves and the American Revolution* (New York: HarperCollins, 2006); Keith Mason, "The American Loyalist Diaspora and the Reconfiguration of the British Atlantic World," in *Empire and Nation: The American Revolution in the Atlantic World*, ed. Peter Onuf and Eliga H. Gould (Baltimore:

Johns Hopkins University Press, 2005), 239–59; Mary Beth Norton, *The British-Americans: The Loyalist Exiles in England, 1774–1789* (Boston: Little, Brown, 1972).

4.   W. Lowndes, ed., *A London Directory or Alphabetical Arrangement . . . Embellished with a Plan of the Royal Exchange* (London, 1795).

5.   While Carolina's imports from England approached absolute prewar levels during the 1780s, the import and export trade with England lagged behind in per capita terms. This was chiefly attributable to the state's rapid population growth in the 1780s, principally through massive immigration to the backcountry. South Carolina's population grew from about 124,000 in 1770 to 249,000 in 1790, when the first federal census was taken, meaning that per capita imports from England approximately halved, from £3.5s.8d. in 1771 to £1.8s.8d. in 1790. The decline in exports to England was even more pronounced, from an average £438,379 per year between 1768 and 1774 (again excluding 1770 as anomalous) to £220,141 per year between 1784 and 1791. In per capita terms, this fall was from £3.7s.6d. in 1771 to £1.0s.4d. in 1790. For further detail, see James F. Shepherd and Gary M. Walton, "Economic Change after the American Revolution: Pre- and Post-War Comparisons of Maritime Shipping and Trade," *Explorations in Economic History* 13.4 (1976): 11–12.

6.   CO391/82/157, National Archives, London.

7.   16 Geo. III c. 5, American Prohibitory Act, in Great Britain, *Statutes at Large*, VIII, 458.

8.   CO5/79/5–6, CO5/116/49, National Archives, London.

9.   CO5/181/65–74, National Archives, London. Clark & Milligan was a successor firm to Graham, Clark & Co., leading London merchants in the prewar Georgia trade. After James Graham withdrew from the firm, John Clark went into partnership with his brother-in-law, Daniel Milligan. See James Habersham to Mary Bagwith, 7 January 1774, in Habersham, *Collections of the Georgia Historical Society*, 233.

10.   CO5/181/192–93, CO5/80/134–35, National Archives, London. The petitioning efforts also reflected how London's American traders, with their direct trade to the colonies curtailed, soon lost the insights and intelligence into American affairs that had defined and built their Atlantic commerce. For example, seven merchants with interests in the Georgia trade, including Greenwood & Higginson, Richard Shubrick, and John Nutt, petitioned the Earl of Carlisle and his peace commissioners in March 1779 for the restoration of civil government in Georgia. The commissioners had just returned from an abortive trip to America, where their peace proposals had been comprehensively rebuffed.

11   20 Geo. III c. 46, in Great Britain, *Statutes at Large*, IX, 101. The law was renewed in 1781 and 1782 as 21 Geo. III c. 29 and 22 Geo. III c. 13 respectively.

12.   CO5/397/357–58, National Archives, London. The petition was signed by (in the order that their names appeared) John Nutt; Greenwood & Higginson; Richard Shubrick; John Shoolbred; Champion & Dickason; Lane, Son & Fraser; and George Bague.

13.   CO5/652/34–38, CO5/397/374–75, National Archives, London.

14.   Figures do not include the comparatively insignificant trade between South Carolina/ Georgia and Scotland. Unknown quantities of British goods entered American ports indirectly, by way of Caribbean entrepôts such as St. Eustatius. With documentary evidence on wartime overseas commerce in Charleston understandably limited, the organization of this trade has received relatively little attention from historians. See Clarence L. Ver Steeg, "Stacy Hepburn and Company: Enterprisers in the American Revolution," *SCHM* 55.1 (1954): 1–6; G. Terry Sharrer, "Indigo in Carolina, 1671–1796," *SCHM* 72.2 (1971): 99–102. For anecdotal accounts of the revival of trade links with Britain during the May 1780 to December 1782 occupation, see Philip Porcher correspondence with William Manning, 1781–82, SCL; William Ancrum to Greenwood & Higginson, 14 May 1780, William Ancrum Letterbook, SCL.

15.   CO5/397/406–7, 409–10, 436–37, National Archives, London.

16.   CO5/8/268–69, National Archives, London. The seven Carolina and Georgia trading houses to sign the April 1782 petition to Shelburne, with prewar losses in South Carolina and

Georgia as self-estimated in 1790 in brackets, were Greenwood & Higginson (£269,760), John Nutt (£103,680), Neufville & Rolleston (£81,600), Clark & Milligan (£60,284), Richard Shubrick (£48,113), Davis, Strachan & Co. (£47,040), and Graham & Simpson (£36,380 claimed by its successor firm, Graham & Johnson).

17. They repeated this claim in their August 1782 petition, CO5/8/268–69, 286–87, National Archives, London.

18. Kim, "Merchants, Politics and the Atlantic Imperial Crisis," 195–96.

19. CO5/8/363–66, 417–18, National Archives, London. The Shelburne quote is from Kim, "Merchants, Politics and the Atlantic Imperial Crisis," 244–45.

20. CO5/8/363–64, National Archives, London.

21. HL to Robert Livingston, 15 March 1783, *PHL*, XVI, 163.

22. *Parliamentary History of England*, XXIII, 602–15, 640–46.

23. *PHL*, XVI, 165n, 174n.

24. Kim, "Merchants, Politics and the Atlantic Imperial Crisis," 246.

25. Those who signed the petition and had involvement in trade to South Carolina included partners Henry Merrtens Bird and Benjamin Savage, Adam Tunno, John Shoolbred, and James Strachan (*London Gazette*, 1 April 1783; Crowley, *Privileges of Independence*, 70–72).

26. See John Baker Holroyd, 1st Earl of Sheffield, *Observations on the Commerce of the American States with Europe and the West Indies* (London, 1783). Sheffield's tract was the leading articulation of postwar mercantilism. See also HL to Charles Thomson, 28 March 1784 (Bourdieu quote), *PHL*, XVI, 423; Kim, "Merchants, Politics and the Atlantic Imperial Community," 133–37; Cooper and McCord, *Statutes at Large of South Carolina*, IV, 596.

27. HL to Robert Livingston, 17 June 1783, *PHL*, XVI, 211; *London Chronicle*, 6 February 1783; *South Carolina Gazette & General Advertiser*, 18 April 1783; *South Carolina Weekly Gazette*, 26 April 1783. Evidence from London newspapers in fact indicated that ships were arriving only sporadically into the capital from American ports during May and June 1783; in these same months, however, numerous ships left Charleston for Great Britain, no doubt encouraged by the favorable press reports of American shipping arriving in the former mother country (*PHL*, XVI, 211n; *South Carolina Gazette & General Advertiser*, 27 and 31 May, 3 and 14 June 1783).

28. Paul H. Smith, ed., *Letters of Delegates to Congress, 1775–1789*, 26 vols. (Washington, D.C.: Library of Congress, 1976–2000), XX, 175–76, 235, 713.

29. 23 Geo. III c. 9 and c. 56, in Great Britain, *Statutes at Large*, IX, 286, 319;

30. The July Order was renewed in December 1783. See HL to John Mathews, 9 March 1784, *PHL*, XVI, 412; Thompson and Lumpkin, *Journals of the House of Representatives, 1783–1784*, 428–29, 594; Cooper and McCord, *Statutes at Large of South Carolina*, IV, 596. For a detailed narrative of postwar British orders and legislation relating to American commerce, see Ritcheson, *Aftermath of Revolution*, 3–21, 126–27.

31. "Peace" by the pseudonymous "Crito," *South Carolina Weekly Gazette*, 21 June 1783.

32. *South Carolina Gazette & General Advertiser*, 10, 20, and 31 May 1783; *London Courant and Daily Advertiser*, 27 January 1783. On ships' arrivals, see inter alia, *Public Advertiser*, 30 August 1783; *General Evening Post*, 11 October 1783; *Gazetteer and New Daily Advertiser*, 31 October 1783. On the arrival of some of the first ships in London from South Carolina after the peace but before the final peace terms had been settled, see also HL to Mary Laurens, 27 November 1783, *PHL*, XVI, 355.

33. HL to James Bourdieu, 30 August 1783, *PHL*, XVI, 275; XVI, 458n. On American merchants' tours to Britain before and after the American Revolution, see Kenneth Morgan, "Business Networks in the British Export Trade to North America, 1750–1800," in *The Early Modern Atlantic Economy*, ed. John J. McCusker and Kenneth Morgan (Cambridge: Cambridge University Press, 2000), 41–46.

34. HL to John Owen, 15 August 1783, *PHL*, XVI, 261.

35. *Public Advertiser*, 1 August 1783.

36. *Public Advertiser*, 6 September 1783.

37. Quoted in Rogers, *Evolution of a Federalist*, 101.

38. RP to William Freeman Sr., undated (quote), Pringle–Freeman Correspondence, SCHS. The letter's contents indicated that it was sent in the first months of 1784. Bankruptcy notices in the London press are a good source in documenting the formation (and failure) of transatlantic partnerships between merchants in Charleston and Britain. See, for example, *London Gazette*, 14 October 1786; *General Evening Post*, 29 July 1788.

39. Articles of Agreement between William Freeman Jr. and Robert Pringle Jr., June 1783, William Freeman Sr. to RP, 13 and 17 November 1783, 20 February 1784 (quote), Pringle-Freeman Correspondence, SCHS; *South Carolina Weekly Gazette*, 19 July 1783.

40. Inter alia, William & James Carson, Cooke & Webb, Dutarque & Smith, Graham & Burt, Kershaw & Riddle, Wayne & Jervey. See *South Carolina & American General Gazette*, 16 and 27 September 1780, 22 November 1780; *Royal South Carolina Gazette*, 8 December 1780, 10 May 1781.

41. Olson, *Making the Empire Work*, 182–83; Thomas M. Doerflinger, *A Vigorous Spirit of Enterprise: Merchants and Economic Development in Revolutionary Philadelphia* (Chapel Hill: University of North Carolina Press, 1986), 242–45.

42. James H. Kettner, *The Development of American Citizenship, 1608–1870* (Chapel Hill: University of North Carolina Press, 1978), 213–32; Douglas Bradburn, *The Citizenship Revolution: Politics and the Creation of the American Union* (Charlottesville: University of Virginia Press, 2009), 57–60.

43. Kellock, "London Merchants and the Pre-1776 American Debts," 141–43.

44. Rogers, *Evolution of a Federalist*, 103.

45. RP to William Freeman Sr., undated [early 1784], Pringle-Freeman Correspondence, SCHS.

46. Thompson and Lumpkin, *Journals of the House of Representatives, 1783–1784*, 253–54; Nadelhaft, *Disorders of War*, 92–94, 150–51.

47. "Arrangements between English and Southern Merchants," [c. June 1790], in Julian P. Boyd et al., eds., *The Papers of Thomas Jefferson*, 42 vols. (Princeton, N.J.: Princeton University Press, 1950–2017, XVI, 528–30.

48. Thomas Jefferson to Samuel House, 18 August 1785, in Boyd et al., *Papers of Thomas Jefferson*, VIII, 402.

49. Brailsford & Morris to Thomas Jefferson, 31 October 1787, in Boyd et al., *Papers of Thomas Jefferson*, XII, 299.

50. George Abbot Hall, 31 December 1784, in Boyd et al., *Papers of Thomas Jefferson*, VIII, 201.

51. RP to William Freeman Sr., undated [early 1784], Pringle-Freeman Correspondence, SCHS.

52. William Cumine to George Ogilvie, 29 May 1786, OFP.

53. William Nicholson to Alexander Fraser, 18 October 1788, Alexander Fraser Papers, SCHS.

54. *South Carolina Weekly Gazette*, 19 July 1783.

55. *Morning Chronicle and London Advertiser*, 24 June 1784.

56. Proclamation of Governor Benjamin Guerard, *South Carolina Gazette & General Advertiser*, 12 July 1783.

57. "A Patriot," *South Carolina Gazette & General Advertiser*, 15 July 1783. According to the writer, some twelve hundred copies of his pamphlet had been distributed, leading it to be reprinted in the *Gazette*.

58. *South Carolina Gazette & General Advertiser*, 10 July 1784.

59. *Morning Post and Daily Advertiser*, 11 September 1783; *London Chronicle*, 9 December 1783 ("darling independence"). Reports of anti-Tory sentiment and protests were also carried

in the British press during the following two years. See, inter alia, *St. James's Chronicle or the British Evening Post*, 19 August 1784; *Whitehall Evening Post*, 4 September 1784; *London Recorder or Sunday Gazette*, 8 May 1785 ("appellation of Tory"); *St. James's Chronicle or the British Evening Post*, 22 November 1785; *Morning Post and Daily Advertiser*, 23 December 1785. See also John Lewis Gervais to HL, 12 February and 17 April 1784, *PHL*, XVI, 391, 431. On the turbulence and partisanship of Charleston politics during the 1780s, see John A. Hall, "Quieting the Storm: The Establishment of Order in Post-Revolutionary South Carolina" (D.Phil. thesis, University of Oxford, 1989), esp. 44–49; Nadelhaft, *Disorders of War*, 71–124; Rogers, *Evolution of a Federalist*, 97–158; E. Stanly Godbold Jr. and Robert H. Woody, *Christopher Gadsden and the American Revolution* (Knoxville: University of Tennessee Press, 1982), 225–46.

60.   Aedanus Burke, *A Few Salutary Hints, Pointing out the Policy and Consequences of Admitting British Subjects to Engross our Trade and Become our Citizens* (Charleston and New York, 1786), quoted in George C. Rogers Jr., "Aedanus Burke, Nathanael Greene, Anthony Wayne, and the British Merchants of Charleston," *SCHM* 67.1 (1966): 79–80.

61.   Holton, *Forced Founders*, 216.

62.   Brailsford & Morris to Thomas Jefferson, 31 October 1787, in Boyd et al., *Papers of Thomas Jefferson*, XII, 301. Their comments anticipated the commercial rationale for federal union expounded just days later in Federalist XI (Hamilton). See also Federalists III and IV (Jay) and VII and XXII (Hamilton) on the necessity of the U.S. Constitution to regulate commerce. See James Madison, Alexander Hamilton, and John Jay, *The Federalist Papers*, ed. Isaac Kramnick (London: Penguin, 1987), 95–96, 98–99, 106–8, 129–33, 177. On the federalist movement in 1780s South Carolina and its opponents, see Rogers, *Evolution of a Federalist*, 124–58; Carl J. Vipperman, *The Rise of Rawlins Lowndes, 1721–1800* (Columbia: University of South Carolina Press, 1978), 240–57; Mark D. Kaplanoff, "How Federalist Was South Carolina in 1787–88?," in Chesnutt and Wilson, *Meaning of South Carolina History*, 67–103.

63.   Brailsford & Morris to Nathaniel Barrett, and to J. J. Berards & Co., October 1787 (enclosures to letter to Thomas Jefferson, 31 October 1787), in Richard Walsh, ed., "The Letters of Morris & Brailsford to Thomas Jefferson," *SCHM* 58.3 (1957): 138–41. The letters appear in heavily edited form in Boyd et al., *Papers of Thomas Jefferson*, XII, 302–3.

64.   On the prewar reputation of Carolinian indigo and colonial suspicions of a metropolitan bias against it, see Edelson, "Character of Commodities," 352–55.

65.   HL to Babut, Fils & Labouchère, 25 February 1786, *PHL*, XVI, 636.

66.   HL to Bridgen & Waller, 31 March 1785, 7 January 1786, *PHL*, XVI, 550n, 626.

67.   HL to Bridgen & Waller, 14 June 1784, 7 January and 1–2 February 1786, *PHL*, XVI, 469–70, 625–28, 628–31.

68.   Ramsay, *History of South* Carolina, II, 237.

69.   Inter alia, *General Evening Post*, 11 September 1784; *St. James's Chronicle or the British Evening Post*, 5 July 1785.

70.   HL to John Woddrop, 29 June 1783, *PHL*, XVI, 220–21. See also John Woddrop to Benjamin Franklin, 17 February 1783 (unpublished), http://www.franklinpapers.org (accessed 2 November 2016).

71.   On Philadelphia's postwar economic crisis, see Doerflinger, *Vigorous Spirit of Enterprise*, 245–50.

72.   George Abbot Hall, 31 December 1784, in Boyd et al., *Papers of Thomas Jefferson*, VIII, 199.

73.   Joseph W. Barnwell, ed., "Diary of Timothy Ford, 1785–1786," *South Carolina Historical and Genealogical Magazine* 13.4 (1912): 194–95.

74.   Robert Pringle Jr. to William Freeman Jr., 7 September 1783, Pringle-Freeman Correspondence, SCHS.

75.   See, for example, William Cumine (Jamaica) to George Ogilvie (Charleston), 29 May 1786, OFP.

76. HL to James Bloy, 9 August 1783; and to James Bourdieu, 9 June 1785, *PHL*, XVI, 255n, 568–69. Laurens also feared the renewal of the slave trade for its social implications. Slave imports had resumed within months of British forces leaving Charleston, leading Laurens to complain that "if continued this will keep them [lowcountry planters] a weak defenceless People, & may one day prove the destruction of the Sea Coast Inhabitants." He continued to express no remorse for his personal involvement in the slave trade as one of Charleston's largest prewar slave importers. See HL to Mary Laurens, 27 November 1783, *PHL*, XVI, 355. On the evolution of Laurens's attitude toward slavery, see Kelly, "Henry Laurens," 82–123.

77. Statistics compiled using the Transatlantic Slave Trade Database, searching "total slaves disembarked" for slave voyages between 1783 and 1787 when South Carolina was the "principal region of slave landing": http://slavevoyages.org/voyages/RAyNL3HL (accessed 31 October 2016). The figure of more than 8,300 slaves therefore excludes slaves brought overland into South Carolina or returned following the British evacuation of Charleston in December 1782. On the suspension of slave imports in 1787, see Klein, *Unification of a Slave State*, 127–28, 131–32.

78. South Carolina's direct balance of trade with England in 1784 was favorable to that of any other American state except Georgia and remained so throughout the 1780s. In Virginia and Maryland exports to England in 1784 were 32.1 percent of the value of imports, in Pennsylvania 10.5 percent, in New York 6.6 percent, and in New England 9.6 percent. Statistics do not include trade between the United States and Scotland. See Carter et al., *Historical Statistics*, V, 710–13.

79. Nash, "South Carolina Indigo," 379; Winberry, "Indigo in South Carolina," 98–99; Chaplin, *Anxious Pursuit*, 205–20.

80. David Ramsay to John Kean, 13 September 1785, in Michael A. Stevens, ed., "'To be a Member of Congress hereafter will be like a Profession': New Letters from David Ramsay, 1785–1793," *SCHM* 116.1 (2015): 62.

81. Ramsay, *History of South Carolina*, II, 237.

82. Klein, *Unification of a Slave State*, 127–28, 131–32; Edgar, *South Carolina: A History*, 247.

83. HL to Mannings & Vaughan, 6 January 1787, *PHL*, XVI, 684. Christopher Gadsen to Thomas Jefferson, 29 October 1781. Boyd, "Papers of Thomas Jefferson," XII, 295.

84. *Public Advertiser*, 16 July 1787.

85. Langford, "British Business Community"; Olson, "London Mercantile Lobby."

86. Oscar J. P. Tapper, "The Brailsford Debt," *Guildhall Miscellany* 2 (1961): 82–83; *Gazetteer and New Daily Advertiser*, 8 January 1772; William Lee to Samuel Brailsford, 19 August 1775, in Ford, *Letters of William Lee*, I, 169–71; *Morning Chronicle and London Advertiser*, 3 October 1775; Edgar and Bailey, *Biographical Directory*, II, 93.

87. *PHL*, X, 136n; XVI, 685n; Elias Ball (in Bristol) to his cousin Elias Ball (in South Carolina), 9 July 1785, Ball Family Papers, SCL; Rogers, *Evolution of a Federalist*, 273–75.

88. HL to Bridgen & Waller, 7 January 1786, *PHL*, XVI, 625–28.

89. Mortimer, *Universal Director* [*Mortimer's Directory*]; *PHL*, II, III, passim; XVI, 104–5n; *Public Advertiser*, 14 April 1772; *Morning Chronicle and London Advertiser*, 23 July 1776; Olson, "London Mercantile Lobby," 26–27; CO5/65/220: 1764, National Archives, London. A Samuel Chollet had traveled in 1779 to St. Eustatius, where he continued to transact business with South Carolina, though it is unclear if the Chollet in question was the partner in Bourdieu & Chollet or his son. See William Ancrum to Samuel Chollet, 27 September 1779, William Ancrum Letterbook, SCL.

90. Manning's connections to Laurens preceded the war. He had become Laurens's principal London correspondent after Laurens returned to South Carolina in late 1774 following a spell in Europe. Laurens shipped his plantation rice to Manning before rice exports were banned by the Provincial Congress in June 1775. Links between the two were reinforced by

the marriage of Laurens's son John to Manning's daughter Martha in London in October 1776. Manning continued to look after Laurens's interests in Britain during the war, effectively acting as his banker and keeping an eye on his younger son, Henry Jr., during his schooling in Britain. See HL to William Manning, 9 May, 26 May, and 8 June 1775; William Manning to HL, 8 July and 3 August 1775, 11 April 1778, *PHL*, X, 117, 147, 166, 211, 275; XII, 105.

91. Manning's political sensibilities did not preclude him from continuing to trade with South Carolina during the British wartime occupation of Charleston, however. See Philip Porcher to Manning, 12 November and 7 December 1781; Manning to Porcher, 6 February and 6 March 1782, Philip Porcher correspondence with William Manning, 1781–82, SCL; Edgar and Bailey, *Biographical Directory*, II, 534–35.

92. Manning's prewar sympathy for American grievances was suggested in his correspondence with Laurens in 1775. See Manning to HL, 17 February and 22 May 1775, *PHL*, X, 68–69, 125–31; "Benjamin Vaughan," *Oxford Dictionary of National Biography*.

93. HL to Benjamin Franklin, 7 April 1783, *PHL*, XV, 551; Bourdieu & Chollet to East India Company, 15 and 23 July 1773, in Drake, *Tea Leaves*, 233–34, 236–37.

94. *London Evening Post*, 17 October 1775, cited in Sainsbury, *Disaffected Patriots*, 173–91. Joseph Nicholson, Charles Ogilvie, and Benjamin Stead were the only other London merchants with interests in the Carolina trade to sign this petition.

95. For Bridgen's links with Americans and American sympathizers in Britain, see Edward Bridgen to Benjamin Franklin, 19 June 1777 and 19 November 1779, in Willcox et al., *Papers of Benjamin Franklin*, XII, 422n; XXIV, 200–201; XXXI, 129–30. On the fund for American prisoners of war, see *Public Advertiser*, 7 January 1778; *Gazetteer and New Daily Advertiser*, 13 January 1778. The fund for prisoners of war is discussed briefly in Sainsbury, *Disaffected Patriots*, 141–42. On how the defeat at Saratoga influenced British opinion toward America, see Stephen Conway, "From Fellow-Nationals to Foreigners: British Perceptions of the Americans, c. 1739–1783," *WMQ* 59.1 (2002): 93–94.

96. *PHL*, XV, 512n; Edward Bridgen to Benjamin Franklin, 23 October 1782, in Willcox et al., *Papers of Benjamin Franklin*, XXXVIII, 243–44; Edward Bridgen to Benjamin Franklin, 2 and 4 August 1785 (quotes) (unpublished), http://www.franklinpapers.org (accessed 2 November 2016).

97. "An Act for confiscating the property of all such persons as are inimical to this or the United States . . .," 18 October 1779; "An Act directing the sale of Confiscated Property," 13 April 1782, in Walter Clark, ed., *State Records of North Carolina* (Goldsboro, N.C., 1899), XXIV, 264, 424.

98. Benjamin Franklin to Alexander Martin, 5 August 1782, in Willcox et al., *Papers of Benjamin Franklin*, XXXVII, 703; Edward Bridgen to Benjamin Franklin, April 1786 (unpublished), http://www.franklinpapers.org (accessed 2 November 2016); *PHL*, XV, 531n; "An Act to Restore to Edward Bridgen, His Heirs and Assigns, all His Property, Real and Personal, in This State," 29 December 1785, in Clark, *State Records of North Carolina*, XXIV, 762.

99. Edward Bridgen to Benjamin Franklin, 4 August 1785 (unpublished), http://www.franklinpapers.org (accessed 2 November 2016). In particular, Bridgen suspected the state's chief justice of seeking to annex his lands since they were contiguous to the justice's own tracts.

100. Cooper and McCord, *Statutes at Large of South Carolina*, IV, 758; Thompson and Lumpkin, *Journals of the House of Representatives, 1783–1784*, 82–83; Roe Coker, "Absentees as Loyalists," 123–24. Baker and his father, the major London merchant Sir William Baker, had been prominent advocates for American rights throughout the 1760s and 1770s. See Bradley, *Popular Politics*, 54, 148; Sainsbury, *Disaffected Patriots*, 66, 75.

101. *General Advertiser and Morning Intelligencer*, 21 February 1782.

102. Brewer, *Sinews of Power*, 114–16. Forty-six men held government contracts to supply provisions and munitions to the British armed forces during the war. Most were London merchants, and a dozen were either involved in the West Indies trade or owned plantations in

the Caribbean. See Norman Baker, *Government and Contractors: The British Treasury and War Supplies* (London: Athlone, 1971), 216–40.

103. *London Courant and Westminster Chronicle*, 6 April 1780, 17 March 1781.

104. HL to Bridgen & Waller, 14 June 1784, *PHL*, XVI, 470. Laurens claimed that, because of a dispute over a prewar debt, Nutt had used his influence with Lord Hillsborough (according to Laurens, Nutt "had His Lordship's Ear at Command") to prolong his imprisonment in the Tower of London so that "my breath and his debt might be extinguished at the same time" (*PHL*, XV, 371).

105. T79/5/133, National Archives, London; Edgar and Bailey, *Biographical Directory*, II, 212. Nutt's assistance to Dupont further exemplified the interplay of interpersonal commerce and politics during the war. Dupont had been one of Nutt's principal prewar correspondents in Charleston and had owed him large debts. Nutt therefore had had a strong vested interest in delivering Dupont from jail and for him to return to productive commerce in South Carolina to enable him to pay off his debts. The plan backfired. Dupont's renunciation of his former Patriot convictions and his loyalism in occupied Charleston led to his estate being confiscated after the war, preventing him from repaying his debt to Nutt.

106. *PHL*, VI, 406n; Rogers, *Evolution of a Federalist*, 98–99.

107. For newspaper reports on the bankruptcy, see *London Chronicle*, 27 December 1785; *London Gazette*, 14 February 1786; Kellock, "London Merchants and the Pre-1776 American Debts," 142–43.

108. Charles Ogilvie to John Chesnut, 25 November 1780, Williams-Chesnut-Manning Papers, SCL.

109. On St. Eustatius's role as an entrepôt for Anglo-American trade during the war and the island's capture by the British, see O'Shaughnessy, *Empire Divided*, 214–27. On British merchants' wartime commerce through St. Eustatius, see George Ogilvie to Alexander Ogilvie, 21 August 1778, and to Peggie Ogilvie, 30 August 1778, OFP; William Ancrum to Greenwood & Higginson, 16 August 1779, and to Samuel Chollet, 27 September 1779, William Ancrum Letterbook, SCL.

110. *London Evening Post*, 17 October 1775; Willcox et al., *Papers of Benjamin Franklin*, XXVIII, 55–57, 76, 166; XXIX, 108.

111. Charles Ogilvie to George Ogilvie, 4 February 1779, OFP.

112. AO12/48/32–47, National Archives, London.

113. Cooper and McCord, *Statutes at Large of South Carolina*, IV, 516–23; *London Chronicle*, 6 July 1782.

114. Charles Ogilvie to Alexander Ogilvie, 17 September 1783, OFP.

115. AO12/47/148, National Archives, London; *PHL*, VIII, 141n; Edgar and Bailey, *Biographical Directory*, II, 141–42.

116. AO12/47/148–50, National Archives, London; *Morning Chronicle and London Advertiser*, 27 December 1780; *Royal Gazette*, 9 January 1782; *London Chronicle*, 6 July 1782.

117. Norton, *British-Americans*, 178–84, 216.

118. William M. Malloy, ed., *Treaties, Conventions, International Acts, Protocols and Agreements between the United States and Other Powers, 1776–1909* (Washington, D.C.: United States Department of State, 1910), 586–90; Francis Kinloch to Thomas Boone, 27 June 1783, in Felix Gilbert, ed., "Letters of Francis Kinloch to Thomas Boone, 1782–1788," *Journal of Southern History* 7 (1942): 95. On legal obstructions in the southern states, see Ritcheson, *Aftermath of Revolution*, 63–64; Holton, *Forced Founders*, 216.

119. Joshua Ward to Isaac King, 14 May 1785, IKL.

120. Stevens, "To be a Member of Congress," 59; Nadelhaft, *Disorders of War*, 155–72.

121. Compensation claim of Strachan & Davis, T79/36/237–38, National Archives, London; Isaac King to Joshua Ward, 8 June 1784 and 2 July 1789, and Joshua Ward to Isaac King, 14 May 1785, IKL.

122. T79/37/250, 289.

123. HL to Christopher Rolleston, 12 December 1785, and to Edward Neufville, 8 December 1787, *PHL*, XVI, 613–22, 748.

124. Charles Ogilvie to George Ogilvie, 27 January 1788, OFP; HL to Edward Neufville, 8 December 1787, *PHL*, XVI, 613n, 748; Isaac King to William Greenwood, 15 March 1790, IKL; Elias Ball (Bristol) to Elias Ball (South Carolina), 14 July 1791, Ball Family Papers, SCL (quote).

125. Isaac King to Robert Smyth, 30 August 1785, IKL.

126. Joshua Ward to Isaac King, 2 January 1789, IKL.

127. Cited in Kellock, "London Merchants and the Pre-1776 American Debts," 139.

128. Rogers, *Evolution of a Federalist*, 121–22, 250–52.

129. John Bassett Moore, ed., *International Adjudications Ancient and Modern*, 6 vols. (New York: Oxford University Press, 1929–33), III, 53–54; Tapper, "Brailsford Debt," 82–83; Kellock, "London Merchants and the Pre-1776 American Debts," 142–43.

130. *Public Advertiser*, 11 December 1786.

131. Marshall, *Remaking the British Atlantic*, 46, n55.

132. The success of an appeal by prewar Indian traders for government compensation further illustrates how significant the balance of power equation in British policy was toward the commercial debtors: where Parliament accepted that responsibility for repayment fell on the British side, it was willing to provide funds. In 1788 a group of former Cherokee traders in South Carolina and Georgia lobbied Parliament for recompense for land in Georgia ceded by the Indians to the Crown in 1773 in lieu of debts owed to the traders. In this case Parliament accepted that compensation to the traders for their losses was its responsibility, and it duly voted in May 1790 to pay them £49,500 in compensation. See *JHC*, XLIII, 179–80, 312; XLV, 458; *Parliamentary Register 1780–1796*, 1788, 136–37.

133. Jasanoff, "Other Side of Revolution," 215–16.

134. Isaac King to Nathaniel Russell, 7 March 1784, IKL.

135. On Lord Cornwallis's aid to Carolinian Loyalists in Britain, see Elias Ball (Bristol) to Elias Ball (South Carolina), 30 January and 6 June 1785, Ball Family Papers, SCL. The former's experience as an exile in Britain is discussed in Ball, *Slaves in the Family*, 236–37.

136. "Petition of the Committee of Merchants trading to North America," 13 April 1787, Add MSS 38221, f. 334, British Library, London; Ritcheson, *Aftermath of Revolution*, 57–58; Norton, *British-Americans*, 208.

137. Nadelhaft, *Disorders of War*, 89; Kellock, "London Merchants and the Pre-1776 American Debts," 113–14; Coclanis, "Hydra Head," 11–12. Jacob Price has highlighted the limitations of the debt claims as a guide to the relative share of debt by colony and British port, since the different organization of different trades affected creditors' ability to reclaim prewar debts. The nature of the Glaswegian retail tobacco trade with planters in Virginia, North Carolina, and Maryland, he suggested, made these debts harder to collect, therefore inflating the Glaswegian share, and by implication tobacco colonies' share, of total debts. If this is correct, it suggests that debts in South Carolina may have been a still higher proportion of the "real" prewar total. See Price, "Who Cared about the Colonies," 410–11.

138. Langford, "British Business Community," 299–305. On the role of nonimportation and the bumper tobacco exports of 1775 in reducing Virginian planters' debts, see also Holton, *Forced Founders*, 119–29.

139. Commercial claims are filed in the T79 American Loyalist Claims Commission records at the National Archives, London. For examples of debts on account, in bond and through loans, see in particular the compensation claims of David & Strachan, T79/36/237–38; Charles Ogilvie, T79/43/177; Thomas Binford, T79/20/285–86.

140. Powell & Hopton's claim was dismissed on the grounds that they had resided in Charleston rather than Britain before the American Revolution and that the claim was

therefore outside the commission's purview (Kellock, "London Merchants and the Pre-1776 American Debts," 141–43).

141. On methods of calculating interest on the debt claims, see in particular T79/5/142–44, National Archives, London: petitions in support of John Nutt's compensation claims, 22 June and 17 August 1804.

142. CO391/82/157, National Archives, London.

143. William Manning to HL, 17 April 1778, *PHL*, XII, 128; *London Gazette and Westminster Chronicle*, 6 April 1780 and 17 March 1781.

144. Greenwood died "after a lingering illness, at his house in Budge-Row [London], in the 53rd year of his age . . . an eminent merchant" (*General Evening Post*, 20 April 1786; Will of William Greenwood, Prob. 11/1142, National Archives, London).

145. Will of Richard Shubrick, Prob. 11/1289, National Archives, London.

146. Will of James Poyas, Prob. 11/1326, National Archives, London; Will of Christopher Rolleston, Prob. 11/1467, National Archives, London.

147. For newspaper reports on the dispute between the government and Richard Atkinson, see *Morning Chronicle and London Advertiser*, 30 March 1784; *Morning Post and Daily Advertiser*, 6 April 1784. The dispute and its eventual resolution are discussed in Baker, *Government and Contractors*, 165–75.

148. *General Evening Post*, 4 July 1786; *Oracle Bell's New World*, 10 July 1789; *Oracle and Public Advertiser*, 9 July 1795.

149. For example, Nutt sat on a committee in 1794 managing an appeal for the relief of widows and children of seamen killed during the Anglo-French warfare, and he was one of the numerous city merchants who in an advert placed in the press by the Bank of England pledged to accept bank notes in all payments in order to support the public credit (*London Chronicle*, 23 June 1794; *Morning Chronicle*, 31 July 1794; *Oracle and Public Advertiser*, 3 March 1797).

150. Campbell and Molleson claimed in 1791 for debts, respectively, of £38,134 in Virginia and Maryland, and £71,038 in Maryland and Pennsylvania. See Kellock, "London Merchants and the Pre-1776 American Debts"; *Morning Post and Daily Advertiser*, 20 March 1783; Olson, *Making the Empire Work*, 179–80.

151. Ralph Izard to Thomas Lynch, 14 February 1775, in Deas, *Correspondence of Mr. Ralph Izard*, I, 47–48.

152. Brailsford & Morris to Thomas Jefferson, 31 October 1787, in Boyd et al., *Papers of Thomas Jefferson*, XII, 298.

153. *Gazetteer and New Daily Advertiser*, 16 February 1785; William Bailey, *List of Bankrupts, Dividends and Certificates, from the Year 1772, to 1793*, 3 vols. (London, 1794), II, 81; Will of Samuel Carne, Prob. 11/1149, National Archives, London.

154. Isaac King to Joshua Ward, 9 October 1790, IKL.

155. South Carolina Court of Common Pleas, Judgement Rolls: 71A, 72A, 276A, 392A, SC-DAH; HL to Isaac King, 30 September 1767, *PHL*, V, 320, and IX, 289n; Maurice A. Crouse, ed., "Papers of Gabriel Manigault, 1771–1784," *SCHM* 64.1 (1963): 7.

156. Isaac King to James Fisher, 16 June 1783, IKL.

157. Isaac King to Joshua Ward, 16 June 1783, and to Nathaniel Russell, 8 June 1784 and 2 September 1785, IKL.

158. Walter E. Minchinton, "Richard Champion, Nicholas Pocock, and the Carolina Trade," *SCHM* 65.2 (1964): 89–91; N. L. Bailey and Elizabeth Ivey Cooper, *Biographical Directory of the South Carolina House of Representatives*, vol. III, 1775–90 (Columbia: University of South Carolina Press, 1981), 136–38.

159. Isaac King to Nathaniel Russell, 23 February 1785, IKL.

CONCLUSION

1. Memorials of 17th and 18th Century South Carolina Land Titles, 1731–75, II, 473, SC-DAH; Isaac King to Joshua Ward, 16 June 1783, 4 March 1786, 18 May 1787; and to Nathaniel Russell, 2 September 1785 (quote), IKL.

2. Isaac King to Joshua Ward, 12 March 1788 and 19 April 1791, IKL.

3. Margaret Colleton to Robert Raper and Francis Kinloch, 13 July 1778, Margaret Colleton Papers, SCL.

4. Will of Margaret Colleton, Prob. 11/1058, National Archives, London.

5. James Nassau Colleton to Benjamin Franklin, 8 November 1782 (unpublished), http://www.franklinpapers.org (accessed 2 November 2016). Whether Franklin replied or forwarded on Nassau Colleton's plea is unknown.

6. William Ancrum to James Edward Colleton, 14 July 1780, Margaret Colleton Papers, SCL.

7. Thomas Boone to Allen Swainston, 19 March 1783, and to James Edward Colleton, 27 July 1783, Margaret Colleton Papers, SCL.

8. Cooper and McCord, *Statutes at Large of South Carolina*, IV, 624–66; VI, 634. Nassau Colleton's struggle to regain his plantations has been described in Kathryn Roe Coker, "The Case of James Nassau Colleton before the Commissioners of Forfeited Estates," *SCHM* 87.2 (1986): 106–16.

9. Aaron Loocock to Allen Swainston, 12 July 1786, Margaret Colleton Papers, SCL. See also Roe Coker, "Absentees as Loyalists," 132.

10. *Morning Post and Daily Advertiser*, 9 February 1788; http://south-Carolina-plantations.com/beaufort/richfield.html (accessed 7 November 2016).

11. T/79/43/142–48, 177, National Archives, London; Charles Ogilvie to George Ogilvie, 27 January 1788, OFP.

12. John Martin Sr. to John Martin Jr., 1 July 1788 (quote) and 26 April 1789, John Martin Papers, SCHS.

13. HL to Bourdieu, Chollet & Bourdieu, 20 October 1785, *PHL*, XVI, 566–67n, 603–4.

14. HL to Mannings & Vaughan, 30 June 1787, *PHL*, XVI, 718; *Public Advertiser*, 7 September 1787. On war damage to New Hope and Broughton Island, see Edelson, *Plantation Enterprise*, 247.

15. *Morning Post and Daily Advertiser*, 7 March 1789; *Gazetteer and New Daily Advertiser*, 20 April 1789.

16. *Morning Chronice and London* Advertiser, 14 February 1789; *Public Advertiser*, 30 April 1789.

17. "An Act for raising and paying into the Public Treasury of this State the Tax therein mentioned, for the use and service thereof," 10 March 1783, in Cooper and McCord, *Statutes at Large of South Carolina*, IV, 528–37.

18. "An Act for the making of Aliens free of this part of the Province," 4 November 1704, repealed in "An Act to confer the rights of Citizenship on Aliens," 26 March 1784, in Cooper and McCord, *Statutes at Large of South Carolina*, II, 251–53; IV, 600–601.

19. Hugh Williamson to Thomas Ruston, 12 February 1784, in Smith, *Letters of Delegates to Congress*, XXI, 352–53. On North Carolina's citizenship requirements, see Kettner, *Development of American Citizenship*, 214.

20. "An Ordinance to encourage subjects of Foreign States to lend money at interest on real estates within this state," 26 March 1784, in Cooper and McCord, *Statutes at Large of South Carolina*, IV, 642–43.

21. Marshall, *Remaking the British Atlantic*, 269.

22. "An Act for the Security of Foreigners who May lend Money at Interest, or on real Estates," 21 February 1785, in Candler and Knights, *Colonial Records of the State of Georgia*, XIX, pt. II, 417–18; HL to Champion & Dickason, 6 October 1785, *PHL*, XVI, 598–99.

23. "An Act for ascertaining the rights of aliens and pointing out a mode for the admission of Citizens" and "An Act for imposing a Tax on the Inhabitants of the State of Georgia and other Persons holding Property real or Personal therein," 7 and 21 February 1785, in Candler and Knights, *Colonial Records of the State of Georgia*, XIX, pt. II, 375–78, 398–416.

24. On the experiences of Loyalists returning to the postwar United States, see Norton, *British-Americans*, 242–49.

25. Elias Ball (Bristol) to Elias Ball (South Carolina), 20 October 1788, Ball Family Papers, SCL.

26. Elias Ball (Bristol) to Elias Ball (South Carolina), 22 November 1784, Ball Family Papers, SCL.

27. Isaac Darnford to John Martin Jr., 10 October 1790; John Martin Jr. to John Bold, 20 June 1791; and Bold to Martin Jr., 6 January 1792, John Martin Papers, SCHS.

28. *St. James's Chronicle or the British Evening Post*, 17 April 1790.

29. Price, "What Did Merchants Do," 274.

30. On the reception of the Jay-Grenville Treaty in South Carolina, see Rogers, *Evolution of a Federalist*, 275–80; Klein, *Unification of a Slave State*, 218–21; Godbold and Woody, *Christopher Gadsden*, 246–47.

31. Kellock, "London Merchants and the Pre-1776 American Debts," 116.

BIBLIOGRAPHY

PRIMARY SOURCES

Archival Sources

Bodleian Library, Oxford
Letterbook of Robert Raper, 1759–70. Microfilm.

British Library, London
Add. MS. 15154–5. Minute Books of the Free British Fishery Society.
Add. MS. 38221.

Essex Record Office, Chelmsford
D/DDa T42. Manorial Records: Deeds of Luxborough estate etc., 1615–1775.
D/DHt T62/9. Deeds of Chigwell.

Guildhall Library, London
Bishopsgate wardmote minutes and agenda, vol. I, 1737–1839.
Candlewick wardmote inquest minutes, 1676–1802.
City of London Land Tax Assessments, 1743–75.
Nathaniel Lewis and Alexander Bailey. Account Book, 1711–12.
Parish of St. Dunstan Stepney, hamlet of Mile End: land tax assessment books, 1750–62.
Rawlinson, Davison and Newman. Account Book, 1753–57.

Hertfordshire Archives, Hertford
A/2709–10: Agreement between Charles Crokatt and Henry Potts for bond in connection with mortgage on Old Bethlem lands and messuage.
A/2807–8: Articles of agreement between Edward Lewis, William Minet and Charles Crokatt in connection with mortgage on land and messuage in Old Bethlem, London.
A/2811: Bond of £4,400 of Charles Crokatt to Henry Potts.

Huntington Library, San Marino, California
Loudon papers.
James Wright correspondence.

London Metropolitan Archives
ACC 0371/013–4: Leases between Richard Shubrick and William Edmundson and William and Benjamin Hodges for land in Enfield.
ACC 0813/012: Lease between Richard Shubrick and William Edmundson, and Thomas Skinner for land in Enfield.
MS. 11936: Sun Fire Insurance Office policy records.

National Archives, London
AO12/46–52: American Loyalists' Claims, series I, evidence, South Carolina.
C12: Court of Chancery: Six Clerks Office: Pleadings, 1758–1800.
CO323/17: Record of the Colonial Office etc: General Colonies, original correspondence—Board of Trade, 1763–64.
CO324/37: Record of the Colonial Office etc: General Entry Books, series I: Commissions, instructions, petitions, grants, orders in council, warrants, letters, etc., 1736–49.
CO391/82: Board of Trade: Minutes.

CO5/116: America: Secretary of State, Original Correspondence, petitions, 1776–79.

CO5/1330–31: Board of Trade and Secretaries of State: America and West Indies, original correspondence—Board of Trade, Virginia, 1760–67.

CO5/181: America: Secretary of State, Original Correspondence, Commissioners to quiet disorders in North America, 1778–79.

CO5/2: Original correspondence, Board of Trade, 1777–1807.

CO5/366–97: Board of Trade and Secretaries of State: America and West Indies, original correspondence—Board of Trade, South Carolina, 1737–38 to 1780–84.

CO5/509–11: Board of Trade and Secretaries of State: America and West Indies, original correspondence—Shipping returns, South Carolina, 1721–35 to 1764–65.

CO5/65: Board of Trade and Secretaries of State: America and West Indies, original correspondence—Secretary of State, Indian affairs, surveys etc., 1760–64.

CO5/651: Board of Trade and Secretaries of State: America and West Indies, original correspondence—Board of Trade, Georgia, 1769–72.

CO5/79–80: America: Secretary of State, Original Correspondence, Indian affairs, defence etc., 1777–79.

Prob. 11/1000. 20 August 1774. Will of Richard Grubb, merchant of St. Edmund the King, London.

Prob. 11/1029. 11 March 1777. Will of James Crokatt.

Prob. 11/1051. 16 March 1779. Will of Margaret Colleton, Hill Street, St. George, Hanover Square, London.

Prob. 11/1058. 6 November 1779. Will of William Stone, merchant of Walsall, Staffordshire.

Prob. 11/1142. 20 May 1786. Will of William Greenwood, merchant of St. Stephen Walbrook, London.

Prob. 11/1149. 2 January 1787. Will of Samuel Carne of Kensington, Middlesex.

Prob. 11/1164. 14 March 1788. Will of Gilbert Ross, merchant of Fenchurch St., London.

Prob. 11/1171. 13 October 1788. Will of Charles Ogilvie, merchant of St. Clement Danes, Middlesex.

Prob. 11/1192. 17 May 1790. Will of Andrew Pringle of Clifton, Gloucestershire.

Prob. 11/1200. 17 January 1791. Will of Nathaniel Newberry, merchant of London.

Prob. 11/1285. 20 February 1797. Will of Isaac King, late merchant, gentleman of St. Michaels Hill, Bristol, Gloucestershire.

Prob. 11/1289. 29 April 1797. Will of Richard Shubrick, of Enfield, Middlesex.

Prob. 11/1326. 20 June 1799. Will of James Poyas, merchant of London.

Prob. 11/1467. 19 September 1807. Will of Christopher Rolleston of Watnall, Nottinghamshire.

Prob. 11/634. 6 December 1729. Will of Stephen Godin, merchant of St. Peter le Poer, London.

Prob. 11/677. 5 June 1736. Will of John Walter of Woking, Surrey.

Prob. 11/703. 28 June 1740. Will of William Payne, gentleman, of Winterbourne, Gloucestershire.

Prob. 11/781. 4 July 1750. Will of John Crokatt, merchant, Charles Town.

Prob. 11/785. 25 January 1751. Will of Samuel Wragg, merchant of Charles Town, South Carolina.

Prob. 11/810. 2 August 1754. Will of John Nickleson, merchant of London.

Prob. 11/810. 8 August 1754. Will of Elizabeth Shubrick, wife of Richard Shubrick.

Prob. 11/879. 16 August 1762. Will of Jane Shubrick, widow of Mile End Green, London.

Prob. 11/900. 8 August 1764. Will of John Beswicke, merchant, London.

Prob. 11/912. 12 September 1765. Will of Richard Shubrick, merchant of St. Stephen Walbrook, London.

Prob. 11/963. 29 January 1771. Will of George Udny of Lincoln's Inn Fields, London

T1/424: Treasury Board Papers and In-Letters.

T1/425: Treasury Board Papers and In-Letters.

T1/441: Treasury Board Papers and In-Letters.
T1/449: Treasury Board Papers and In-Letters.
T1/453: Treasury Board Papers and In-Letters.
T1/480: Treasury Board Papers and In-Letters.
T79/10: Treasury, American Loyalist Claims Commission Records.
T79/11: Treasury, American Loyalist Claims Commission Records.
T79/20: Treasury, American Loyalist Claims Commission Records.
T79/21: Treasury, American Loyalist Claims Commission Records.
T79/30: Treasury, American Loyalist Claims Commission Records.
T79/36: Treasury, American Loyalist Claims Commission Records.
T79/37: Treasury, American Loyalist Claims Commission Records.
T79/38: Treasury, American Loyalist Claims Commission Records.
T79/43: Treasury, American Loyalist Claims Commission Records.
T79/5: Treasury, American Loyalist Claims Commission Records.

South Carolina Department of Archives and History, Columbia
Journals of His Majesty's Council, 1721–74. Microfilm.
Letterbook of Charles Garth, 1766–75. Microfilm.
Letterbook of James Wright and Charles Garth, 1758–66. Microfilm.
Memorials of South Carolina Land Titles, 1731–75.
Middleton Family Papers. Microfilm.
Miscellaneous Records. Microfilm.
Public Register, South Carolina, Conveyance books [Charleston Deeds].
St. Philip's Parish, Charleston. Church Wardens' Account Book, 1725–52. Microfilm.
St. Philip's Parish, Charleston. Parish Registers, 1714–1810. Microfilm.
St. Philip's Parish, Charleston. Vestry Minutes, 1732–74. Microfilm.
South Carolina Court of Common Pleas, Judgement Rolls.

South Carolina Historical Society, Charleston
Alexander Fraser Papers.
Peter Manigault Papers.
John Martin Papers.
Middleton Family Papers.
Ogilvie-Forbes Papers.
Pinckney Family Papers. Microform.
Pringle-Freeman Correspondence.
Pringle Garden Family Papers.
William Loughton Smith Papers.

South Caroliniana Library, University of South Carolina, Columbia
William Ancrum Account Book (of Fesch and Guinand), 1757–58.
William Ancrum Letterbook and Accounts, 1776–82.
Ball Family Papers.
Colleton Family Papers.
Margaret Colleton Papers.
James Glen Papers, 1757–66.
James Grant Papers.
Isaac King Letterbook, 1783–97.
Isaac King Papers.
Manigault Family Papers, 1753–56.
Will of Sarah Nicholson, 1770.
Charles Pinckney Papers.

Philip Porcher Account Book, 1778–80.
Philip Porcher correspondence with William Manning, 1781–82.
Robert Raper Account Book.
Alexander Rose Papers.
Taylor Family Papers.
Williams-Chesnut-Manning Papers, 1766–1805.
Samuel Wragg Papers.

Newspapers

Craftsman or Says Weekly Journal (London).
Daily Advertiser (London).
Gazetteer and New Daily Advertiser (London).
General Advertiser (London).
General Advertiser and Morning Intelligencer (London).
General Evening Post (London).
Lloyd's Evening Post (London).
London Chronicle.
London Courant and Westminster Chronicle.
London Evening Post.
London Gazette.
London Recorder or Sunday Gazette.
Middlesex Journal and Evening Advertiser (London).
Morning Chronicle and London Advertiser.
Morning Herald and Daily Advertiser (London).
Morning Post and Daily Advertiser (London).
Oracle and Public Advertiser (London).
Oracle Bell's New World (London).
Public Advertiser (London).
Public Ledger or The Daily Register of Commerce and Intelligence (London).
Read's Weekly Journal or British Gazetteer (London).
Royal Gazette (Charleston).
Royal South Carolina Gazette (Charleston).
St. James's Chronicle or the British Evening Post (London).
South Carolina and American General Gazette (Charleston).
South Carolina Gazette (Charleston).
South Carolina Gazette and Country Journal (Charleston).
South Carolina Gazette and General Advertiser (Charleston).
South Carolina Weekly Gazette (Charleston).
Whitehall Evening Post or London Intelligencer (London).
World (London).

Other Printed Primary Sources

Adams, Lark E., and Rosa S. Lumpkin. *The State Records of South Carolina: Journals of the House of Representatives, 1785–1786.* Columbia: University of South Carolina Press, 1979.

[Anon.]. *American Husbandry. Containing an Account of the Soil, Climate, Production and Agriculture, of the British Colonies in North-America and the West-Indies; with Observations on the Advantages and Disadvantages of settling in them, compared with great Britain and Ireland.* 3 vols. London: Printed for J. Bew, 1772.

[Anon.]. *Ill-Judged Bounties tend to Beggary on both Sides or, Observations on a Paper intituled Reasons for laying a Duty on French and Spanish Indico, and granting a Bounty on what is made in the British Plantations.* London: Printed by E. Owen, 1748.

Archdale, John. *A New Description of that Fertile and Pleasant Province of Carolina.* London: Printed for John Wyat, 1707.

Bailey, William. *List of Bankrupts, Dividends and Certificates, from the Year 1772, to 1793.* 3 vols. London, 1794.

Barnwell, Joseph W., ed. "Diary of Timothy Ford, 1785–1786." *South Carolina Historical and Genealogical Magazine* 13.3/4 (1912): 132–47, 181–204.

Boyd, Julian P., et al., eds. *The Papers of Thomas Jefferson.* 42 vols. Princeton, N.J.: Princeton University Press, 1950–2017.

Bull, William. "Representation of the Colony, 1770." In *The Colonial South Carolina Scene: Contemporary Views, 1697–1774*, ed. H. Roy Merrens, 254–69. Columbia: University of South Carolina Press, 1977.

Burke, William. *An Account of the European Settlements in America. In six parts.* 2 vols. 2nd ed. London: Printed for R. and J. Dodsley, 1758.

Candler, Allen D., and Lucian Lamar Knights, eds. *Colonial Records of the State of Georgia.* 26 vols. Atlanta: Franklin Printing and Publishing, 1904–16.

Carter, Susan B., et al., eds. *Historical Statistics of the United States: Millennial Edition.* New York: Cambridge University Press, 2006.

Champion, Richard. *Considerations on the Present Situation of Great Britain and the United States of America.* London: Printed for J. Stockdale, 1784.

Chesnutt, David R., et al., eds. *The Papers of Henry Laurens.* 16 vols. Columbia: University of South Carolina Press, 1968–2003.

Clark, Walter, ed. *State Records of North Carolina.* 30 vols. Goldsboro, N.C., 1899.

Colyer-Ferguson, Thomas, ed. *The Marriage Registers of St. Dunstan's, Stepney, in the County of Middlesex, 1697–1719.* Canterbury, 1898.

Committee Appointed for Relieving the Poor Germans. *Proceedings of the Committee Appointed for Relieving the Poor Germans, who were brought to London and there left Destitute in the Month of August 1764.* London: Printed by J. Haberkorn, 1765.

Cooper, Thomas, and David J. McCord, eds. *The Statutes at Large of South Carolina.* 10 vols. Columbia, S.C.: A. S. Johnson, 1836–41.

[Crokatt, James.] *Observations concerning indigo and cochineal.* London, 1746.

[Crokatt, James, ed.] *Further observations intended for improving the culture and curing of indigo, &c. in South-Carolina.* London, 1747.

Crouse, Maurice A., ed. "Papers of Gabriel Manigault, 1771–1784." *SCHM* 64.1 (1963): 1–12.

[Decker, Sir Matthew.] *An Essay on the Causes of the Decline in Foreign Trade, consequently of the Value of the Lands in Britain, and on the Means to Restore both.* 2nd ed. London, 1750.

Donnan, Elizabeth, ed. *Documents Illustrative of the History of the Slave Trade to America.* Vol. IV, *The Border Colonies and the Southern Colonies.* Washington, D.C.: Carnegie Institute, 1935.

Drake, Francis S., ed. *Tea Leaves: Being a Collection of Letters and Documents Relating to the Shipment of Tea to the American Colonies in the Year 1773, by the East India Company.* Boston, 1884.

Easterby, J. H., and R. Nicholas Olsberg, eds. *Journal of the Commons House of Assembly of South Carolina.* 14 vols., 1736–57. Columbia: Historical Commission of South Carolina, 1951–89.

Edgar, Walter B., ed. *The Letterbook of Robert Pringle, 1737–45.* 2 vols. Columbia: University of South Carolina Press, 1972.

Ford, Worthington C., ed. *Letters of William Lee: Sheriff and Alderman of London; Commercial Agent of the Continental Congress in France; and Minister to the Courts of Vienna and Berlin, 1766–1783.* 3 vols. Brooklyn: Historical Printing Club, 1891.

Garstin, Crosbie, ed. *Samuel Kelly: An Eighteenth Century Seaman, whose days have been few and evil, to which is added remarks, etc., on places he visited during his pilgrimage in this wilderness.* London: C. Cape, 1925.

Gee, Joshua. *The Trade and Navigation of Great-Britain Considered.* 3rd ed. London: Printed by Sam. Bockley, 1731.

Gibbes, R. W. *Documentary History of the American Revolution consisting of letters and papers relating to the contest for liberty chiefly in South Carolina, from originals in the possession of the editor, and other sources, 1764–1776.* New York, 1855.

Gilbert, Felix, ed. "Letters of Francis Kinloch to Thomas Boone, 1782–1788." *Journal of Southern History* 7.1 (1942): 87–105.

Glen, James. "An Attempt towards an Estimate of the Value of South Carolina, for the Right Honourable the Lords Commissioners for Trade and Plantations, 1751." In *The Colonial South Carolina Scene: Contemporary Views, 1697–1774,* ed. H. Roy Merrens, 177–91. Columbia: University of South Carolina Press, 1977.

[Glen, James]. *A description of South Carolina; containing, many curious and interesting particulars relating to the civil, natural and commercial history of that colony, viz. . . . To which is added, a very particular account of their rice-trade for twenty years, with their exports of raw silk and imports of British silk manufactures for twenty-five years.* London: Printed for R. and J. Dodsley, 1761.

[Gordon, Lord Adam]. "Journal of an Officer who Travelled in America and the West Indies in 1764 and 1765." In *Travels in the American Colonies,* ed. N. D. Mereness, 367–453. New York: Macmillan, 1916.

Great Britain. *Calendar of State Papers, Colonial Series.* 45 vols. London: Longman, Green, Longman and Roberts, 1860–1994 .

——. *Calendar of Treasury Books and Papers, 1729–1745.* 5 vols. London: His Majesty's Stationary Office, 1897–1903.

——. *Calendar of Treasury Papers, 1702–1728.* Vols. 3–6. London: Longman, Green, Reader, and Dyer, 1868–89.

——. *Journal of the Commissioners for Trade and Plantations, from April 1704 to May 1782.* 14 vols. London: H.M.S.O, 1920–28.

——. *Journal of the House of Commons.* Vols. 18–29, 43–45. London: H.M.S.O., 1802.

——. *Journal of the House of Lords.* 42 vols. London: H.M.S.O., 1767–1830.

——. *The Statutes at Large, from Magna Charta, to the Twenty Fifth Year of the Reign of King George the Third, Inclusive.* 14 vols. London: Eyre and Strahan, 1786.

Habersham, James. *Collections of the Georgia Historical Society.* Vol. VI, *The Letters of the Hon. James Habersham, 1756–1775.* Savannah: Georgia Historical Society, 1906.

Hanway, Jonas. *An Account of the Marine Society, recommending the piety and policy of the institution, and pointing out the advantages accruing to the nation. . . .* 6th ed. London, 1759.

——. *Motives for a subscription towards the relief of the sufferers at Montreal in Canada, by a dreadful fire on the 18th of May 1765, in which 108 houses . . . were destroyed. . . .* 2nd ed. London, 1766.

Hemphill, William E., and Wylma A. Wates, eds. *Extracts from the Journals of the Provincial Congresses of South Carolina, 1775–1776.* Columbia: South Carolina Archives Department, 1960.

Hewitt, Alexander. *An Historical Account of the Rise and Progress of the Colonies of South Carolina and Georgia.* 2 vols. London, 1779.

Hewitt, John. *The Universal Pocket Companion.* London, 1741.

Howe, Mark A. DeWolfe, ed. "Josiah Quincy Jr., London Journal 1774–5." *Proceedings of the Massachusetts Historical Society* 50 (1916–17): 433–71.

Hutchinson, William T., et al., eds. *The Papers of James Madison. Congressional Series,* 17 vols. Chicago: Chicago University Press; Charlottesville: University of Virginia Press, 1962–91.

Izard Deas, Anne, ed. *Correspondence of Mr. Ralph Izard, of South Carolina, from the Year 1774 to 1804; with a Short Memoir.* 3 vols. New York: C.S. Francis, 1844.

Johnston, George Milligen. *A Short Description of the Province of South-Carolina, with an Account of the Air, Weather, and Diseases, at Charles-Town. Written in the year 1763.* London: Printed for J. Hinton, 1770.

Kent, Henry. *Kent's Directory.* 21st, 29th, 30th eds. London, 1754, 1762, 1763.

Lawson, John. *A New Voyage to South Carolina, containing the exact description and natural history of that country: together with the present state thereof.* London, 1709.

Ledyard, John. *Methods for Improving the Manufacture of Indigo: Originally Submitted to the Consideration of the Carolina Planters; And Now published for the Benefit of all the British Colonies, whose Situation is favorable to the Culture of Indigo. . . .* Devizes: Printed for the author by T. Burrough, 1776.

Lowndes, W., ed. *A London Directory or Alphabetical Arrangement . . . Embellished with a plan of the Royal Exchange.* London, 1795.

Madison, James, Alexander Hamilton, and John Jay. *The Federalist Papers.* Ed. Isaac Kramnick. London: Penguin, 1987.

Magdalen Hospital. *The rules, orders and regulations, of the Magdalen House, for the reception of penitent prostitutes. . . .* London: Printed by W. Faden, 1760.

Malloy, William M., ed. *Treaties, Conventions, International Acts, Protocols and Agreements between the United States and Other Powers, 1776–1909.* Washington, D.C.: United States Department of State, 1910.

Miller, Philip. *The Gardener's Dictionary.* London, 1733.

Moore, Caroline T., and Agatha Aimar Simmons, eds. *Abstracts of Wills of the State of South Carolina.* Charleston, S.C., 1960.

Moore, John Bassett, ed. *International Adjudications Ancient and Modern: History and Documents.* Modern Series, vol. III. New York: Oxford University Press, 1931.

Mortimer, Thomas. *The Universal Director, or, The nobleman and gentleman's true guide to the masters and professors of the liberal and polite arts and sciences, and of the mechanic arts, manufactures, and trades, established in London and Westminster and their environs . . . to which is added, a distinct list of the booksellers, distinguishing the particular branches of their trade.* London, 1763.

Oldmixon, John. *The History of Carolina, being an Account of that Colony, originally published in the History of the British Empire in America.* London, 1708.

[Osborn, J.]. *A Complete Guide to All Persons who have any Trade or Concern with the City of London, and Parts Adjacent.* 2nd–16th eds. London, 1740–83.

Pace, Antonio, trans. and ed. *Luigi Castiglioni's Viaggio: Travels in the United States of North America, 1785–1787.* Syracuse: Syracuse University Press, 1983.

Parker, Thomas, of Lincoln's Inn. *The laws of shipping and insurance, with a digest of adjudged cases; containing the acts of parliament relative to shipping, insurance and navigation . . . from Trinity term 1693, to Michaelmas term 1774.* London: Printed by W. Strahan and M. Woodfall, 1775.

Perceval, John, Earl. *Manuscripts of the Earl of Egmont: Diary of Viscount Percival, afterwards First Earl of Egmont.* 3 vols. London: H.M.S.O., 1920–23.

Pinckney, Elise, ed. *The Letterbook of Eliza Lucas Pinckney, 1739–1762.* Chapel Hill: University of North Carolina Press, 1972.

Ramsay, David. *History of South Carolina, from Its First Settlement in 1760, to the Year 1808.* 2 vols. 1809; repr., Spartanburg, S.C.: Reprint Co., 1959.

Robins, Walter L., trans. and ed. "John Tobler's Description of South Carolina (1753–1754)." *SCHM* 71.3/4 (1970): 141–61, 257–65.

Royal Society of Arts. *Museum rusticum et commerciale: or, Select papers on agriculture, commerce, arts, and manufactures. Drawn from experience, and communicated by gentlemen engaged in these pursuits . . . Volume the Fifth.* London, 1765.

Salley, A. S., ed. *Journal of the Commons House of Assembly of South Carolina, February 23rd 1724/5 to 1st June 1725.* Columbia: Historical Commission of South Carolina, 1945.

———. *Journal of the Commons House of Assembly of South Carolina, November 8th 1734 to June 7th 1735.* Columbia: Historical Commission of South Carolina, 1945.

Scots Hospital of King Charles II. *A Short Account of the Institution, Progress, and Present State of the Scottish Corporation in London.* London: Printed for W. and A. Strahan, 1777.

Sheffield, John Baker Holroyd, 1st Earl of. *Observations on the Commerce of the American States with Europe and the West Indies.* London, 1783.

Sketchley, James. *Sketchley's Bristol Directory; including Clifton, Bedminster, and the out-parishes of St. James and St. Philip.* Bristol, 1775.

Smith, Paul H., ed. *Letters of Delegates to Congress, 1774–1789.* 26 vols. Washington, D.C.: Library of Congress, 1976–2000.

Stevens, Michael, ed. "'To be a Member of Congress hereafter will be like a Profession': New Letters from David Ramsay, 1785–1793." *SCHM* 116.1 (2015): 55–79.

Stork, William. *An Account of East-Florida. With remarks on its future importance to trade and commerce.* London, 1766.

Thompson, Theodora J., and Rosa S. Lumpkin, eds. *The State Records of South Carolina: Journals of the House of Representatives, 1783–1784.* Columbia: University of South Carolina Press, 1977.

Tobias, Thomas J., ed. "Charleston in 1764." *SCHM* 67.2 (1966): 63–74.

Van Horne, J. C., and G. Reese, eds. *The Letterbook of James Abercromby, Colonial Agent, 1751–1773.* Richmond: Virginia State Library and Archives, 1991.

Walsh, Richard, ed. "The Letters of Morris & Brailsford to Thomas Jefferson." *SCHM* 58.3 (1957): 129–44.

Webb, Benjamin. *The Complete Negociator: or, tables for the arbitration and combination of the exchanges of all the trading countries in Europe, and for reducing the same to par.* London: Printed for C. Rivington, 1767.

Webber, Mabel L., ed. "Josiah Smith's Diary, 1780–1781." *South Carolina Historical and Genealogical Magazine* 33 (1932): 1–28, 79–116, 197–207, 281–89; 34 (1933): 32–39, 67–84, 138–48, 194–210.

[Webster, Pelatiah]. "Journal of a Visit to Charleston, 1765." In *The Colonial South Carolina Scene: Contemporary Views, 1697–1774,* ed. H. Roy Merrens, 218–26. Columbia: University of South Carolina Press, 1977.

Willcox, William B., Leonard W. Labaree, et al., eds. *The Papers of Benjamin Franklin.* 42 vols. New Haven, Conn.: Yale University Press, 1959–2017.

Withington, Lothrop, ed. "South Carolina Gleanings in England." *South Carolina Historical and Genealogical Magazine* 6.3 (1905): 117–25.

Wright, Louis B., and Marion Tinling, eds. *Quebec to Carolina in 1785–1786, Being the Travel Diary and Observations of Robert Hunter, Jr., a Young Merchant of London.* San Marino, Calif.: Huntington Library, 1943.

Yonge, Francis. *A View of the Trade of South Carolina, with Proposals Humbly Offer'd for Improving the same.* London, c. 1722.

SECONDARY SOURCES

Books and Journal Articles

Andrew, Donna. *Philanthropy and Police: London Charity in the Eighteenth Century.* Princeton, N.J.: Princeton University Press, 1989.

Andrews, Charles M. *The Colonial Period of American History.* Vol. IV, *England's Commercial and Colonial Policy.* New Haven, Conn.: Yale University Press, 1938.

Appleby, Joyce. *Inheriting the Revolution: The First Generation of Americans.* Cambridge, Mass.: Belknap Press, 2000.

Armitage, David. "Greater Britain: A Useful Category of Historical Analysis?," *American Historical Review* 104.2 (1999): 427–55.

Armitage, David, and Michael Braddick, eds. *The British Atlantic World, 1500–1800*. Basingstoke: Palgrave, 2002.

Atkins, Peter J. *The Directories of London, 1677–1977*. London: Mansell, 1990.

Bailey, N. L., and Elizabeth Ivey Cooper, eds. *Biographical Directory of the South Carolina House of Representatives*. Vol. III, 1775–90. Columbia: University of South Carolina Press, 1981.

Bailyn, Bernard. *Atlantic History: Concept and Contours*. Cambridge, Mass.: Harvard University Press, 2005.

——. "The Idea of Atlantic History." *Itinerario* 20.1 (1996): 19–44.

——. *The Ideological Origins of the American Revolution*. Enlarged ed., Cambridge, Mass.: Harvard University Press, 1967; enlarged ed., 1992.

——. *The New England Merchants in the Seventeenth Century*. Cambridge, Mass.: Harvard University Press, 1955.

——. *Voyagers to the West: A Passage in the Peopling of America on the Eve of the American Revolution*. New York: Knopf, 1986.

Baker, Norman. *Government and Contractors: The British Treasury and War Supplies, 1775–1783*. London: Athlone Press, 1971.

Ball, Edward. *Slaves in the Family*. London: Penguin, 1999.

Barker, Eirlys M. "Indian Traders, Charles Town and London's Vital Link to the Interior of North America, 1715–1755." In *Money, Trade, and Power: The Evolution of Colonial South Carolina's Plantation Society*, ed. Jack P. Greene, Rosemary Brana-Shute, and Randy J. Sparks, 141–65. Columbia: University of South Carolina Press, 2001.

Baugh, Daniel A. "Great Britain's 'Blue Water' Policy, 1689–1815." *International History Review* 10.1 (1988): 33–58.

——. "Maritime Strength and Atlantic Commerce: The Uses of 'A Grand Marine Empire.'" In *An Imperial State at War: Britain from 1689 to 1815*, ed. Lawrence Stone, 185–223. London: Routledge, 1994.

Beard, Charles A. *Economic Origins of Jeffersonian Democracy*. 2nd ed. New York: Macmillan, 1927.

Beer, George Louis. *The Commercial Policy of England towards the American Colonies*. New York: Columbia College, 1893.

Behrendt, Stephen D. "Markets, Transactions Cycles, and Profits: Merchant Decision Making in the British Slave Trade." *WMQ* 58.1 (2001): 171–204.

Bellows, Barbara L. "Eliza Lucas Pinckney: The Evolution of an Icon." *SCHM* 106.2/3 (2005): 147–65.

Bickman, Troy. *Making Headlines: The American Revolution as seen through the British Press*. DeKalb: Northern Illinois University Press, 2009.

Bowen, H. V. *Elites, Enterprise and the Making of the British Overseas Empire, 1688–1775*. Basingstoke: Macmillan, 1996.

Bradburn, Douglas. *The Citizenship Revolution: Politics and the Creation of the American Union*. Charlottesville: University of Virginia Press, 2009.

Bradley, James. *Popular Politics and the American Revolution in England: Petitions, the Crown and Public Opinion*. Macon, Ga.: Mercer, 1986.

Breen, Timothy H. "'Baubles of Britain': The American and Consumer Revolutions of the Eighteenth Century." *Past and Present* 119 (1988): 73–104.

——. "An Empire of Goods: The Anglicization of Colonial America, 1690–1776." *Journal of British Studies* 25.4 (1986): 467–99.

——. *The Marketplace of Revolution: How Consumer Politics Shaped American Independence*. Oxford: Oxford University Press, 2004.

——. *Tobacco Culture: The Mentality of the Great Tidewater Planters on the Eve of the Revolution.* 2nd ed. Princeton, N.J.: Princeton University Press, 2001.

Brewer, John. *The Sinews of Power: War, Money, and the English State, 1688–1783.* Oxford: Oxford University Press, 1989.

Bridenbaugh, Carl. "Charlestonians at Newport, 1767–1775." *South Carolina Historical and Genealogical Magazine* 41.1 (1940): 43–47.

Bull, Henry D. "Kinloch of South Carolina." *South Carolina Historical and Genealogical Magazine* 46.2 (1945): 63–69.

Burnard, Trevor. "Passengers Only: The Extent and Significance of Absenteeism in Eighteenth-Century Jamaica." *Atlantic Studies* 1.2 (2004): 178–95.

Byrd, Michael D. "The First Charles Town Workhouse, 1738–1775: A Deterrent to White Pauperism?" *SCHM* 110.1/2 (2009): 35–52.

Calhoun, Jeanne A., Martha A. Zierden, and Elizabeth A. Paysinger. "The Geographic Spread of Charleston's Merchant Community, 1732–67." *SCHM* 86.3 (1985): 182–220.

Canny, Nicholas. "Writing Atlantic History, or, Reconfiguring the History of Colonial British America." *Journal of American History* 86 (1999): 1093–1114.

Carp, Benjamin L. *Rebels Rising: Cities and the American Revolution.* Oxford: Oxford University Press, 2007.

Cashin, Edward J. *Guardians of the Valleys: Chickasaws in Colonial South Carolina and Georgia.* Columbia: University of South Carolina Press, 2009.

Chaplin, Joyce E. *An Anxious Pursuit: Agricultural Innovation and Modernity in the Lower South, 1730–1815.* Chapel Hill: University of North Carolina Press, 1993.

Chesnutt, David R. "South Carolina's Penetration of Georgia in the 1760s: Henry Laurens as a Case Study." *SCHM* 73.4 (1972): 194–208.

Christie, Ian R. *British Non-elite MPs, 1715–1820.* Oxford: Clarendon, 1995.

Clark, Dora Mae. "The Impressment of Seamen in the American Colonies." In *Essays in Colonial History Presented to Charles McLean Andrews by His Students,* 198–224. New Haven, Conn.: Yale University Press, 1931.

——. *The Rise of the British Treasury: Colonial Administration in the Eighteenth Century.* New Haven, Conn.: Yale University Press, 1960.

Clayton, J. Glen. "South Carolina Baptist Records." *SCHM* 85.4 (1984): 319–27.

Cleary, Patricia. "'Who shall say we have not equal abilitys with the Men when Girls of 18 years of age discover such great capacitys?': Women of Commerce in Boston, 1750–1776." In *Entrepreneurs: The Boston Business Community, 1700–1850,* ed. Conrad Edick Wright and Katheryn P. Viens, 39–61. Boston: Massachusetts Historical Society, 1997.

Clowse, Converse D. *Economic Beginnings in Colonial South Carolina, 1670–1730.* Columbia: University of South Carolina Press, 1971.

——. *Measuring Charleston's Overseas Commerce, 1717–1767.* Washington, D.C.: University Press of America, 1981.

Cockburn, J. S., and T. F. T. Baker, eds. *The Victoria History of the County of Middlesex.* Vol. IV. Oxford: Oxford University Press, 1971.

Coclanis, Peter A. "Bitter Harvest: The South Carolina Low Country in Historical Perspective." *Journal of Economic History* 45 (1985): 251–59.

——. "*Esse Est Percipi:* The Strange Case of Early American Economic History." *Journal of Southern History* 73.3 (2007): 589–602.

——. "Global Perspectives on the Early Economic History of South Carolina." *SCHM* 106.2 (2005): 130–46.

——. "How the Low Country was Taken to Task: Slave-Labour Organization in Coastal South Carolina and Georgia." In *The South, the Nation and the World: Perspectives on Southern Economic Development,* ed. David L. Carlton and Peter A. Coclanis, 24–34. Charlottesville: University of Virginia Press, 2003.

——. "The Hydra Head of Merchant Capital: Market and Merchants in Early South Carolina." In *The Meaning of South Carolina History: Essays in Honor of George C. Rogers, Jr.*, ed. David R. Chesnutt and Clyde N. Wilson, 1–12. Columbia: University of South Carolina Press, 1991.

——. Introduction. In *The Atlantic World during the Seventeenth and Eighteenth Centuries: Organization, Operation, Practice, Personnel*, ed. Peter A. Coclanis, xi–xix. Columbia: University of South Carolina Press, 2005.

——. "Rice Prices in the 1720s and the Evolution of the South Carolina Economy." *Journal of Southern History* 48.4 (1982): 531–44.

——. *The Shadow of a Dream: Economic Life and Death in the South Carolina Lowcountry, 1670–1920*. New York: Oxford University Press, 1989.

Cohen, Hennig. *The South Carolina Gazette, 1732–1775*. Columbia: University of South Carolina Press, 1953.

Cohen, Joanna. "'The Right to Purchase is as Free as the Right to Sell': Defining Consumers as Citizens in the Auction House Conflicts of the Early Republic." *Journal of the Early Republic* 30.1 (2010): 25–62.

Colley, Linda. *Britons: Forging the Nation, 1707–1837*. New Haven, Conn.: Yale University Press, 1992.

Conway, Stephen. "From Fellow-Nationals to Foreigners: British Perceptions of the Americans, c. 1739–1783." *WMQ* 59.1 (2002): 65–100.

——. "'A Joy Unknown for Years Past': The American War, Britishness and the Celebration of Rodney's Victory at the Battle of the Saints." *History* 86.2 (2001): 180–99.

Coon, David L. "Eliza Lucas Pinckney and the Reintroduction of Indigo Culture in South Carolina." *Journal of Southern History* 42.1 (1976): 61–76.

Crane, Verner W. *The Southern Frontier, 1670–1732*. Ann Arbor: University of Michigan Press, 1956.

Craton, Michael. "Reluctant Creoles: The Planters' Word in the British West Indies." In *Strangers within the Realm: Cultural Margins of the First British Empire*, ed. Bernard Bailyn and Philip Morgan, 314–62. Chapel Hill: University of North Carolina Press, 1991.

Crouse, Maurice A. "Cautious Rebellion: South Carolina's Opposition to the Stamp Act." *SCHM* 73.2 (1972): 59–71.

——. "Gabriel Manigault: Charleston Merchant." *SCHM* 68.4 (1967): 220–31.

Crowley, John E. *The Privileges of Independence: Neomercantilism and the American Revolution*. Baltimore: Johns Hopkins University Press, 1993.

David, Huw. "James Crokatt's 'Exceeding Good Counting House': Ascendancy and Influence in the Transatlantic Carolina Trade." *SCHM* 111.3–4 (2010): 151–74.

Davis, Ralph. "The Rise of Protection in England, 1689–1786." *Economic History Review* 19.2 (1966): 306–17.

Devine, T. M. *The Tobacco Lords: A Study of the Tobacco Merchants of Glasgow and Their Trading Activities, c. 1740–1790*. Edinburgh: Edinburgh University Press, 1975.

Dickson, Peter G. M. *The Financial Revolution in England, 1688–1756*. London: Macmillan, 1967.

Doerflinger, Thomas M. "Philadelphia Merchants and the Logic of Moderation, 1760–1775." *WMQ* 50.2 (1983): 197–226.

——. *A Vigorous Spirit of Enterprise: Merchants and Economic Development in Revolutionary Philadelphia*. Chapel Hill: University of North Carolina Press, 1986.

Dunn, Richard S. "The English Sugar Islands and the Founding of South Carolina." *SCHM* 72.2 (1971): 81–93.

——. "The Trustees of Georgia and the House of Commons, 1732–1752." *WMQ* 11.4 (1954): 551–65.

Earle, Peter. *The Making of the English Middle Class: Business, Society and Family Life in London, 1660–1730*. London: Methuen, 1989.

Edelson, S. Max. "Beyond 'Black Rice': Reconstructing Material and Cultural Contexts for Early Plantation Agriculture." *American Historical Review* 115.1 (2010): 125–35.

——. "Carolinians Abroad: Cultivating English Identities from the Colonial Lower South." In *Britain and the American South: From Colonialism to Rock and Roll*, ed. Joseph P. Ward, 81–105. Jackson: University Press of Mississippi, 2003.

——. "The Character of Commodities: The Reputations of South Carolina Rice and Indigo in the Atlantic World." In *The Atlantic Economy during the Seventeenth and Eighteenth Centuries: Organization, Operation, Practice, Personnel*, ed. Peter A. Coclanis, 344–60. Columbia: University of South Carolina Press, 2005.

——. *Plantation Enterprise in Colonial South Carolina*. Cambridge, Mass.: Harvard University Press, 2006.

Edgar, Walter B. *Partisans and Redcoats: The Southern Conflict That Turned the Tide of the American Revolution*. New York: Perennial, 2003.

——. "Robert Pringle and His World." *SCHM* 76.1 (1975): 1–11.

——. *South Carolina: A History*. Columbia: University of South Carolina Press, 1998.

——, ed. *The South Carolina Encyclopedia*. Columbia: University of South Carolina Press, 2006.

Edgar, Walter B., and N. L. Bailey, eds. *Biographical Directory of the South Carolina House of Representatives*. Vol. II, *The Commons House of Assembly, 1692–1775*. Columbia: University of South Carolina Press, 1977.

Egnal, Marc. *New World Economies: The Growth of the Thirteen Colonies and Canada*. Oxford: Oxford University Press, 1998.

Egnal, Marc, and Joseph A. Ernst. "An Economic Interpretation of the American Revolution." *WMQ* 29.1 (1972): 3–32.

Eltis, David, Philip Morgan, and David Richardson. "Black, Brown or White? Color-Coding American Commercial Rice Cultivation with Slave Labor." *American Historical Review* 115.1 (2010): 164–71.

Evans, Chris, and Göran Rydén. *Baltic Iron in the Atlantic World in the Eighteenth Century*. Leiden: Brill, 2007.

Ferguson, Niall. *The Ascent of Money: A Financial History of the World*. London: Penguin, 2009.

Finger, Simon. "'A Flag of Defiance at the Masthead': The Delaware River Pilots and the Sinews of Philadelphia's Atlantic World in the Eighteenth Century." *Early American Studies* 8.2 (2010): 386–409.

Fischer, David Hackett. *Albion's Seed: Four British Folkways in America*. Oxford: Oxford University Press, 1989.

Flavell, Julie. "American Patriots in London and the Quest for Talks, 1774–1775." *Journal of Imperial and Commonwealth History* 20.3 (1992): 335–69.

——. *When London Was Capital of America*. New Haven, Conn.: Yale University Press, 2010.

French, Christopher J. "Crowded with Traders and a Great Commerce: London's Domination of English Overseas Trade, 1700–1775." *London Journal* 17 (1992): 27–35.

Gallay, Alan. *The Formation of a Planter Elite: Johnathan Bryan and the Southern Colonial Frontier*. Athens: University of Georgia Press, 1989.

——. *The Indian Slave Trade: The Rise of the English Empire in the American South, 1670–1717*. New Haven, Conn.: Yale University Press, 2002.

Games, Alison. "Atlantic History: Definitions, Challenges, and Opportunities." *American Historical Review* 111.3 (2006): 741–57.

Gauci, Perry. *Emporium of the World: The Merchants of London, 1660–1800*. London: Continuum, 2007.

——. *The Politics of Trade: The Overseas Merchant in State and Society, 1600–1720*. Oxford: Oxford University Press, 2001.

Glaisyer, Natasha. "Networking, Trade and Exchange in the Eighteenth Century British Empire." *Historical Journal* 47.2 (2004): 451–76.

Godbold, E. Stanly, and Robert H. Woody. *Christopher Gadsden and the American Revolution*. Knoxville: University of Tennessee Press, 1982.

Gould, Eliga H. *The Persistence of Empire: British Political Culture in the Age of the American Revolution.* Chapel Hill: University of North Carolina Press, 2000.

Gray, Lewis C. *A History of Agriculture in the Southern United States to 1860.* 2 vols. Washington, D.C.: Carnegie Institution, 1933.

Greene, Jack P. "Bridge to Revolution: The Wilkes Fund Controversy in South Carolina, 1769–1775." *Journal of Southern History* 29.1 (1963): 19–52.

——. "Colonial South Carolina and the Caribbean Connection." *SCHM* 88.4 (1987): 192–210.

——. "Early Modern Southeastern North America and the Broader Atlantic and American Worlds." *Journal of Southern History* 73.3 (2007): 525–38.

——. "Empire and Identity from the Glorious Revolution to the American Revolution." In *The Oxford History of the British Empire: The Eighteenth Century,* ed. Peter J. Marshall, 208–30. Oxford: Oxford University Press, 1998.

——. *Pursuits of Happiness: The Social Development of the Early Modern British Colonies and the Formation of American Culture.* Chapel Hill: University of North Carolina Press, 1988.

——. *The Quest for Power: The Lower Houses of Assembly in the Southern Royal Colonies, 1689–1776.* Chapel Hill: University of North Carolina Press, 1963.

Greene, Jack P., and J. R. Pole. *Colonial British America: Essays in the New History of the Early Modern Era.* Baltimore: Johns Hopkins University Press, 1984.

Guillery, Peter. *The Small House in Eighteenth-Century London: A Social and Architectural History.* New Haven, Conn.: Yale University Press, 2004.

Gwyn, Julian. *The Enterprising Admiral: The Personal Fortune of Sir Peter Warren.* Montreal: McGill-Queen's University Press, 1974.

Habakkuk, John. *Marriage, Debt, and the Estates System: English Landownership 1650–1950.* Oxford: Oxford University Press, 1994.

Hadden, Sally. *Slave Patrols: Law and Violence in Virginia and the Carolinas.* Cambridge, Mass.: Harvard University Press, 2001.

Hancock, David. "The British Atlantic World: Co-ordination, Complexity, and the Emergence of an Atlantic Market Economy, 1651–1815." *Itinerario* 23.2 (1999): 107–26.

——. *Citizens of the World: London Merchants and the Integration of the British Atlantic Community, 1735–1785.* Cambridge: Cambridge University Press, 1995.

——. "Commerce and Conversation in the Eighteenth-Century Atlantic: The Invention of Madeira Wine." *Journal of Interdisciplinary History* 29.2 (1998): 197–219.

——. *Oceans of Wine: Madeira and the Emergence of American Taste and Trade.* New Haven, Conn.: Yale University Press, 2009.

——. "'A Revolution in the Trade': Wine Distribution and the Development of the Infrastructure of the Atlantic Market Economy, 1703–1807." In *The Early Modern Atlantic Economy,* ed. John J. McCusker and Kenneth Morgan, 105–53. Cambridge: Cambridge University Press, 2000.

——. "Transatlantic Trade in the Era of the American Revolution." In *Anglo-American Attitudes: From Revolution to Partnership,* ed. Fred M. Leventhal and Roland E. Quinault, 38–75. Aldershot: Ashgate, 2000.

Harden, William. "Basil Cowper's Remarkable Career in Georgia." *GHQ* 1.1 (1917): 24–35.

Harris, Bob. "'American Idols': Empire, War and the Middling Ranks in Mid-Eighteenth Century Britain." *Past and Present* 150 (1996): 111–41.

——. "Patriotic Commerce and National Revival: The Free British Fishery Society and British Politics, c. 1749–58." *English Historical Review* 114 (1999): 285–313.

——. *Politics and the Nation: Britain in the Mid-Eighteenth Century.* Oxford: Oxford University Press, 2002.

——. "War, Empire and the 'National Interest' in Mid-Eighteenth Century Britain." In *Britain and America Go to War: The Impact of War and Warfare in Anglo-America, 1754–1815,* ed. Stephen Conway and Julie Flavell, 13–40. Gainesville: University Press of Florida, 2004.

Hart, Emma. *Building Charleston: Town and Society in the Eighteenth Century British Atlantic World*. Charlottesville: University of Virginia Press, 2010.

——. "'The Middling Order are Odious Characters': Social Structure and Urban Growth in Colonial Charleston, South Carolina." *Urban History* 34.2 (2007): 209–26.

Haw, James. "'Everything Here Depends upon Opinion': Nathanael Greene and Public Support in the Southern Campaigns of the American Revolution." *SCHM* 109.3 (2008): 212–31.

——. "The Rutledges, the Continental Congress, and Independence." *SCHM* 94.4 (1993): 232–51.

Haywood, C. Robert. "Mercantilism and South Carolina Agriculture, 1700–1763." *SCHM* 60.1 (1959): 15–27.

Hepper, David. *British Warship Losses in the Age of Sail, 1650–1859*. Rotherfield: Jean Boudinot, 1994.

Herring, George C. *From Colony to Superpower: U.S. Foreign Relations since 1776*. Oxford: Oxford University Press, 2008.

Heyward, Duncan Clinch. *Seed from Madagascar*. Chapel Hill: University of North Carolina Press, 1937.

Higgins, W. Robert. "Charles Town Merchants and Factors Dealing in the External Negro Trade, 1735–75." *SCHM* 66.4 (1965): 205–17.

Higman, B. W. *Plantation Jamaica, 1750–1850: Capital and Control in a Colonial Economy*. Kingston: University of the West Indies Press, 2008.

Hilton, Boyd. *A Mad, Bad, and Dangerous People? England, 1783–1846*. Oxford: Oxford University Press, 2006.

Holton, Woody. *Forced Founders: Indians, Debtors, Slaves and the Making of the American Revolution in Virginia*. Chapel Hill: University of North Carolina Press, 1999.

Hoppit, Julian. "Patterns of Parliamentary Legislation, 1600–1800." *Historical Journal* 39.1 (1996): 109–31.

James, Francis G. "The Irish Lobby in the Early Eighteenth Century." *English Historical Review* 81 (1966): 543–57.

Jasanoff, Maya. *Liberty's Exiles: How the Loss of America Made the British Empire*. London: Harper, 2011.

——. "The Other Side of Revolution: Loyalists in the British Empire." *WMQ* 65.2 (2008): 205–32.

Johnson, Lloyd. *The Frontier in the Colonial South: South Carolina Backcountry, 1736–1800*. Westport, Conn.: Greenwood Press, 1997.

Jones, Alice Hanson. *Wealth of a Nation to Be: The American Colonies on the Eve of the Revolution*. New York: Columbia University Press, 1980.

Kammen, Michael G. *Empire and Interest: The American Colonies and the Politics of Mercantilism*. Philadelphia: Lippincott, 1970.

———. *A Rope of Sand: The Colonial Agents, British Politics and the American Revolution*. Ithaca, N.Y.: Cornell University Press, 1968.

Kaplanoff, Mark D. "How Federalist Was South Carolina in 1787–88?" In *The Meaning of South Carolina History: Essays in Honor of George C. Rogers, Jr.*, ed. David R. Chesnutt and Clyde N. Wilson, 67–103. Columbia: University of South Carolina Press, 1991.

Kellock, Katherine A. "London Merchants and the Pre-1776 American Debts." *Guildhall Studies* 1.3. (1974): 109–49.

Kelly, Joseph P. "Henry Laurens: The Southern Man of Conscience in History." *SCHM* 107.2 (2006): 82–123.

Kettner, James H. *The Development of American Citizenship, 1608–1870*. Chapel Hill: University of North Carolina Press, 1978.

Klein, Herbert S., Stanley L. Engerman, Robin Haines, and Ralph Shlomowitz. "Transoceanic Mortality: The Slave Trade in Comparative Perspective." *WMQ* 58.1 (2001): 93–118.

Klein, Rachel N. *Unification of a Slave State: The Rise of the Planter Class in the South Carolina Backcountry, 1760–1808*. Chapel Hill: University of North Carolina Press, 1990.

Langford, Paul. "The British Business Community and the Later Nonimportation Movements, 1768–76." In *Resistance, Politics and the American Struggle for Independence*, ed. Walter H. Conser Jr., 278–324. Boulder: L. Rienner, 1986.

——. "London and the American Revolution." In *London in the Age of Reform*, ed. John Stevenson, 55–78. Oxford: Blackwell, 1977.

——. *A Polite and Commercial People: England, 1727–1783*. Oxford: Oxford University Press, 1989.

——. "Property and 'Virtual Representation,' in Eighteenth-Century England." *Historical Journal* 31.1 (1988): 83–115.

Lillywhite, Bryant. *London Coffee Houses: A Reference Book of Coffee Houses of the Seventeenth, Eighteenth, and Nineteenth Centuries*. London: Allen and Unwin, 1963.

Littlefield, Daniel C. *Rice and Slaves: Ethnicity and the Slave Trade in Colonial South Carolina*. Baton Rouge: Louisiana State University Press, 1981.

——. "The Slave Trade to Colonial South Carolina: A Profile." *SCHM* 91.2 (1990): 68–99.

Lonn, Ella. *The Colonial Agents of the Southern Colonies*. Chapel Hill: University of North Carolina Press, 1945.

Malcomson, A. P. W. "Absenteeism in 18th Century Ireland." *Irish Economic and Social History* 1 (1974): 15–35.

Mancall, Peter C., Joshua L. Rosenbloom, and Thomas Weiss. "Indians and the Economy of Eighteenth-Century Carolina." In *The Atlantic Economy during the Seventeenth and Eighteenth Centuries: Organization, Operation, Practice, Personnel*, ed. Peter A. Coclanis, 297–322. Columbia: University of South Carolina Press, 2005.

Marsh, Ben. *Georgia's Frontier Women: Female Fortunes in a Southern Colony*. Athens: University of Georgia Press, 2007.

Marshall, Peter J. "Britain without America—A Second Empire?" In *The Oxford History of the British Empire: The Eighteenth Century*, ed. Peter J. Marshall, 576–95. Oxford: Oxford University Press, 1998.

——. *Remaking the British Atlantic: The United States and the British Empire after American Independence*. Oxford: Oxford University Press, 2012.

——. "Who Cared about the Thirteen Colonies? Some Evidence from Philanthropy." *Journal of Imperial and Commonwealth History* 27.2 (1999): 53–67.

Mathias, Peter. "Risk, Credit and Kinship in Early Modern Enterprise." In *The Early Modern Atlantic Economy*, ed. John J. McCusker and Kenneth Morgan, 15–35. Cambridge: Cambridge University Press, 2000.

Matson, Cathy D. *Merchants and Empire: Trading in Colonial New York*. Baltimore: Johns Hopkins University Press, 1998.

Matson, Cathy D., and Peter S. Onuf. *A Union of Interests: Political and Economic Thought in Revolutionary America*. Lawrence: University Press of Kansas, 1990.

McCann, Alison. "The Letterbook of Robert Raper." *SCHM* 82.2 (1981): 111–17.

McCusker, John J. *Money and Exchange in Europe and America, 1600–1775: A Handbook*. Chapel Hill: University of North Carolina Press, 1978.

McCusker, John J., and Russell R. Menard. *The Economy of British America, 1607–1789*. Chapel Hill: University of North Carolina Press, 1985.

McDonough, Daniel. *Christopher Gadsen and Henry Laurens: The Parallel Lives of Two American Patriots*. London: Associated University Press, 2000.

McInnes, Maurie D., ed. *In Pursuit of Refinement: Charlestonians Abroad, 1740–1860*. Columbia: University of South Carolina Press, 1999.

Menard, Russell R. "Financing the Lowcountry Export Boom: Capital and Growth in Early South Carolina." *WMQ* 51.4 (1994): 659–76.

Mercantini, Jonathan. "The Great Carolina Hurricane of 1752." *SCHM* 103.4 (2002): 351–65.

——. *Who Shall Rule at Home? The Evolution of South Carolina Political Culture, 1748–1776*. Columbia: University of South Carolina Press, 2007.

Meroney, Geraldine. "The London Entrepôt Merchants and the Georgia Colony." *WMQ* 25.2 (1968): 230–44.

Merrens, H. Roy, and George D. Terry. "Dying in Paradise: Malaria, Mortality and the Perceptual Environment in Colonial South Carolina." *Journal of Southern History* 50.4 (1984): 533–50.

Middlekauff, Robert. *The Glorious Cause: The American Revolution, 1763–1789.* Oxford: Oxford University Press, 1982.

Minchinton, Walter E. "Richard Champion, Nicholas Pocock, and the Carolina Trade." *SCHM* 65.2 (1964): 87–97.

Moody, T.W., ed. *A New History of Ireland: Eighteenth Century Ireland, 1691–1800.* Oxford: Clarendon Press, 1986.

Moore, W. O., Jr. "The Largest Exporters of Deerskins from Charles Town, 1735–1775." *SCHM* 74.3 (1973): 144–50.

Morgan, Kenneth. *Bristol and the Atlantic Trade in the Eighteenth Century.* Cambridge: Cambridge University Press, 1993.

———. "Business Networks in the British Export Trade to North America, 1750–1800." In *The Early Modern Atlantic Economy*, ed. John J. McCusker and Kenneth Morgan, 36–62. Cambridge: Cambridge University Press, 2000.

———. "The Organization of the Colonial American Rice Trade." *WMQ* 52.3 (1995): 433–52.

Nadelhaft, Jerome J. *The Disorders of War: The Revolution in South Carolina.* Orono: University of Maine Press, 1981.

Namier, Lewis B. "Charles Garth and His Connexions." *English Historical Review* 54 (1939): 443–70, 632–52.

———. *The Structure of Politics at the Accession of George III.* 2nd ed. London: Macmillan, 1957.

Namier, Lewis B., and John Brooke, eds. *The House of Commons, 1754–1790.* 3 vols. London: H.M.S.O, 1964.

Nash, Robert C. "The Organization of Trade and Finance in the Atlantic Economy: Britain and South Carolina, 1670–1775." In *Money, Trade, and Power: The Evolution of Colonial South Carolina's Plantation Society*, ed. Jack P. Greene, Rosemary Brana-Shute, and Randy J. Sparks, 74–107. Columbia: University of South Carolina Press, 2001.

———. "The Organization of Trade and Finance in the British Atlantic Economy, 1670–1830." In *The Atlantic Economy during the Seventeenth and Eighteenth Centuries: Organization, Operation, Practice, Personnel*, ed. Peter A. Coclanis, 95–151. Columbia: University of South Carolina Press, 2005.

———. "South Carolina and the Atlantic Economy in the Late 17th and 18th Centuries." *Economic History Review* 45.4 (1992): 677–702.

———. "South Carolina Indigo, European Textiles and the British Atlantic Economy in the Eighteenth Century." *Economic History Review* 63.2 (2010): 362–92.

———. "Trade and Business in Eighteenth Century South Carolina: The Career of John Guerard, Merchant and Planter." *SCHM* 96.1 (1995): 6–29.

———. "Urbanization in the Colonial South: Charleston, South Carolina, as a Case Study." *Journal of Urban History* 19.1 (1992): 3–29.

Newell, Margaret E. "A Revolution in Economic Thought: Currency Development in Eighteenth Century Massachusetts." In *Entrepreneurs: The Boston Business Community, 1700–1850*, ed. Conrad Edick Wright and Katheryn P. Viens, 1–21. Boston: Massachusetts Historical Society, 1997.

Norton, Mary Beth. *The British-Americans: The Loyalist Exiles in England, 1774–1789.* Boston: Little, Brown, 1972.

O'Brien, Patrick K. "Inseparable Connections: Trade, Economy, Fiscal State, and the Expansion of Empire, 1688–1815." In *The Oxford History of the British Empire: The Eighteenth Century*, ed. Peter J. Marshall, 53–77. Oxford: Oxford University Press, 1998.

Olsberg, R. Nicholas. "Ship Registers in the South Carolina Archives, 1734–1780." *SCHM* 74.4 (1973): 189–299.

Olson, Alison G. "The Board of Trade and London-American Interest Groups in the Eighteenth Century." *Journal of Imperial and Commonwealth History* 8.2 (1980): 33–50.

——. "Coffee House Lobbying." *History Today* 41.1 (1991): 35–41.

——. "The London Mercantile Lobby and the Coming of the American Revolution." *Journal of American History* 69.1 (1982): 21–41.

——. *Making the Empire Work: London and American Interest Groups, 1690–1790.* Cambridge, Mass.: Harvard University Press, 1992.

——. "The Virginia Merchants of London: A Study in Eighteenth Century Interest Group Politics." *WMQ* 40.3 (1983): 363–88.

Olwell, Robert. *Masters, Slaves and Subjects: The Culture of Power in the South Carolina Low Country, 1740–1790.* Ithaca, N.Y.: Cornell University Press, 1998.

O'Shaughnessy, Andrew J. *An Empire Divided: The American Revolution and the British Caribbean.* Philadelphia: University of Pennsylvania Press, 2000.

——. "The Formation of a Commercial Lobby: The West Indies Interest, British Colonial Policy and the American Revolution." *Historical Journal* 40.1 (1997): 71–95.

——. "The West India Interest and the Crisis of American Independence." In *West Indies Accounts: Essays in the History of the British Caribbean in Honour of Richard Sheridan,* ed. Roderick A. McDonald, 126–48. Kingston: University of the West Indies Press, 1996.

Pares, Richard. "A London West India Merchant House, 1740–69." In *The Historian's Business and Other Essays,* ed. R. A. Humphreys and Elizabeth Humphreys, 198–226. Oxford: Clarendon, 1961.

——. *War and Trade in the West Indies, 1739–1763.* Oxford: Oxford University Press, 1936.

Peters, Marie. "Early Hanoverian Consciousness: Empire or Europe?" *English Historical Review* 122 (2007): 632–68.

Pettigrew, William A. "Free to Enslave: Politics and the Escalation of Britain's Transatlantic Slave Trade, 1688–1714." *WMQ* 64.1 (2007): 3–38.

Pitman, Frank. *The Development of the British West Indies, 1700–1763.* New Haven, Conn.: Yale University Press, 1917.

Price, Jacob M. *Capital and Credit in British Overseas Trade: The View from the Chesapeake, 1700–1776.* Cambridge, Mass.: Harvard University Press, 1980.

——. *Perry of London: A Family and a Firm on the Seaborne Frontier, 1615–1753.* Cambridge, Mass.: Harvard University Press, 1992.

———. "The Transatlantic Economy." In *Colonial British America: Essays in the New History of the Early Modern Era,* ed. Jack P. Green and J. R. Pole, 18–42. Baltimore: Johns Hopkins University Press, 1984.

——. "What Did Merchants Do? Reflections on British Overseas Trade, 1660–1790." *Journal of Economic History* 49.2 (1989): 267–84.

——. "Who Cared about the Colonies? The Impact of the Thirteen Colonies on British Society and Politics, c. 1714–1775." In *Strangers within the Realm: Cultural Margins of the First British Empire,* ed. Bernard Bailyn and Philip Morgan, 395–436. Chapel Hill: University of North Carolina Press, 1991.

Price, Jacob M., and Paul G. E. Clemens. "A Revolution in Overseas Trade: British Firms in the Chesapeake Trade, 1675–1775." *Journal of Economic History* 47.1 (1987): 1–43.

Ramsey, William L. "'All and Singular the Slaves': A Demographic Profile of Indian Slavery in Colonial South Carolina." In *Money, Trade, and Power: The Evolution of Colonial South Carolina's Plantation Society,* ed. Jack P. Greene, Rosemary Brana-Shute, and Randy J. Sparks, 166–86. Columbia: University of South Carolina Press, 2001.

Raven, James. *London Booksellers and American Customers: Transatlantic Literary Community and the Charleston Library Society, 1748–1811.* Columbia: University of South Carolina Press, 2002.

Richardson, David. "The British Slave Trade to Colonial South Carolina." *Slavery and Abolition* 12.3 (1991): 125–72.

Ritcheson, Charles R. *Aftermath of Revolution: British Policy towards the United States, 1783–1795.* Dallas: Southern Methodist University Press, 1969.

Roberts, William I., III. "Samuel Storke: An Eighteenth-Century London Merchant Trading to the American Colonies." *Business History Review* 39.2 (1965): 147–70.

Roe Coker, Kathryn. "Absentees as Loyalists in Revolutionary War South Carolina." *SCHM* 96.2 (1995): 119–34.

———. "The Case of James Nassau Colleton before the Commissioners of Forfeited Estates." *SCHM* 87.2 (1986): 106–16.

Rogers, George C., Jr. "Aedanus Burke, Nathanael Greene, Anthony Wayne, and the British Merchants of Charleston." *SCHM* 67.1 (1966): 75–83.

———. *Charleston in the Age of the Pinckneys.* Norman: University of Oklahoma Press, 1969.

———. "The Charleston Tea Party: The Significance of December 3, 1773." *SCHM* 75.3 (1974): 153–68.

———. *Evolution of a Federalist: William Loughton Smith of Charleston, 1758–1812.* Columbia: University of South Carolina Press, 1962.

———. *The History of Georgetown County, South Carolina.* Columbia: University of South Carolina Press, 1970.

———. "The Papers of James Grant of Ballindalloch Castle, Scotland." *SCHM* 77.3 (1976): 145–60.

Rogers, Nicholas. "Brave Wolfe: The Making of a Hero." In *A New Imperial History: Culture, Identity and Modernity in Britain and the Empire, 1660–1840,* ed. Kathleen Wilson, 239–59. Cambridge: Cambridge University Press, 2004.

———. *The Press Gang: Naval Impressment and Its Opponents in Georgia Britain.* London: Continuum, 2007.

Rogers, Nicholas, and Gerald Jordan. "Admirals as Heroes: Patriotism and Liberty in Hanoverian England." *Journal of British Studies* 28.3 (1989): 201–24.

Rosenblatt, Samuel M. "The Significance of Credit in the Tobacco Consignment Trade: A Study of John Norton & Sons, 1768–1775." *WMQ* 19.3 (1962): 383–99.

Roseveare, Henry. "Property versus Commerce in the Mid-Eighteenth Century Port of London." In *The Early Modern Atlantic Economy,* ed. John J. McCusker and Kenneth Morgan, 65–85. Cambridge: Cambridge University Press, 2000.

Rudé, George. "The Anti-Wilkite Merchants of 1769." *Guildhall Miscellany* 2.7 (1965): 283–304.

Rutter, Owen. *At the Three Sugar Loaves and Crown: A Brief History of the Firm of Messrs. Davison, Newman & Company, now incorporated with the West Indian Produce Association Limited.* London: Davison, Newman & Co., 1938.

Sainsbury, John. *Disaffected Patriots: London Supporters of Revolutionary America, 1769–1782.* Toronto: McGill-Queen's University Press, 1987.

Schama, Simon. *Rough Crossings: Britain, the Slaves and the American Revolution.* London: HarperCollins, 2005.

Schlesinger, Arthur M. *The Colonial Merchants and the American Revolution, 1763–1776.* New York: Columbia University Press, 1918.

Scott, Kenneth. "Sufferers in the Charleston Fire of 1740." *SCHM* 64.4 (1963): 203–11.

Sedgwick, Romney, ed. *The House of Commons, 1715–1754.* 2 vols. London: H.M.S.O, 1970.

Sharrer, G. Terry. "Indigo in Carolina, 1671–1796." *SCHM* 72.2 (1971): 94–103.

Shepherd, James F., and Gary M. Walton. "Economic Change after the American Revolution: Pre- and Post-War Comparisons of Maritime Shipping and Trade." *Explorations in Economic History* 13.4 (1976): 397–422.

Sheridan, Richard B. "Planters and Merchants: The Oliver Family of Antigua and London, 1716–84." *Business History* 13.2 (1971): 104–13.

Sherman, Richard. *Robert Johnson, Proprietary and Royal Governor of South Carolina.* Columbia: University of South Carolina Press, 1966.

Shy, John. *Toward Lexington: The Role of the British Army in the Coming of the American Revolution*. Princeton, N.J.: Princeton University Press, 1965.

Sirmans, M. Eugene. *Colonial South Carolina: A Political History, 1663–1763*. Chapel Hill: University of North Carolina Press, 1966.

——. "The South Carolina Royal Council, 1720–1763." *WMQ* 18.3 (1961): 373–92.

Smith, Henry A. M. "The Baronies of South Carolina." *South Carolina Historical and Genealogical Magazine* 18.1 (1917): 3–36.

——. "The Colleton Family in South Carolina." *South Carolina Historical and Genealogical Magazine* 1.4 (1900): 325–41.

Smith, Marion B. "South Carolina and 'The Gentleman's Magazine'." *SCHM* 95.2 (1994): 102–29.

Smith, S. D. "The Atlantic History Paradigm." *New England Quarterly* 79.1 (2006): 123–33.

——. "British Exports to Colonial North America and the Mercantilist Fallacy." *Business History* 37.1 (1995): 45–63.

——. "Gedney Clarke of Salem and Barbados: Transatlantic Super-Merchant." *New England Quarterly* 76.4 (2003): 499–549.

——. "Merchants and Planters Revisited." *Economic History Review* 55.3 (2002): 434–65.

——. "Reckoning the Atlantic Economy." *Historical Journal* 46.3 (2003): 749–64.

Smith, S. D., and T. R. Wheeley. "'Requisites of a Considerable Trade': The Letters of Robert Plumsted, Atlantic Merchant, 1752–8." *English Historical Review* 124 (2009): 545–70.

Smyth, William D. "Travelers in South Carolina in the Early Eighteenth Century." *SCHM* 79.2 (1978): 113–25.

Sosin, Jack M. *Agents and Merchants: British Colonial Policy and the Origins of the American Revolution, 1763–1775*. Lincoln: University of Nebraska Press, 1965.

Starr, Rebecca. *A School for Politics: Commercial Lobbying and Political Culture in Early South Carolina*. Baltimore: Johns Hopkins University Press, 1998.

Stumpf, Stuart O. "Implications of King George's War for the Charleston Mercantile Community." *SCHM* 77.3 (1976): 161–88.

——. "South Carolina's Importers of General Merchandise, 1735–1765." *SCHM* 84.1 (1983): 1–10.

Swanson, Carl E. "American Privateering and Imperial Warfare, 1739–1748." *WMQ* 42.3 (1985): 357–82.

Tapper, Oscar J. P. "The Brailsford Debt." *Guildhall Miscellany* 2 (1961): 82–94.

Taylor, C. James. "A Member of the Family: Twenty-five Years with Henry Laurens." *SCHM* 106.2 (2005): 117–29.

Thomas, P. D. G. *The House of Commons in the Eighteenth Century*. Oxford: Clarendon, 1971.

Thoms, D. W. "The Mills Family: London Sugar Merchants of the Eighteenth Century." *Business History* 11.1 (1969): 3–10.

Van Ruymbeke, Bertrand. "The Huguenots of Proprietary South Carolina: Patterns of Migration and Integration." In *Money, Trade, and Power: The Evolution of Colonial South Carolina's Plantation Society*, ed. Jack P. Greene, Rosemary Brana-Shute, and Randy J. Sparks, 26–48. Columbia: University of South Carolina Press, 2001.

Ver Steeg, Clarence L. "Stacy Hepburn and Company: Enterprisers in the American Revolution." *SCHM* 55.1 (1954): 1–6.

Vipperman, Carl J. *The Rise of Rawlins Lowndes, 1721–1800*. Columbia: University of South Carolina Press, 1978.

Waddell, Gene. *Charleston Architecture, 1670–1860*. Charleston, S.C.: Wyrick, 2003.

Wallace, David Duncan. *The Life of Henry Laurens*. New York: G. P. Putnam, 1915.

——. *South Carolina: A Short History, 1520–1948*. Chapel Hill: University of North Carolina Press, 1951.

Waterhouse, Richard. "The Development of Elite Culture in the Colonial American South: A Study of Charles Town, 1670–1770." *Australian Journal of Politics and History* 28 (1982): 391–404.

——. "England, the Caribbean, and the Settlement of South Carolina." *Journal of American Studies* 9.3 (1975): 259–81.

——. "Merchants, Planters and Lawyers: Political Culture and Leadership in Colonial South Carolina, 1721–1775." In *Power and Status: Officeholding in Colonial America*, ed. Bruce C. Daniels, 146–72. Middletown, Conn.: Wesleyan University Press, 1986.

——. *A New World Gentry: The Making of a Planter and Merchant Class in South Carolina, 1670–1770*. 2nd ed. Charleston, S.C.: History Press, 2005.

Webber, Mabel L. "The Mayrant Family." *South Carolina Historical and Genealogical Magazine* 27.2 (1926): 81–90.

Weir, Robert M. *Colonial South Carolina: A History.* New York: KTO Press, 1983.

——. "'The Harmony We Were Famous For': An Interpretation of Pre-Revolutionary South Carolina Politics." *WMQ* 26.4 (1969): 473–501.

——. "Who Shall Rule at Home: The American Revolution as a Crisis for Legitimacy for the Colonial Elite." *Journal of Interdisciplinary History* 6.4 (1976): 679–700.

Williams, George W. *St. Michael's, Charleston, 1751–1951.* Columbia: University of South Carolina Press, 1951.

Williams, Glyn. *The Prize of All the Oceans: The Triumph and Tragedy of Anson's Round the World Voyage.* London: HarperCollins, 2000.

Wilson, Kathleen. "Empire of Virtue: The Imperial Project and Hanoverian Culture, c. 1720–1785." In *An Imperial State at War: Britain from 1689 to 1815*, ed. Lawrence Stone, 128–64. London: Routledge, 1994.

——. "Empire, Trade and Popular Politics in Mid-Hanoverian Britain: The Case of Admiral Vernon." *Past and Present* 212 (1988): 74–109.

———. "Introduction: Histories, Empires, Modernities." In *A New Imperial History: Culture, Identity and Modernity in Britain and the Empire, 1660–1840*, ed. Kathleen Wilson, 1–26. Cambridge: Cambridge University Press, 2004.

——. *The Sense of the People: Politics, Culture and Imperialism in England, 1715–1785.* Cambridge: Cambridge University Press, 1995.

Winberry, John J. "Indigo in South Carolina: A Historical Geography." *Southeastern Geographer* 19.2 (1979): 91–102.

——. "Reputation of Carolina Indigo." *SCHM* 80.3 (1979): 242–50.

Wood, Betty. *Slavery in Colonial Georgia, 1730–1775.* Athens: University of Georgia Press, 1984.

Wood, Peter H. *Black Majority: Negroes in Colonial South Carolina from 1670 through to the Stono Rebellion.* New York: Norton, 1974.

Woods, Michael. "The Culture of Credit in Colonial Charleston." *SCHM* 99.4 (1998): 358–80.

Zahedieh, Nuala. *The Capital and the Colonies: London and the Atlantic Economy, 1660–1700.* Cambridge: Cambridge University Press, 2010.

Theses

Beaumont, Andrew D. M. "'Ambitious Men of Modest Means': Colonial Administration under the Earl of Halifax, 1748–1761." University of Oxford, 2007.

Edelson, Scott David. "Colour and Enterprise: South Carolina Indigo and the Atlantic Economy, 1745–1795." University of Oxford, 1994.

Hall, John A. "Quieting the Storm: The Establishment of Order in Post-Revolutionary South Carolina." University of Oxford, 1989.

Kim, Daeryoon. "Merchants, Politics and the Atlantic Imperial Community, 1763–1783." University of Oxford, 2006.

Pettigrew, William A. "Free to Enslave: Politics and the Escalation of Britain's Transatlantic Slave Trade, 1688–1714." University of Oxford, 2007.

Sandy, Laura. "Between Planter and Slave: The Social and Economic Role of Plantation Overseers in Colonial Virginia and South Carolina." University of Manchester, 2006.

INDEX

Page numbers in *italics* refer to illustrations; those in **bold type** denote tables.

Champion, Richard, 158, 173

Charles Town (Charleston), 6–7, *23;* and absentees, 72, 76, 81–84, 86, 87; anti-British sentiment, 147–51; auctions, 38, *39,* 147; becomes a city, xviii; British share of foreign shipping, **156,** 157; buildings, 82; civil government, xviii; coastal shipping, 119–20; commercial equilibrium, 147; fire (1740), 91; incorporation, 149; overstocking of goods, 152–53, 168; population, 22–23, 82; postwar trade, 144; property ownership, 81–83, 86, 87, 88; recapture by British forces (1780), xvii, 131, 133, 136; rents, 81, 82–83; riots, 148, 149, 150; St Michael's Church, 91, 124; St Philip's Church, 35; site of, xv, 4, 22; Stamp Act (1765), reactions to, 102–3; stores, 23, 31, 33, 88; tea party (1773), 125–27; trading in Charles Town, 30–35; unsuitable merchandise, 191n20; wharves, 143, *180,* 195n7. *See also* merchants, Charles Town

Charleywood Plantation, 80

Child, Josiah, *New Discourse on Trade,* 71

Chollet, Samuel, 159, 178, 222n89

citizenship, 145, 146, 166, 179–80, 181–82

Clark & Milligan, 136, 161, 218–19n16, 218n9

Clark, John, 103, 137

Clinton, Sir Henry, 133, 136

Coclanis, Peter, 4–5

Coercive Acts [Intolerable Acts] (1774), xvii, 4, 128–29

coffeehouses: Carolina Coffee House, 53; Garraway's Coffee House, 179

Colleton family, 77, 85

Colleton, James Edward, 90, 99, 176

Colleton, James Nassau, 176–77

Colleton, John, 79–80, 83, 84, 85

Colleton, Margaret, 80; absentee landownership, 75, 84, 85–86; confiscation of land, 176–77

colonial agents, 14, 50; and absenteeism, 88–93; background, 98; co-ordination of lobbying, 89–90, 98–102, 103–4; Crokatt, James as, xvi, 66, 67–68, 69–70, 88–89; duties, 20; Fury, Peregrine as, 59, 62, 66, 193n41; Garth, Charles as, 95–96, 98–102, 105, 116

Colonial Debt Recovery Act (1732), 108

Columbia, 143, 179

Confiscation Acts (1782), 163, 180, 205n14

Connecticut, 14

Continental Congress, xxi, 126, 216n107

Corbett, Thomas, 143

Cornwallis, Lord, 164, 167

cotton, 62–63

Cowes, 45, 95, 115

Crokatt, Charles, xx, 44, 50, 52, 108, 123, 124

Crokatt, Daniel, 23

Crokatt, Elizabeth, 23

Crokatt, James, 7, 43, 44, 47, 48, 66, 73, 106, 197n117; advertisements, *34, 35,* 38–9; agent for South Carolina, xvi, 6, 67–68, 69–70, 88–89; agricultural innovation, 123; background, xx, 23; civic duties in Charles Town, 35; credit, 31; death, 124; debtors, 31, 38–40, 123; evidence to Parliament, 62, 66, 67, 89, 100, 103; and Henry Laurens, 25, 66, 69, 124; Indian trade, 31–32; indigo, 51, 63–70; lobbying and petitioning, 62–63, 63–70; London premises, 110; Luxborough Hall, 88, 108, 123; marriage, 34; partnerships, 40, 50, 51–52, 76–77; philanthropy, 49, 91; potash lobbying, 67; property in South Carolina, 30, 76–77, 83, 87, 88; relocation to London, 36, 38–41, *40,* 52; retirement, 123; salt lobbying, 68; silk lobbying, 66–67; slave trade, 47; slavery, 33–34; and the Stamp Act, 102–3; store in Charles Town, 23; success of, 94; taxes, 110

Crokatt, John, 23

Crokatt, (nee Gaillard), Esther, 34

Crowfield Plantation, 163

Crugar, Henry, 158

Cumine, Alexander, 28

Dartmouth, Earl of, 126

Davis & Strachan, 160–61, **171,** 218–19n16

Decker, Sir Matthew, *Essay on the Causes of the Decline of the Foreign Trade,* 71

deerskins, 3, 31–32, 45, 113, **114,** 152, 198n15, 214n65

DeSaussure, Daniel, 161–62

Dinwiddie, Robert, 67

Drayton, John, 77

Dupont Jr., Gideon, 161, 224n105

duties, 18, 19, 42, 61, 62; rice, 116, 119, 142; slave trade, 16, 47; tobacco, 142; Townshend duties, xvii, 121, 122, 127, 129